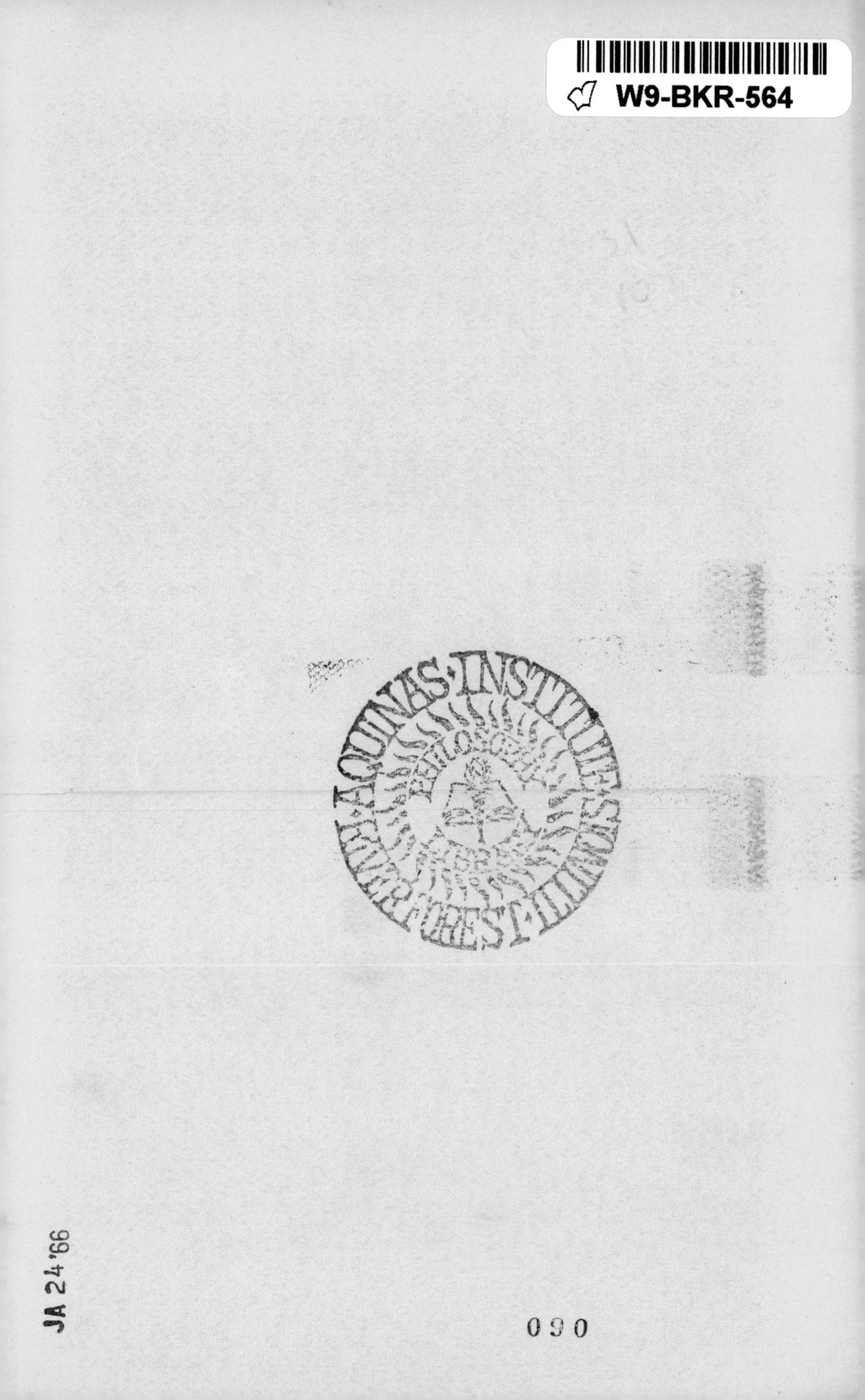
W9-BKR-564
AQUINAS INSTITUTE
090

STATE ADMINISTRATIVE LAW

VOLUME ONE

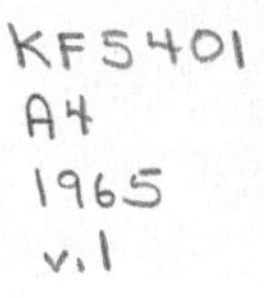

STATE ADMINISTRATIVE LAW

BY FRANK E. COOPER
of the Detroit Bar
Professor of Law, University of Michigan

VOLUME ONE

A RESEARCH PROJECT OF THE
AMERICAN BAR FOUNDATION AND
THE UNIVERSITY OF MICHIGAN LAW SCHOOL

THE BOBBS-MERRILL COMPANY, INC.

Library of Congress Catalog Card Number: 65-20272
Printed in the United States of America
FIRST PRINTING

THE BOBBS-MERRILL COMPANY, INC.
A SUBSIDIARY OF HOWARD W. SAMS & CO., INC.
PUBLISHERS • INDIANAPOLIS • KANSAS CITY • NEW YORK

AMERICAN BAR FOUNDATION

THE UNIVERSITY OF MICHIGAN LAW SCHOOL

FOREWORD

THE AMERICAN BAR FOUNDATION AND THE UNIVERSITY OF MICHIGAN LAW SCHOOL present this work on *State Administrative Law* with the hope and expectation that it will fill a long-felt need for a comprehensive text treatment of the subject. Moreover, since it parallels in large measure the Revised Model State Administrative Procedure Act promulgated by the Conference of Commissioners on Uniform State Laws, the study will be of service to state legislators and others concerned with the statutory improvement of state practices.

From 1939 to 1946 when the Conference of Commissioners prepared its original Model State Administrative Procedure Act, general discussions of the subject matter were virtually nonexistent. State administrative law was a dreary wasteland of unorganized detail. It is true that, in 1942, one outstanding treatment of administrative law in one state, New York, came to hand. Entitled "Administrative Adjudication in the State of New York," it was written by Robert M. Benjamin, a member of the New York Bar, who prepared it as Commissioner under official appointment from the Governor of the State. It was a valuable and unique contribution—a light shining in the wilderness; and it was most useful in the shaping of the Model State Act which finally was adopted and promulgated by the Conference of Commissioners in 1946.

Then followed a decade of experience with the Act. It was adopted, or at least served as a reference source and guide, in a considerable number of states that were beginning to improve their administrative procedures. In the light of this experience, in 1958 the Conference of Commissioners again undertook to examine the subject, and in due course it prepared a Revised Model State Administrative Procedure Act, which was duly adopted and promulgated in 1961. Although the federal field had, between 1940 and 1960, been covered generously both in law reviews and treatises, the Conference of Commissioners Committee was again confronted with a dearth of discussion of state administrative procedure. Statutes and judicial decisions were, of course, available in quantity, but they could be unearthed only by diligent use of the individual indices of the fifty states—a monumental task to say the least. The plain fact was that state administrative procedure had not invited the scholarship lavished upon the federal scene. Literature was scarce. Moreover, the state systems were variant; in fact they were more or less of a crazy quilt of provisions, with vague boundaries, uncertain precedents, and all too often wide gaps in coverage. Those of us who worked on the original Model Act and later on the Revised Act of the Conference of Commissioners were continuously conscious of the difficulties of achieving fertility in the largely unplowed field of state administrative law.

Fortunately the Conference Committee in charge of the Revised Act was able to enlist as a consultant Frank E. Cooper of the Detroit Bar. Mr. Cooper was able to bring many talents to the task. Since graduation from the University of Michigan Law School in 1934, he had practiced law in Detroit with the leading firm of Beaumont, Smith and Harris. Known as one of Detroit's able trial lawyers, much of his experience had been connected with administrative agencies—the National Labor Relations Board, the Michigan Employment Security Commission, and other federal and state agencies, as well as the courts. In addition on a part-time basis he had taught administrative law for a dozen years at the University of Michigan Law School. A former Ross Essay prize winner, he had written extensively on administrative law and procedure in law reviews and bar journals. He had also written and published several volumes, *Administrative Agencies and the Courts* (1951), *The Lawyer and Administrative Agencies* (1957), *Living the Law* (1958), *Writing in Law Practice* (1963), and, jointly with the undersigned, he had edited *Cases on Administrative Tribunals* (3d Edition 1957). With this background Mr. Cooper became an important contributor to the Revised Model Act which the Conference of Commissioners after extensive study promulgated in 1961.

When the American Bar Foundation undertook to prepare a treatise on State Administrative Procedure to fill the need that seemed obvious, we counted ourselves fortunate to find that Mr. Cooper had long had just such a project in mind as his next venture into legal literature. Accordingly an arrangement was made with him and with the University of Michigan Law School, which, with its William W. Cook Research Funds, joined the American Bar Foundation in promoting the project and arranging for the necessary research and clerical assistance.

This fortunate combination of talents is precisely the kind sought by the American Bar Foundation. The Foundation seeks to marshal the practical experience of the bar and to unite it with the research and literary skills of members of the teaching branch of the profession, to produce legal literature possessed of the best qualities of each area of endeavor. In this instance the Foundation has captured both sets of talents in one person and it gratefully acknowledges its indebtedness to Mr. Cooper for his fine cooperation and his extraordinary productivity in completing the project. Moreover, the Michigan Law School cooperation has been most gratifying and is deeply appreciated.

Especial appreciation is also expressed for the many helpful comments received from Robert M. Benjamin of the New York Bar and Roger C. Cramton of the University of Michigan Law Faculty, both of whom have generously assisted with suggestions and advice with reference to the manuscript.

The Bar Foundation expresses its hope that this volume will prove of service to members of the bar as well as to legal scholars and others concerned with state administrative processes. Interest in the subject is growing rapidly. Some twenty-five states have in recent years adopted comprehensive state administrative procedure legislation based to a greater or lesser extent upon either the original Model Act or the Revised Act. The subject is coming of age, and we hope that this work will serve the cause of further maturing of a most important field of the law.

E. Blythe Stason
SPECIAL ADVISER

Chicago
July 1965

PREFACE

THE PURPOSE of this study is primarily to analyze the statutory and case law of the several states bearing upon problems of administrative procedure. The analysis has been made in light of the provisions of the Revised Model State Administrative Procedure Act, as drafted and promulgated by the Commissioners on Uniform State Laws in 1961.

It is thought that an analysis of the state laws and court decisions, in terms of the provisions of the Revised Model State Act, will serve to demonstrate the desirability and importance of enacting, in states where no adaptation of the Model Act is in effect, legislation following the general pattern of that Act.

The adoption of such administrative procedure acts, it is believed, will afford a means of significantly improving the performance of those agencies which now carry on their work without the guiding direction such legislation affords. An attempt to document this conclusion is made in the following pages.

But this is not the sole purpose of the survey. Rather, there are three other objectives which are deemed to be of even greater importance.

First, there are a number of areas (such as the delegability of legislative and judicial powers, and the constitutional requirements of notice and hearing) with respect to which the Revised Model State Act makes no provision. An attempt has been made to present an accurate and up-to-date analysis of the law in these areas. Hopefully, such a statement may be of assistance to the courts, the agencies, and the practicing bar.

Second, the analysis of the decisional law indicates that in some states, the courts—through seeming unawareness of important social considerations involved—have in certain instances failed to require some of the agencies (particularly those called, inappropriately, the "minor" agencies) to adhere to the basic procedural rules that are necessary to guarantee fair treatment to the respondents and to assure fully informed decisions. It is hoped that by bringing to the attention of judges and agency officials and attorneys the importance of these basic tenets of fair procedure, the study may in some measure serve to instill in the minds of all concerned a determination to insist vigorously on adherence to the basic requirements of fair play in agency rule-making and adjudication.

Third, it is hoped that the study may serve as a useful treatise on the principles of state administrative law, by making readily available a summary of the statutory and case law of the several states.

Financial support for this study was provided by the American Bar Foundation and the University of Michigan Law School. However, the analyses, conclusions, and opinions contained herein are those of the author, and do not constitute an expression of views by the American Bar Foundation, the American Bar Association, or the University of Michigan. Some of the ideas suggested in the following pages appear in more or less similar form in the author's earlier books, *Administrative Agencies and the Courts* (University of Michigan Law School, 1951); *The Lawyer and Administrative Agencies* (Prentice-Hall, Inc., 1957); and in Stason and Cooper, *Cases and Other Materials on Administrative Tribunals* (Third Edition, Callaghan & Company, 1957); and acknowledgment to those publishers is gratefully made.

Much of the credit for whatever merit this work may possess belongs to E. Blythe Stason, Dean Emeritus of the University of Michigan Law School and Administrator of the American Bar Foundation during the period that these volumes were written, who gave generously of his wise counsel on problems concerning the scope and techniques of research. Further, his careful reading and editing of the manuscript resulted in the correction of many errors, and the addition of many significant observations.

Mrs. John H. Holmes diligently checked the state reports of most of the states on a page-by-page basis for the period from 1950 to 1963, in order to find decisions relevant to administrative procedure which were not so indexed in the digests. She also prepared the comparative statutory studies.

In the final steps leading up to publication, members of the staff of the American Bar Foundation have been very helpful.

William Braithwaite was immediately responsible for the work on the manuscript which was done at that institution, and prepared the tables of cases, statutes and index.

Frank E. Cooper

Independence Day, 1965

SUMMARY CONTENTS

VOLUME I

VOLUME II

TABLE OF CONTENTS

VOLUME II

CHAPTER XVII TIMING OF THE APPLICATION FOR JUDICIAL REVIEW 561

CHAPTER I

IMPORTANCE OF ADMINISTRATIVE AGENCIES IN STATE GOVERNMENT: HISTORICAL PERSPECTIVE

Section 1

Distinguishing Characteristics of State Administrative Agencies

In marked contrast to the incandescent glare of investigation and debate, which since 1941[1] has been focused on the functions of federal administrative agencies (a glare which has at times produced more heat than light), comparatively little attention has been paid to the multiform agencies operating within the states.

It is strange that this neglect should exist. The personal privileges and property rights of most persons are more frequently and vitally affected by the rules and orders of state agencies than by the actions of federal agencies. Most lawyers, too, are more often concerned with state than with federal administrative proceedings. While matters before the federal agencies are, in the main, handled by a comparatively small segment of the bar (often specialists in the work of a single agency), almost every general practitioner has occasion from time to time to appear before state agencies.

In point of sheer numbers, the proliferation of state agencies is impressive. In several states, as many as sixty or seventy independent agencies make rules and adjudicate contested cases affecting in varied ways the lives, health, fortunes, safety, labor,

[1] The 1941 report of the Attorney General's Committee (*Administrative Procedure in Government Agencies,* S. DOC. No. 8, 77th Cong., 1st Sess.) may be cited as the critical bench-mark, if not the starting point, because the suggested code of administrative procedure appended to the separate statement of Messrs. McFarland, Stason, and Vanderbilt pointed the way to the Administrative Procedure Act of 1946, 5 U.S.C. § 1000 et seq.; F.C.A. 5 § 1000 et seq., which in turn became the foundation for the plethora of investigation, recommendation, and debate that has filled thousands of pages during the ensuing years.

and the business of millions of citizens. At a conservative estimate, more than 2000 state administrative agencies are exercising legislative and judicial functions. In carrying out their duties, they are to a large degree independent of the legislatures and the courts. Further, they are significantly independent of each other.[2] This self-assertive independence of the state agencies is reflected not only in the baffling heterogeneity of procedural rules, which is a source of needless confusion but, more importantly, in the widely disparate approaches to related problems, and in the application of variant principles and philosophies of economic and social control.

Even the briefest catalog of the principal agencies found in state governments indicates the broad areas of governmental activity committed to administrative control. In most states, agencies are depended on for supervision and regulation of agriculture (there may be five or ten agencies in this field), air pollution, banking, civil rights, civil service, conservation, corporations, some aspects of divorce law, fair employment practices, fisheries, highways, horse racing, insurance, labor, licensing (here, too, a single state may have a large number of agencies determining who may engage in a wide variety of businesses and pursuits, from driving a car to growing Christmas trees), liquor control, mediation, occupational permits (which may be required for barbers, druggists, contractors, optometrists, peddlers, plumbers, and many other occupations), parole of prisoners, professional licensing, public health, public utilities, public welfare, railroads, revenue, securities, taxation, trucking, unemployment, unfair competition, veterans' affairs, water resources, workmen's compensation, zoning, and literally dozens of other fields of activity.

Significance attaches, furthermore, not only to the number of agencies and to the broad spheres of governmental control committed to them, but also to the breadth of the powers delegated to them. In the field of corporation law, the lawyer is more concerned with administrative agencies than with the

---

[2] Witness the political maelstrom that attended the efforts of the Michigan legislature to implement the provisions of Section 2 of Article V of the Constitution of 1963, providing for the grouping of all state agencies into not more than twenty principal departments. Each agency was intensely jealous of its own prerogatives, and objected to proposals to subordinate its autonomy to any outside department head.

courts. Problems of labor law, which in recent years have assumed unique social importance, are likewise delegated primarily to administrative agencies, although in this field doctrines of preemption have led to the substantial displacement of state power in favor of federal administrative control. A substantial segment of the law of torts is now a matter of administrative adjudication. Even in the private law realm of contracts, administrative agencies are important. Administrative techniques have reached still further. In matters of criminal law and domestic relations, such agencies as probation offices and public "friends of the court" have assumed ever-increasing importance.

In many fields, property rights of substantial value are determined with a considerable degree of finality by administrative decision. A determination by a state tax commission as to the methods to be used in fixing property values for purposes of *ad valorem* taxation may add to the tax burden of every property owner in the state, aggregating millions of dollars in a single year. It has been suggested that a decision by a public service commission approving a rate increase for an electric or telephone utility may bulk larger, in point of the dollars involved, than all the decisions handed down by the state supreme court during the same year.

The determinations of administrative agencies significantly affect the personal life of every citizen. Many men can avoid "court trouble," but few indeed can avoid the administrative agencies. Like death and taxes (both of which, incidentally, are matters of agency concern) the agencies reach everyone.

While comparable to the federal agencies in point of importance, the state agencies differ from their federal counterparts in many respects, presenting unique problems which require their own solutions.

The most characteristic difference—and the most significant—is that of size. Compared with the massive institutional structure of the federal agencies, staffed sometimes with hundreds of lawyers and technicians, state agencies are small and loosely organized. A state agency may, for example, consist of three commissioners, who devote only a part of their time to the duties of their office, who depend for legal advice on an assistant attorney general (who may be assigned as counsel to a number of agencies), and who have no assistance other than that of a miniscule staff—perhaps one investigator and a few clerks and secretaries.

The differences resulting from the characteristically smaller size of the state agencies are many. Their procedures are more informal, and this means that a procedural code as complex as that of the Federal Administrative Procedure Act[3] would be unduly cumbersome. A more simple set of procedural standards is needed—one which concerns basic principles rather than procedural minutiae, and which is adaptable to the variant needs of both larger and smaller agencies. There exist wide differences in the operational methods of different state agencies. For example, a workmen's compensation commission, which may have a number of hearing officers and an administrative board of appeals all operating under the general superintending control of the commissioners, and hearing several thousand cases annually, necessarily exhibits a more complex procedural pattern than a state board of chiropractic examiners, which may be concerned only with issuing licenses to candidates who pass a prescribed examination, and revoking the licenses of those who violate prescribed statutory rules. But certain basic procedural standards, such as those set forth in the Revised Model State Administrative Procedure Act, can beneficially be applied to all.

Not only are state agencies smaller in point of personnel than the federal agencies, but their geographical jurisdictions are much more narrow. This circumstance, too, produces meaningful results. For one thing, counsel involved in a case are not infrequently acquainted personally with one or more of the members of the agency. It is a simple matter, therefore, in the case of some state agencies, to telephone the agency member, or call at his office, and discuss in *ex parte* informality the merits of the case, and undertake to work out a mutually satisfactory adjustment. Moreover, the agency members and staff employees are frequently acquainted personally with the parties appearing before the agency, and have a personal familiarity with their backgrounds and methods of operation. This circumstance may lead to delicate and difficult questions concerning possible favoritism or bias.

---

[3] 5 U.S.C. § 1000 et seq.; F.C.A. 5 § 1000 et seq.

The aura of professionalism and claimed expertise which is so pervasive a characteristic of the federal agencies is not so uniformly encountered in the case of the state agencies. This situation reflects a composite of many factors: the fact that state agencies frequently operate without the assistance of large permanent staffs; the fact that the commissioners, whose terms in office are often short, frequently do not bring to their assignments any particular professional or technical background; and the fact that in many instances there is an awareness that the state courts will have little hesitation in overriding the agency's determination, if it appears clearly wrong, on questions of fact as well as of law.

Because of these important differences between the state and the federal agencies, and the fact that no comprehensive survey has hitherto been made of the operations of the state agencies, the research committees of the American Bar Foundation and the University of Michigan Law School concluded in 1961 to sponsor the study which has resulted in these volumes.

Adopting the Revised Model State Administrative Procedure Act (promulgated in 1961 by the Commissioners on Uniform State Laws) as a convenient frame of reference, an attempt has been made to compare the statutory enactments of the several states as they bear on basic principles governing agency activities and judicial review thereof, and to analyze the leading decisions of the state courts since 1950 which establish general procedural rules.

A word should be said as to the reason for the voluminous statutory citations which have been included. It is realized that it would be an impossible task to present a complete, thorough, and accurate survey of all the statutory law in the fifty states.[4] Every lawyer will of course consult the current supplements to his own state code to determine the applicable statutory law of his state. But it was believed that a large-scale sampling of state legislation, as of 1963-1964, would help to identify significant legislative trends, and in this way assist statutory draftsmen and other students of the subject.[5]

---

[4] During the course of the preparation of these volumes, five states (Alaska, Georgia, Minnesota, Oklahoma, and West Virginia) adopted far-reaching statutory amendments, and there will doubtless be other significant amendments before this work is printed.

[5] In view of the importance of the field of state administrative law, it is strange that so few broad-scale studies have been made. For many years, the monumental

In the field of state administrative procedure, as in other fields, the problems of the present day can be properly understood only from the viewpoint of historical perspective. There is accordingly included in this introductory chapter a history of the last thirty years of administrative procedure reform. The statement was prepared by E. Blythe Stason, Dean Emeritus of the University of Michigan Law School and Administrator of the American Bar Foundation during the period that this study was conceived and carried out. No one is so well qualified as Dean Stason to write this historical review, for he has had a unique personal participation in that history.

As one of the members of the Attorney General's Committee of 1941, Dean Stason joined with Messrs. McFarland and Vanderbilt in a "Statement of Additional Views and Recommendations" attached to which was a "Code of Standards of Fair Administrative Procedure," drafted in large part by Dean Stason. This code was of particular historical importance, for its provisions, and the views set forth in the "Statement of Additional Views" rather than the views expressed in the majority report, became the basis of the Federal Administrative Procedure Act of 1946. Dean Stason was also the principal draftsman, for the Conference of Commissioners of Uniform State Laws, of the first Model State Administrative Procedure Act, promulgated in 1946, the same year that the Congress adopted the Federal Administrative Procedure Act.

---

work of Robert M. Benjamin, *Administrative Adjudication in the State of New York* (1942) which is a classic example of what may be accomplished by careful analysis and perceptive diagnosis of the problem, stood as the sole beacon light in a tempestuous sea. In more recent years, a general awakening of interest may be noted. Whitney R. Harris wrote a notable comparative analysis in 1953: Harris, *Administrative Practice and Procedure: Comparative State Legislation,* 6 OKLA. L. REV. 29. The newly-formed Division of State Administrative Law of the Administrative Law Section of the American Bar Association, under the chairmanship of Dan M. Byrd, Jr., of Atlanta, has accomplished much in a short time. Not the least of its achievements was a notable symposium on the Revised State Administrative Procedure Act, 16 *Administrative Law Review* 50 (1963), setting forth the respective views of academicians, administrators, appellate judges, and legislators with respect to the provisions of the act. Professor Maurice H. Merrill, who had a great deal to do with the drafting of the Oklahoma Administrative Procedure Act (1963) is the author of an article which not only describes the details of the Oklahoma statute but includes a perceptive analysis of the problems of the legislative draftsman in this area. Merrill, *Oklahoma's New Administrative Procedure Act,* 17 OKLA. L. REV. 1 (1964). Mr. Charles M. Harrison published a careful and scholarly review of the 1964 West Virginia Act which also deserves the careful attention of any lawyer who may be faced with the problem of adapting to his own state the general principles of the Revised Model State Act. Harrison, *The West Virginia Administrative Procedure Act,* 66 W. VA. L. REV. 159 (1964).

Not only did Dean Stason play a leading role in the writing of the Federal Act and the Model State Act, but he has been in the forefront of efforts to improve both statutes.

As a member of the Task Force on Legal Services and Procedure of the Second Hoover Commission, he contributed in large measure to the drafting of the report of that committee[6] and the subjoined Administrative Code. The following year, as chairman of a drafting committee of the Administrative Law Section of the American Bar Association, Dean Stason prepared a draft of an amended Federal Administrative Procedure Act, which became the basis for the American Bar Association bill that in turn served as the foundation for several bills now pending in Congress.

Shortly after the completion of this effort, Dean Stason accepted the chairmanship of the committee charged with the preparation of the Revised Model State Administrative Procedure Act, completed and published in 1961.

Section 2

Three Decades of Administrative Procedure Reform

Administrative procedure reform, which, at the state level, is the principal subject of study in this book, had its origins more than thirty years ago and has evolved during the intervening years in a long series of intensive studies of administrative procedure, both federal and state. In large measure, the movement originated in the American Bar Association, primarily in the Association's Special Committee on Administrative Law. This Special Committee was created by the Executive Committee of the American Bar Association at the May meeting in 1933. Later that year, under the chairmanship of Louis G. Caldwell, the Committee submitted an initial report dealing with what was called "the growing multiplicity of administrative tribunals and the apparently irresistible tendency to delegate the promulgation of regulations and the hearing and determination of controversies to such tribunals."[7]

Subsequently, under the successive chairmanships of Louis Caldwell in 1934 and 1935,[8] and O. R. McGuire in 1936, 1937,

[6] Commission on Organization of the Executive Branch of the Government, TASK FORCE REPORT ON LEGAL SERVICES AND PROCEDURE (1955).

[7] 58 REPORTS OF THE AMERICAN BAR ASSOCIATION 407-27 (1933).

[8] 59 REPORTS OF THE AMERICAN BAR ASSOCIATION 539-64 (1934) and 60 *id.* at 136-43 (1935).

1938, and 1939,[9] a gradual evolution of thinking was revealed with respect to administrative law and procedure. Moreover, these reports were in reality a reflection of many other concurrent studies and reports that began to emerge from bar associations, law faculty members, and government officials. Together they precipitated a chain reaction in the form of massive research and aggressive development of the administrative process, paralleling in time, but lagging somewhat behind, the notable proliferation of administrative agencies in the middle 1930's, created to regulate almost all business, commerce, and even individual affairs. The ultimate outcome was the Federal Administrative Procedure Act of 1946, the Model State Administrative Procedure Act of the same year, and eventually corresponding legislation in a large number of states.

In connection with the 1939 report of the American Bar Association Committee, an administrative procedure bill was presented, one of the earliest of the many to come. This bill included provisions for judicial review of all administrative decisions by petition to the United States Court of Appeals for the District of Columbia serving as an administrative court of appeal.

The American Bar Association Committee reports, together with other related activities, eventually resulted in congressional action. In 1939, the Walter-Logan Administrative Procedure Bill, S.915, was favorably reported and was adopted by Congress. In the meantime, however, President Roosevelt had directed the appointment of an Attorney General's Committee on Administrative Procedure to make further studies and recommendations. Pending report from this Committee, the President vetoed the Walter-Logan Bill and stated in his veto message that he wished to await the report and recommendations of the Committee before approving any measure in this complicated field.

In 1941, the Attorney General's Committee presented its final report, with a so-called supplemental report prepared by three of the twelve members of the Committee. This supplemental report included a draft "Code of Fair Administrative Procedure" which code, with many changes made along the way, finally became the Federal Administrative Procedure Act of 1946.

---

[9] 61 REPORTS OF THE AMERICAN BAR ASSOCIATION 720-93 (1936); 62 *id.* at 789-845 (1937); 63 *id.* at 331-68 (1938); 64 *id.* at 575-620 (1939).

With the foregoing as a background in the federal field, it was inevitable that consideration should be given to state administrative agencies and their procedures. Although not so large in terms of staff size, the state agencies are even more numerous than federal agencies, for they are multiplied fifty times over. In the several state and local governments, we find agencies touching almost every phase of business and many phases of private life. In setting up this vast array of agencies, the legislatures have, in general, concentrated on the substance of the intended regulation, and paid little or no attention to the procedural aspects of their activities. All too frequently the development of rules of procedure has been left to the whims of agency personnel.

Conscious of this state of affairs and, also, cognizant of the developments with respect to the procedures of federal administrative agencies, the Section of Judicial Administration of the American Bar Association, in 1937, created a Committee on Administrative Agencies and Tribunals. In 1938, this Committee, under the chairmanship of Ralph M. Hoyt of Milwaukee, presented a report concerning judicial review of state administrative action in state courts,[10] a report that drew much favorable comment. Again in 1939, at the winter Section meeting, the same Committee reported, this time setting forth a draft of a proposed act dealing with certain major phases of state administrative procedure. The act was prepared to serve as a model for state legislation.[11]

In accordance with established practice, this draft act was referred by the Section to the National Conference of Commissioners on Uniform State Laws, and at its 1939 meeting a Conference Committee was appointed for the purpose of further study and development of the measure. In the Conference and its Committee the draft act was subjected to intensive research over a long period of time.

During 1939-1940, the Conference Committee met with the Committee of the Section on Judicial Administration, and numerous changes in the original draft were mutually agreed upon. A revised draft was then presented at the 1940 session of the Conference, and after careful revision it was adopted and forwarded to the House of Delegates of the American Bar Association for

[10] 63 *id.* at 623-31 (1938).
[11] 64 *id.* at 407-42 (1939).

approval. However, in January of 1941, before action was taken by the House of Delegates, the United States Attorney General's Committee on Administrative Procedure, after two years of study, filed its final report on the subject of federal administrative law, setting forth both majority and minority drafts of bills for the regulation of federal administrative procedure. Thereafter, the Executive Committee of the Conference decided that, in view of the Attorney General's Committee Report, it was advisable to give still further consideration to the Conference measure. Accordingly, it was recalled from the House of Delegates and recommitted to the Conference Committee for further research and reconsideration.[12]

In March of 1942, the so-called Benjamin Report was submitted to the Governor of New York. This report, entitled "Administrative Adjudication in the State of New York," was prepared by Robert M. Benjamin of the New York Bar, who served as commissioner appointed under the Executive Law of New York. It consisted of a study of the exercise of quasi-judicial and rule-making functions of boards, commissions, and departments of New York State, and judicial review thereof. It was a thorough critique of state administrative practice not only in New York, but also on the general subject of state administrative procedure. It did for state administrative procedure what the Attorney General's Committee Report did for federal procedure.

With the new light afforded by these two significant reports, the Conference Committee prepared a completely revised and much improved draft of a Model State Administrative Procedure Act and submitted it for consideration at the 1942 session of the Conference. There it was re-examined and was again recommitted for final study. During the succeeding year, the act was widely distributed to members of state administrative commissions, to bar associations, and to other interested persons and groups in every state of the union. Hundreds of helpful suggestions were received and studied by the Committee. Parenthetically, in 1943

[12] Dean E. Blythe Stason, Chairman of the Committee, discussed the matter on the floor of the conference at its meeting in September, 1941. He pointed out that the report of the Attorney General's Committee and the two bills connected therewith had thrown considerable additional light upon the proper principles of administrative procedure. He, also, pointed out that the Benjamin Report on the state administrative agencies of New York State was soon to be forthcoming, and under these circumstances the Conference Committee wished to reconsider its earlier draft. NATIONAL CONFERENCE OF COMMISSIONERS ON UNIFORM STATE LAWS 134-35 (1941).

the then current draft of the measure was enacted almost verbatim by the state legislature of Wisconsin, where it received much favorable comment. Again, at its 1943 session, the Conference repeated its section by section, line by line examination, and the measure was ready for final action. This action was delayed, however, because of the fact that the Federal Administrative Procedure Bill was pending in Congress. Some persons felt apprehensive lest differences in terminology in the two measures might result in question about and delay of the Federal Bill.

The Federal Bill was finally enacted by Congress in June, 1946, and thereafter the Model State Administrative Procedure Act, after having been held in abeyance pending congressional action, was approved by the National Conference of Commissioners at its October, 1946, annual meeting. Following its adoption and for the last eighteen years, the Model Act has been available as a guide for state legislation and it has been widely used in connection therewith.

Moreover, during the intervening years since the adoption of the original federal legislation and the Model State Act, further study has been constantly given the subject of administrative procedure at both federal and state levels. In fact, the consideration given the subject constitutes one of the truly massive research activities in the history of the law.[13]

On April 29, 1953, the President of the United States, at the instance of the Chief Justice of the United States in his capacity as chairman of the Judicial Conference, called a conference for the purpose of considering the unnecessary delays, expense, and volume of records in adjudication and rule-making proceedings in the federal agencies. Some fifty-six agencies were represented in this conference, the chairman of which was Judge E. Barrett Prettyman of the Court of Appeals of the District of Columbia. Also present were members of the federal judiciary, federal trial examiners, and the practicing bar. The conference formulated its recommendations (twenty-two in number) and reported them to the President in March, 1955. It was a massive collaborative effort, pulling together the knowledge, skill, experience, and ability of a host of experts in federal administrative law. A second such conference under the same chairman was called by President Kennedy in 1961 and it reported its thirty recommendations in

[13] See Stason, *Research in Administrative Law*, 16 AD. L. REV. 99-107 (1964).

1962. These two reports added many new and useful ideas to the aggregate of knowledge of administrative law and procedure.

On July 10, 1953, Congress, by Public Law 108, established the Commission on Organization of the Executive Branch of the Government, known as the "Second Hoover Commission." One of the task forces of this Commission was the Task Force on Legal Services and Procedure, consisting of fourteen members under the chairmanship of James M. Douglas, former Chief Justice of the Supreme Court of Missouri. This group undertook and carried forward a major study of the procedure of federal administrative agencies. Its final report included some seventy-four recommendations with appropriate commentary, together with proposed legislation for complete recodification of the federal law concerning legal services and administrative procedures. The report was submitted to Congress with the Hoover Commission Report under the date of March 28, 1955.

Subsequently, in May of 1955, the Board of Governors of the American Bar Association established a Special Committee on Legal Services and Procedure, under the chairmanship of Ashley Sellers, Esq., a member of the Washington, D.C., Bar, and a long-time student of as well as a practitioner before administrative agencies. This Committee, in cooperation with the Section on Administrative Law of the American Bar Association, undertook a thorough re-examination of the Federal Administrative Procedure Act in the light of the recommendations of the Hoover Commission Task Force. As a result, a new "Code of Federal Administrative Procedure" has been prepared and introduced into Congress.

In view of all this ferment, the National Conference of Commissioners concluded that its Model State Administrative Procedure Act of 1946 deserved reconsideration and revision. Accordingly, in 1958, a special committee was constituted by the Conference for the purpose. In 1959, and again in 1960, drafts of a revision were presented to the Conference and were given consideration in great detail. Finally, in 1961, the draft was given Conference approval as its Revised Model Act.[14] It is this measure that is now being utilized by state legislatures as a guide to administrative procedure reform.

[14] NATIONAL CONFERENCE OF COMMISSIONERS ON UNIFORM STATE LAWS 199-223 (1961).

The major principles embraced in the Model Act and the Revised Act include such fundamental matters as the requirement that each agency adopt essential procedural as well as substantive rules; that all rule making be accompanied by proper notice and opportunity to submit views; that there be proper assurance of publicity for all administrative rules; that provision be made for declaratory judgments and rulings; that there be assurance of fundamental fairness in administrative adjudicative hearings, particularly as to notice, rules of evidence, taking official notice, separation of functions, and the assurance of personal familiarity with the evidence on the part of responsible deciding officers; and, finally, that provision be made for adequate judicial review. These are basic principles of fairness in procedure.

Over the years since the adoption of the original Model Act in 1946, the measure has been studied by the legislatures in a very considerable number of states. It has been widely used for the purpose for which it was intended, namely, as a model to assist state legislators who are interested in designing legislation appropriate for their own purposes. Moreover, in a number of states the act has been adopted almost verbatim. Legislation in about twenty-five jurisdictions has been founded to a greater or lesser extent upon either the original Model Act of 1946 or the Revised Act of 1961.[15] This widespread use of the Act in the preparation of state legislative coverage of the subject is indicative of the fact that state administrative procedure is no longer to be left largely to the state agencies themselves, but is to be regulated by statute in accordance with the basic principles of common sense, justice, and fairness that have been found over the years to be worthy in connection with administrative action.

As a result of the vast ferment of the past thirty years and the immense amount of research, deliberation, and skillful draftsmanship that has been devoted to the subject, administrative procedure is coming of age. It is the result of this maturing process that is set forth in these volumes.

---

[15] Arizona, Connecticut, Florida, Georgia, Hawaii, Illinois, Indiana, Iowa, Kentucky, Maine, Maryland, Massachusetts, Michigan, Minnesota, Missouri, Nebraska, New Mexico, North Carolina, North Dakota, Oregon, Rhode Island, Virginia, Washington, West Virginia, Wisconsin.

CHAPTER II

SEPARATION OF POWERS

Section 1

Historical Perspective

(A) Introduction

The history of the separation of powers doctrine has apparently been one of rapid retreat, if not rout. It has been described as an anachronistic vestige. Analogic applications of Montesquieuian concepts, and nostalgic attachment to governmental philosophies of the eighteenth and early nineteenth century, have given way, it is said, to the harsh necessities of modern government.

But a more searching analysis suggests that the ideals of an earlier day have not been renounced totally. Their basic values have been preserved, and some hints may be found that the paths to be followed by the state governments in the future may lead to insistence on a greater separation of the respective powers of declaring legislative policy, of executing and administering the law as declared by the legislature, and of adjudicating disputes as to the respective boundaries of public and private right.

(B) The Classical View

It has been recognized by most political scientists since James Madison that the doctrine of separation of powers does not forbid the exercise by one department of powers that could appropriately be exercised by another department—that there may be a "blending" of disparate powers—as when a legislature tries impeachment proceedings, or when a court legislates rules of practice.

Montesquieu's statement was:

> When the legislative and executive powers are united in the same person, or in the same body of magistracy, there can be then no lib-

> erty; because apprehensions may arise, lest the same monarch or senate should enact tyrannical laws, to execute them in a tyrannical manner.
>
> Again, there is no liberty, if the power of judging be not separated from the legislative and executive powers. Were it joined with the legislative, the life and liberty of the subject would be exposed to arbitrary control; for the judge would then be the legislator. Were it joined to the executive power, the judge might behave with all the violence of an oppressor.[1]

Discussing these passages in *The Federalist,* Madison proclaimed that Montesquieu

> . . . did not mean that these departments ought to have no *partial agency* in, or no *control* over, the acts of each other. His meaning, as his own words import, and still more conclusively as illustrated by the example in his eye, can amount to no more than this, that where the *whole* power of one department is exercised by the same hands which possess the *whole* power of another department, the fundamental principles of a free constitution are subverted.[2]

In other words, the real thrust of the separation of powers philosophy is that each department of government must be kept free from the control or coercive influence of the other departments.[3] An agency whose members are appointed by the governor must not be given rule-making powers as plenary as those of the legislature; nor may its adjudicatory determinations be given a degree of conclusiveness so great as to denigrate the powers of the courts. Restated in these terms, the doctrine of separation of powers continues to be accorded a hospitable reception by the state courts.

(C) Current Attitude of State Courts

The state courts, by and large, are not ready to agree with the strictures of those who dub the whole separation of powers concept as an unhappy anachronism, the product of an "Aristotelian theoretician."[4] Neither, it is fair to say, do they agree fully with

[1] XI L'Esprit des Lois 215-17 (1750); See Ehrlich, *Montesquieu and Sociological Jurisprudence,* 29 Harv. L. Rev. 582 (1916).

[2] Madison, The Federalist, No. XLVII (1788) (Lodge ed. 1906), 301-302.

[3] Humphrey's Ex'r v. United States, 295 U.S. 602, 79 L. Ed. 1611, 55 Sup. Ct. 869 (1935), at p. 874: "The fundamental necessity of maintaining each of the three general departments of government entirely free from the control or coercive influence, direct or indirect, of either of the others, has often been stressed and is hardly open to serious question."

[4] *E.g.,* Landis, The Administrative Process 1-2 (1938).

those who proclaim that "the doctrine [of separation of powers] must be universal in its application if stability and liberty are to be sought and obtained."[5]

Rather, the state courts have inclined to the view that combination of legislative, prosecutory, and adjudicatory functions in a single agency will be countenanced where a practical necessity therefor exists, but only so long as workable checks and balances (such as reservation of superintending control in the legislature, or the availability of reasonably broad judicial review) exist to guard against abuses of administrative discretion. In the absence of such safeguards, the state courts are still prepared to strike down statutes which grant an agency powers so unlimited as to enable the agency in practical effect to displace the legislature and the courts.

There is thus discernible a difference in attitude between the state courts and the federal courts. The state courts are inclined on the whole to take a less charitable view than that entertained by the federal courts as to the propriety of according a large measure of finality to determinations of agencies which combine legislative, prosecutory, and adjudicatory functions.

It is principally in connection with claims as to the finality of administrative action that the question as to separation of powers becomes critical. So long as the legislature can effectively change the agency's rules, and the courts can effectively correct errors made in the adjudication of cases, it is of comparatively little concern that an agency's powers possess at once legislative and judicial characteristics. Indeed, it could almost be called an identifying characteristic of agencies that they combine the powers of rule making and of adjudication. The mere existence of blended powers has not been a cause of concern.[6] It is only when the blending of functions creates a danger of unchecked power that concern arises.

The reason for the circumstance that state courts have on the whole been more vigilant than have the federal courts to extirpate combinations of power which threaten to produce ungovernable administrative omnipotence may very well be, as sug-

---

[5] VANDERBILT, THE DOCTRINE OF THE SEPARATION OF POWERS AND ITS PRESENT-DAY SIGNIFICANCE 144 (1953).

[6] As Justice Jackson put the matter, in characteristically trenchant phrase: "Courts have differed in assigning a place to these seemingly necessary bodies in our constitutional system. Administrative agencies have been called quasi-legisla-

gested by Judge Vanderbilt,[7] that the state courts have been better equipped to take the necessary corrective measures. The powers of the state courts to grant relief from arbitrary administrative action derive, in part at least, from the constitutional right of the individual to obtain review of administrative determinations through the great prerogative writs or their modern substitutes. These have remained generally available in the state courts, and have provided an access to the courts even in cases where the legislature has not provided for judicial review.[8] On the other hand, the powers of the federal courts in controversies arising in federal agencies, and the extent of review accorded by the Congress, or provided by the federal courts in the absence of statute,[9] is often less efficacious than the review afforded by the state courts.[10]

Aided by their inherent powers, most state courts have evinced an attitude in large measure responsive to a criticism made by three members of the Attorney General's Committee on Administrative Procedure:

> In the administrative process . . . these stages of making and applying law have been telescoped into a single agency. In this concentration customary and separate procedures have disappeared. The legislature no longer prescribes the rules but in large part leaves this function to the administrative agency. . . . The agency which prescribes rules is also the investigator, the prosecutor, the judge, and to a large extent the appellate tribunal. It is given a staggering load of work and must necessarily delegate many of these functions to subordinates. One employee acts as prosecutor, another as presiding judge, and another as appellate judge. There is no jury. The litigant often feels that, in this combination of functions within a single tribunal or agency, he has lost all opportunity to argue his case to an

---

tive, quasi-executive or quasi-judicial, as the occasion required, in order to validate their functions within the separation-of-powers scheme of the Constitution. The mere retreat to the qualifying 'quasi' is implicit with confession that all recognized classifications have broken down, and 'quasi' is a smooth cover which we draw over our confusion as we might use a counterpane to conceal a disordered bed." Federal Trade Comm'n v. Ruberoid Co., 343 U.S. 470, 487, 96 L. Ed. 1081, 72 Sup. Ct. 800 (1952)—Dissent.

[7] VANDERBILT, *op. cit. supra* note 5, at p. 112.

[8] Foster v. Goodpaster, 290 Ky. 410, 161 S.W.2d 626, 140 A.L.R. 1044 (1942); Cofman v. Ousterhous, 40 N.D. 390, 168 N.W. 826, 18 A.L.R. 219, (1918); Sabre v. Rutland R.R., 86 Vt. 347, 85 Atl. 693 (1913).

[9] *E.g.,* Estep v. United States, 327 U.S. 114, 90 L. Ed. 567, 66 Sup. Ct. 423 (1946).

[10] Vanderbilt, *Administrative Law,* 1944 ANNUAL SURVEY OF AMERICAN LAW 169, 205-13 (1946).

unbiased official and that he has been deprived of safeguards he has been taught to revere.[11]

State legislatures, too, have evinced a sympathy with the complaint voiced by these three distinguished scholars. They have taken many steps to ameliorate the conditions decried in the report of these members of the Attorney General's Committee. They have, for example, in a significant number of cases, required agencies to submit their rules to legislative oversight. They have required agencies to follow rules of evidence more court-like than those observed in many federal agencies. They have required state agencies to adopt procedures designed to assure personal mastery of the record by those officials charged with the responsibility for making the decision. Often, they have provided for review in trial courts, where a leisurely reexamination of the entire case produces a more searching review than that available under a procedure pursuant to which a written record is submitted to an appellate court on the basis of a brief oral argument. More to the point, they have often, meeting a need which was expressed by the Task Force on Legal Services and Procedure of the Second Hoover Commission,[12] provided for an internal separation of powers more rigorous than that commonly encountered in the federal agencies.

(D) The Future Path

It may well be that the states will lead the way to a more complete separation of prosecutory and adjudicatory functions by creating separate and independent tribunals to pass upon cases prosecuted by the agencies—a proposal urged by the Task Force with respect to immigration, labor, trade, and tax matters.[13] In fact, a number of states have already taken steps in this direction. It is commonly provided in unemployment insurance matters, for example, that a completely independent appeals tribunal will review agency determinations as to the allowance of benefits. The same is sometimes true of workmen's compensation

---

11 Statement of Messrs. McFarland, Stason, and Vanderbilt, S. Doc. No. 8, 77th Cong., 1st Sess. 204 (1941).

12 Commission on Organization of the Executive Branch of the Government, Task Force Report on Legal Services and Procedure 176 (1955).

13 *Id.* at 248, 435, 439.

appeals. Similarly, in a number of states independent tax courts, or courts of claims, exercise final authority in the adjudicatory phase of those administrative activities. This trend may well go further, and possibly the states may set an example which in time will be imposed upon the federal agencies.

The administrative agency is often created to meet new problems which may at the outset require an experimental approach where, perhaps, rules can be formulated only on the basis of experience gained by deciding cases for a period of time on an *ad hoc* basis. Broad administrative discretion and a union of functions may be necessary at the outset. But in many such cases where agencies were originally created to meet emergency situations, and accordingly were granted not only executive and legislative powers but judicial powers as well, later experience has suggested a refinement of the early approach to the problem. On the basis of further studies, and in the light of experience, it has sometimes proved wise to create special tribunals to exercise adjudicatory powers. Thus, adjudicatory functions of the Customs Bureau came after a time to be vested in a Court of Customs and Patent Appeals. Similarly, the responsibilities of the Bureau of Internal Revenue in passing administratively on claims for refunds or objections to tax assessments were in later years vested in a separate Board of Tax Appeals, which in due course became the Tax Court.

These lessons of history teach that, in fields where administrative agencies engage contentiously with the private parties appearing before them, it is in the interest of good government to eliminate the combinations of prosecuting and judicial powers. The process is gradual. Change does not come overnight. But the highway of past experience points the way into the uncharted future.

Ernst Freund, whose voice in the early 1920's was that of a prophet in the wilderness, insofar as American administrative law was concerned, predicted long ago that administration of regulatory laws would gravitate from discretion to rule. He phrased the thought as follows:

> A comprehensive view of administrative discretion discloses a tendency toward standardization with a small residual margin for flexibility which approximates the inevitable question of fact. The function of discretion would then be not to displace rule but to prepare

> the way for it. On any other terms administrative discretion would be an anomaly. It would mean that administrative authorities are superior to courts in their capacity to deal with private rights, or that under modern conditions the public welfare demands personal government instead of government by law.[14]

In the context of the developments in state administrative law during the last half century, it is interesting in retrospect to consider the prediction Freund made when, addressing the St. Louis Bar Association in 1923, he said:

> What we cannot say of administrative power in general we can say of discretionary administrative power over individual rights, namely that it is undesirable *per se* and should be avoided as far as may be, for discretion is unstandardized power and to lodge in an official such power over person or property is hardly conformable to the "Rule of Law."
>
> Is it then possible to establish in our administrative statutes a tendency toward the elimination of discretion? . . . I am inclined to think that . . . the gradual and rather unconscious drift is toward displacement of discretion. I do not overlook the new advent of the unstandardized power over capital issues and the certificates of convenience and necessity; but the importance of these matters will force standardization in a relatively short time.[15]

Section 2

State Court Decisions Respecting Separation of Powers

(A) PRESERVING ESSENTIAL INDEPENDENCE OF DEPARTMENTS OF GOVERNMENT

Illustrative of the principle that a combination of prosecutory and adjudicatory powers in an agency will be held invalid if it produces a concentration of power so great as to threaten the independence of other departments of government is a decision of the Illinois court.[16] A statute requiring assessment of a retailer's occupation tax provided that the department of revenue could issue a jeopardy assessment under stated circumstances, that notice of the jeopardy assessment would be given the taxpayer, and that a certified copy of the assessment would be immediately

---

[14] FREUND, ADMINISTRATIVE POWERS OVER PERSONS AND PROPERTY 102 (1928).

[15] FREUND & OTHERS, THE GROWTH OF AMERICAN ADMINISTRATIVE LAW 22-23 (1923).

[16] People *ex rel.* Isaacs v. Johnson, 26 Ill. 2d 268, 186 N.E.2d 346 (1962).

filed with the clerk of court, whereupon it became the duty of the clerk to enter judgment on the assessment. Noting that the contemplated procedure cut off the right of the taxpayer to a hearing before the court on the legality of the assessment—thus circumventing the power of the court to check what it might deem to be an abuse of power by the agency—the court held that the statute offended the very essence of due process, by placing unbridled discretionary power in the agency.

An attempt by the legislature to exercise coercive control over the executive department of government is equally offensive to the separation of powers doctrine. Thus, when the New Jersey Legislature attempted to interpose its will upon the state's governor by extending the term of office of the incumbent director of the state rent control office, thereby depriving the governor of his power to make an appointment to that office, the statute was held invalid.[17] Highlighting the point of the decision is another case decided by the New Jersey court in the same year[18] involving a similar legislative action extending the term of office of incumbent members of an agency. But in the second case the agency involved (the state law enforcement council) was deemed by the court to be a legislative arm of the government, its principal duty being to recommend legislative action designed to minimize crime. Since the functions served by the agency were primarily designed to aid the legislature in its own tasks, it was found that there was no invasion of the reserved powers of the executive department in depriving the governor of appointive control. Indeed, in the latter case, the governor's insistence on the right to control the personnel of the agency might properly be viewed as an improper interference with the right of the legislature to be free of the coercive control of the executive department.

The reasons which persuade the state courts to insist on this residual application of the separation of powers philosophy were well stated in a dictum of the Alabama court[19] in a decision upholding the validity of a statutory provision authorizing the state's trial courts to consider *de novo* an appeal from an administrative agency. It was argued that to permit the trial courts to

---

[17] Richman v. Ligham, 22 N.J. 40, 123 A.2d 372 (1956).

[18] Richman v. Neuberger, 22 N.J. 28, 123 A.2d 217 (1956).

[19] *Ex parte* Darnell, 262 Ala. 71, 76 So. 2d 770 (1955); *Cf.*, Ball v. Jones, 272 Ala. 305, 132 So. 2d 120 (1961).

reconsider *de novo* the executive decision of a state personnel board to discharge a public employee violated the provision of the state constitution which declared that the judiciary should never exercise legislative or executive powers. In rejecting the contention, the court held that the separation of powers doctrine requires only that the entire power of one governmental department should not be exercised by the same body that possesses the entire power of either of the other departments; and the court added: ". . . an administrative commission need not be exclusively a branch of the executive, the legislative, or the judicial department. It can partake of the nature and powers of all three."[20]

In other words, the real thrust of the separation of powers doctrine, as now applied in the state courts, is that there must remain, either in the legislature or the courts, effective power to correct any abuses resulting from the grant of combined powers to a single agency. This point was emphasized by Chief Justice Vanderbilt of the New Jersey court, in a case holding that the state division of workmen's compensation was not a court and that accordingly under the New Jersey constitution the supreme court was without jurisdiction to consider a question certified to it by the agency (for only courts could so certify questions to the supreme court). After noting that "the doctrine of separation of powers is the great contribution of Anglo-American lawyers to the prevention of absolutism and the preservation of the rights of the individual against the state," the court pointed out that "the proper delegation of legislative power to administrative agencies within the executive department" was not a violation of the separation of powers provision of the New Jersey constitution (which declared that no person belonging to one branch of the government shall exercise any of the powers properly belonging to either of the others) for the reason that "what the Legislature delegates it may at any time withdraw." The court further pointed out that no violation of the constitutional

[20] In an earlier day, when the doctrine of separation of powers was more rigidly construed, a contrary result was reached in Illinois holding that a statute authorizing the state supreme court to review, on certiorari, questions of law involved in a decision of the workmen's compensation commission, was invalid because the supreme court could not consider a non-judicial question, *i.e.,* one not decided by a judicial tribunal. Courter v. Simpson Constr. Co., 264 Ill. 488, 106 N.E. 350 (1914).

provision is involved in the grant to administrative agencies of the power to adjudicate cases, "for every administrative adjudication is subject to the doctrine of the supremacy of law" and "nowhere is the right of judicial review of administrative determinations more strictly enforced than in this State."[21]

Other cases invalidating delegations to administrative agencies on the basis that the grants of power have violated separation of power precepts reflect, in the main, the principles and philosophies of the cases above cited.

For example, the New Hampshire court relied on the separation of powers doctrine in holding invalid a proposed statute providing a system of compensation for injuries to person or property arising out of automobile accidents and vesting in an administrative commission the determination of claims thereunder.[22] The decision was predicated on the proposition that the judicial functions delegated to the board amounted to a clear derogation of the traditional power of the courts, and ran counter to the proposition that none of the departments of government should be subject to the coercive control of another department. The court said:

> It is consistent with the Constitution that executive officers should be vested with some judicial power. . . . As a rule which meets most situations, when an executive board has regulatory functions, it may hear and determine controversies which are incidental thereto, but if the duty is primarily to decide questions of legal right between private parties, the function belongs to the judiciary. Courts of justice, in their popular sense, may not be set up and established in the executive organization. They pertain exclusively to the branch of the judiciary. . . . The creation of an executive board is justified if its service is to determine and maintain a public right or interest. To accomplish its purposes judicial powers may be necessarily exerted. But they must concern matters of an executive character. They are proper if it may fairly be said that there is need of them in order to produce an efficient and effective administrative enforcement of the public interest. . . . However . . . the vesting of the control of private litigation in an administrative board . . . is not permissible. It is as much forbidden as it is to require a court to take on executive functions.

---

21 Mulhearn v. Federal Shipbuilding & Dry Dock Co., 2 N.J. 356, 364, 66 A.2d 726 (1949).

22 *In re* Opinion of the Justices, 87 N.H. 492, 493-95, 179 Atl. 344, 110 A.L.R. 819 (1935). The decision is believed by some students to go too far in insisting on a rigid separation of powers.

Again in California, the delegation of judicial powers to administrative agencies not possessing other significant administrative or regulatory responsibilities has been condemned. In an early case,[23] it was held that the power to grant compensation to dependents because of death by industrial accident could not be vested in an administrative tribunal, unless authorized by special constitutional provision. The point was re-emphasized in a later case[24] holding that in the absence of special constitutional authority only a court may exercise the state's judicial power.

The Indiana court has likewise been insistent on comparatively strict application of classical separation of powers doctrine, holding unconstitutional a statute which named legislators serving on the legislature's budget committee as members of an agency created to supervise the financing and operation of a state office building.[25]

(B) Delegation of Combined Powers to Agencies

Except in the comparatively rare cases, such as those noted above, where a combination of powers in a single agency was deemed to threaten, in some measure, the respective primacies of the legislature or of the courts, the states have sustained the delegation of combined legislative, prosecutory, and judicial powers to agencies.

If the state legislature so ordains, the same agency may legislate the rules that implement a general statute, then look for violations of such rules, and (if it discovers a suspected violation) prosecute a hearing at which it sits as judge to determine whether it has proved its allegations to its own satisfaction. Contrary though this may seem to the ancient maxim that no man should be judge in his own case, there seems to be no constitutional impediment to such combination of powers within a single agency.

Typical of the general approach is a decision of the Connecticut court[26] holding it proper to authorize a dental commission to investigate, prosecute, and adjudicate charges against dentists

---

23 Western Metal Supply Co. v. Pillsbury, 172 Cal. 407, 156 Pac. 491 (1916).

24 Standard Oil Co. of California v. State Bd. of Equalization, 6 Cal. 2d 557, 59 P.2d 119 (1936).

25 Book v. State Office Bldg. Comm'n, 238 Ind. 120, 149 N.E.2d 273 (1958).

26 Ramanov v. Dental Comm'n, 142 Conn. 44, 111 A.2d 9 (1955).

charged with unprofessional conduct. Similarly, the Massachusetts court held[27] that selectmen of a town could be authorized to prefer charges against elected officials and, after hearing, decide whether the charges should be sustained, and the official removed from office.

Yet it is this delegation of combinations of power, rather than the delegation of either legislative or judicial power alone to a single agency, which is at the bottom of much of the criticism directed against the operation of state agencies. Correction must come from the state legislatures. An initial step in this direction is provided by those provisions of the Revised Model State Act[28] which, by prohibiting certain *ex parte* consultations, command in minimal degree an internal separation of functions. As noted above, several state legislatures have seen fit to provide a greater separation of the prosecuting and judicial functions in such fields as workmen's compensation, unemployment compensation, and state taxation. In other states, the processes of judicial review are utilized to provide safeguards against the dangers inherent in such combinations of functions. As noted in Chapter XIX, *infra,* state courts exhibit a tendency to probe more deeply in examining the fairness of administrative procedures where such combinations of functions exist.

(C) Conferring Non-Judicial Power on Courts

Reflecting what Justice Vanderbilt[29] described as "an instinctive desire to seek an impartial and independent tribunal for the handling of a wide variety of matters deemed vital to the welfare of the community," the legislatures have frequently, in blithe disregard of strict separation of powers concepts, delegated non-judicial functions to the state courts.[30]

In cases where performance of the delegated duties would make the courts subject to the supervision of another branch of the government, the courts have held invalid the attempted delegations. Thus, a New York statute casting on a justice of its supreme court the mandatory duty of investigating charges

---

27 Collins v. Selectmen of Brookline, 325 Mass. 562, 91 N.E.2d 747 (1950).

28 Section 13.

29 VANDERBILT, *op. cit. supra* note 5, at p. 115.

30 An intriguing catalog of the wide variety of non-judicial functions imposed on American judges in former years is found in POUND, ORGANIZATION OF COURTS 5-6 (1940).

against a public official, and reporting his findings and conclusions to the governor for the latter's consideration, was held unconstitutional.[31]

The courts have also refused to accept invitations to perform non-judicial functions in instances where carrying them out would interfere with the judicial work of the courts, either by demanding too much of the judges' time and attention[32] or by involving the judiciary in situations that might reflect on the judges' reputations for independence and freedom from politics.[33] In this category may be included such decisions as those of the Michigan court holding invalid a statute which would have required judges to sit as arbitrators in certain labor disputes.[34]

A particular problem which has proved troublesome has arisen in connection with statutes vesting in the courts power to grant *de novo* review of agency determinations predicated essentially on legislative or political considerations. Sometimes, the courts hold such statutes invalid as attempts to vest non-judicial duties in the courts.[35] Occasionally, the courts say that conferring of powers to review *de novo* administrative decisions, whatever their character, is quite proper.[36] Most frequently, the courts say that they will review the administrative decision in question, but will limit the review to typically judicial questions, *e.g.,* whether the agency's conclusions of law reflect an erroneous interpretation of the governing statute, or whether its findings of fact have no substantial evidence to support them.[37] The state courts not uncommonly strain to discover a means of interpreting the statutes providing for judicial review in a way which will authorize a more limited type of review than a literal reading of the statute would indicate, *i.e.,* review limited to typically judicial questions. Thus, in one Michigan case, the statute ex-

---

31 *In re* Richardson, 247 N.Y. 401, 160 N.E. 655 (1928).

32 *Cf.* Voss, *Exercise of Non-Judicial Functions by Courts and Judges,* 7 KAN. B. BULL. 172 (1939).

33 State *ex rel.* White v. Barker, 116 Iowa 96, 89 N.W. 204 (1902); Sartin v. Snell, 87 Kan. 485, 125 Pac. 47 (1912).

34 Local 170, Transport Workers Union v. Gadola, 322 Mich. 332, 34 N.W.2d 71 (1948).

35 Ball v. Jones, 272 Ala. 305, 132 So. 2d 120 (1961); Vissering Mercantile Co. v. Annunzio, 1 Ill. 2d 108, 115 N.E.2d 306, *appeal dismissed,* 347 U.S. 949, 98 L. Ed. 1096, 74 Sup. Ct. 680 (1953).

36 *Ex parte* Darnell, 262 Ala. 71, 76 So. 2d 770 (1955).

37 State *ex rel.* Public Serv. Comm'n v. Johnson Circuit Court, 232 Ind. 501, 112 N.E.2d 429 (1953); Russo v. Governor, 22 N.J. 156, 123 A.2d 482 (1956); Fentress County Beer Bd. v. Cravens, 209 Tenn. 679, 356 S.W.2d 260 (1962).

plicitly provided that decisions of a fair employment practices commission would be subject to review *de novo* before the trial courts, with a right to trial by jury on the appeal. The state supreme court, after observing that to grant a truly *de novo* review would involve the trial courts in the unconstitutional exercise of administrative functions, construed the statute as meaning that the scope of review should be limited to that available on an appeal in the nature of certiorari, restricting the reviewing court to reversing for "legal error or arbitrary action."[38] Similarly, the West Virginia court went far in interpreting a statute of that state as providing for only a limited degree of review. The statute provided that on appeal from an order of the state water commission, finding that there had been an actionable pollution of river waters, the trial court should make a finding as to whether the act complained of was a statutory pollution. The trial court, relying on earlier West Virginia cases[39] held this provision void as an attempt to confer non-judicial powers on a court. But the state supreme court said that the real intent of the legislature was to give the trial courts power only to decide whether the administrative finding constituted an abuse of power, or excess of power, or was arbitrary in nature; and concluded that, so construed, the statute was not void for delegating non-judicial powers to a court.[40]

The reasons which persuade the courts to accept the task of granting review in these cases (at the same time limiting the scope of review to issues deemed judicially cognizable) appear clearly in the last cited case.[41] The court pointed out that if the sections of the statute providing for judicial review were declared invalid, the result would be that the administrative agency would have power to enter orders, and that those aggrieved by the orders would have no practicable or effective means whatsoever of obtaining judicial review.

In other cases, the willingness of state courts to assume duties which might technically be described as non-judicial (and it may

[38] Lesniak v. Fair Employment Practices Comm'n, 364 Mich. 495, 111 N.W.2d 790 (1961).

[39] State v. Huber, 129 W. Va. 198, 40 S.E.2d 11 (1946); Danielley v. City of Princeton, 113 W. Va. 252, 167 S.E. 620 (1933); Hodges v. Public Serv. Comm'n, 110 W. Va. 649, 159 S.E. 834 (1931).

[40] City of Huntington v. State Water Comm'n, 135 W. Va. 568, 64 S.E.2d 225 (1951).

[41] *Ibid.*

be noted that the state courts on the whole are more accommodating to legislative desires in this connection than are the federal courts),[42] is apparently to be ascribed to the circumstance that if the delegation of administrative duties to judges has been assumed for several years without challenge, the courts feel it best to let the practice continue. As the West Virginia court put it[43] "This practice has been pursued in such a great number of cases and over so many years, that we are of the opinion it should not be disturbed now." But this deference to practice is not without limitations. The West Virginia court added: "However . . . we feel no obligation because of submission thereto, to approve the further delegation of legislative functions to the judiciary."

In short, where performance of administrative duties will not interfere with the proper fulfillment of the court's higher responsibilities—and especially where the assumption of such duties will provide a check against possibilities of abuse of administrative discretion that otherwise would be remediless—the state courts are not loath to accept responsibilities which are not purely judicial but involve some measure of executive or even legislative responsibility.

---

42 *Cf.* Federal Radio Comm'n v. General Elec. Co., 281 U.S. 464, 74 L. Ed. 964, 50 Sup. Ct. 389 (1930).

43 Hodges v. Public Serv. Comm'n, *supra* note 39.

CHAPTER III

DELEGATION OF POWERS— THE NECESSITY OF CONTROLLING ADMINISTRATIVE DISCRETION

While discretion has been described by enthusiastic administrators as the lifeblood of the administrative process, it is viewed with less enthusiasm by many state courts which regard it as a virus which may infect the process.

State courts have exhibited an inclination significantly greater than that of the federal courts to hold invalid delegations of power which vest an agency with untrammeled and uncontrolled discretionary power.

Section 1

The Need For Controls

To understand the reasons for this attitude, and formulate a basis on which to predict whether a particular delegation of rule making or adjudicatory power would be upheld, it is helpful to examine: (1) the sources of discretionary power; (2) the results of delegating broad discretionary powers to the agencies; (3) the resulting problems faced by the courts; (4) the legal bases on which delegation of discretionary power is challenged. These topics will be examined in this section. Later sections of this chapter will discuss the approaches which the courts have utilized in considering the validity of challenged delegations of power, and will suggest the factors which it is believed preponderantly motivate decision.

(A) The Sources of Discretionary Power

Discretion is a word of many meanings. It is sometimes used to describe the quality of discreetness—characterized by circumspection and judiciousness. It is not in this sense, ordinarily, that the term is applied to administrative agencies. Rather, it is used to refer to an area within which agencies may choose freely between alternate courses of action, basing decision on *ad hoc* considerations.

The principal sources from which agencies derive this type of discretionary power are threefold:

(1) Discretion in Promulgating Rules

First, the agency may be granted the power to adopt substantive rules, having for most purposes the force of law, compelling or prohibiting action on the part of those subject to the agency's jurisdiction. Thus, a state railroad commission may adopt a rule prohibiting pullman porters from collecting tickets from sleeping car passengers,[1] or a zoning commission may prescribe the shape and size of houses that must be built in a particular area, or a labor commissioner may prescribe what safety appliances shall be put on machinery in factories, or what rest room facilities should be furnished.

In these cases, an administrative agency acts like a "little legislature" and, within the limits of the authority delegated to it, exercises the same sort of discretionary powers as those exercised by a legislature. When the limits imposed by the legislature's delegation of power are loose and ill-defined, the agency is in effect enabled not only to fill in the interstices of the legislative fabric (acting "interstitially," in Justice Holmes' phrase) but to go much further and fashion new legislative policies.

This result obtains when the only limits imposed by the legislature on the scope of the agency's discretion are expressed in such vague and nebulous concepts as "adequate," "advisable," "appropriate," "beneficial," "competent," "convenient," "detrimental," "expedient," "equitable," "indispensable," "necessary," "practicable," and the like. When an agency is empowered to adopt any rule that it finds "appropriate" to assure the most "adequate" level of benefits that are "practicable" in the "public interest," there are few, if any, judicially enforceable limits on the agency's discretionary powers.

---

[1] Railroad Comm'n of Texas v. Pullman Co., 312 U.S. 496, 85 L. Ed. 971, 61 Sup. Ct. 643 (1941).

(2) Discretion in Adjudication

Secondly, a broad measure of discretionary power results where an agency is given a vague, indefinite standard to apply in the adjudication of individual cases. For example, an agency may be empowered to decide, in contested cases involving applications for unemployment benefits, whether an employee who quit had "good cause" for leaving (in which case the disqualification attached to voluntary quitting is removed). So broad a standard permits an agency to decide in its own discretion the fundamental policy question as to whether an individual who leaves his job for reasons of purely personal convenience has "good cause" for leaving.

It is worth noting that this second source of discretionary power is more subtle than the first. When an agency is empowered to adopt rules, there is no attempt to conceal the fact that it is making policy. The agency is acting in the open; its actions are subject to vigilant scrutiny and critical review; the legislature is likely to revoke a rule which appears to be at odds with the legislative purpose.

On the other hand, when an agency is acting in a judicial capacity, the trend of decision does not so clearly appear in the individual adjudications. The agency (in terms of the example stated above) merely rules in specific cases whether or not "good cause" exists. It may say very little about the reasons which support the conclusion, and the concept of "good cause" may gradually be enlarged until it is transmuted into an equivalent of "plausible excuse." In this way, agencies engaged in adjudication may be enabled to exercise their discretionary powers to reach results which go far beyond, and which may even be quite at odds with, the underlying legislative purpose. It is not meant to imply that agencies always stretch the legislative fabric. However, the freedom to exercise discretion in deciding individual cases on a basis of *ad hoc* adjudication may enable them at times to read new and unanticipated meanings into legislative language, when the agency heads feel that the accomplishment of their broad social purposes will be furthered thereby.

(3) Sub-delegated Discretion

Third, the process of sub-delegation within an agency sometimes results in the vesting of broad discretionary powers in a single anonymous subordinate. When a statute is adopted delegating to a five-member board the responsibility of deciding, for example, whether it is in the public interest to grant liquor licenses to clubs, hotels, or restaurants, it is often assumed that the combined wisdom and judgment of the five distinguished citizens comprising the board will be reflected in the decisions that are made. In practice, however, it often does not work that way. The members of the board (particularly in those cases where, as is true in many state agencies, the members devote only a part of their time and efforts to the discharge of their public responsibilities) may find that so much time is required to attend to other important official duties (such as policy meetings and agenda meetings) and to discharge administrative responsibilities (such as considering staff appointments and promotions), and to make speeches and other public appearances, that they do not have time for joint consideration of the several hundred license applications that are made annually.

This circumstance may necessitate the board's delegating to each of its five separate members the power to consider cases individually and to "recommend" to the other four members (who know little of the case beyond the recommendation of their colleague) what decision should be made. Each of the board members, in turn, may find himself too busy to make a detailed study of the cases assigned to him, and accordingly he may ask his staff assistants to make the detailed study and advise him what decision should be made, so that he may pass the recommendation along to the other members of the board for their approval.

Such sub-delegation of authority necessarily results in vesting broad discretionary powers in staff assistants, whose decisions in individual cases will in large part reflect their personal ideas and judgments, rather than the combined group judgment of the principal officers of the agency.

The discretion resulting from delegation of responsibilities to individual staff members within an agency has a character and genre which differentiates it from the discretion exercised by board members acting in consultation. When a group of publicly responsible officials pool their efforts in hammering out a decision on a question, the discipline of group consultation provides a safeguard against hasty decisions. But this safeguard is not present when the discretionary power reposed by law in the agency is delegated to a single anonymous member of the agency staff. His decisions may mirror his personal prejudices or predilections.

(B) Results of Delegating Discretionary Power to Agencies

The granting of appropriate discretionary power to administrative agencies is necessary to the effective performance of their tasks. Typically, they function in areas where social or economic controls of private activity are deemed desirable, but where the legislature despairs of formulating a general rule which will be capable of precise and equitable application to all the contingencies that are anticipated. It would be impossible, for example, for a legislature to prescribe a general rule which could be equitably applied to determine in exactly what cases a variance from the details of the applicable zoning regulation should be permitted, or to determine how many common carrier truck lines should be permitted to operate between given termini. In such cases, granting too little discretionary power would forestall the achievement of the very purpose sought to be accomplished in creating the agency.

Another important reason for entrusting agencies with discretionary powers—and one which is predominantly applicable in cases of agency adjudication—is the circumstance that the legislatures have from time to time desired that the legislative codes of conduct be applied and interpreted by governmental organs with attitudes different from those of the judges sitting on the appellate courts at the time of the creation of the agency. Thus, in the congressional debates at the time of the adoption of the Federal Trade Commission Act in 1914[2] the thought was expressed that it would further the underlying congressional purpose of condemning all unfair methods of competition if the fairness of challenged competitive methods were adjudged by

[2] See 51 Cong. Rec. 11384.

commissioners who did not harbor the pro-business sympathies which the congressmen attributed to the federal judiciary of that day. The same attitude has influenced state legislatures, in numerous instances. When "Little Wagner" acts were adopted in many states in the late 1930's (designed to apply to intra-state employers the proscriptions against unfair labor practices embodied in the National Labor Relations Act), it was generally believed that an interpretation calculated to achieve the basic purpose of promoting union organization and collective bargaining could be better achieved by vesting in an agency, rather than in the state courts, the responsibility of applying the provisions of the Act in specific case situations. Conversely, when the early workmen's compensation acts were adopted half a century ago, the reason that led some conservatively minded state legislatures to limit the scope of judicial review was the belief that the administrative interpretation would be more favorable to employers than would that of election-conscious judges. Surely, this may be recorded as a noteworthy instance of false prophecy!

On the whole, a strong argument can be made in favor of granting broad discretionary powers in the two categories above described, *i.e.*, where there is a need for devising rules of specific applicability to govern a multitude of variant factual situations which cannot all be covered by a single general rule of universal application, or where there is a legislative desire to make sure that adjudications will be made by officials particularly aware of and in sympathy with a new social policy adopted by the legislature.

But where powers have been delegated to administrative agencies in cases where neither of these two justifications has existed, the granting of unnecessarily broad discretionary powers may produce troublesome problems. In many cases, legislatures have delegated extensive legislative and judicial powers to agencies only because it was easier to let some agency decide what the rule should be than to resolve difficult policy questions within the legislature. When the legislature feels that "there ought to be a law" to provide for some troublesome problem, but the legislators are not sure what the law should provide, great attraction has been found in the deceptively innocuous-appearing device of creating an agency, and handing it the problem. Moreover, in some cases where it appears that the number of individual adjudications under a new law will be large, it has been deemed economical to vest the judicial function in comparatively low-paid administrative staffs, rather than to increase the number of judges to permit the state courts to take care of the added case load that would result from vesting the responsibility of adjudication in the courts.

If broad discretionary powers are unnecessarily vested in administrative agencies—and if the administrators are not discreet in the exercise of their prerogative—a number of questionable results may follow. A recapitulation of these results is a convenient method of describing the desirability of imposing reasonable controls to limit the freedom of administrative discretion, and of suggesting the type of limitations which should be considered.

To grant a larger measure of discretionary power than is required by the circumstances of the case is to take a long step away from the historic Anglo-American ideals of government by law and toward a concept of government by non-elective officers formulating policy. The difference between applying law and formulating policy is significant.

The significance is disclosed by examining the seven principal results that may follow. It is not suggested that these results always follow, or even that they usually follow the delegation of broad discretionary powers to agencies. But they have in fact sometimes followed; and attention may therefore be briefly directed to the untoward possibilities that can ensue from unwise grants of discretionary powers, in the absence of a demonstrable need therefor. These possibilities, it is believed, are considered by the courts in passing upon the validity of delegations. They may wisely be considered by those engaged in the drafting of legislative standards designed to channel administrative discretion.

(1) Legislature Effectively Displaced

First, when broad discretionary power is vested in an agency to formulate rules having the effect of law, to a large extent that agency is enabled to displace the legislature in the ordinary day-to-day control of that segment of governmental activity included within the jurisdiction of the agency. For example, if a board of agriculture is given power to make rules as to the grading of grass seed, and a group of local seed producers importunes the agency to adopt a rule which will have the effect of interfering with the retail sale, within the state, of lawn seed produced by an out-state competitor, then the decision of a basic underlying policy—whether the state will discriminate against out-state producers—is committed to the agency. The agency (through the device, for example, of adopting a rule which requires the out-state producer's seed to be labelled "Grade B" or "inferior quality," even though it is rated of highest quality in the other forty-nine states) may effectively discriminate against out-state producers, even though the members of the legislature, had they been given a voice in the matter, might have emphatically opposed such discrimination.

(2) Diminution of Powers of Courts

Second, the vesting of broad discretionary powers in an agency may result in a corresponding diminution of the powers of the judiciary, in the areas committed to agency control. To the extent that authority is delegated to rely on administrative discretion in the resolution of individual cases as they arise, the power of judicial review is curtailed. Where the course of agency action is reposed in agency discretion, there is little for the courts to review except the question of whether there has been an abuse of discretion. It makes little difference whether the agency has properly interpreted the statute, if its decision is predicated not on what the statute says but on what administrative intuition or experience suggests to be the best solution of a knotty problem. The most the courts can do is to ascertain whether the administrative action has exceeded the limits of the delegated discretion. In short, judicial control of administrative action varies inversely with the scope of administrative discretion.[3] Thus, if a state tax commission has completely discretionary power to either approve or disapprove a "separate accounting method" by which a corporation proposes to effect an allocation between out-state and intra-state business for purposes of state income or intangibles or

[3] "As the field of discretion of the council in regard to circumstances which dictate granting of consent is enlarged, opportunity for the intervention of the courts becomes restricted. Into the field of legislative or administrative discretion the courts may not enter." Larkin Co. v. Schwab, 242 N.Y. 330, 335, 151 N.E. 637 (1926).

franchise taxation, and the commission elects to disapprove a method proposed by the corporate taxpayer, the courts are powerless to intervene. Even though the court may be of the opinion that the disapproved method fairly reflected the proper allocation, it has no power to reverse or modify the commission's action—unless, of course, it can find an "abuse of discretion"; and in the circumstances described it is almost impossible to establish that an abuse of discretion exists.

(3) Relaxation of Procedural Standards

Third, delegation of broad discretionary powers can result in relaxation, if not abandonment, of procedural standards. Discretion can be exercised more freely if procedures are varied to meet the exigencies of the pending case. Indeed, administrative discretion can be most freely exercised if there are no rules of procedure at all—a condition which some state agencies appear ambitious to approximate. Some of them have no published rules of procedure. In one state, when a statute was adopted some years ago providing for the publication by the Secretary of State of all rules of all state agencies, publication of the compilation was delayed some two years beyond the required date—for the reason that several of the agencies had difficulty finding the official copies of their respective rules. They had been adopted and filed, but had apparently been thereafter neglected.

The procedural rules adopted by state agencies tend sometimes to be restricted to (1) a description of forms used by the agency, and (2) a sterile recital of the bare requirements of practice. They may touch upon the high spots of formality without disclosing the essential patterns of the procedures utilized by a given agency in a given type of case.[4] Such tendencies have serious implications. Attorneys practicing before an agency which has adopted this course do not know precisely what steps to take in order to make sure that their contentions are properly presented at the proper time, at the proper place, in the most appropriate manner, and to the persons whose discretion will determine the result. This contingency can present a substantial threat to the goal of attaining equal justice under law. As the

[4] The Attorney General's Committee which investigated the operations of the federal agencies, 1939-1941, found this to be true at that time of the federal agencies. S. DOC. No. 8, 77th Cong., 1st Sess. 27 (1941).

Supreme Court has pointed out, the history of American freedom has been in no small measure the history of insistence on procedural standards.[5]

(4) Limitation of Hearings

Fourth, the delegation of broad discretionary powers may beget an inclination to decide a case without a full hearing, or without hearing both parties. If an agency's discretionary powers were unlimited, it could logically take the position that there was no need whatever to hear respondent's proofs, because the evidence he might offer would not influence the agency's judgment as to what disposition of the matter was most desirable to effectuate the agency's concept of the public interest.

The threat of this extreme position does not often occur. Rarely does a legislature see fit to vest in an administrative agency unlimited discretionary powers; and rarely is an attempt made to deny a party respondent all semblance of a hearing. But often the degree of delegated discretion is such as to engender in an agency some impatience with the time-consuming course of deciding each case on the basis of careful and painstaking consideration of all the evidence produced in the slow-moving process of a contested hearing. Discretion can be exercised more freely when the hearing procedure is minimized. The greater the measure of discretion accorded an agency, the more it is subjected to the temptation of deciding without a full hearing, or of treating respondent's proofs in somewhat cavalier fashion.

The classic example, perhaps, among state agencies is that afforded by the Kansas State Board of Medical Examination.[6] In a case involving proceedings to revoke a physician's license, one of the members of the Board (a doctor) after listening to testimony for three days, said that he had made up his mind. He sought permission to cast his vote and to be excused from the hearing, so that he could attend to his patients. But the chairman refused to excuse him, ruling that no vote could be cast until all the testimony was in. Thereupon, the court noted, "the impatient member assented, and resumed his task."

---

[5] Malinski v. New York, 324 U.S. 401, 89 L. Ed. 1029, 65 Sup. Ct. 781 (1945).

[6] Brinkley v. Hassig, 130 Kan. 874, 289 Pac. 64 (1930).

In cases where the issuance of the complaint reflects the conclusion which the agency has reached on the basis of *ex parte* study of information obtained by its investigators, as to what charges can be sustained, the issuance of the complaint constitutes a certificate of probable cause. In such circumstances, the document initiating formal proceedings sometimes takes on almost the character of an order *nisi.* It indicates what decision will be entered unless respondent shows good cause why the agency's initial *ex parte* appraisal of the case is erroneous. In such an atmosphere, the existence of discretion in the agency to frame its order—without the constraint imposed by the necessity of applying objective legal standards—in such form as it conceives will best serve the agency's basic purposes, tends to minimize the utility of the hearing procedure.

(5) Secrecy as to Standards of Decision

Fifth, reliance on the role of discretion has disinclined some agencies to make available for the use of interested parties any useful statements of the criteria relied on by the agency in deciding cases. Discretion can be exercised more freely if the agency has reserved the privilege of deciding each case on its "merits," permitting such departures from prior criteria of decision as may seem expedient.

The problem of requiring agencies to make available, as a matter of public information, statements describing the policies and criteria on which decisions are based, will be considered in greater detail in Chapters VI and VIII, *infra.*

(6) Tendency to Expand Jurisdiction

Sixth, possession of discretionary powers affords agencies an opportunity and a temptation to extend their jurisdiction so as to include within the ambit of the agency's powers persons and business enterprises which the legislature did not intend to subject to the control of the agency. The observation of Justice Jackson in one case[7] that the agency there involved, "like most administrative agencies, has looked with favor on the oppor-

---

[7] Great Atl. & Pac. Tea Co. v. Supermarket Equip. Corp., 340 U.S. 147, 156, 95 L. Ed. 162, 71 Sup. Ct. 127 (1950).

tunity which the exercise of discretion affords to expand its own jurisdiction" applies to state, as well as to federal agencies.

(7) Tendency to Extend Philosophy of Statute

Seventh, the heady exuberance produced in administrative officials by the delegation to them of broad discretionary powers may lead them to broaden the policy of the statute, stretching the legislative rubric to cover situations which are not included in the statute but which it is thought need correction just as badly as those which the legislature has specified.[8]

Sometimes, in the exercise of their discretionary power to fix policies, agencies adopt criteria of decision or promulgate rules that not only extend the legislative purpose but are in fact at odds with the original legislative intent. Illustrative cases are collected in Chapter IX, Section 3; Chapter XIX, Section 4; and Chapter XX, Section 2.

(C) The Problems Faced by the Courts in Attempting to Reconcile Administrative Discretion With the Rule of Law

The argument of Aristotle that government should be by law, and not by men, represented a protest directed toward the earlier Grecian systems of despotically controlled administrative law.[9]

Aristotle was protesting the results of delegating discretionary powers to administrators; he urged that the executive department of the government should be subjected to the rule of law. It can be so subjected only through the courts, for as the venerable A. V. Dicey observed three quarters of a century ago[10] the very concept of the Rule of Law "means in the last resort the right of the judges to control the executive government."

Essentially, the problem of the courts has been to discover a method of reconciling the practical necessity of granting broad measures of discretionary power to administrative agencies with the inexorable imperative, demanded by the Rule of Law, that

---

8 Weber v. Board of Health, 148 Ohio St. 389, 74 N.E.2d 331 (1947).

9 The classic phrase found in Part I, § 30, of the Massachusetts Constitution (1780), was borrowed from Harrington [*Oceana* 2-29 (1656)] who acknowledged his indebtedness to Aristotle's *Politics* III, xvi, 4-5.

10 Dicey, The Law of the Constitution 401 (2d ed. 1886).

adjudicated cases be decided on the basis of general principles and standards known to the parties and applicable to all cases.

The necessity of achieving such a reconciliation has proved a more pervasive problem in the state courts than in the federal courts: partly for the reason that many of the state courts have been more insistent on adherence to classical Rule of Law concepts than have the federal courts; and, more importantly, for the reason that the problems resulting from delegation of legislative and judicial powers to administrative agencies have been presented in their most aggravated form to the state courts. Their problem has thus been a more difficult one than that of the federal courts. The greater difficulty has resulted from a number of factors.

For one thing, delegations are too often made by state legislatures in casual and careless fashion. When the United States Congress creates an administrative agency, the enabling statute almost always contains at least an articulated statement of the objectives which are entrusted to the agency, drafted with skill and care. While the statement of policy sometimes fails to furnish a rigid, clearly defined, or objective standard, it at least charts the direction of the path which the agency is required to follow. On the other hand, some state legislatures are prone, in turning a problem over to an agency, to give that agency complete carte blanche as to the policies to be achieved, *e.g.,* directing a labor board to determine, by compulsory arbitration, the terms and conditions of employment in the public utilities industries;[11] or telling an agency to determine on such basis as it pleases the license fee to be charged for the use of public buildings;[12] or authorizing a labor commissioner to make such exceptions as he thinks advisable in a law prescribing hours of work.[13]

Further, the procedural provisions imposed upon federal agencies by the Administrative Procedure Act[14] tend in an important degree to provide checks and balances upon the excesses that may accompany unsupervised exercise of discretionary power. The minimal requirements concerning public information, and

---

11 State v. Traffic Tel. Workers' Fed'n, 2 N.J. 335, 66 A.2d 616 (1949).

12 Maryland Theatrical Corp. v. Brennan, 180 Md. 377, 24 A.2d 911 (1942).

13 Holgate Bros. Co. v. Bashore, 331 Pa. 255, 200 Atl. 672, 117 A.L.R. 639 (1938).

14 5 U.S.C. §§ 1005, 1006; F.C.A. 5 §§ 1005, 1006.

notice and hearing procedures set forth in the federal act afford the interested parties an opportunity of influencing in some degree the course of administrative decision. In many states, comparable procedural restraints are lacking as to some or all of the more important state agencies.

Finally, if only because of the restricted territorial jurisdiction of the state agencies, and the resulting likelihood that in a large percentage of the cases there will exist personal acquaintanceship between the agency members and the other parties to the agency proceedings, there is greater danger in state agencies that decision will reflect friendships or personal antipathies or political affiliations.

The task of the state courts is formidable, involving as it does the responsibility of undertaking to subject to an overriding Rule of Law the operations of agencies created carelessly and casually, without clearly defined objectives, without useful standards to guide their course of decision, without even a clearly defined course of procedure to follow.

The difficulties of the task have not been lightened by the circumstance that the courts have been compelled to recognize the overpowering practical necessity of delegating to administrative agencies many of the most important functions of modern state government. The state courts have, in the main, intervened only where the need to do so is clear, in order to avoid readily perceived dangers.

In cases of demonstrated need, they have interposed their authority to insist on minimal guaranties of the right of individuals to be notified and to be heard before an administrative order is entered against them. They have insisted on certain requirements of fair procedure. They have accorded a measure of judicial review—somewhat broader, on the whole, than that commonly available in the federal courts—to set aside administrative action which violates constitutional or statutory provisions, which is without evidentiary support, or which is arbitrary or capricious. Only in instances where the above described approaches seem plainly inadequate do the state courts resort to the device of declaring the delegation itself invalid.

(D) THE LEGAL BASES ON WHICH DELEGATIONS OF DISCRETIONARY POWER MAY BE CHALLENGED

It is difficult to discover the legal genealogy of the time-worn cliche that legislative and judicial powers may not be delegated, or (as most courts put it today) that they may be delegated only in certain circumstances and on certain conditions.

As discussed more fully in Chapter II, *supra,* there is no fixed constitutional requirement prescribing the separation of the powers of government, or proscribing delegations of power. The federal constitution does not require the several states to observe in their internal organization the limitations imposed by the separation of powers doctrine.[15] Neither the provision of article IV, section 4, of the federal constitution, providing that the United States shall guarantee to every state a republican form of government, nor the fourteenth amendment, has been held to necessitate a rigid separation of powers.[16]

The separation of powers doctrine (as noted in Chapter II, *supra*) affords an obstacle to delegation of power to state agencies only insofar as the constitution of a particular state may require such separation.[17]

Yet, despite the widely disparate provisions of state constitutions in this respect, the great majority of the state courts have traditionally spoken with almost uniform voice in declaring that legislative and judicial powers may not be delegated.

Many judicial opinions refer to the maxim *delegata potestas non potest delegare* as affording a basis for the doctrine of non-delegability of legislative and judicial powers. The theory seems to be that the people have delegated legislative and judicial powers to the legislature and to the courts, respectively, and that such grants are not susceptible of sub-delegation to executive agencies. But there appears to be little sound historical basis for this suggestion.

---

[15] Consolidated Rendering Co. v. Vermont, 207 U.S. 541, 552, 52 L. Ed. 327, 28 Sup. Ct. 178 (1908); Sandstrom v. California Horse Racing Bd., 31 Cal. 2d 401, 189 P.2d 17, *cert. denied,* 335 U.S. 814, 93 L. Ed. 369, 69 Sup. Ct. 31 (1948).

[16] Ohio *ex rel.* Bryant v. Akron Metropolitan Park Dist., 281 U.S. 74, 79-80, 74 L. Ed. 710, 50 Sup. Ct. 228, 266 A.L.R. 1460 (1930); Reetz v. Michigan, 188 U.S. 505, 507, 47 L. Ed. 563, 23 Sup. Ct. 390 (1903).

[17] Neblett v. Carpenter, 305 U.S. 297, 83 L. Ed. 182, 59 Sup. Ct. 170, *reh. den.,* 305 U.S. 675, 83 L. Ed. 437, 59 Sup. Ct. 355 (1938); Pacific States Box & Basket Co. v. White, 296 U.S. 176, 186, 80 L. Ed. 138, 56 Sup. Ct. 159, 101 A.L.R. 853 (1935).

Occasionally, it is suggested that delegation of uncontrolled powers to administrative agencies violates due process requirements.[18] While the language of due process guaranties can aptly be applied where delegation of judicial power is involved, it does not so well fit cases of delegation of legislative power. In either case, reference to the requirements of due process appears to constitute essentially a make-weight argument. If the delegation is held invalid, it is sometimes said that to permit it would result in deprivation of due process; *per contra,* where the delegation is sustained, no denial of due process is perceived.[19]

The lack of substantial support in basic legal concepts for the precepts prohibiting delegation of legislative or judicial powers is presumably the reason for the circumstance that, while some state courts continue to repeat the time-worn phrases, the doctrine prohibiting such delegations has become so attentuated that it rarely, if ever, affords the actual basis for decision on the question whether a particular delegation of discretionary power to an administrative agency will be upheld.

Section 2

Demise of Doctrines of Non-Delegability

It was for a long time maintained both by eminent textwriters[20] and by the courts[21] that legislative powers cannot be delegated to administrative tribunals.

---

18 Buehman v. Bechtel, 57 Ariz. 363, 114 P.2d 227, 134 A.L.R. 1374 (1941); Drummey v. State Bd. of Funeral Directors & Embalmers, 13 Cal. 2d 75, 87 P.2d 848 (1939); Smithberger v. Banning, 129 Neb. 651, 262 N.W. 492, 100 A.L.R. 686 (1935); Abelson's, Inc. v. New Jersey State Bd. of Optometrists, 5 N.J. 412, 75 A.2d 867, *modifying* 65 A.2d 644 (1950).

19 P. F. Petersen Baking Co. v. Bryan, 290 U.S. 570, 78 L. Ed. 505, 54 Sup. Ct. 277, 90 A.L.R. 1285 (1934); Miami Laundry Co. v. Florida Dry Cleaning & Laundry Bd., 134 Fla. 1, 183 So. 759, 119 A.L.R. 956 (1938).

20 *E.g.,* COOLEY, I CONSTITUTIONAL LIMITATIONS 224 (8th ed. 1927): "One of the settled maxims in constitutional law is that the power conferred upon the legislature to make laws cannot be delegated by that department to any other body or authority."

21 *E.g.,* Dowling v. Lancashire Ins. Co., 92 Wis. 63, 68, 65 N.W. 738, 31 L.R.A. 112 (1896): "That no part of the legislative power can be delegated by the legislature to any other department of the government, executive or judicial, is a fundamental principle in constitutional law, essential to the integrity and maintenance of the system of government established by the Constitution."

Similarly, it was long asserted with equal vigor that the legislature is powerless to delegate judicial duties to administrative officers.[22]

But candor compels recognition of the hard fact that these statements have become mere shibboleths, shattered by the hard course of decision—reverently repeated, but not followed in practice.

If judicial power be conceived as the sort of power which a court exercises (applying the general rule of a statute, for example, to particular factual situations, and declaring the rights of the parties), it must be conceded that judicial powers are delegated to administrative agencies. Similarly, if legislative power be conceived as the sort of power which a legislature exercises (determining, for example, what types of conduct shall be prohibited), then it must likewise be conceded that legislative powers are delegated to administrative tribunals.

There is no generic distinction between the function of a workmen's compensation commission adjudicating a claim of an injured employee and that of a court adjudicating a claim under some other statute imposing liability without fault. In either case, the adjudicatory body determines the facts and then assesses their legal significance in light of the terms of the statute. The mental processes of a workmen's compensation commissioner in determining whether the claimant was an employee, whether there was an "accident," and whether the accident arose "in the course of" his employment, are no different than the mental processes of a judge, in a claim under a wage discrimination statute, in determining whether the woman plaintiff was an "employee," whether she performed work "like that performed by male employees," and whether she was paid a lower hourly rate.

Similarly, when a public utilities commission determines that there must be a pullman conductor, as well as a pullman porter, on trains with a single sleeping car,[23] or determines that each

---

[22] Whitten v. California State Bd. of Optometry, 8 Cal. 2d 444, 65 P.2d 1296, 115 A.L.R. 1 (1937); Reid v. Smith, 375 Ill. 147, 30 N.E.2d 908, 132 A.L.R. 1286 (1940); *e.g., In re* Opinion of the Justices, 87 N.H. 492, 179 Atl. 344, 110 A.L.R. 819 (1935).

[23] Railroad Comm'n of Texas v. Pullman Co., 312 U.S. 496, 85 L. Ed. 971, 61 Sup. Ct. 643 (1941).

freight train must have a caboose,[24] its policy-framing functions are not of a different genre than that exercised by the legislature in deciding that each train must carry a full crew.

There was a time when many state courts insisted that constitutional doctrines precluded the delegation of legislative or judicial powers to administrative agencies, and as a result many early grants of power to state agencies were held invalid.[25] But that time has long passed. Gradually, the sheer, hard logic of the early cases retreated in the face of the felt necessities of the times. Though the old rubrics prohibiting delegation are still occasionally repeated, they no longer shape decision.

(A) Falsity of the "True Tests"

The path of retreat was not orderly. It was unfortunate that this was so, for, as pointed out in a perceptive opinion by Justice Rosenberry of the Wisconsin Supreme Court:[26]

> The essential facts upon which courts, legislatures, and executives, as well as students of the law, agree is that there is an over-powering necessity for a modification of the doctrine of separation and non-delegation of powers of government. In the face of that necessity, courts have upheld laws granting legislative powers under the guise of the power to make rules and regulations; have upheld laws delegating judicial power under the guise of power . . . to find facts. . . . The public interest would be greatly advanced and our law clarified if the situation as it exists were frankly recognized.

One of the fictions employed to conceal the retreat was the enunciation of "true tests" to distinguish between the "truly" legislative or judicial powers, which could not be delegated, and those merely "administrative" powers which could be entrusted to agencies.

The earliest of the "true tests," which apparently originated in the opinion of Justice Ranney in *Cincinnati, W. & Z. R.R.*

---

24 Akron & B. Belt R.R. v. Public Utils. Comm'n, 148 Ohio St. 282, 74 N.E.2d 256 (1947).

25 Tighe v. Osborne, 149 Md. 349, 131 Atl. 801, 43 A.L.R. 819 (1925)—holding invalid a delegation of limited authority to a zoning commission. *E.g.*, Dowling v. Lancashire Ins. Co., 92 Wis. 63, 65 N.W. 738, 31 L.R.A. 112 (1896)—holding invalid a delegation of power to an insurance commissioner to prescribe a standard form of policy which was to conform to the New York standard policy "as near as the same can be made applicable."

26 State *ex rel.* Wisconsin Inspection Bureau v. Whitman, 196 Wis. 472, 498, 220 N.W. 929 (1928).

v. Clinton County Commissioners,[27] and which has been reverently repeated thousands of times,[28] asserts that an administrative tribunal may not be given power to make the law, but may be given discretion as to the execution of the law. While this criterion possesses, in certain case situations, the advantages of glib plausibility, it does not serve as a basis of decision. Its fallacies were pointed out as long ago as 1928 by Justice Rosenberry of Wisconsin in *State ex rel. Wisconsin Inspection Bureau v. Whitman,*[29] overruling earlier cases[30] in which the court had predicated decision on this "true test." Its inutility is further demonstrated by the circumstance that in one of the very few cases in which the United States Supreme Court has held a delegation of power invalid[31] literal application of this "test" would have upheld the delegation, because in that case Congress had "made the law" by prohibiting interstate transportation of "hot" oil, and had delegated to administrative officers no more than "discretion as to the execution of the law," by permitting them to decide whether or not, and on what terms and conditions, the prohibition would be enforced.

A second "true test" which has been stated in many opinions asserts that an administrative agency may not be vested with discretionary power to determine policies, but may be empowered only to determine the facts to which the legislatively-declared policy will apply. The fallacy of this suggestion (which likewise was skillfully exposed in Judge Rosenberry's landmark opinion in *State ex rel. Wisconsin Inspection Bureau v. Whitman*[32]) is apparent when one considers the many areas in which policy determination is in fact a principal reason for the creation of an administrative agency, *e.g.,* the many cases where a licensing function is delegated to a board guided only by its conception of what the "public interest" requires. Nevertheless, the language of this second "true test", which first gained popularity in con-

[27] 1 Ohio St. 77 (1852).

[28] Comparatively recent repetitions of this "true test" include Carolina-Virginia Coastal Highway v. Coastal Turnpike Authority, 237 N.C. 52, 74 S.E.2d 310 (1953), and Archbishop O'Hara's Appeal, 389 Pa. 35, 131 A.2d 587 (1957).

[29] See note 26 *supra.*

[30] Dowling v. Lancashire Ins. Co., 92 Wis. 63, 65 N.W. 738, 31 L.R.A. 112 (1896).

[31] Panama Ref. Co. v. Ryan, 293 U.S. 388, 79 L. Ed. 446, 55 Sup. Ct. 241 (1935). The statute prohibited interstate transportation of oil produced in excess of stated quotas, but allowed the agency to waive the prohibition.

[32] See note 26 *supra.*

nection with cases testing the validity of delegation of rate-making powers to public utility commissions, where it was said that in determining a reasonable rate, the agency was only finding a fact, continues to muddy judicial opinions[33] and, occasionally, to muddy judicial thinking.

A third "true test", cast in less precise and therefore safer language, asserts that administrative tribunals may be empowered only to fill in details by making subordinate rules within prescribed limits.[34] This suggestion has the security of vague ambiguity. To what must the administrative rule be subordinate? By what standards must the limits of its discretion be prescribed? The rule is little more than a restatement of the problem. In practice, courts have without hesitation found compliance with this "rule" in cases where the "detail" left to the agency's discretion included such broad questions of legislative policy as that of deciding whether there should or should not be a regulation. Similarly, it appears that the requirement of "subordination" to the statute means only that the administrative regulation must not be directly contrary to the statute, and that the "limits" need be no tighter than those of "fairness" or "equity" which, as is well known, varies with the length of the chancellor's foot. As was well said by Judge Rosenberry: "It only leads to confusion and error to say that the power to fill up the details and promulgate rules and regulations is not legislative power."[35]

(B) "QUASI" NOT A TOUCHSTONE

Recognition of the artificiality of the "true tests" led a number of courts to employ, as a convenient fiction, the diminutive prefix "quasi." This approach adopted as an implicit major premise the proposition that "pure" legislative or judicial powers could not be delegated to an agency, but that functions which were merely "quasi-legislative" or "quasi-judicial" could be delegated without running afoul of constitutional guaranties. This fiction afforded a convenient means of describing the result reached by a court in a given case. Whenever a delegation was sustained, it was labelled merely "quasi" legislative or judicial.

---

[33] *Cf.*, McDonough v. Goodcell, 13 Cal. 2d 741, 91 P.2d 1035, 123 A.L.R. 1205 (1939); Commonwealth of Pennsylvania Water & Power Resources Bd. v. Green Springs Co., 394 Pa. 1, 145 A.2d 178 (1958).

[34] *E.g.*, Whittle v. Nesmith, 255 Ala. 193, 51 So. 2d 6 (1951).

[35] State *ex rel.* Wisconsin Inspection Bureau v. Whitman, note 26 *supra.*

But no court ever succeeded—indeed, none seriously tried—to discover a logical basis for distinguishing between "pure" and "quasi" legislative or judicial powers. Utilization of the diminutive "quasi" furnished no touchstone for decision. Thus, the determination of the issue of "wanton misconduct" would be a "pure" judicial function in a guest-passenger automobile case (because the decision was made by a court) but only a "quasi" judicial function in a workmen's compensation case (because that decision was made by an agency). In many cases, powers which were originally held to be "purely" legislative were later discovered to be merely "quasi" legislative. Thus, attempts to delegate to state agencies the power to apportion between conflicting claimants the use of water rights in a stream were at first viewed with disfavor, and statutes delegating such powers were held unconstitutional on the ground that the function involved was "purely" legislative. But twenty years later, as the practical necessity of utilizing administrative devices to apportion water rights compelled the courts to reverse their earlier view, it was found, on further reflection, that the function was merely "quasi" legislative, and the delegation was therefore perfectly all right.[36]

In short, then, it appears:

1) Neither federal nor state constitutional requirements preclude the delegation of legislative and judicial powers to administrative agencies, in appropriate instances.

2) The problem of determining in what instances such delegation is "appropriate" cannot be solved by utilization of any of the "true tests" which have been suggested in judicial opinions.

3) No more can the convenient diminutive "quasi" be relied upon as a touchstone.

(C) Vestigial Effects

Nevertheless, for reasons which it is difficult to assess [perhaps the explanation is to be found at least in part in the practice of some judges to utilize, in their opinion writing, the style which Justice Cardozo delicately described as "agglutinative"—a name derived from "the shears and the paste pot which are its implements and emblems"] the language of the discredited "true tests" and the terminology of the "quasi" fiction continue to be repeated

36 See Pound, Administrative Law 32 et seq. (1942).

in court opinions and in some texts. They have become a part of our legal jargon—like the phraseology of medieval conveyancing which still persists in so many deeds, even though the beautiful language (*e.g.*, "grant, bargain, sell, remise, release, alien, and confirm forever") has lost its meaning and application. For this reason, the language used by the courts of yesterday, in attempting to utilize separation of powers doctrines in fashioning a method to control the exercise of administrative discretion, cannot be forgotten.

There are, indeed, more substantial reasons which preclude today's student of the law from cavalierly ignoring the applicability to administrative adjudication of the separation of powers philosophy. In certain limited respects, these doctrines retain a significant measure of vitality.

First, (as discussed in greater detail in Chapter II, *supra*) the courts continue to recognize the "fundamental necessity of maintaining each of the three general departments of government entirely free from the control or coercive influence, direct or indirect, of either of the others."[37] When an attempt is made to vest in an administrative agency powers which could be exercised in such a way as to deprive the legislature or the courts of their constitutional prerogatives, the delegation is held invalid. Thus, where an attempt was made to delegate to the Pennsylvania Department of Labor power to prescribe "variations" from a statutory limitation on the maximum number of hours that certain employees would be allowed to work in any one day, and the delegation was so unlimited as to permit the department of labor to set at nought the legislatively declared policy, the delegation was held invalid.[38] There can be no doubt, it seems safe to assume, that the courts would not sustain the delegation to an administrative agency of the power to amend the corporation code of a state, or to repeal legislative enactments. The fact that courts have sustained the delegation of many legislative and judicial powers does not mean that all such powers may be delegated. The point is only that the criterion to distinguish between delegable and non-delegable powers cannot be premised upon

---

[37] Humphrey's Ex'r v. United States, 295 U.S. 602, 609, 79 L. Ed. 1611, 55 Sup. Ct. 869 (1935).

[38] Holgate Bros. Co. v. Bashore, note 13 *supra*.

the characterization of the delegated power as legislative or judicial.

Second, the doctrine of separation of powers still retains vitality in connection with the principle, espoused by many state courts, that constitutional courts may not be required to exercise non-judicial functions.[39]

Third, there are still encountered occasional opinions in which delegation of powers to an administrative agency is held invalid on the grounds that the agency has been vested with legislative, or judicial, power. While the death certificate may have been signed, the ghost of these old cases still walks, and at times haunts judicial chambers. In 1957, for example, the New Mexico court, in an opinion reminiscent of those filed by many courts half a century earlier, held that the state workmen's compensation act was unconstitutional because ". . . the legislature has attempted to create an executive agency, clothe it with judicial power, on a parity with district courts, and invest it with state-wide jurisdiction."[40]

Subject, however, to these few limited exceptions, it may safely be concluded that principles of non-delegability of legislative and judicial powers are no longer useful tools to the state courts in their task of finding a workable method of imposing sound and proper limits on the exercise of discretionary powers by state agencies.

Rather, decision as to what limits shall be placed on such delegations must be predicated on a painstaking, case-by-case appraisal, weighing the advantages of such delegation against the hazards involved. The fundamental criteria were well stated in a dissenting opinion of Mr. Justice Harlan.[41] He said that the principle that authority granted to administrative agencies must

---

[39] State *ex rel.* Chernesky v. Civil Serv. Comm'n, 141 Conn. 465, 106 A.2d 713 (1954), and see discussion in Chapter II, *supra*; State *ex rel.* Waterworth v. Harty, 278 Mo. 685, 213 S.W. 443 (1919); Hodges v. Public Serv. Comm'n, 110 W. Va. 649, 159 S.E. 834 (1931); Gerbitz v. Joint County School Comm., 274 Wis. 396, 80 N.W.2d 377 (1957).

[40] State *ex rel.* Hovey Concrete Prods. Co. v. Mechem, 63 N.M. 250, 254, 316 P.2d 1069 (1957). Some of the California decisions contain strong language respecting the non-delegability of judicial powers, absent specific constitutional sanction; *E.g.*, Standard Oil Co. of California v. State Bd. of Equalization, 6 Cal. 2d 557, 59 P.2d 119 (1936); Rudolph v. Athletic Comm'n, 177 Cal. App. 2d 1, 1 Cal. Rptr. 898 (1960).

[41] State of Arizona v. State of California, 373 U.S. 546, 626, 10 L. Ed. 2d 542, 83 Sup. Ct. 1468 (1963).

be limited is a sound principle, and that it serves two primary functions:

> First, it insures that the fundamental policy decisions in our society will be made not by an appointed official but by the body immediately responsible to the people. Second, it prevents judicial review from becoming merely an exercise at large by providing the courts with some measure against which to judge the official action that has been challenged.

His point was underscored by the piquant observation in the dissenting opinion of Mr. Justice Douglas in the same case (which involved the delegation to the Secretary of the Interior of power to apportion the waters of the Colorado River). He protested that the delegation was too broad, because under it "one can receive his priority because he is the most worthy Democrat or Republican, as the case may be."[42]

Section 3

Inutility of Attempts to Control Administrative Discretion by Insisting on Imposition of "Standards"

Starting some thirty years ago, and coincident with the abandonment of the "true tests" discussed in the preceding section, the state courts began the formulation of a doctrine that delegation of legislative or judicial power to administrative agencies must be limited by the imposition of legislatively prescribed standards. Such standards serve the purpose of stating the general policy which must be followed, thereby serving as a guide to the agency, directing and channeling its discretion.

The doctrine early gained, and currently retains, widespread popularity. Almost all judicial opinions which undertake to articulate the reasons which have persuaded the court to sustain or invalidate a grant of power to an agency, are cast in terms of assaying the sufficiency of the standard imposed to limit or control administrative discretion. It is apparently regarded by most courts, at the present time, as the real "true test" by which validity of delegations must be judged.

It is believed, however (for reasons which will be pointed out, see subsection (C) of this section, in connection with an exam-

[42] *Id.* 373 U.S. at 630.

ination of cases in which courts have felt compelled to sustain the delegation of legislative or judicial powers even in the absence of a standard supplying any meaningful degree of guidance or control), that while the doctrine has proved a useful tool and has provided a means of imposing workable controls on administrative discretion, nevertheless it cannot be relied upon as a basis for predicting judicial decision. For these reasons, it is suggested that in time the insistence upon the existence of legislative standards, in connection with delegations of power to administrative agencies, will disappear; and that this "true test" will meet the fate of the "true test" devised by Justice Ranney in 1852.[43]

But, before proceeding to a criticism of the "standards" test, and in recognition of the fact that most state courts continue to apply it whenever its application squares with the result deemed desirable in a particular case, there should be first examined typical instances of judicial definition of the test, and typical instances of its application.

(A) Definitions of the "Standards" Test

A typical enunciation of the "standards" test is that of the Connecticut court:[44]

> In order to render admissible such delegation of legislative power, however, it is necessary that the statute declare a legislative policy, establish primary standards for carrying it out, or lay down an intelligible principle to which the administrative officer or body must conform, with a proper regard for the protection of the public interest and with such degree of certainty as the nature of the case permits.

In other words, under the "standards" test it is said in effect that the question as to the extent to which legislative or judicial powers may be delegated to administrative bodies resolves itself into a question as to what sort of standard the legislature must set up to limit administrative discretion: if not appropriately limited, the delegation is invalid.

Thus, in sustaining the delegation to a municipal corporation of the power to determine the boundaries of a proposed redevel-

---

[43] Cincinnati, W. & Z. R.R. v. Clinton County Comm'rs, note 27 *supra*, declaring that administrative agencies may not be given power to make the law, but may be given discretion as to the execution of the law.

[44] State v. Stoddard, 126 Conn. 623, 628, 13 A.2d 586 (1940).

opment area, the Wisconsin court said: ". . . by its enactment, the legislature has declared the policy and fixed the standard for the administration of the law."[45] The Pennsylvania court declared: ". . . such authority and discretion may not be conferred by the legislature except under the limitations of a prescribed standard."[46]

Other statements of the princple may be found in the encyclopedias. Thus, it is said in *American Jurisprudence:*[47] ". . . when the legislature states the purpose of the law and sets up standards to guide the agency which is to administer it, there is no constitutional objection to vesting discretion as to its execution in the administrators." Similarly, in *Corpus Juris Secundum,* it is stated:[48] ". . . where executive officers or bodies are charged with the administration of statutes, the legislature must ordinarily prescribe a policy, standard, or rule for their guidance and must not vest them with an arbitrary or uncontrolled discretion with regard thereto. . . ."

(B) Typical Applications of the "Standards" Test

The significance and practical operation of the "standards" test can best be seen in cases where a court invalidates a grant of power to an agency because of the lack of an appropriate standard to limit the agency's discretionary power. It is only in such instances that the determination of the sufficiency of the standard becomes really critical.

An instructive example of the formulation and application of the "standards" test is afforded by an opinion of the Pennsylvania court.[49] In that case, in which the court held invalid a statutory provision requiring Public Utility Commission approval of every contract between a public utility company and any "affiliated interest," the court observed:

> There is no explicit standard set up . . . to guide the Commission. . . . Its power to approve or disapprove is untrammeled by any conditions. Even if we were to consider that public interest can be implied as the standard for approval, that term would not be a

---

[45] David Jeffrey Co. v. Milwaukee, 267 Wis. 559, 590, 66 N.W.2d 362 (1954).

[46] Archbishop O'Hara's Appeal, 389 Pa. 35, 47-48, 131 A.2d 587 (1957).

[47] 42 Am. Jur. *Public Administrative Law* § 45 (1942).

[48] 16 C.J.S. *Constitutional Law* § 138.

[49] Bell Tel. Co. v. Driscoll, 343 Pa. 109, 115, 21 A.2d 912 (1941).

proper standard unless further defined and limited in its meaning. . . . The phrase "public interest" as used in this connection is a "concept without ascertainable criterion."

Another case in which the complete absence of standards was held to invalidate a delegation of power is *Maryland Theatrical Corporation v. Brennan*[50] in which the court considered a statute that authorized a police commissioner to impose a license fee of not less than $5.00 and not more than $100 per day for dances and certain other public entertainments. In this case, it was too obvious for argument that the police commissioner was given an opportunity to favor some licensees on purely personal grounds and to discriminate against others—an opportunity which was perhaps highlighted by the fact that out of more than 40,000 licenses issued, all were at the rate of $5.00 per day except in 40 instances, in all of which the fee had been arbitrarily set at $100. The court found the delegation invalid.

Similar apprehension of the possible dangers inherent in the exercise of untrammeled discretionary powers in a politically delicate situation persuaded the New Jersey court to invalidate a statute delegating power to a state labor board to arbitrate labor disputes affecting public utilities, without prescribing any standard to delineate the factors that were to guide the agency in determining wage rates and other conditions of employment.[51] Thereafter, the legislature amended the statute, to require that the board consider: (1) the public welfare, (2) comparative wage levels, (3) security of employment of utility employees, and (4) such other factors as "are normally or traditionally taken into consideration." The amended statute was upheld[52] on the grounds that the standards were "adequately definitive"; the court apparently concluded that it was impractical to insist upon a more precise delineation of the factors which were to limit the agency's discretion in the volatile field in which it was to operate.

The standards considered in the last-mentioned New Jersey case verged close to the area in which courts have struck down "illusory" standards which, although purporting to create a guide

50 180 Md. 377, 24 A.2d 911 (1942).
51 State v. Traffic Tel. Workers' Fed'n, note 11 *supra.*
52 New Jersey Bell Tel. Co. v. Communications Workers of America, 5 N.J. 354, 371, 75 A.2d 721 (1950).

to channel and direct administrative discretion, used phrases so vague as to really provide no limits at all. Thus, in an early Maryland case,[53] an ordinance was held invalid which authorized a municipal building inspector to refuse a building permit upon consideration of a large number of criteria, including not only such matters as the character of adjoining buildings, and the density of population, and the location of subsurface structures, but also "such other matters as may, in the judgment of the zoning commissioner . . . be necessary to determine whether the proposed building . . . or use . . . would be prejudicial to the public welfare." The court observed:

> These provisions are supposed to supply adequate rules, regulations, and standards to define, guide, and limit the powers given the zoning officials. . . . But in our opinion they have the contrary effect. . . . The "public welfare" . . . could include matters which would have no tangible or physical relation to [protection of the public].

Similarly, the Kansas court[54] held invalid, for lack of a meaningful standard, the delegation to school authorities of the power to reorganize school districts. The court said:

> It is true that the . . . statute sets out a general outline of the various elements which might ordinarily be considered by the legislature in enacting legislation providing for the reorganization of school districts but the general outline contains nothing in the nature of a basis upon which the reorganization committee is instructed to act. . . . They are free to select as they choose from the many and various elements suggested by the legislature.

In cases where the nature of the problem is such that it would plainly be practicable for the legislature to lay down a meaningful standard, its failure to do so may result in the invalidation of the delegation. Thus, the Louisiana court[55] held invalid an ordinance authorizing the chief of police to determine in his sole discretion how long vehicles could be parked on the public streets, because it would not have been impracticable to have laid down a rule to guide the exercise of his discretion.

---

[53] Tighe v. Osborne, 149 Md. 349, 355, 131 Atl. 801, 43 A.L.R. 819 (1925).

[54] State *ex rel.* Donaldson v. Hines, 163 Kan. 300, 312-14, 182 P.2d 865 (1947).

[55] City of Baton Rouge v. Shilg, 198 La. 994, 5 So. 2d 312 (1941).

Other typical cases invalidating delegation of legislative or judicial powers to administrative agencies, on the ground that the statute delegating the power failed to impose adequately definite tests to limit administrative discretion, include:

Kerth v. Hopkins County Board of Education[56]—delegation of power to determine "prevailing wage rates"; *Holgate Bros. Co. v. Bashore*[57]—state department of labor authorized to allow variations from a statutory forty-four hour week where the statutory requirement "imposes an unnecessary hardship and violates the intent and purpose of this act."

South Carolina State Highway Department v. Harbin[58]—highway department authorized to suspend drivers' licenses "for cause satisfactory" to it;

State Board of Dry Cleaners v. Thrift-D-Lux Cleaners, Inc.[59]—agency authorized to establish minimum prices for cleaning and pressing, on consideration of the public health and safety and "all the conditions affecting the business";

Carolina-Virginia Coastal Highway v. Coastal Turnpike Authority[60]—agency authorized, without limiting standard, to prescribe terms for operation of a toll road;

People's Federal Savings and Loan Association v. Franchise Tax Board[61]—agency given uncontrolled choice, in making rules applicable to building and loan associations, to make computation on basis of (a) state-wide average rates, or (b) average rates in a particular locality;

Harvell v. Scheidt, Commissioner of Motor Vehicles[62]—Commissioner of vehicles authorized to revoke drivers' licenses of "habitual violators" of traffic laws;

State ex rel. Continental Oil Co. v. Waddill[63]—city planning committee given unlimited power, without a guiding standard, to grant or deny building permits in certain cases;

---

[56] 346 S.W.2d 737 (Ky. 1961).
[57] 331 Pa. 255, 263, 200 Atl. 672 (1938).
[58] 226 S.C. 585, 597, 86 S.E.2d 466 (1955).
[59] 40 Cal. 2d 436, 254 P.2d 29 (1953).
[60] 237 N.C. 52, 74 S.E.2d 310 (1953)—other defects also involved.
[61] 110 Cal. App. 2d 696, 243 P.2d 902 (1952).
[62] 249 N.C. 699, 107 S.E.2d 549 (1959); *contra,* Anderson v. Commissioner of Highways, 126 N.W.2d 778 (Minn. 1964).
[63] 318 S.W.2d 281 (Mo. 1958).

Colorado Anti-Discrimination Commission v. Case[64]—authority to order "such other action as in the judgment of the commission will effectuate the purposes of this article";

Lane Distributors, Inc. v. Tilton[65]—statute requiring certain wholesalers to keep a stock of cigarettes and "related merchandise" authorized agency to decide what was "related merchandise";

Weiner v. Borough of Stratford[66]—power to deny license to establish an auction store, without a guiding standard;

State ex rel. Associated Land and Investment Corporation v. City of Lyndhurst[67]—standard of "parking space reasonably adequate for commercial vehicles."

State v. Marana Plantations, Inc.[68]—board of health authorized to "regulate sanitation and sanitary practices in the interests of public health."

Krebs v. Thompson[69]—the term "professional engineering" was held too imprecise a standard;

Osius v. City of St. Clair Shores[70]—standard of "public health, safety, and general welfare" held insufficient in a grant of power to a zoning commission, because the standard was not "as reasonably precise as the subject matter requires or permits," and constituted "an open door to favoritism and discrimination."

School District No. 39 v. Decker[71]—authorized to "formulate rules and regulations" for the conduct of public high schools, the state superintendent of public instruction had insisted upon a teacher-pupil ratio of 1-5 for most high schools, but had waived the requirement for other high schools under similar situations.

The number of cases in which courts have held delegations invalid, on the ground that there was no standard imposed (or that the standard was formulated in terms too vague to provide a sufficient restriction on administrative discretion) is long and impressive. But the circumstance that decisions are often ex-

---

64 380 P.2d 34 (Colo. 1962).
65 7 N.J. 349, 81 A.2d 786 (1951).
66 15 N.J. 295, 104 A.2d 659 (1954).
67 168 Ohio St. 289, 154 N.E.2d 435 (1958).
68 75 Ariz. 111, 252 P.2d 87 (1953).
69 387 Ill. 471, 56 N.E.2d 761 (1944).
70 344 Mich. 693, 699-700, 75 N.W.2d 25 (1956).
71 159 Neb. 693, 68 N.W.2d 354 (1955); *cf.,* Lewis Consol. School Dist. v. Johnston, 127 N.W.2d 118 (Iowa 1964).

plained in terms of the "standard" test does not establish its utility. In former years, equally large numbers of decisions were justified in light of then-prevailing "true tests" which have since been repudiated.

As will be noted in the next section, many courts have recently come to recognize the inutility of the "standards" test. As in the case of the "quasi" fiction that was once in vogue, the determination of the sufficiency of the standard is often merely a description of the results, rather than the real basis of decision. The fundamental question is: why is a given standard deemed sufficient and proper in one situation, although the same standard would be ruled too vague in another situation? This question will be considered in Section 4, following an examination of cases in which the courts have recognized the inutility of the "standards" test as workable basis of decision.

(C) JUDICIAL RECOGNITION OF INUTILITY OF "STANDARDS" TEST

While the courts have found attractive the idea that administrative discretion can be controlled and kept within proper limits by insistence upon legislative imposition of appropriate standards, this approach has failed to furnish a criterion capable of precise or equitable application.

In the areas in which governmental controls are commonly delegated to administrative officials, it is not ordinarily possible (nor would it be desirable) to prescribe a standard characterized by the unbending rigidity of mathematical rules. Yet, to the extent that the standard is not susceptible to objective testing, discretionary power is conferred upon the administrative officers.

The central difficulty, therefore, is to determine how tight the standard must be—to what extent the courts should insist that administrative discretion be held in check by rigid, objective standards. The courts soon came to recognize that the test must necessarily vary with the nature of the power conferred. It is quite all right to insist, with exactly measurable precision, that a liquor control commission may not license a dramshop within 500 feet of a church or school; but when the question is how many customers a contract motor carrier may serve, a greater measure of discretion must be accorded the agency, to permit it to fulfill the purpose for which it was created.

It has been recognized that loose and imprecise standards—referable to such elusive concepts as "adequacy" of a service, or "appropriateness" of a bargaining unit, or other criteria not susceptible of proof or disproof by objective tests—are valid whenever it is impracticable to lay down more precise controls. This concession has meant that the legislature may delegate such measure of discretionary power as the court considers wise and proper in the circumstances of a particular case. Thus, determinations of the validity of the delegation are governed not by any jurisprudential analysis of the sufficiency or precision of the standard selected by the legislature, but rather by *ad hoc* assessment of variable and imponderable desiderata.

Judicial retreat from the "standards" test may be seen, further, in opinions proclaiming that "the exigencies of modern government have increasingly dictated the use of general, rather than minutely detailed standards";[72] in cases holding that the perceived purpose of the statute supplies a standard, even though none is enunciated; and in decisions where the court itself supplied a standard by interpolation, in order to sustain a delegation.

To demonstrate the extent to which the utilization of these devices has served to rob the standards test of any real significance, reference may be had to typical cases showing how far the courts are willing to go (in cases where delegation of a wide measure of discretion is deemed desirable) in discovering "standards" that would escape detection upon a mere reading of the statute.

(1) Required Degree of Certainty Depends on Nature of Subject Matter

In the area of zoning, it is difficult to devise meaningful standards. Yet, the desirability of vesting a considerable measure of discretion in zoning commissions has persuaded most courts (although there is by no means unanimous agreement) to sustain delegations of broad discretionary powers to zoning commissions. Noting the imprecision of the standard, the courts have said that a standard which might not be tight enough if applied to other areas of governmental control will be sustained in zoning cases.

[72] State v. Hotel Bar Foods, Inc., 18 N.J. 115, 124, 112 A.2d 726 (1955).

A typical case is *Burnham v. Board of Appeals of Gloucester*[73] where the only limit placed on the zoning board's discretion was the provision that "no permit shall be granted . . . without considering the effect upon the neighborhood and the City at large." The court upheld the delegation. In reply to the argument that there was no limit to what the zoning board might do under the loosely permissive language of the statute, the court observed: "The degree of certainty with which standards for the exercise of discretion are set up must necessarily depend on the subject matter and the circumstances." In case of zoning regulations, the court further observed: "It would have been difficult, if not impossible, to specify in what circumstances permits should be granted and in what circumstances denied. That would depend on numerous unforeseeable factors."

Where health or public safety is involved, the courts have similarly approved grants of extremely broad discretionary authority, and justified the result on the basis that the nature of the subject matter excuses the need for objective standards. Thus, in sustaining the delegation to an agency of the power to draft a "safety code" to reduce fire hazards in a downtown hotel, the Connecticut court[74] said:

> While it is true that the law-making power is in the legislative branch of our government and cannot be delegated, we have recognized the place of administrative agencies in modern society. The General Assembly in passing a law designed to accomplish a particular purpose may expressly create an administrative agency. The statutes under consideration have as their avowed purpose, "reasonable safety from fire, smoke and panic." Sec. 3665. This is a legislative policy certainly within the police power of the state. . . . The code, even at points where it merely requires safeguards which are "proper" or "adequate," established standards adequate to guide the enforcement of it. Regulations or orders might be reasonable as applied to one situation but not to another.

The language of the court explains the result which was reached; but it does not explain the reason for the result. Such explanation must lie in the circumstance that the courts are willing to approve a much broader delegation of discretionary power in

---

73 333 Mass. 114, 118, 128 N.E.2d 772 (1955).

74 Len-Lew Realty Co. v. Falsey, 141 Conn. 524, 528, 530, 107 A.2d 403 (1954).

cases where the public safety is significantly involved, than in cases where the need for administrative discretion is less apparent.

When the desirability of establishing minimum milk prices and regulating the milk industry impressed itself upon a large number of state legislatures in the "depression years" of the early 1930's, questions of delegability faced a severe test, for most legislatures found it impracticable to establish any meaningful guides to assist the agencies in fixing prices. While there was disagreement among the courts, most of them found it possible to justify the delegation, despite the lack of a definite standard.

An example of how slight a standard is deemed sufficient, where the practical need appears great, is afforded by *Elite Dairy Products v. Ten Eyck*[75] where the judgment of the Appellate Division was reversed by the New York Court of Appeals. The statute prohibited the acquisition of new plants or new facilities by milk dealers except in cases where the Commissioner of Agriculture was satisfied that the applicant was qualified "by character, experience, financial responsibility and equipment to properly conduct the proposed business." On appeal from denial of a license, the Appellate Division declared the delegation invalid for lack of a standard, and proclaimed:

> The statute does not point out what character is requisite for a milk dealer, nor does it suggest that any particular financial responsibility is necessary, what plant and equipment are adequate. . . . Even though it were competent for the legislature to prescribe such conditions, and to fix such standards, . . . they have not been prescribed. On the contrary, the Commissioner is free to follow his own judgment, notion, or whim in determining whether any or all of these conditions (as he may define them) have been met.

While the Court of Appeals did not quarrel with this rather trenchant analysis, it sustained the delegation on the convenient principle that the standard need not be strict or precise, where the nature of the case makes it impracticable to draft a tight standard.

Similarly, a Connecticut statute which authorized a milk administrator to fix minimum prices upon consideration of "cost factors which should influence the determination of such prices,"

---

75 271 N.Y. 488, 492, 3 N.E.2d 606 (1936), *reversing* 247 App. Div. 443, 288 N.Y.S. 162 (1936).

was sustained on the ground that the standard need have only "such degree of certainty as the nature of the case permits."[76]

As noted above, a standard cast in very similar terms was held to be insufficiently precise in the case of delegation of authority to fix prices for dry cleaning.[77] The difficulty of framing a standard, clearly, is the same whether the prices to be fixed relate to the sale of milk or the sale of dry cleaning. The cases cannot be distinguished on the basis that it is possible to fix a more precise standard for one type of price-fixing than for another. The reason for the disparate results must lie in the circumstance that the courts believe governmental control of private business activities can be justified by over powering social necessities in the case of milk, but not in the case of dry cleaning.

In another type of price-fixing, involving delegation to a state liquor control board of the power to fix prices at which wine would be sold, the court upheld the delegation and excused the lack of standards by saying it was impossible to fix standards.[78] The decision appears sound if justified in terms of the special position of the liquor business, vis-á-vis state control, and the desirability of delegating a broad measure of discretion to administrative agencies in this particular field. But it is impossible to reconcile these three price-fixing decisions on the basis that it is necessary to have objective, restrictive standards in cases where they can be drawn but unnecessary where no such standard can be devised.

On the ground that it would be "difficult to provide a more specific standard," the Supreme Court of Washington upheld the delegation to the Supervisor of Banks of discretionary power to reject applications to engage in the small loan business, if the applicant did not possess the necessary financial responsibility, experience, character, and general fitness, or if the granting of the license would not promote the convenience and advantage of the community.[79]

Where a state agency was granted power to condemn land and to construct and operate airports, its discretion not being limited by any legislatively imposed standard, the court held

---

[76] State v. Stoddard, 126 Conn. 623, 625, 628, 13 A.2d 586 (1940).

[77] State Bd. of Dry Cleaners v. Thrift-D-Lux Cleaners Inc., note 59 *supra.*

[78] The Pompei Winery, Inc. v. Board of Liquor Control, 167 Ohio St. 61, 146 N.E.2d 430 (1957).

[79] Kelleher v. Minshull, 11 Wash. 2d 380, 119 P.2d 302 (1941).

that while it approved, in general, the rule it had earlier declared[80] that "delegation of discretionary power to an administrative body must be accompanied by adequate standards . . . sufficient to guide its exercise", nevertheless "this general rule should not be applied . . . where important public interests are involved, and on account of the inherent nature of the power delegated, standards applicable generally throughout the State cannot be set up."[81]

In another case in which delegation of broad discretionary powers was deemed desirable, the Ohio court observed that it was "not only impractical but impossible" to prescribe specific standards of conduct to guide a state highway commissioner; and that since it was essential that the highway commissioner be authorized to make a great many discretionary decisions in the exercise of "his manifold duties," a delegation of power "in general terms, depending upon the judgment of the one to whom the powers are delegated, is justified."[82]

On similar grounds, the New York court authorized delegation of a broad measure of discretion to a water pollution control board, observing that if the state legislature had insisted on a strict statutorily imposed standard, the agency could not effectively exercise its power to control pollution, since conditions varied widely in different parts of the state.[83]

If further demonstration be needed that the "standards" test is a slender reed, when modified by the caveat that the standard need be only such as the necessities of the case permit, such demonstration is afforded by cases holding that although the standard itself was satisfactory, yet administrative action thereunder constituted such an abuse of discretion as to compel the court to invalidate the administrative act. Such a case is *Weber v. Board of Health.*[84] There, the statute authorized county boards of health to make such regulations as the respective boards deemed necessary for the public health, the prevention of disease,

---

[80] Chapman v. Huntington Housing Authority, 121 W. Va. 319, 336, 3 S.E. 2d 502 (1939).

[81] Meisel v. Tri-State Airport Authority, 135 W. Va. 528, 545, 64 S.E.2d 32 (1951).

[82] City of Lakewood v. Thormyer, 171 Ohio St. 135, 143, 168 N.E.2d 289 (1960).

[83] City of Utica v. Water Pollution Control Bd., 5 N.Y.2d 164, 182 N.Y.S.2d 584, 156 N.E.2d 301 (1959).

[84] 148 Ohio St. 389, 396, 74 N.E.2d 331 (1947).

and the prevention of nuisances. The court held that the standard was a valid one, declaring:

> . . . [T]here are many occasions where the nature of the problem makes it impossible to lay down standards, and as a result rule-making bodies must be allowed a wide discretion without anything as their guide except the general policy of the law-making body and the law that such bodies must not legislate or make rules which are unreasonable, discriminatory, or contrary to constitutional rights.

However, when faced with the rule which a particular board of health had promulgated—prohibiting the transportation of garbage for feeding animals, except as licensed by the health commissioner—the court held that the rule was so unreasonable as to be unenforceable.

(2) Generality in Fixing of Standards Deemed Helpful

Not only have the courts uniformly recognized that precision of statement will not be required in cases where it is difficult to state the standard precisely; they have gone further and recognized that in many cases the attainment of the basic purposes of administrative control can best be achieved by the adoption of broad standards, so as to permit the agencies to exercise a necessary and desirable degree of discretion. Thus, the New Jersey court[85] in upholding a statute which delegated the power to license solicitors and canvassers on the basis of a showing that the applicant possessed "satisfactory character and business responsibility," observed: ". . . the exigencies of modern government have increasingly dictated the use of general rather than minutely detailed standards."

Similarly, the Washington court,[86] sustaining the delegation to a state budget director of the power to make such rules as he found necessary to carry out the purposes of the act, observed:

> The fact that the standards and limitations are not immediately apparent to every layman casually perusing the statute does not establish their non-existence. . . . The complexity and character of the subject matter of legislation is to be considered in determining whether there has been an unlawful delegation of legislative power.

---

85 Moyant v. Borough of Paramus, 30 N.J. 528, 154 A.2d 9 (1959).
86 Yelle v. Bishop, 55 Wash. 2d 286, 302, 347 P.2d 1081 (1959).

Similarly, the New Jersey court[87] spoke approvingly of the delegation of a broad measure of discretionary power, not limited by any narrow standard, where "reasonably needful to insure a well-qualified constabulary."

The California court noted with approval, in sustaining the delegation of discretionary power to an agency charged with making regulations for the spacing of oil wells, that "in the interest of providing for flexibility" the legislature "did not desire to lay down minutely defined standards."[88]

The Missouri court has noted that recent cases indicate a trend toward broadening of the permissible scope of discretion where the questioned legislation is of a police nature.[89]

The desirability of having standards phrased only in general terms, so as to permit broad exercise of administrative discretion, in cases involving the protection of the public health, has also been noted.[90]

Other cases recognize, in a variety of situations, that it is sometimes better if the legislature does not inhibit administrative discretion by the imposition of strict standards.[91]

(3) The Purpose of the Statute May be Sufficient as a Standard

In cases where the court cannot discover any standard whatever in the language of the statute, delegations of power are not infrequently sustained on the theory that the apparent purpose of the statute itself may be utilized to supply an implicit "standard." While it may be argued that such decisions are not necessarily inconsistent with the "standards" test, they do demonstrate that it is not insisted that the legislature formulate any explicit standard.

In a California case involving the delegation to a police officer of discretionary power to designate certain areas in the streets

[87] Cammarata v. Essex County Park Comm'n, 26 N.J. 404, 413, 140 A.2d 397, 46 N.J. Super. 262, 134 A.2d 604 (1957).

[88] Wotton v. Bush, 41 Cal. 2d 460, 469, 261 P.2d 256 (1953).

[89] State *ex rel.* Priest v. Gunn, 326 S.W.2d 314 (Mo. 1959).

[90] Butterworth v. Boyd, 12 Cal. 2d 140, 82 P.2d 434, 126 A.L.R. 838 (1938); Quesenberry v. J. S. Estep, 142 W. Va. 426, 95 S.E.2d 832 (1956).

[91] State *ex rel.* Wright v. Casey, 225 Ark. 149, 279 S.W.2d 819 (1955); West v. Egan, 142 Conn. 437, 115 A.2d 322 (1955); Levitt & Sons, Inc. v. Division Against Discrimination in State Dep't of Educ., 31 N.J. 514, 158 A.2d 177, 56 N.J. Super. 542, 153 A.2d 700 (1959); Matter of Old Republic Ins. Co. v. Wikler, 9 N.Y.2d 524, 175 N.E.2d 147 (1961); Board of Medical Examiners v. Mintz, 233 Ore. 441, 378 P.2d 945 (1963).

as taxicab stands for the exclusive use of particular cab companies, the absence of a standard was held not to be fatal, because an implied standard was "inherent in the reasons which must have led to the adoption of the ordinance. In the present case, it is clear that the purpose of controlling taxicab stands by issuance of permits is to make satisfactory and orderly taxicab service readily available to the public without unnecessary obstruction of traffic. This purpose supplies standards."[92]

Similarly, the Minnesota court declared that it was enough "if the law furnishes a reasonably clear policy or standard of action which controls and guides the administrative officers." On this basis, delegation of power to a Board of Barber Examiners to determine by examination whether aspirants to barber licenses had proficiency in specified subjects, was sustained on the basis that the obvious purpose of the statute was that only a *reasonable* degree of proficiency could be required.[93]

The New Jersey court observed that "standards do not need to be set out in express terms if they can be inferred from the statutory scheme as a whole";[94] and in another case noted that vague standards may "acquire content from the overall objective of the statute."[95] Similarly, the Missouri court found that the mere description of the agency's function may provide a sufficient standard.[96]

(4) The Standard May be Supplied by Court

Even in cases where the statute does not imply a standard, the delegation is sometimes sustained by judicial interpolation of a standard. For example, where a police official was authorized to revoke licenses of private detectives "for cause," the court said that the term "cause" should be equated to the standard fixed for the issuance of the license, and that by such equation the statute would be construed as authorizing revocation only for "deficiency with respect to good character, competency, or in-

---

92 *In re* Petersen, 51 Cal. 2d 177, 185, 331 P.2d 24 (1958).

93 Lee v. Delmont, 228 Minn. 101, 113, 36 N.W.2d 530 (1949).

94 Schierstead v. City of Brigantine, 20 N.J. 164, 119 A.2d 5 (1955).

95 Elizabeth Fed. Sav. & Loan Ass'n v. Howell, 30 N.J. 190, 152 A.2d 359 (1959).

96 Ross v. City of Kansas City, 328 S.W.2d 610 (Mo. 1959).

tegrity." So construed, the court added, the statute "does not admit of arbitrary action," and the delegation was sustained.[97]

In another licensing case (this one affecting the operators of hand-trucks in Manhattan's "garment district"), the New York Court of Appeals supplied a standard not apparent in the legislative enactment by declaring:

> There can be no disputing the general rule that any discretionary powers exercised by an administrative officer must be delegated to him by statute and that such delegation must be accompanied by standards to guide the exercise of administrative discretion. With respect to licensing officials, however, it is equally well settled that the power to withhold a license for good cause, as well as the standards defining good cause, need not be *expressly* delegated where, by fair implication, in light of the statutory purpose, such power has been implicitly delegated.[98]

(5) Constitutional Limitations Non-Existent

Finally, there are cases where delegation of power is sustained even though the statute does not state a standard, and none can be implied from the statutory purpose, and the court does not choose to interpolate a standard by interpretation. Thus, the courts have long sustained delegation of completely unfettered discretionary powers in such cases as the granting of licenses to dredge in state-owned waters,[99] or prohibiting fishing in certain areas,[100] or regulating the non-traffic use of city streets.[101] In such cases, the requirement of a "standard" is frankly abandoned.

---

[97] Berardi v. Rutter, 42 N.J. Super. 39, 125 A.2d 877 (1956), *aff'd,* 23 N.J. 485, 129 A.2d 705 (1957).

[98] Matter of Barton Trucking Corp. v. O'Connell, 7 N.Y.2d 299, 307, 197 N.Y.S.2d 138, 165 N.E.2d 163 (1959).

[99] State *ex rel.* Port Royal Mining Co. v. Hagood, 30 S.C. 519, 9 S.E. 686, 3 L.R.A. 841 (1889).

[100] McMillan v. Sims, 132 Wash. 265, 231 Pac. 943, *reversing* 129 Wash. 516, 225 Pac. 240 (1925).

[101] Wilson v. Eureka City, 173 U.S. 32, 43 L. Ed. 603, 19 Sup. Ct. 317 (1899).

Section 4

Factors That Motivate Decision as to Sufficiency of Limitation on Administrative Discretion

(A) No Logical Test Available

The pervasive desire of judges and lawyers to find order in uncertainty—the desire that has long led them on a will-o-the-wisp pursuit of a "true test" to determine the delegability of legislative and judicial powers—lends great attraction to the "standards" test. There is great appeal in the suggestion that, as a condition of the validity of delegation, the legislature must establish a standard, to guide and limit administrative discretion, in terms as specific as the nature of the case will permit.

The idea is unquestionably sound. It has commended itself to the state courts and to the state legislatures for some forty years. However, as demonstrated by the cases in the preceding section, the "standards" test affords no sure touchstone to the courts in the decision of cases. Logical and sound though the principle is, it does not provide a practical working tool because there is no logical basis for determining how far the nature of the case permits or prohibits the fashioning of a specific standard.

This question is basically a problem for the legislatures. When the legislative draftsmen decide upon the terms of the delegation, it is for them to decide whether the legislature shall set the policy in definitive terms, or whether on the other hand the legislative enactment shall express its general purpose only in terms of a pious wish, delegating to an administrative agency the responsibility of actually determining the working policies by which the generally-phrased legislative desire should be attained.

Thus, in enacting an unemployment compensation act, the legislature could set a definite policy by declaring that as a condition of establishing eligibility for unemployment benefits, the claimant must prove that he had actively searched for work. This would be a comparatively definite standard.

On the other hand, the legislature could provide merely that benefits should be paid only to claimants found to be available for work. Such an expression would delegate the real policy-making function to the agency. Under such a standard, the agency could (subject to the residual power of the courts to define the meaning of the term "available" as a matter of law) choose to require that the claimant must show that he had actively searched for work; or could, at the opposite extreme, require only that the claimant must not refuse to accept a job offer tendered him by the agency; or could adopt a number of intermediate policy positions.

If the legislature chooses the latter alternative—and authorizes the agency to grant benefits whenever it finds the claimant available for work—the legislature has in effect expressed its judgment that this vague suggestion is the most definite standard which the nature of the case permits. When a court is later asked to displace the legislature's judgment, the court faces a most delicate task.

There is no purely analytical or logical test by which a court can determine whether the legislature should have adopted the tighter standard. The court can do no more than to balance the public interest in administrative control against the countervailing private interest, in the context of the particular case, and then express its judgment whether the consequences of granting very broad discretionary power to the agency to allow benefits to anyone whom the agency considers "available," will lead to social consequences so undesirable as to be abhorrent to the court's sense of justice. Unless the court reaches this conclusion, it will not say that it would have been possible for the legislature to have adopted a more specific standard, although as a matter of logical fact, it would have actually been possible (as demonstrated above) for the legislature to have adopted a more specific standard. This is true not only in the case of unemployment compensation statutes, but in every case wherein the court is asked to decide whether the delegation is invalid because of the looseness of the standard.

In other words, what the courts are really called on to decide is not whether the legislature *could* have prescribed a more specific standard; but whether the legislature *should* have prescribed a more definite standard. The courts are reluctant to displace the legislative judgment on this point, unless they feel absolutely compelled to do so by the factors discussed in the succeeding subsections of this section.

(B) Practical Considerations Motivate Decision

In the following subsections, there are suggested eleven factors that are believed to play a predominant part in the actual course of judicial decision, when a court is asked to determine whether a grant of legislative or judicial power to an administrative agency is invalid because of the absence of proper limitations upon the agency's discretion. The list does not purport to be exhaustive. Nor does it purport to furnish a convenient rule of thumb by reference to which counsel can determine what the decision of a court would be, in a particular case situation. Still less does it purport to be a touchstone on which courts can rely to ease the delicate and difficult burden which is theirs in determining whether to upset a legislative judgment as to how broad a scope of discretion should be delegated.

Rather, the eleven factors mentioned are intended only as an indication of the general character of the basic considerations—most often not articulated in judicial opinions (although sometimes, with refreshing candor, specified as the basis of decision) that sway the course of judicial decision.

It is not suggested that these eleven factors afford any sort of a "true test"; nor is it implied that by adding up pluses and minuses, as these eleven tests are applied to a given case situation, a seven-to-four score will determine how a case must be decided. Indeed, if one chose to, he could expand this list of eleven criteria to a list twice as long. The attempt is only to suggest the sort of factors that are persuasive to the courts. It is believed that one's opinions as counsellor will be more accurate, and his arguments as advocate more compelling, if they are predicated upon an appraisal of these earthy, pragmatic considerations, rather than on a coldly logical analysis of the practicability of having prescribed a more definite standard. In some cases, it will be clear that the presence of only one of these eleven factors will, for all practical purposes, control the decision. In other cases, one must search for factors not included on this list (but nevertheless of the same general character as the factors here mentioned) which will be effective in persuading a court that a particular delegation should or should not be sustained.

(C) Analysis of Factors That Motivate Decision

The innominate, imponderable factors that do, in fact, motivate decision cannot be catalogued. Their nature and relative importance vary from one case to another. Further, it must be recognized that in this field judgment is somewhat temporal, reflecting to a substantial degree contemporaneous economic and political thinking. Likewise, the attitude of the particular court must be considered. The admonitions found in some opinions, that administrative tribunals must be recognized as agencies that are coordinate with (and not inferior to) the courts in the administration of law and justice, are not accorded universal acquiescence. Courts are not equally receptive to this philosophy. Despite all these difficulties, it appears possible to describe the character of the most important factors that influence decision by the courts as to the sufficiency of the limitations imposed on administrative discretion.

(1) Delegation Sustained, Where Reference to Established Legal Concepts Has Effect of Limiting Discretion

If a seemingly vague standard is susceptible of definition by reference to well-established legal concepts, it will usually be sustained. Some phrases commonly employed in formulating standards to guide administrative action have, by constant use and judicial interpretation, acquired what the courts consider to be a well-defined meaning. While it is true that in applying the standard, the agencies may sometimes disregard the judicial interpretations which over the years have been placed upon the phrase in question, and may read into it concepts and implications which a court would not have perceived; nevertheless, the courts feel that if the standard is phrased in terms of established legal concepts, it should be upheld.

In this class, for example, are such expressions as "reasonable rates," "unreasonable preferences," "discrimination," "monopoly." In the field of rate regulation, the term "reasonable" takes on fairly ascertainable meaning when viewed in the light of hundreds of judicial decisions construing the term "reasonable rate" as applied in utility regulation. The same term would presumably be held to be an insufficient limitation on administrative discretion if a taxing agency were authorized to impose a variable rate of tax, depending on what was deemed a "reasonable rate" in light of the profits of the taxpayer. Again, the power of an agency to proscribe "unfair methods of competition" can be defined in substantial degree by reference to common-law tests, and is therefore sustained although delegation of power to compel companies to follow whatever the agency deemed to be "fair methods of competition" might not be sustained.[102]

The importance of this factor is sometimes acknowledged by the courts. Thus, the Vermont court[103] said:

> In order that a statute may be held valid, the duty imposed by it must be prescribed in terms definite enough to serve as a guide to those who have the duty imposed upon them. Such definiteness may be produced by words which have a technical or other special meaning well enough known to permit compliance therewith, or words which have an established meaning at common law through decisions.

Likewise, the Minnesota court,[104] in sustaining the delegation to a state board of power to revoke a practitioner's license for "unprofessional conduct," adverted to the fact that through long professional experience and judicial interpretation the meaning of this phrase had become well established.[105]

The Missouri court, similarly, in approving a delegation of authority to fix the "fair value" at which land could be sold, observed that no improperly broad discretion was vested in the agency because "The phrase, 'fair value,' has a well known meaning."[106]

(2) The Tradition in a Particular Field May Control Decision

In areas where the delegation of broad discretionary powers to administrative agencies is supported by long tradition, delegations cast in terms that leave the agency wide discretion are

---

[102] Indeed, such delegation was held invalid in A. L. A. Schechter Poultry Corp. v. United States, 295 U.S. 495, 79 L. Ed. 1570, 55 Sup. Ct. 837, 97 A.L.R. 947 (1935).

[103] State v. Auclair, 110 Vt. 147, 163, 4 A.2d 107 (1939).

[104] Reyburn v. Minnesota State Bd. of Optometry, 247 Minn. 520, 78 N.W.2d 351 (1956).

[105] Half a century earlier, the Kentucky court had reached the opposite conclusion, holding that the standard of "unprofessional conduct" was insufficient because of the danger that the board might rule something to be unprofessional which the defendant would have had no reason to suspect might be so considered. Matthews v. Murphy, 23 Ky. L. Rep. 750, 63 S.W. 785, 54 L.R.A. 415 (1901).

[106] State *on inf.* Dalton v. Land Clearance Authority, 364 Mo. 974, 270 S.W. 2d 44 (1954).

often upheld. In these cases, delegations of legislative and judicial power are upheld that would be held invalid in other fields of administrative activity. Where tradition favors delegation, it is enough if the legislature, either expressly or by implication—and silence is sufficient implication—sets up a general standard of reasonableness (the same standard by which the legislature itself is controlled).

Thus, apparently for the reason that, as the United States Supreme Court once phrased it,[107] banking and money-lending comprise "one of the longest regulated and most closely supervised of public callings," delegations of extremely broad discretionary powers to state banking commissioners are unquestioningly upheld. Such "standards" as "the convenience and advantage of the community"[108] or "adequacy of banking facilities"[109] are acceptable where banks are the subject of the regulation, although it seems reasonably clear that if an attempt were made to vest a similar measure of discretion in an agency authorized to license grocery stores, the delegation would be held invalid by most state courts.[110]

The selling of milk long has been subject to administrative controls designed to impose regulations suitable for the preservation of the public health, and the courts are generally willing to sustain the delegation of broad discretionary powers to administrative agencies to fix the price of milk[111] although attempts to delegate to administrative authorities the power to fix prices in the cleaning and pressing business, under substantially the same "standards," have been held invalid.[112]

Indeed, in the regulation of the milk industry, delegations have been upheld even where the standards to be applied were those to be stated by private groups,[113] although ordinarily[114]

107 Fahey v. Mallonee, 332 U.S. 245, 250, 91 L. Ed. 2030, 67 Sup. Ct. 1552 (1947).

108 Kelleher v. Minshull, 11 Wash. 2d 380, 119 P.2d 302 (1941).

109 Dauphin Deposit Trust Co. v. Myers, 388 Pa. 444, 130 A.2d 686 (1957).

110 State *ex rel.* Makris v. Superior Court of Pierce County, 113 Wash. 296, 193 Pac. 845 (1920).

111 Elite Dairy Products v. Ten Eyck, 271 N.Y. 488, 3 N.E.2d 606 (1936); Noyes v. Erie & Wyoming Farmers Co-operative Corp., 281 N.Y. 187, 22 N.E.2d 334, *reversing* 170 Misc. 42, 10 N.Y.S.2d 114 (1939); Rohrer v. Milk Control Bd., 322 Pa. 257, 186 Atl. 336 (1936).

112 State Bd. of Dry Cleaners v. Thrift-D-Lux Cleaners Inc., 40 Cal. 2d 436, 254 P.2d 29 (1953).

113 Natural Milk Producers Ass'n v. San Francisco, 20 Cal. 2d 101, 124 P.2d 25 (1942).

the courts refuse to permit delegation of legislative or judicial power to private groups.

Similarly, delegation of broad discretionary powers to agencies regulating the activities of those engaged in various professions, and in occupations deemed to bear a critical relationship to the public health or morals, has long been sustained.

There has been a long tradition of delegating to administrative agencies a free hand in the regulation of such businesses as the operation of saloons or dance halls.[115] Where the standard for the licensing of junk dealers was made to depend on the agency's finding that the applicant was a "suitable person," the Connecticut court held that the delegation was proper.[116] Similarly, in the conduct of the liquor business, agencies may be empowered to decide, without guidance of a statutory standard, what is "good cause."[117]

The tradition of permitting governing boards composed of members of a learned profession to exercise a broad measure of discretion in granting or revoking licenses to practice[118] has gradually been extended to other fields involving professional competence or activities which involve a high degree of public interest. Thus, in the case of optometry, it has been held that a standard of "unprofessional conduct" is proper.[119] But if the standard is made to depend on the personal opinions of the members of the licensing board, rather than on generally accepted traditions of the profession, the result may be different.[120]

---

114 See subsec. (7) *infra.*

115 State v. Sherow, 87 Kan. 235, 123 Pac. 866 (1912), where the court upheld a standard which authorized the agency to grant licenses for the operation of poolhalls, "whenever in their judgment it shall be to the interest of their respective townships to grant the same." The court observed that so broad a grant of discretionary powers would not have been sustained if the statute had applied to "some useful trade or business, like keeping a pharmacy."

116 Clapp v. Ulbrich, 140 Conn. 637, 103 A.2d 195 (1954).

117 Schwartz v. Kelly, 140 Conn. 176, 99 A.2d 89, *appeal dismissed,* 346 U.S. 891, 98 L. Ed. 394, 74 Sup. Ct. 227 (1953).

118 Such delegations, despite a few early doubts—*e.g.,* Matthews v. Murphy, 23 Ky. L. Rep. 750, 63 S.W. 785, 54 L.R.A. 415 (1901)—have long been upheld. See 5 A.L.R. 94 (1920).

119 Reyburn v. Minnesota State Bd. of Optometry, 247 Minn. 520, 78 N.W.2d 351 (1956).

120 In Abelson's, Inc. v. New Jersey State Bd. of Optometrists, 5 N.J. 412, 75 A.2d 867, *modifying* 65 A.2d 644 (1950), a delegation which permitted revocation of licenses for any conduct which "in the opinion of the board" was likely to deceive the public, was held invalid.

The tradition permitting the delegation of broad discretionary power in the regulation of occupations has been extended to teachers,[121] to real estate brokers,[122] and even to general contractors.[123]

While the trend to urban planning through the delegation of broad discretionary powers to zoning commissions and redevelopment boards is of more recent origin, this field has been added to those wherein, without any critical or searching study of the sufficiency of the standards, delegations of broad discretionary power are normally upheld. Thus, in zoning cases, such standards as "protecting the character of the neighborhood," "promoting the health, safety, morals, or general welfare," or "substantial depreciation of property values" are held proper.[124]

However, many courts have concluded that in one aspect of zoning regulation (one that constitutes a departure from traditions in the field)—that having to do with the vesting of discretionary power in a zoning board to grant variances from the prescribed rules—somewhat greater caution is necessary. Sensing that in this area there is a danger that members of a local board, politically appointed, might "pick and choose the recipients of their favors,"[125] several courts have invalidated attempts to bestow upon local agencies uncontrolled discretionary powers to

---

121 Laba v. Board of Educ., 23 N.J. 364, 129 A.2d 273 (1957), where the standard was "inefficiency, incapacity, conduct unbecoming a teacher or other just cause."

122 Lewis Realty, Inc. v. Wisconsin Real Estate Brokers' Bd., 6 Wis. 2d 99, 94 N.W.2d 238 (1959)—standard of "improper, fraudulent, or dishonest dealing"; Wall v. Wisconsin Real Estate Brokers' Bd., 4 Wis. 2d 426, 90 N.W.2d 589 (1958)—standard of "persons who are trustworthy and competent to transact such business."

123 Tasco Developing & Bldg. Corp. v. Long, 212 Tenn. 96, 368 S.W.2d 65 (1963).

124 Gohld Realty Co. v. Hartford, 141 Conn. 135, 104 A.2d 365 (1954); Burnham v. Board of Appeals of Gloucester, 333 Mass. 114, 128 N.E.2d 772 (1955); Krupp v. Building Comm'r, 325 Mass. 686, 92 N.E.2d 242 (1950); Porporis v. City of Warson Woods, 352 S.W.2d 605 (Mo. 1962); State v. Guffey, 306 S.W.2d 552 (Mo. 1957); Ward v. Scott, 11 N.J. 117, 93 A.2d 385 (1952); Fifty-Fourth St. Center, Inc. v. Zoning Bd. of Adjustment, 395 Pa. 338, 150 A.2d 335 (1959); National Maritime Union of America, AFL-CIO v. City of Norfolk, 202 Va. 672, 119 S.E.2d 307 (1961); State *ex rel.* Saveland Park Holding Corp. v. Wieland, 269 Wis. 262, 69 N.W.2d 217, *cert. denied,* 350 U.S. 841, 100 L. Ed. 750, 76 Sup. Ct. 81 (1955).

125 Osius v. City of St. Clair Shores, 344 Mich. 693, 698, 75 N.W.2d 25 (1956).

grant variances.[126] But, even here, some courts sustain a grant of broad discretion in the allowance of variances.[127]

There are, however, some limits. Where an attempt was made to vest a veto power in a single elected official, dependent on his personal caprice, to cancel a permit issued in ordinary course by a director of public service, it was held that the granting of so untrammeled a measure of discretion was invalid.[128]

In short, areas where administrative controls have been so long exercised as to have become traditional must be put in a class by themselves. Delegations which are sustained in such areas as public utility regulation, banking, zoning, and the like, are sustained because they have become, so to speak, a part of the political or judicial mores. When an attempt is made to extend to fields in which administrative control is not an accustomed thing, the same broad discretionary power which is accepted in the former type of case, the courts—depending on experience rather than logic—are likely to upset the attempt.

(3) Discretion Must Be More Strictly Limited Where Substantial Property Interests Are Involved

The courts exhibit unwillingness to sustain vague standards where the arbitrary exercise of an agency's discretionary powers could have calamitous effects on substantial rights of property.

Thus, despite the fact that the phrase "public interest" has long been deemed to provide a satisfactory standard when used as a condition for licensing a telephone company by a public utility commission, yet when an attempt was made to authorize a public utility commission to require the rescission of any contract between a telephone company and its affiliates which the commission deemed to be contrary to the "public interest," the court held the discretion was greater than could be tolerated, protesting that "the phrase 'public interest' as used in this context is 'a concept without ascertainable criteria.' "[129]

---

126 Aloe v. Dassler, 303 N.Y. 878, 105 N.E.2d 104 (1952); Little v. Young, 299 N.Y. 699, 87 N.E.2d 74 (1949); State *ex rel.* Selected Properties, Inc. v. Gottfried, 163 Ohio St. 469, 127 N.E.2d 371 (1955).

127 Nelson v. Donaldson, 255 Ala. 76, 50 So. 2d 244 (1951); Ward v. Scott, 11 N.J. 117, 93 A.2d 385 (1952).

128 Northern Boiler Co. v. David, 157 Ohio St. 564, 106 N.E.2d 620 (1952).

129 Bell Tel. Co. of Pennsylvania v. Driscoll, 343 Pa. 109, 21 A.2d 912 (1941).

Obviously, the court was concerned with the grave consequences inherent in a situation in which contracts involving millions of dollars, and on which the security of employment of hundreds of employees depended, could be set aside if three commissioners, for reasons of their own, found that some term of the contract was contrary to the "public interest."

For similar reasons, the Kentucky court held that the legislature could not delegate to an agency, without any guiding criterion, the power to establish "prevailing wage schedules," the establishment of which would substantially affect the rights of large numbers of employers and employees.[130]

Similarly, delegation of power to fix minimum prices for dry cleaning was held void.[131]

In licensing cases, much less discretion may be delegated as to revocation of licenses to carry on a substantial business of a type not affected by a high degree of public interest[132] than in cases where the license permits one to engage in activity of a type which the legislature might entirely prohibit, such as running a poolroom[133] or a business which so immediately affects the public interest that close and continuous supervision is deemed desirable.[134]

Attempts to vest broad discretion in an agency to resolve the outcome of labor disputes, or determine the rights of parties thereto—cases where not only the amount of money involved but also the intrinsic social significance of the determinations make the courts fearful of delegating uncontrolled discretion to agencies—have been either held invalid[135] or carefully limited.[136]

---

130 Kerth v. Hopkins County Bd. of Educ., 346 S.W.2d 737 (Ky. 1961).

131 State Bd. of Dry Cleaners v. Thrift-D-Lux Cleaners Inc., note 112 *supra.*

132 People v. Brown, 407 Ill. 565, 95 N.E.2d 888 (1951); Kentucky Alcoholic Beverage Control Bd. v. Jacobs, 269 S.W.2d 189 (Ky. 1954); McKibben v. Michigan Corp. & Sec. Comm'n, 369 Mich. 69, 119 N.W.2d 557 (1963); Livesay v. Tennessee Bd. of Examiners in Watchmaking, 204 Tenn. 500, 322 S.W.2d 209 (1959); State *ex rel.* Makris v. Superior Court of Pierce County, 113 Wash. 296, 193 Pac. 845 (1920).

133 State v. Sherow, 87 Kan. 235, 123 Pac. 866 (1912); Mehlos v. Milwaukee, 156 Wis. 591, 146 N.W. 882, 51 L.R.A. (n.s.) 1009 (1914).

134 *E.g., In re* Petersen, 51 Cal. 2d 177, 331 P.2d 24 (1958)—regulation of taxicabs; Lee v. Delmont, 228 Minn. 101, 36 N.W.2d 530 (1949)—barbering; Berardi v. Rutter, 23 N.J. 485, 129 A.2d 705 (1957)—license to carry weapons; Moyant v. Borough of Paramus, 30 N.J. 528, 154 A.2d 9 (1959)—solicitors and canvassers; Barton Trucking Corp. v. O'Connell, 7 N.Y.2d 299, 197 N.Y.S.2d 138, 165 N.E.2d 163 (1959)—hand trucks in garment center.

135 State *ex rel.* Standard Oil Co. v. Review Board, 230 Ind. 1, 101 N.E.2d 60 (1951); State v. Traffic Tel. Workers' Fed'n, 2 N.J. 335, 66 A.2d 616 (1949).

136 State *ex rel.* Board of Mediation v. Pigg, 362 Mo. 798, 244 S.W.2d 75

(4) Broad Discretionary Powers May Be Delegated, Where Judicial Review Is Available to Correct Abuses

Where provisions for judicial review permit the courts to exercise a large measure of superintending control over the agency, the courts are more easily persuaded that a broad measure of discretion should be sustained, for the courts feel confident that if unfair procedures be imposed, or arbitrary decisions made, they could be corrected on appeal to the courts. Thus, in *Matthews v. State,*[137] after observing that in matters substantially affecting the public safety, health, or morals, a wide measure of discretion may be delegated, the court said: "Under this rule, general standards will be sufficient here, provided there is an opportunity for a court revision of possible arbitrary or capricious action" by the agency.

It is not the mere availability of judicial review that is the determinant factor here. Rather, it is the scope of review. If the court is limited, as in typical certiorari proceedings, to determining questions of law that arise upon the face of the record, this is not enough to induce the court to relax its insistence upon limitation of administrative discretion. But if the court can exercise a scope of review that permits it to re-examine factual determinations and questions as to the fairness of the administrative procedure, then it is commonly felt that because of these safeguards, no irreparable harm is likely to attend the vesting of broad discretionary powers in the agencies.

This approach is clearly evident in a decision of the New Jersey court[138] where the court was divided as to the validity of the delegation to a zoning board of the power to grant variances. The dissenting judges would have held the delegation invalid, because of the lack of a meaningful standard. But the majority upheld the delegation, relying in substantial measure upon the circumstance that "judicial review of the administrative action is afforded as of right . . . and our courts have not hesitated to set it aside where it lacked reasonable basis."

Again, the Washington court[139] relied upon the availability of broad judicial review, in the nature of a hearing *de novo,* in

(1951); New Jersey Bell Tel. Co. v. Communications Workers of America, 5 N.J. 354, 75 A.2d 721 (1950).

137 237 Ind. 677, 682, 148 N.E.2d 334 (1958).

138 Ward v. Scott, 11 N.J. 117, 93 A.2d 385 (1952).

139 Kelleher v. Minshull, 11 Wash. 2d 380, 119 P.2d 302 (1941).

sustaining delegation of a large measure of discretion to a board empowered to grant licenses to engage in the small loan business.

The Ohio court,[140] while sustaining the delegation of a broad power to make rules, in the same opinion decreed that the rule which the agency had made was void because it was unreasonable. One wonders: Would the court have held the delegation invalid, if it had been without the power to pass upon the validity of the challenged rule?

In other cases, availability of a broad scope of judicial review has been an important factor in persuading the courts to permit delegation of discretionary power, not subject to well-defined legislative standards.[141]

(5) Broad Delegations Sustained Where Statute Requires Notice and Hearing and Fair Administrative Procedure

Broad standards are often upheld because of the circumstance that those to be affected by the administrative edict are assured an opportunity to present their views fully to the agency before official action is taken. Especially does this tendency manifest itself if the administrative hearing procedures appear well devised to guarantee that agency action will be predicated upon a fair and fully informed consideration of the views of the affected parties. Contrariwise, the courts exhibit a greater readiness to insist on well-defined, objective standards where there appears to be a danger that agency action might be premised upon *ex cathedra* pronouncements, or might be made without hearing the parties, or upon the basis of *ex parte* consultations.

One of the reasons given by the United States Supreme Court for the invalidation of the National Industrial Recovery Act was the absence of provision for participation, by those subject to the rules, in the process of formulating them.[142] Other federal cases have indicated that absence of an opportunity for hearing is one

---

140 Weber v. Board of Health, 148 Ohio St. 389, 74 N.E.2d 331 (1947).

141 West Realty Co. v. Ennis, 147 Conn. 602, 164 A.2d 409 (1960); Jennings v. Connecticut Light & Power Co., 140 Conn. 650, 103 A.2d 535 (1954); People *ex rel.* Armstrong v. Huggins, 407 Ill. 157, 94 N.E.2d 863 (1950); State v. Stehlek, 262 Wis. 642, 56 N.W.2d 514 (1953).

142 A.L.A. Schechter Poultry Corp. v. United States, 295 U.S. 495, 79 L. Ed. 1570, 55 Sup. Ct. 837, 97 A.L.R. 947 (1935).

of the factors that influences the court in deciding whether delegations of discretionary power, unlimited by restrictive standards, will be sustained.[143]

While this factor is not often articulated in state court decisions, it is no doubt a matter importantly considered. Illustrative are two decisions by the Illinois court. Originally, a section of a zoning ordinance which delegated power to grant variances was held unconstitutional.[144] Thereafter, the statute was amended, to require that every order allowing a variance must be accompanied by a finding of fact, explaining why the variance had been allowed. This requirement of fact finding served to assure that each petition would be considered on the basis of the facts, and that a variation would be allowed only where the facts amply demonstrated its fairness. The amended statute was upheld.[145]

Similarly, in overruling objections based on the argument that too broad discretionary power was vested in a public utilities commission which acted (as the court put it) "as informer, prosecutor, jury, and judge," the California court relied upon the fact that "due process as to the commission's initial action is provided by the requirement of adequate notice to a party affected and an opportunity to be heard, [and] . . . is further afforded by the right of petition for a writ of review to this court."[146]

(6) Broad Delegations Are Upheld Where There Is an Obvious Need for Expertise

Courts show a readiness to sustain delegations of virtually unlimited discretionary power if the sphere of regulation is characterized by baffling technicalities so complex that the judges entertain doubts as to the adequacy of judicial knowledge and techniques to deal with the matter effectively, or if they sense a need for experimentation in a new and untrodden field. Thus, looser standards would be tolerated in a statute dealing with the regulation of intrastate transportation of atomic isotopes than in a statute dealing with the licensing of candy stores.

---

143 *E.g.,* Southern Ry. Co. v. Virginia, 290 U.S. 190, 78 L. Ed. 260, 54 Sup. Ct. 148 (1933).

144 Speroni v. Board of Appeals, 368 Ill. 568, 15 N.E.2d 302 (1938).

145 Downey v. Grimshaw, 410 Ill. 21, 101 N.E.2d 275 (1951).

146 People v. Western Air Lines, Inc., 42 Cal. 2d 621, 632, 268 P.2d 723 (1954).

As the Virginia court put it,[147] the delegation may be in "general terms" if those terms "get precision from the technical knowledge or sense and experience of men and thereby become reasonably certain."

The need for expertise has been cited in support of broad delegations to zoning commissions[148] and to budget commissions,[149] and in determinations as to sanity.[150]

(7) Delegation of Power to Private Groups Is Frowned Upon

Where a legislature undertakes to vest legislative or judicial powers in a body dominated by self-interested groups, the courts understandably are loathe to tolerate the delegation of any broad discretionary powers, for fear they will be exercised not in the public interest, but rather in the private interests of those who have an axe to grind.

Thus, a Mississippi statute which in effect delegated to fire insurance companies doing business in that state the power to determine, by majority vote, the rate of commission to be paid local insurance agents, was held invalid.[151]

An attempt by the New York legislature to delegate to a "Jockey Club" (a private organization) the power to exercise licensing functions in connection with horse racing was held to be "such an abdication as to be patently an unconstitutional relinquishment of legislative power."[152]

The Oregon court held that a statutory requirement that electrical installations must meet the standards set forth in a code published by the American Standards Association (a private organization) was an invalid delegation of legislative power.[153]

Similarly, a licensing statute which conferred upon presently licensed dispensing opticians an unlimited and unguided power to exclude from their profession any and all persons, was held invalid.[154]

---

147 Ours Properties, Inc. v. Ley, 198 Va. 848, 852, 96 S.E.2d 754 (1957).

148 Burnham v. Board of Appeals of Gloucester, note 124 *supra*.

149 Yelle v. Bishop, 55 Wash. 2d 286, 347 P.2d 1081 (1959).

150 Caritativo v. Teets, 47 Cal. 2d 304, 303 P.2d 339 (1956).

151 State v. Allstate Ins. Co., 231 Miss. 869, 97 So. 2d 372 (1957).

152 Fink v. Cole, 302 N.Y. 216, 225, 97 N.E.2d 873 (1951).

153 Hillman v. Northern Wasco County People's Util. Dist., 213 Ore. 264, 323 P.2d 664 (1958).

154 Blumenthal v. Board of Medical Examiners, 57 Cal. 2d 228, 368 P.2d 101, 18 Cal. Rptr. 501 (1962).

Attempts to delegate to private groups the power to determine price levels,[155] or wage levels,[156] or permissible land uses,[157] have likewise been held invalid.

Similarly, the delegation of broad regulatory powers to a milk marketing board, four-fifths of whose members were privately engaged in the milk business, was held invalid, the court apparently believing there was danger of unfairness in view of the circumstance that certain actions on the part of the board were challenged by a distributor of milk whose business methods differed sharply from those of his competitors who controlled the board.[158]

(8) Broad Discretionary Powers May Be Delegated Where Public Health, Safety, or Morals Are Significantly Involved

Where the court is convinced that there exists in fact a genuine and substantial threat to the public health or safety, or the public morals, unless broad discretionary powers are vested in an administrative agency, the court will go far in sustaining delegations which might under other circumstances be held invalid.

When a court is convinced that a case fits into this category, it uses language like that employed by the Ohio court in holding that a public utilities commission could be empowered to decide, in its own discretion, whether and under what circumstances freight trains would be required to carry cabooses:

> As a general rule a law which confers discretion on an executive officer or board without establishing any standards for guidance is a delegation of legislative power and unconstitutional; but, when the discretion to be exercised relates to a police regulation for the protection of the public morals, health, safety, or general welfare, and it is impossible or impracticable to provide such standards, and to do so would defeat the legislative object sought to be accomplished, legislation conferring such discretion may be valid and constitutional without such restrictions and limitations.[159]

---

155 Bradley v. Casey, 415 Ill. 576, 114 N.E.2d 681 (1953).

156 State Bd. of Dry Cleaners v. Thrift-D-Lux Cleaners, Inc., note 131 *supra.*

157 State *ex rel.* Sims v. Eckhardt, 322 S.W.2d 903 (Mo. 1959).

158 Michigan Milk Marketing Bd. v. Johnson, 295 Mich. 644, 295 N.W. 346 (1940).

159 Akron & B. Belt R.R. v. Public Utils. Comm'n, 148 Ohio St. 282, 287, 74 N.E.2d 256 (1947).

On this basis, state courts are generally willing to sustain delegations of broad discretionary powers to boards of health,[160] and to agencies exercising powers commonly associated with police measures.[161] In one such case, the Indiana court said: "Courts generally are less strict in requiring specific standards to guide the licensor when the subject matter . . . is closely related to the public safety, health, morals, or general welfare."[162]

While opinion is not unanimous, most state courts are willing to sustain almost any standard in delegations of power intended to permit agencies to deal effectively with matters of traffic safety.[163]

Again, in fields where the agency is directly concerned with the preservation of public morality, broad delegations of discretion are sustained.[164]

More difficult problems arise when it is suggested that agencies whose operations affect the "public welfare" should be included in the same category, for this purpose, as agencies whose work is closely connected with the public safety, health, and morals. The difficulty arises from the circumstance that every agency can plausibly put forth a claim that, in a general sense at least, it is concerned with the public welfare. Courts recognize that to sustain grants of virtually unfettered discretionary power in every case where the agency is concerned with the "public welfare" would remove the limits completely. However, in fields where there is a long tradition of far-reaching administrative controls, *e.g.*, banking, the courts often rely in part upon the make-weight

[160] Housing Authority of County of Los Angeles v. Dockweiler, 14 Cal. 2d 437, 94 P.2d 794 (1939); Len-Lew Realty Co. v. Falsey, 141 Conn. 524, 107 A.2d 403 (1954); Board of Health v. New York Cent. R.R., 4 N.J. 293, 72 A.2d 511 (1950); Chiropractic Ass'n of New York, Inc. v. Hilleboe, 12 N.Y.2d 109, 237 N.Y.S.2d 289, 187 N.E.2d 756 (1962); Weber v. Board of Health, 148 Ohio St. 389, 74 N.E.2d 331 (1947); State v. Bunner, 126 W. Va. 280, 27 S.E.2d 823 (1943).

[161] Lane v. Holderman, 23 N.J. 304, 129 A.2d 8 (1957).

[162] Matthews v. State, 237 Ind. 677, 682, 148 N.E.2d 334 (1958).

[163] Whittle v. Nesmith, 255 Ala. 193, 51 So. 2d 6 (1951); Franklin v. Scurlock, 224 Ark. 168, 272 S.W.2d 62 (1954); *In re* Petersen, 51 Cal. 2d 177, 331 P.2d 24 (1958); People v. Warren, 11 Ill. 2d 420, 143 N.E.2d 28 (1957); Ross v. MacDuff, 309 N.Y. 56, 127 N.E.2d 806 (1955). *But see, contra,* Automobile Club of Missouri v. City of St. Louis, 334 S.W.2d 355 (Mo. 1960).

[164] Boehl v. Sabre Jet Room, Inc., 349 P.2d 585 (Alaska 1960); Gilman v. City of Newark, 73 N.J. Super. 562, 180 A.2d 365 (1962); Kingsley International Pictures Corp. v. Regents of University of New York, 4 N.Y.2d 349, 175 N.Y.S.2d 39, 151 N.E.2d 197 (1958); Commercial Pictures Corp. v. Board of Regents of University of New York, 305 N.Y. 336, 113 N.E.2d 502 (1953).

argument that broad delegation should be sustained, where the agency's work importantly affects the general welfare.[165]

(9) Delegations of Power to Fix Penalties Are Not Favored

Constitutional rights of jury trial preclude the delegation to administrative agencies of the power to determine guilt or innocence in criminal cases. This difficulty may sometimes be avoided by description of the penalty as a "civil penalty,"[166] but—impelled apparently by some doubts as to the judicious impartiality of administrative officials—state courts generally look with jaundiced eye upon attempts to vest in administrative agencies the power, unrestricted by specific statutory standards, to determine and impose penalties.

Where a state income tax law provided that if the tax were not paid when due, the tax commissioner "may, in his discretion, impose for such delinquency a penalty of not less than ten percentum (10%) and not more than twenty-five percentum (25%) of the delinquent sum," the court refused to uphold the delegation, declaring:

> . . . the determination of the amount of a penalty to be imposed for non-compliance with the requirements of law is a legislative function, which may not be delegated to an administrative officer or agency, with power, in his discretion, to impose such penalties, within broad limits, as he may see fit to impose.

The court added that it would have been proper for the legislature to have provided the penalties, and authorized the tax commissioner to impose them under conditions prescribed by the legislature, but that the legislature could not surrender its own discretion to the commissioner as to determining the amount of the penalty.[167]

A similar statute, delegating to a tax commission the power to determine the penalty to be assessed against persons failing to affix the required stamps to packages of cigarettes, was held invalid where the only limit on administrative discretion was

[165] Dauphin Deposit Trust Co. v. Myers, 388 Pa. 444, 130 A.2d 686 (1957); Kelleher v. Minshull, 11 Wash. 2d 380, 119 P.2d 302 (1941).

[166] Wycoff Co. v. Public Serv. Comm'n, 13 Utah 2d 123, 369 P.2d 283 (1962), and see Schwenk, *The Administrative Crime,* 42 MICH. L. REV. 51 (1943).

[167] Broadhead v. Monaghan, 238 Miss. 239, 254, 256, 117 So. 2d 881 (1960).

that the penalty was to be not less than $10.00 nor more than $299.[168]

Strict standards, limiting administrative discretion within narrow limits, are insisted upon where power is delegated to fix the penalty to be imposed for non-compliance with a statute,[169] or to prescribe rules whose violation carries criminal penalties.[170] Where the "penalty" is in effect an award of damages to be paid to an injured complainant—in the nature of the reparations claims which have long been within the competence of the Interstate Commerce Commission—the courts may allow an agency to determine the amount to be paid, even though it is denominated a "penalty."[171]

Also, it should be noted that parole boards may be given what is in effect the power to determine or adjust penalties, under indeterminate sentence laws; but here unique considerations are involved.[172]

(10) Courts Insist on Preserving Essential Independence of the Departments of Government

As noted in Chapter II, the real thrust of the separation of powers doctrine, as applied currently by the state courts, is that each department of government must be kept free from the control or coercive influence of the other departments.[173] So applied, the separation of powers philosophy is intimately connected with certain aspects of the question as to the extent to which legislative or judicial powers may be delegated to administrative agencies, without legislatively imposed controls designed

168 Tite v. State Tax Comm'n, 89 Utah 404, 57 P.2d 734 (1936). It is interesting to note, as bearing upon the willingness of the courts to sustain broad delegations where the scope of judicial review is equally broad, that in State Tax Comm'n v. Stanley, 234 Ala. 66, 173 So. 609 (1937), a somewhat similar statute was upheld where provision was made for de novo judicial review.

169 Memorial Trusts, Inc. v. Beery, 144 Colo. 448, 356 P.2d 884 (1960); Lewis Consolidated School Dist. v. Johnston, 127 N.W.2d 118 (Iowa 1964); Broadhead v. Monaghan, 238 Miss. 239, 117 So. 2d 881 (1960); Lincoln Dairy Co. v. Finigan, 170 Neb. 777, 104 N.W.2d 227 (1960).

170 State v. Williams, 253 N.C. 337, 117 S.E.2d 444 (1960).

171 State v. Atlantic Coast Line R.R., 56 Fla. 617, 47 So. 969, 32 L.R.A. (n.s.) 639 (1908); Southern Ry. Co. v. Melton, 133 Ga. 277, 65 S.E. 665 (1909).

172 *In re* Larsen, 44 Cal. 2d 642, 283 P.2d 1043 (1955); Cohn v. Ketchum, 123 W. Va. 534, 17 S.E.2d 43 (1941).

173 Humphrey's Ex'r v. United States, 295 U.S. 602, 609, 79 L. Ed. 1611, 55 Sup. Ct. 869 (1935).

to curb administrative discretion. That is to say, administrative agencies are permitted to exercise powers which logically belong to the courts, or to the legislatures, so long as the independence of the courts or of the legislatures is not impaired. But when an attempt is made to vest in an administrative agency, or when an agency claims, powers which could be exercised in such a way as to deprive the legislatures or the courts of their constitutional responsibilities, there has been a violation of the essential constitutional precept.

This principle, which has been stated in federal cases[174] is recognized and not infrequently applied by the state courts.

An interesting instance is *State ex rel. Spencer v. Montgomery County Board of Elections.*[175] The Ohio legislature had originally decreed that where voting machines were used, there must be one machine for each 800 voters. After some experience, it became plain that more machines were required. Instead of determining what the number should be—and no doubt believing that the proper ratio would vary from one voting district to another—the legislature delegated to county election boards the responsibility "to arrange for a sufficient number of voting machines to accommodate the number of electors in each precinct." Fearful that some county boards might attempt to disenfranchise some voters, by providing an insufficient number of voting machines, and noting that the matter was "packed with political implications," the court concluded that the agencies would be required to follow the standard provided indirectly by another section of the statutes, which required that in precincts where voting machines were not used, there must be one voting compartment for each 100 electors. The court ruled that there must be one voting machine for each 100 electors, and declared that if the number of machines to be used in each precinct were "left to the caprice and whim" of the election boards in the several counties, it would amount to an unlawful delegation of legislative power.

In other words, where the court senses a substantial danger that an agency might be put in a position, as a result of delegation

---

174 *Cf.,* Humphrey's Ex'r v. United States, note 173 *supra,* and Myers v. United States, 272 U.S. 52, 71 L. Ed. 160, 47 Sup. Ct. 21 (1926).

175 102 Ohio App. 51, 141 N.E.2d 195 (1956), *appeal dismissed as moot,* 166 Ohio St. 147, 140 N.E.2d 312 (1957).

of too broad discretionary power, to displace the courts or the legislature, the delegation will be held invalid.

Similarly, where a state department of labor was authorized to prescribe variations from a maximum hour law, the court, observing that "the hours may be shortened to six a day or extended to 10 or 12 a day," and that "there are no boundaries" to the power of the board to amend the legislative mandate, held the delegation invalid.[176]

The same result followed when a legislature undertook to grant school authorities unrestricted powers as to the reorganization of school districts;[177] and when a legislature attempted to grant a state department of revenue powers which the court concluded must properly be reserved to the legislature itself.[178]

The state courts also show an inclination to strike down attempts to hobble the power of the state legislatures by providing that the application of state law will depend on future amendments to federal laws.[179]

(11) Broad Discretionary Powers May Be Delegated Where Proprietary Functions Are Involved

Where power is delegated to an agency to carry on proprietary functions—or where it is engaged in the conduct of the public business, rather than in the regulation of private business—the state courts sustain delegations of broad discretionary powers, unlimited by any meaningfully restrictive standards. Thus, an agency may be given power, unguided by any statutory standard, to grant or deny permits to fill in a lake.[180] Similarly, grant of the power to lease state lands, subject only to the standard that the leases should not exceed a term of fifteen years, and should contain proper covenants to guard against trespass and waste, was held valid.[181] On similar grounds, courts have upheld broad delegations of power to determine whether turnpikes should be constructed;[182] to determine the wages to be paid on public works;[183]

---

176 Holgate Bros. Co. v. Bashore, 331 Pa. 255, 200 Atl. 672, 117 A.L.R. 639 (1938).

177 State *ex rel.* Donaldson v. Hines, 163 Kan. 300, 182 P.2d 865 (1947).

178 Giebelhausen v. Daley, 407 Ill. 25, 95 N.E.2d 84 (1950).

179 Crowly v. Thornbrough, 226 Ark. 768, 294 S.W.2d 62 (1956).

180 State v. Public Serv. Comm'n, 275 Wis. 112, 81 N.W.2d 71 (1957).

181 State *ex rel.* Evjue v. Seyberth, 9 Wis. 2d 274, 101 N.W.2d 118 (1960).

182 State *ex rel.* Thomson v. Giessel, 265 Wis. 207, 60 N.W.2d 763 (1953).

183 City of Joplin v. Industrial Comm'n, 329 S.W.2d 687 (Mo. 1959).

to fix charges for public services;[184] or to waive mandatory retirement plans for civil service employees.[185]

(D) Summary as to Application of Factors That Motivate Decision

As above noted, the discussion of the eleven categories which have been described does not attempt to do more than to suggest the general character of the factors which the courts consider. These eleven categories do not afford a comprehensive test. If any attempt were made to formulate all-embracing criteria of decision, many other factors would have to be added to the list, and it would be necessary to determine a "point value" for each criterion. Obviously, this cannot be done, for a factor which bulks all-important on one set of facts would fade into insignificance, under other factual circumstances.

It is probably true that a delegation will ordinarily be held invalid if there are no standards to limit the agency's discretion, and if the agency is empowered to make orders affecting substantial property rights without notice or hearing, without assurance that fair procedures will be used, and without adequate judicial review, in a field where there is doubt as to the true expertise of the board.

On the other hand, almost any extent of discretionary power may be delegated if public safety is significantly involved, and if there is need for the exercise of an expert judgment which the agency undoubtedly possesses, and if its procedures afford fair hearings, and adequate judicial review is provided.

Most cases, of course, fall between these two extremes, and must be resolved not by application of any convenient "true test," but by an agonizing weighing of the competing demands of the private against the public interests involved.

---

184 Hartman v. Aurora Sanitary Dist., 23 Ill. 2d 109, 177 N.E.2d 214 (1961).

185 Jordan v. Metropolitan Sanitary Dist., 15 Ill. 2d 369, 155 N.E.2d 297 (1958).

Section 5

Sub-Delegation of Authority

The statutes usually bestow authority upon a commission or the head of an agency, but these individuals often cannot perform personally the multifarious duties delegated to them. There frequently exists a clear necessity for the sub-delegation of discretionary power to employees of the agency.

The governing statutes often recognize this situation, and make appropriate provision therefor. Failure to do so has sometimes produced untoward results.

The courts have at times invalidated unauthorized attempts of agency heads to delegate to their subordinates powers vested by statute in the heads of the agency.[186]

On other occasions, the problem has been avoided by reliance on the presumption of regularity that attends official action, which as here applied means merely that it is hard to prove that the responsible official did not personally perform his duty.[187]

In many cases, the courts, appreciating the necessity of a limited degree of such delegation, find authority therefor implicit in the statutory language.[188]

Decision in each case depends on the court's judgment as to whether the nature of the particular power exercised is so important, requiring the exercise of judgment on matters of policy, as to preclude the likelihood that the legislature would have been willing to have the particular power exercised by anyone other than the ultimate authority within the agency.

Regardless of the limits on sub-delegation to agency employees of power to pass finally on matters of importance, the fact re-

---

[186] *Cf.*, Vita-Pharmacals, Inc. v. Board of Pharmacy, 110 Cal. App. 2d 826, 243 P.2d 890 (1952); Muench v. Public Serv. Comm'n, 261 Wis. 492, 53 N.W. 2d 514 (1952); School Dist. No. 4 v. Industrial Comm'n, 194 Wis. 342, 216 N.W. 844 (1927).

[187] Hackley-Phelps-Bonnell Co. v. Industrial Comm'n, 173 Wis. 128, 179 N.W. 590 (1921).

[188] See Grundstein, *Subdelegation of Administrative Authority,* 13 GEO. WASH. L. REV. 144 (1945). Among cases sustaining subdelegation of authority are: Rockland County Anti-Reservoir Ass'n v. Duryea, 282 App. Div. 457, 123 N.Y.S.2d 445 (1953). Warren v. Marion County, 222 Ore. 307, 353 P.2d 257 (1960). Cases holding subdelegation invalid include: Horsman Dolls v. State Unemployment Compensation Comm'n, 134 N.J.L. 77, 45 A.2d 681 (1946); State *ex rel.* Board of Governors of Registered Dentists v. Rifleman, 203 Okla. 294, 220 P.2d 441 (1950).

mains that power to recommend the decision in any matter can be and ordinarily is so delegated.[189] The distinction is more theoretical than practical. The higher officers are so little inclined to reverse the recommendation of their subordinates that the latters' recommendation often carries the weight to sway and determine final agency action in any close case, especially where the determination relates not to a general policy but to the appraisal of a particular factual situation.

A great danger resulting from this necessary practice of delegating within the agency the powers of the agency heads is that decision may be made by an employee whose compelling personal interest is to make such a determination as he thinks will please his superior, in the hope of obtaining promotion. If the employee is impressed with a belief that the agency likes decisions which find an employer guilty of unfair labor practices, or a commercial concern guilty of unfair trade practices, or an employee entitled to receive workmen's compensation, then great strength of mind and character are required to avoid the making of decisions which it is thought will please the officials who will pass upon the employee's personal advancement.

Agency heads face the difficult problem of making free delegation to staff employees as to matters where there is little need for close supervision by agency heads—such as matters of internal management, disposition of routine matters, initiation of proceedings, disposition of matters by consent, executing binding stipulations of fact, and the like—in order that they may devote more time and attention to reviewing the work of subordinates in matters affecting the rights of parties appearing before the agency. In the latter connection, much might be accomplished by (1) careful formulation, for the guidance of agency employees, of instructions for the application of those policies which have been crystallized; (2) consideration by the agency heads of cases where the application of established policies is difficult or where policies have not been definitely formulated; and (3) the requirement of periodic and informative reports by those employees entrusted with power to make decision.

---

189 Vita-Pharmacals, Inc. v. Board of Pharmacy, note 186 *supra.*

Section 6

Problems of Draftsmanship in Formulating Standards

Obviously, effective administrative action may be expedited or hampered by the language adopted in the controlling statute as the standard by which the agency's actions must be guided. Sometimes, as Dean Landis has pointed out,[190] legislative draftsmen formulate too elaborate standards, under a misapprehension as to the clarity of the outlines of the problem at hand, and condition administrative action in such detail as to make it difficult to dispose effectively of pressing problems. On the other hand, the legislature may sometimes be tempted to evade responsibility by an ill-defined transfer to an administrative agency of the duty to provide, by such regulations "as the public interest may require" a determination of fundamental policy in a highly controversial field.

A standard which attempts to anticipate every possible situation is likely to defeat the whole purpose of delegation. On the other hand, one which reflects the empty generalities of "reasonableness" or "public interest"—criteria which would be supplied by implication in any event—tends to substitute a government by men for one of laws.

The tendency of the courts to sustain broad delegations of discretionary power emphasizes the importance of wisely drafting the statutory standards. Relief from unsatisfactory administrative action must often come through the legislature, rather than the courts. It may be necessary, upon venturing into a new field of governmental regulation, to grant the agency wide discretionary powers. It must, perhaps, have some authority to experiment. But as experience defines the contours of the problem involved, opportunities may be afforded to redefine the standards which guide administrative action, terminating the agency's authority to perpetuate unsuccessful experiments. To the extent that it is practicable or desirable for the legislature to specify standards that are definite and capable of objective proof, the courts are enabled to assert a greater power of review over administrative action than they possess when the standards are cast in vague, subjective terminology.

---

190 LANDIS, THE ADMINISTRATIVE PROCESS 55 (1938).

CHAPTER IV

DEFINITIONS

Section 1

Agencies

(A) Need for Definition

Definitions are dull and tiresome—and extremely important. It has been the experience of more than one drafting committee engaged in the writing of a code of administrative procedure that the definition section was found to be the most difficult to write. Indeed, almost every group of lawyers who have undertaken the drafting of such a code have discovered that after the first draft was completed, it was necessary to go back and make a number of changes in the "definitions" section, because the content of the definitions significantly control the operation of the substantive sections.

Obviously, the definition of "agency" is of prime importance. In this initial section of an administrative procedure act, there are settled the questions—thorny and difficult ones—whether certain "old line" long-established state agencies should be excluded; and whether, conversely, county, city, and other local agencies should be included. Many other equally perplexing problems must be settled. If they are not settled by definition, uncertainty as to the actual operative effect of the code will persist for many years.

Such questions as whether the term "rule" should include agency statements of particular rather than general applicability, and whether rate-making should be classified as rule making or as adjudication, and whether applications for licenses should be put in the category of contested cases for procedural purposes, and a host of other like questions, all point to the intense practical importance of the definitions used in administrative procedure acts.

Their importance therefore justifies a careful and thorough exploration of the choices available, and an examination of the choices which different states have made. Moreover, a statement of definitions is necessary to permit accuracy of statement in the later chapters which discuss the details of administrative procedure, for the subsequent discussion is in substantial degree predicated upon the definitions set forth in this chapter.

Indicative of the pressing need for statutory codification within the several states of basic principles of state administrative law is the fact that there is no general agreement as to precisely what governmental authorities are to be deemed administrative agencies. Indeed, uncertainty exists within the several states as to which of their administrative tribunals and officers are to be included within the definition of "administrative agency." The untoward consequences that may flow from such uncertainty and confusion are illustrated by a decision in Texas[1] holding that a statute authorizing direct appeals to the state supreme court from certain orders of any state "board" or "commission" did not apply to such an order promulgated by the securities commissioner, because such officer was neither a "board" nor a "commission." Difficult questions could arise under this interpretation, if for example, an order issued on behalf of a multimember commission were signed by the chief commissioner. The existence of similar uncertainties in other states is eloquent evidence of the need for reasonably precise and workable definitions.

In broadest outline, it is generally said that the term "administrative agency" includes all those governmental organs (other than the legislature or the courts) which possess authority to make rules affecting private rights or to adjudicate contested cases. But the very generality of this definition suggests its inadequacy. What of the governor? What of elected or appointed state officials who, in the exercise of executive powers, make decisions that substantially affect private rights? What of municipal corporations or county boards lacking statewide jurisdiction? There is no general agreement on any of these points, and even within individual states the answer is often uncertain.

---

1 Standard Sec. Serv. Corp. v. King, 161 Tex. 448, 341 S.W.2d 423 (1960).

(B) Approach of Revised Model State Act

The definition of "agency" in the Revised Model State Act is drafted in purposefully general terms in recognition of the fact that the question as to the proper scope of a state administrative procedure code is one on which differences of opinion can be expected, in view of varying conditions and differing philosophies of government in different states. The Revised Model Act provides: "Agency" means each state [board, commission, department, or officer], other than the legislature or the courts, authorized by law to make rules or to determine contested cases.

This definition includes all commissions created by state government which exercise rulemaking and adjudicatory powers.[2] Its applicability to executive officers exercising such powers would seemingly depend (at least if the above-cited decision of the Texas court were followed) upon whether the term "officer," listed in the Revised Model State Act, were included by legislative enactment within a particular state.[3] The definition does not include municipal corporations; such organizations typically delegate rulemaking and adjudicatory powers to their own administrative agencies. Thus, agencies created within city or county governments, being creatures of local government rather than of the state government, are not normally within the provisions of the state act.

A need exists for legislation prescribing procedural standards for such municipal and county agencies. In view of the particular problems and limitations they encounter (arising out of many factors; including, among others, the fact that they are often created on an *ad hoc* basis, the fact that they often have only the most fragmentary organizational structure, and the

---

2 The Federal Administrative Procedure Act, 5 U.S.C. § 1001(a); F.C.A. 5 § 1001(a), defines "agency" as "each authority (whether or not within or subject to review by another agency) of the Government of the United States, other than Congress, the courts, or the governments of the possessions, Territories, or the District of Columbia." On its face, the language of the federal Act would be broad enough to include governmental authorities which had neither rule-making nor adjudicatory powers. This has seemingly created no problems in the federal government. But it might well do so within the framework of state government, where the necessity for legislatively prescribed procedures arises principally in connection with those organs of government that exercise rule-making or adjudicatory power.

3 Throughout the Model Act, as in other model acts promulgated by the Commissioners on Uniform State Laws, the inclusion of particular words or phrases within brackets indicates that the bracketed words or phrases may be inappropriate in some states.

fact that because of their limited staff facilities they are often compelled to operate in an informal manner), it is generally thought that it would be impracticable to make them conform to all the formal procedures required of state agencies. The courts do require, as will be noted, that such municipal and county agencies conduct their activities in a manner consistent with the requirements of procedural due process. But it would serve the public interest to provide a simplified procedural code for all municipal and county agencies exercising rulemaking or adjudicatory powers, and providing a uniform method of judicial review. The "Commentary" on the Revised Model State Act, published by the Commissioners on Uniform State Laws, points out (p. 11) that it may be desirable to include some of the city or county agencies within the state act.

(C) General Approaches Utilized in State Statutes

State legislatures have in the main adopted three approaches to the definition of "administrative agency."

1) Some states have adopted generally phrased definitions, frequently in terms much like those of the Revised Model State Act.

2) Other states have adopted general definitions which are limited by specific exceptions.

3) Still other state legislatures have chosen to list the particular agencies to which the state act will apply.

That the best approach is that of the Revised Model State Act is persuasively indicated by the experience in Wisconsin which is one of the pioneers in the field of state administrative law. It has taken full advantage of acquired experience by amending its statute from time to time to reflect the lessons time has taught. Earlier Wisconsin statutes had listed specific agencies to which the Act applied. In 1955, however, this approach was abandoned in favor of a definition providing that agency means "any board, commission, committee, department or officer in the state government, except the governor or any military or judicial officer of this state."[4] A committee note explained the reasons for the 1955 amendment.[5] The note expressed legis-

[4] WIS. STAT. § 227.01.
[5] *Ibid.*

lative belief that enumeration of specific agencies "is unnecessary and might cast doubt on the inclusion of agencies which are included within the general terms of the definition but which are in a different class than those which are enumerated." The committee note further recited that the purpose of the statute "is to make all governmental agencies at the state level of government subject to the administrative procedure act except as such agencies have been excluded by express provision."

(D) STATES HAVING BROAD STATUTORY DEFINITION

In addition to Wisconsin, the following states have adopted broad and comprehensive definitions of "agency":

Alaska—"Agency" means and includes all departments, offices, agencies and other organizational units of the executive branch, except as may be expressly excluded by this Act . . . or otherwise by law, but does not include an agency in the judicial or legislative departments of the state government.[6]

Arizona—"Agency" means every agency, board, commission, or department authorized by law to exercise rulemaking powers or to adjudicate contested cases, whether created by constitutional provision or legislative enactment, but does not include an agency in the judicial or legislative departments of state government.[7]

Colorado—"Agency" means each board, bureau, commission, department, institution, division, section or officer of the state, except those in the legislative or judicial branches. Courts martial, military commissions and arbitration and mediation functions shall be excluded from the operation of this article.[8]

Florida—"Agency" means any state board, commission, department, or officer authorized by law to make rules, except the legislative and judicial departments of government, the military, and the governor.[9] Another section includes as "agencies": "The governing body of any state board, commission, or department, or state officer who constitutes the agency authorized by law to

---

6 ALASKA STAT. § 44.62.640(a)(4).

7 ARIZ. REV. STAT. ANN. § 41-1001.

8 COLO. REV. STAT. ANN. § 3-16-1(1)(b).

9 FLA. STAT. § 120.021(1).

adjudicate any party's legal rights, duties, privileges or immunities, except the legislature, courts, and the governor."[10]

Hawaii—"Agency" means each state or county board, commission, department, or officer authorized by law to make rules or to adjudicate contested cases, except those in the legislative or judicial branches.[11]

Illinois—One act, dealing with rules, defines agency to include "any State board, commission, department or officer of State government, other than those in the legislative or judicial branch, authorized to administer or interpret any statute of the State of Illinois or any portion thereof."[12] Another act, relating to judicial review, is applicable to any agency where the Act creating the agency adopts the provisions of the Judicial Review Act.[13]

Iowa—"Agency" means each state board, commission, bureau, division, officer, or department which has statewide jurisdiction, except those in the legislative or judicial departments.[14]

Kentucky—"State Agency" includes any officer, department, bureau, division, board, authority, agency, commission or institution of this State except the judicial and the legislative branches.[15]

Minnesota—"Agency" means any state officer, board, commission, bureau, division, department, or tribunal, other than a court, having a statewide jurisdiction and authorized by law to make rules or to adjudicate contested cases.[16]

Missouri—"Agency" means any administrative officer or body existing under the constitution or by law and authorized by law to make rules or to adjudicate contested cases.[17]

Nebraska—"Agency" means each board, commission, department, officer, division, or other administrative office or unit of the state government authorized by law to make rules, except the courts and the Legislature.[18]

---

10 *Ibid.*
11 HAWAII SESS. LAWS 1961, Act 103, § 1(a).
12 ILL. REV. STAT. ch. 127, § 263.
13 ILL. REV. STAT. ch. 110, § 265.
14 IOWA CODE § 17A.1-1.
15 KY. REV. STAT. § 13.080(1).
16 MINN. STAT. § 15.0411. (The statute contains certain exceptions from this broad definition.)
17 MO. REV. STAT. § 536.010(1).
18 NEB. REV. STAT. § 84-901(1).

North Carolina—"Agency" shall mean any state officer, committee, authority, board, bureau, commission, or department authorized by law to make administrative decisions, except those agencies in the legislative or judicial branches and except those whose procedures are governed by Ch. 150 of the General Statutes, or whose administrative decisions are made subject to judicial review under some other statute or statutes containing adequate procedural provisions therefor.[19]

North Dakota—"Agency" shall include any officer, board, commission, bureau, department or tribunal other than a court, having statewide jurisdiction and authority to make any order, finding, determination, award, or assessment which has the force and effect of law and which by statute is subject to review in the courts of this State.[20]

Oklahoma—"Agency" means any state board, commission, department, authority, bureau or officer authorized by the constitution or statutes to make rules or to formulate orders.[21] [There are seven stated exceptions].

Pennsylvania—"Agency" means any department, departmental administrative board or commission, independent administrative board or commission, officer or other agency of this Commonwealth, now in existence or hereafter created, having statewide jurisdiction, empowered to determine or affect private rights, privileges, immunities or obligations by regulation or adjudication, but shall not include a court of record nor a magistrate, alderman, or justice of the peace.[22]

Rhode Island—"Agency" includes each state board, commission, department, or officer, other than the legislature or the courts, authorized by law to make rules or to determine contested cases.[23]

Texas—"Agency" means any state board, commission, department, or officer, authorized by law to make rules, except those in the legislative or judicial branches or institutions of higher education.[24]

---

19 N.C. GEN. STAT. § 143-306(1).
20 N.D. CENT. CODE § 28-32-01(1)
21 OKLA. STAT. tit. 75, § 301(1).
22 PA. STAT. ANN. tit. 71, § 1710.2(b).
23 R.I. GEN. LAWS ANN. § 42-35-1(a).
24 TEX. REV. CIV. STAT. art 6252-13, § 1(a).

Vermont—"State Agency" includes any officer, board, department, commission, authority, or agency of this state except the judicial and legislative branches.[25]

Washington—"Agency" means any state board, commission, department, or officer, authorized by law to make rules or to adjudicate contested cases, except those in the legislative or judicial branches.[26]

West Virginia—"Agency" means any state board, commission, department or officer authorized by law to make rules or adjudicate contested cases, except those in the legislative or judicial branches.[27]

(E) States Limiting Broad Definition by Specific Exceptions

The following states have adopted generally phrased definitions which are limited by specific exceptions, excluding particular agencies. The agencies most commonly excepted are the Workmen's Compensation Commission, the Unemployment Compensation Commission, the Public Utility Commission, and the State Department of Taxation:

Georgia—"Agency" means each state board, bureau, commission, department, activity or officer authorized by law expressly to make rules and regulations or to determine contested cases except the General Assembly, the judiciary, the Governor, the Board of Pardons and Paroles, the State Board of Probation, the Board of Bar Examiners, the Board of Corrections and its penal institutions, the State Board of Workmen's Compensation, the Public Service Commission, all Public Authorities, the State Personnel Board (Merit System), the State Supervisor of Purchases (Purchasing Department), the regulation of liquor and alcoholic beverages, or any school, college, hospital or other such educational, eleemosynary or charitable institution, or any agency when its action is concerned with the military or naval affairs of this State.[28]

Massachusetts—"Agency" includes any department, board, commission, division or authority of the state government, or

---

[25] Vt. Stat. Ann. tit. 3, § 701(1).
[26] Wash. Rev. Code § 34.04.010(1).
[27] W. Va. Code Ann. § 258(1), as amended by ch. 1, Acts of 1964.
[28] Ga. Code § 3A-101—March 10, 1964.

subdivision of any of the foregoing, or official of the state government, authorized by law to make regulations or to conduct adjudicatory proceedings, but does not include the following: the legislative and judicial departments; the governor and council; military or naval boards, commissions or officials; the department of correction; the youth service board and the division of youth service in the department of education; the parole board; the division of industrial accidents of the department of labor and industries; the division of child guardianship of the department of public welfare; and the division of civil service.[29]

Michigan—In a statute applicable to administrative rule making, "state agency" is defined to include any officer, department, bureau, division, board, authority, agency, commission, or institution of this state, except the judicial and legislative branches.[30] In the Administrative Procedure Statute, "agency" means any state board, commission, department, bureau, or officer, authorized by law to make rules or to adjudicate contested cases, except the workmen's compensation commission, the employment security commission, the department of revenue, the public service commission and those in the legislative and judicial branches.[31]

Indiana—"Agency" shall mean and include any officer, board, commission, department, division, bureau or committee of the State of Indiana other than courts, the governor, military officers, or military boards of the state, state colleges or universities supported in whole or part by state funds, benevolent, reformatory or penal institutions, the industrial board, alcoholic beverage commission, state board of tax commissioners, and the public service commission. The State Department of Revenue is also excluded.[32]

Maryland—"Agency" means any state board, commission, department, or officer authorized by law to make rules or to adjudicate contested cases, except those in the legislative or judicial branches, and except the Department of Parole and Probation, the State Industrial Accident Commission, the State Insur-

---

29 MASS. GEN. LAWS ANN. ch. 30A, § 1(2)

30 MICH. COMP. LAWS § 3.560(7)(1).

31 MICH. COMP. LAWS § 3.560(1).

32 IND. ANN. STAT. § 63-3002 (*cf.*, § 60-1503).

ance Department, the Public Service Commission, the Employment Security Board, and the State Tax Commission.[33]

Oregon—"State Agency" is defined in a statute relating to the publication of orders to include the governor or any executive department, independent board, establishment, bureau, agency, institution, commission or separate office of the administrative branch of the government of the state of Oregon, but does not include the legislative or judicial branches of the government.[34] Under a general administrative procedure statute, "agency" means any state board, commission, department, or division thereof, or officer authorized by law to make rules or to adjudicate contested cases, except those in the legislative and judicial branches, and except the state board of parole and probation, the public utility commissioner, the state tax commission, the civil service commission, department of finance and administration, department of motor vehicles, and state industrial accident commission.[35]

Virginia—"Agency" means any state department, commission, board or officer, having statewide jurisdiction, authorized by law to make rules or to adjudicate contested cases, except those pertaining to the legislative or judiciary departments, and except the department of workmen's compensation, state corporation commission, state board of education, commission of game and inland fisheries, and department of education.[36]

(F) STATES LISTING AGENCIES TO WHICH ADMINISTRATIVE PROCEDURE ACT APPLIES

The following states have adopted statutes which list particular agencies to which the State Administrative Procedure Act will apply:

California—"Agency" includes the state boards, commissions, and officers enumerated in Sec. 11501 and those to which this chapter is made applicable by law, except that wherever the word "agency" alone is used, the power to act may be delegated by the agency and wherever the words "agency itself" are used, the power to act shall not be delegated unless the statutes relating

---

[33] MD. ANN. CODE art. 41, § 244(a).
[34] ORE. REV. STAT. § 183.010(2).
[35] ORE. REV. STAT. § 183.310(1).
[36] VA. CODE ANN. § 9-6.2(a).

to the particular agency authorize the delegation of the agency's power to hear and decide.[37]

Maine—"Agency" means the following state boards, commissions, departments or officers authorized by law to make rules or to adjudicate contested cases: [Followed by a list of agencies].[38]

New Mexico—A licensing act is applicable to specified state agencies granting occupational licenses.[39]

New Hampshire—"Commission" as here used means the public utilities commission, the water resources board, the milk control board, or any state department or official concerning whose decision a rehearing or appeal is sought in accordance with the provisions of the chapter.[40]

Ohio—"Agency" is defined as meaning (a) any official, board, or commission within six listed departments of the state government having power to adopt rules or decide contested cases; (b) functions of other departments specifically made subject to the act; and (c) licensing functions. Other named agencies and certain functions of agencies are specifically exempted.[41]

(G) Court Decisions

The courts have, in general, accorded a hospitable reception to the broad definition of "agency" found in most state statutes. By and large, the courts have recognized the desirability of extending the applicability of the procedural requirements as broadly as the statutory language permits.

This attitude is most interestingly evinced in cases in which the courts have imposed the basic procedural requirements intended to assure fair trials and informed decisions even in cases where there were substantial doubts as to the applicability of the Act, if literally construed, to the agency in question.

Thus, in *Bartosh v. Board of Osteopathic Examiners*,[42] the California Appellate Court ruled that although the agency was

---

[37] Cal. Gov't Code § 11500(a).
[38] Me. Rev. Stat. Ann. ch. 20-A, § 1.1.
[39] N.M. Stat. Ann. § 67-26-2.
[40] N.H. Rev. Stat. Ann. § 541:1.
[41] Ohio Rev. Code Ann. § 119.01(A).
[42] 82 Cal. App. 486, 186 P.2d 984 (1947). A notable instance of the imposition of the standards included in a state administrative procedure act on a municipal agency is Lewis v. City of Grand Rapids, 222 F. Supp. 349 (D.C. Mich. 1963).

created by an initiative act, it would still be required to follow the Administrative Procedure Act subsequently enacted by the state legislature. Again, in *Housing Authority of City of Los Angeles v. City of Los Angeles,*[43] the court determined that a city, when acting under a state "housing authorities" law, is acting as an agency of the state.[44]

The Supreme Court of Missouri[45] reviewed an order of the Civil Service Commission of the City of St. Louis under the Administrative Procedure Act. Similarly, the Missouri court held[46] that the Board of Trustees of the Police Retirement System of the City of St. Louis is an administrative body included in the provisions of the Administrative Procedure Act.[47]

The California court ruled[48] that the office of lieutenant governor is included in the term "state agency." In Indiana, it was held[49] that the State Board of Bar Examiners is an agency within the meaning of the statute. Again, the Massachusetts court[50] treated the Metropolitan District Commission as an agency.

However, it is generally held that county and municipal boards are not "agencies" within the strict meaning of the statute and cannot be required to comply with all the statute-prescribed procedures even though (as above noted) they may be required by virtue of court decision to comply with the basic procedural requirements envisaged in the statutes. Typical rulings include decisions that the State Administrative Procedure Act is not applicable to a local board of health;[51] that a county superintendent of schools is not an "agency";[52] that a municipal civil

---

[43] 38 Cal. 2d 853, 242 P.2d 515 (1952).

[44] *Cf.,* Los Angeles Metropolitan Transit Authority v. Brotherhood of R.R. Trainmen, 54 Cal. 2d 684, 355 P.2d 905 (1960), noting that the Los Angeles Metropolitan Transit Authority is not a state agency but a public corporation.

[45] Riley v. Holland, 362 Mo. 682, 243 S.W.2d 79 (1951).

[46] Miller v. Police Retirement Sys., 296 S.W.2d 78 (Mo. 1956).

[47] As to the status of the Missouri "county courts" under the provisions of the 1945 Missouri Constitution and the Missouri statute, *cf.* Kansas City v. Rooney, 363 Mo. 902, 254 S.W.2d 626 (1953) and *In re* Roadway in Section 21, Township 60, Range 6, West, 357 S.W.2d 919 (Mo. 1962).

[48] Treu v. Kirkwood, 42 Cal. 2d 602, 268 P.2d 482 (1954).

[49] *In re* Petition of McDonald, 241 Ind. 239, 171 N.E.2d 691 (1961).

[50] Hayeck v. Metropolitan Dist. Comm'n, 335 Mass. 372, 140 N.E.2d 210 (1957).

[51] Board of Health of Woburn v. Sousa, 338 Mass. 547, 156 N.E.2d 52 (1959).

[52] Kessler v. Board of Educ. of City of Fessenden, 87 N.W.2d 743 (N.D. 1958).

service board is not within the Administrative Procedure Act;[53] that a local irrigation district is not an "agency";[54] that a municipal board of education is not within the Administrative Procedure Act;[55] that a city is not within the Administrative Procedure Act.[56]

Absent clear statutory definition, it is a difficult question whether a tribunal created by action of the state, but possessing a limited geographical jurisdiction, should be deemed a "state agency" for purposes of statutes relating to administrative procedure. It would seem, under the definition proposed in the Revised Model State Act, that such agencies should be included. Absent such definition, a contrary result was reached in a Texas case.[57]

Contrariwise, it is held in Connecticut that town boards of education are agencies of the state, and hence subject to the Administrative Procedure Act, despite their limited geographical jurisdiction.[58] Similarly, it has been held in Massachusetts that a "metropolitan district commission" is an agency subject to the Administrative Procedure Act.[59]

A different sort of problem—again indicative of the need of comprehensive and precise statutory definition—faced the Minnesota court in a case involving the question whether the Board of Regents of the state university was an administrative agency. Holding that the Regents were "more than an agency," the court ruled the state act inapplicable.[60]

Section 2

Rule

To achieve a successful and workable definition of the term "rule," the statute should incorporate certain basic inclusions and certain equally important exclusions.

---

[53] Hansen v. Civil Serv. Bd., 147 Cal. App. 2d 732, 305 P.2d 1012 (1957).

[54] Stark v. Heart River Irrigation Dist., 78 N.D. 302, 49 N.W.2d 217 (1951).

[55] State *ex rel.* Wasilewski v. Board of School Directors of City of Milwaukee, 14 Wis. 2d 243, 111 N.W.2d 198 (1961).

[56] Sloven v. Olsen, 98 N.W.2d 115 (N.D. 1959).

[57] Bryson v. High Plains Underground Water Conservation Dist. No. 1, 156 Tex. 405, 297 S.W.2d 117 (1956).

[58] Fowler v. Town of Enfield, 138 Conn. 521, 86 A.2d 662 (1952); Norwalk Teachers' Ass'n v. Board of Educ., 138 Conn. 269, 83 A.2d 482 (1951).

[59] Hayeck v. Metropolitan Dist. Comm'n, note 50 *supra.*

[60] State *ex rel.* Sholes v. University of Minnesota, 236 Minn. 452, 54 N.W.2d 122 (1952).

(A) What Should Be Included Within Definition

Among the elements which should be included in the definition, the following are of particular importance:

First, the concept should be described in broadly inclusive terms (the word "statement" has been most popular). This has proved necessary to defeat the inclination shown by some agencies to label as "bulletins," "announcements," "guides," "interpretive bulletins," and the like, announcements which, in legal operation and effect, really amount to rules; and then to assert that their promulgations are not technically rules but merely policy statements, and hence may be issued without observance of the procedures required in connection with the adoption of rules.[61]

A second element which is important is that the term "rule" be confined, by definition, to statements of general applicability. The definition in the Federal Administrative Procedure Act,[62] it is true, includes certain rulings which apply to a single person or a small well defined group. This, however, results from the particular form of distinction between rule making and adjudication adopted in the federal act. Substantially all of the state legislatures are in agreement with the concept of the Revised Model State Act, that rule making should be restricted to statements of a legislative nature and of general applicability. Many states add to this a requirement that the rules must be of future effect. It is doubtful whether this addition has any great significance, for there would be few cases if any where an agency statement of general applicability did not have future effect.

A third essential inclusion in any workable definition of the term "rule" is a provision that the term includes all statements which implement, interpret or prescribe law or policy. Thus, the term includes not only so-called substantive regulations but also all statements setting forth the agency's position on questions of statutory interpretation and questions of policy.

---

61 In Michigan, for example, in the early days of the Michigan Unemployment Compensation Commission, the statute required that there be a hearing in case of the adoption of rules but permitted the adoption of regulations without public hearing. Over a period of several years the Commission adopted more than twenty regulations but only two rules.

62 5 U.S.C. § 1001(c); F.C.A. 5 § 1001(c).

A fourth essential is that the term "rule" include all statements describing the procedure or practice requirements of the agency.

Fifth, and closely related to the fourth requirement, is the desirability of including within the definition of rule any statement which describes the organization of an agency. Frequently, those doing business with an agency find that an initial difficulty is to learn how the agency staff may properly be approached, and this can be known only if the organization of the agency is a matter of public knowledge.

Finally, it is important to include, within the definition of "rule," amendments or repeals of rules, because obviously the amendment or repeal of a rule can have just as important an effect as the adoption of a new rule. All of these essentials are included in the definition found in Section 1(7) of the Revised Model State Act, quoted in subsection (C) *infra.*

A majority of the states having adopted definitions of the term "rule" have included most of the above-described essentials.

(B) Exclusions Needed to Sharpen Definition

To achieve a workable definition of the term "rule," it is also important that the definition should exclude statements concerning only the internal management of an agency and not affecting private rights or procedures available to the public. If a state statute authorizes the issuance of declaratory rulings as to the applicability of rules, it is helpful to exclude such declaratory rulings from the definition. It is prudent, also, to exclude from the definition intra-agency memoranda (other than those which by their promulgation affect private rights) because otherwise it might be deemed illegal for a staff member to write a memorandum on a question of policy without complying with the rule making requirements of the statute. Many state legislatures, as will be noted below, have deemed it advisable to add many other particular exclusions.

(C) Comparative Analysis of State Statutes, in Terms of Inclusionary Provisions of Model Act

Definitions of the term "rule" found in the statutes of the several states vary widely. Some are so narrow as to deprive the intended beneficiaries of the full enjoyment of the rights which are meant to be made available to members of the public through the substantive provisions concerning rule-making procedures and the requirements concerning publicity for rules. Conversely, some definitions are so broad that if the agencies were compelled to follow literally the procedural and publicity requirements, with respect to every statement falling within the definition of rule, then the agencies could properly complain that the result was to impose onerous and unnecessary burdens on agency staffs.

One of the most narrow definitions encountered[63] provides that the term "rule" includes only "rules and regulations promulgated or adopted by any agency governing or relating to rules of procedure or practice before such agency, or to govern its organization or procedure," and the statute further provides that the term "rule" does not include "rules, regulations, orders, rates, standards or classifications adopted, promulgated or prescribed by any agency to properly perform its statutory duties or to implement or make specific the law enforced or administered by any such agency."

Under such a definition, only the regulations setting up procedural provisions (such as details concerning the filing of papers and noticing of cases for hearing) are treated as *rules.* If the term is so narrowly defined, this means, of course, that agencies are free to adopt substantive rules of general applicability, prescribing law and policy, without giving notice to those affected that the agency proposed to adopt such rules and without giving the affected parties an opportunity to be heard as to the contents of the rules, and, indeed, without notifying the parties of the fact that the rules had been adopted.

One of the broadest statutory definitions encountered is found in Pennsylvania[64] which refers to "any rule, regulation, or order in the nature of a rule or regulation, of general application and future effect, promulgated by an agency under statutory authority in the administration of any statute administered by or relating to the agency, or prescribing the practice or procedure before such agency."

Without suggesting any criticism of the Pennsylvania statute, which apparently has worked very well, the conclusion is none-

---

63 TEX. REV. CIV. STAT. art. 6252-13, § 1(b).
64 PA. STAT. ANN. tit. 71, § 1710.2(e).

theless suggested that so broad a definition, if literally applied, could be a source of difficulty in that it would require agencies to afford the public an opportunity to participate in the formulation of rules which concern matters relating solely to the internal management of an agency, such as rules creating seniority rights for agency employees.

Indicative of the fact that best results can be achieved by careful periodic revisions of the statutory definition of the term "rule," based upon the experience in the particular state, is the circumstance that Wisconsin, starting out in 1943 with a comparatively short definition of rule, found as a result of careful studies by its Joint Legislative Council that it was in the public interest to adopt a number of carefully formulated and specific exceptions. The net result is that the present Wisconsin definition is bifurcate, the initial phrase encompassing every statement of general application interpreting or implementing laws administered by the agency, and subsequent phrases excepting from this broad definition those particular types of rule making with respect to which legislative experience has shown that the public interest does not require formal public hearings precedent to the adoption of the rule. Thus, for example, among eighteen exceptions are those for regulations respecting the use of highways made known to the public by means of signs or signals, and decisions relating to the curriculum to be offered in public schools.[65]

The history in Wisconsin suggests clearly the approach that state legislatures may best follow to obtain optimum results. The program should begin with the adoption of a fairly broad definition of the term "rule," with only the classical exceptions found in the Model Act. This will initially impose a substantial burden upon agencies, but the preponderating public good can well justify the temporary burden. The result will be that in adopting all statements of general applicability interpreting or implementing or applying the statute it is administering (or devising procedures to be used in administering the statute), the agency will be required to advise all interested persons of the fact that it proposes to adopt such a statement or standard, and the agency will be compelled to afford all interested parties an opportunity to make their views known, and finally the agency will be compelled to give appropriate publicity to its determination of prac-

---

[65] WIS. STAT. § 227.01(3) et seq.

tice or policy—all as provided by appropriate sections of the statute. This will afford private persons a valuable opportunity, which in most states they do not now enjoy, of being able to participate in the process by which the agency adopts its interpretations and implements the statute—substantively and procedurally.

The benefits will not be one-sided, for it is fair to assume that agency officials, whose experience is often less broad than that of those who are regulated, can benefit from the suggestions and advice made to them by those who will be required to comply with the rules and regulations. Finally, after experience of five to ten years, if it appears that adherence to the formal rule-making requirements imposes an undue burden with respect to some types of rules, the legislature may, as it did in Wisconsin, make such exceptions as experience has disclosed to be advisable.

In general, most state legislatures have chosen to follow quite closely the main outlines of the Model Act which defines a rule as follows: "Rule" means each agency statement of general applicability that implements, interprets, or prescribes law or policy, or describes the organization, procedure, or practice requirements of any agency. The term includes the amendment or repeal of a prior rule, but does not include (A) statements concerning only the internal management of an agency and not affecting private rights or procedures available to the public, or (B) declaratory rulings issued pursuant to Section 8, or (C) intra-agency memoranda.[66]

A reference to a requirement that to be a rule the statement must be of "general applicability" is found in many states.[67]

A few states do not require that the statement be of "general applicability" in order that it be classified as a rule. This approach

---

66 Section 1(7).

67 Alaska (STAT. § 44.62.640(a)(2)); Arizona (REV. STAT. ANN. § 41-1001 (3)); California (GOV'T CODE § 11371(b)); Colorado (REV. STAT. ANN. § 3-16-2(d)); Connecticut (GEN. STAT. REV. § 4-41); Florida (STAT. § 120.021 (2)); Illinois (REV. STAT. ch. 127, § 264); Iowa (CODE § 17A.1(3)); Maine (REV. STAT. ANN. ch. 20-A, § 1-III; Maryland (ANN. CODE art. 41, § 244 (b)); Massachusetts (GEN. LAWS ANN. ch. 30A, § 1(5)); Michigan (COMP. LAWS § 3.560); Missouri (REV. STAT. § 536.010(2)); Nebraska (REV. STAT. § 84-901(2)); North Dakota (CENT. CODE § 28-32-01(2)); Ohio (REV. CODE ANN. § 119.01(C)); Oklahoma (STAT. tit. 75, § 301(2)); Pennsylvania (STAT. ANN. tit. 71, § 1710.2(e)); Rhode Island (GEN. LAWS ANN. § 42-35-1(g)); Virginia (CODE ANN. § 9-6.2(b)); Washington (REV. CODE § 34.04.010(2)); West Virginia (CODE ANN. § 258(1), amended by ch. 1, Acts of 1964); Wisconsin (STAT. § 227.01(3)).

is interesting because it should serve to avoid arguments, which might be advanced by those agencies which may be reluctant to comply with the rule-making requirements, that many of their statements of policy implementing or interpreting the underlying statute are of limited rather than general applicability.[68]

One state provides that the term "rule" includes statements of "particular" as well as "general applicability."[69]

Many state statutes provide that the definition of rule applies only to statements which, in addition to having general applicability, have "future effect." Approximately an equal number of state statutes do not include this requirement of future effect. Its inclusion would seem to be unimportant except as a rhetorical nicety, and its omission of little significance, because if statements of general applicability prescribing law or policy do not have future effect they would seem to have little effect at all.[70]

The overwhelming majority of state legislatures adopting administrative procedure acts have made it a basic concept of the definition of rule that, as suggested by the Revised Model State Act, the term include all statements which "implement, interpret, or prescribe law or policy."[71]

---

68 See Indiana (ANN. STAT. § 60-1503); Kentucky (REV. STAT. § 13.080); Minnesota (STAT. § 15.0411(3)); Oregon (REV. STAT. § 183.310(3)); Vermont (STAT. ANN. tit. 3, § 701(2)).

69 HAWAII SESS. LAWS 1961, Act 103, § 1(d).

70 States which include the reference to "future effect" include: Arizona (REV. STAT. ANN. § 41-1001(3)); Colorado (REV. STAT. ANN. § 3-16-1(d)); Hawaii (SESS. LAWS 1961, Act 103, § 1(d)); Maine (REV. STAT. ANN. ch. 20-A, § 1-III); Maryland (ANN. CODE art. 41, § 244(b)); Massachusetts (GEN. LAWS ANN. ch. 30A, § 1(5)); Michigan (COMP. LAWS § 3.560(2)); Missouri (REV. STAT. § 536.010(2)); Oklahoma (STAT. tit. 75, § 301(2) (1961)); Pennsylvania (STAT. ANN. tit. 71, § 1710.2(e)); Virginia (CODE ANN. § 9-6.2(b)); Washington (REV. CODE § 34.04.010(2)); West Virginia (CODE ANN. § 258(1), amended by ch. 1, Acts of 1964). States not containing the requirement that the statement have "future effect" include: Alaska (STAT. § 44.62.640(a)(2)); California (GOV'T CODE § 11371(b)); Connecticut (GEN. STAT. REV. § 4-41); Florida (STAT. § 120.021(2)); Georgia (CODE ANN. § 3A-101); Illinois (REV. STAT. ch. 127, § 264); Iowa (CODE § 17A.1(3)); Kentucky (REV. STAT. § 13080(2)); Minnesota (STAT. § 15.14011(3)); Nebraska (REV. STAT. § 84-901(2)); North Dakota (CENT. CODE § 28-32-01(2)); Ohio (REV. CODE ANN. § 119.01(C)); Oregon (REV. STAT. § 183.310(3)); Rhode Island (GEN. LAWS ANN. § 42-35-1(g)); Vermont (STAT. ANN. tit. 3, § 701(2)); Wisconsin (STAT. § 227.01(3)).

71 Such provisions are found in the following states: Alaska (STAT. § 44.62.-640(2)); Arizona (REV. STAT. ANN. § 41-1001(3)); California (GOV'T CODE § 11371(b)); Colorado (REV. STAT. ANN. § 3-16-1(d)); Connecticut (GEN. STAT. REV. § 4-41); Florida (STAT. § 120.021(2)); Georgia (CODE ANN. § 3A-101; Hawaii (SESS. LAWS 1961, Act 103, § 1(d)); Maine (REV. STAT. ANN. ch. 20-A, § 1-III); Maryland (ANN. CODE art. 41, § 244(b)); Massachusetts

Although two states[72] exclude from the statutory definition of rule those regulations relating to the organization of the agency, most states, following the suggestion of the Revised Model State Act, include within the definition of rule those statements that describe either the organization or the procedure or practice requirements of an agency.[73]

Likewise, most of the state legislatures have found it advisable to include within the definition of "rule" agency actions which amend or repeal former rules. Obviously, the amendment or repeal of a rule carries all the implications involved in the original adoption of the rule.[74]

(GEN. LAWS ANN. ch. 30A, § 1(5)); Michigan (COMP. LAWS § 3.560(1)); Minnesota (STAT. § 15.0411(3)); Missouri (REV. STAT. § 536.010(2)); Nebraska (REV. STAT. § 84-901(2)); North Dakota (CENT. CODE § 28-32-01(2)); Oklahoma (STAT. tit. 75, § 301(2)); Rhode Island (GEN. LAWS ANN. § 42-35-1(g)); Virginia (CODE ANN. § 9-6.2(b)); Washington (REV. CODE § 34.04.010(2)); West Virginia (CODE ANN. § 258(1), amended by ch. 1, Acts of 1964); Wisconsin (STAT. § 227.01(3)).

72 Kentucky (REV. STAT. § 13.080(2)), and Vermont (STAT. ANN. tit. 3, § 701(2)).

73 Specific references to "organization" are found in the statutes of Arizona (REV. STAT. ANN. § 41-1001(3)); Florida (STAT. § 120.021(2)); Georgia (CODE ANN. § 3A-101); Hawaii (SESS. LAWS 1961, Act 103, § 1(d)); Illinois (REV. STAT. ch. 127, § 264); Maine (REV. STAT. ANN. ch. 20-A, § 1-III); Maryland (ANN. CODE art. 41, § 244(b)); Michigan (COMP. LAWS § 3.560(2)); Minnesota (STAT. § 15.0411(3)); Missouri (REV. STAT. § 536.010(2)); Nebraska (REV. STAT. § 84-901(2)); Rhode Island (GEN. LAWS ANN. § 42-35-1(g)); Texas (REV. CIV. STAT. art. 6252-13, § 1(b)); Washington (REV. CODE § 34.04.010(2)); West Virginia (CODE ANN. § 258(1), amended by ch. 1, Acts of 1964); and Wisconsin (STAT. § 227.01(3).

Statutes not relating specifically to agency "organization," and referring only to "statements describing procedure or practice" are found in Alaska (STAT. § 44.62.640(a2)); California (GOV'T CODE § 11371(b)); Colorado (REV. STAT. ANN. § 3-16-1(d)); Indiana (ANN. STAT. § 60-1503); Iowa (CODE § 17A.1(3)); North Dakota (CENT. CODE § 28-32-01(2)); Oklahoma (STAT. § 301(2)); Oregon (REV. STAT. § 183.310(3b)); and Pennsylvania (STAT. ANN. tit. 71, § 1710.2(e)).

74 Alaska (STAT. § 44.62.640(a2)); Arizona (REV. STAT. ANN. § 41-1001(3)); California (GOV'T CODE § 11371(b)); Florida (STAT. § 120.021(2)); Georgia (CODE ANN. § 3A-101); Illinois (REV. STAT. ch. 127, § 264); Iowa (CODE § 17A.1(3)); Maine (REV. STAT. ANN. ch. 20-A, § 1-III); Maryland (ANN. CODE art. 41, § 244(b)); Michigan (COMP. LAWS § 3.560(1)); Minnesota (STAT. § 15.0411(3)); Missouri (REV. STAT. § 536.010(2)); Nebraska (REV. STAT. § 84-901(2)); North Dakota (CENT. CODE § 28-32-01(2)); Oklahoma (STAT. tit. 75, § 301(2)); Rhode Island (GEN. LAWS ANN. § 42-35-1(g)); Texas (REV. CIV. STAT. art. 6252-13, § 1(b)); Vermont (STAT. ANN. tit. 3, § 701(2)); Virginia (CODE ANN. § 9-6.2(b)); Washington (REV. CODE § 34.04.010(2)); West Virginia (CODE ANN. § 258(1), amended by ch. 1, Acts of 1964); Wisconsin (STAT. § 227.01(3)).

(D) Additional Inclusions in Definition of "Rule"

A number of states have incorporated in their statutes other provisions, including stated types of agency statements within the definition of rule.

Two are of particular interest. The Alaska statute[75] includes "manuals, policies, instructions, guides to enforcement, interpretive bulletins, interpretations, and the like, which have the effect of rules, orders, regulations, or standards of general application; and this and similar phraseology shall not be used to avoid or circumvent this chapter." In view of the tendency of many administrative officers to avoid compliance with the rule-making requirements of the applicable statutes by utilizing a name other than "rule" or "regulation" to describe agency statements which have the effect of rules, legislative draftsmen might well be interested in including the language found in the Alaska statute, although it could be argued that the courts should construe the language of the Revised Model State Act to achieve the same result.

The Nebraska statute[76] provides that every agency statement, even though purportedly relating to the internal management of the agency "which shall prescribe a penalty" shall be presumed to have general applicability or to affect private rights and interests so as to come within the rule-making provisions. This provision closes, or at least narrows, a loophole by which agencies sometimes seek to avoid the procedural requirements applicable to rule making by describing a rule as one relating to internal management.

(E) Comparative Analysis of State Statutes, in Terms of Exclusionary Provisions of Model Act

The state legislatures have not so uniformly conformed with the suggestions of the Revised Model State Act as to exclusions, from the statutory definition, of certain activities that might otherwise be deemed to be rule making. As noted above, the Revised Model State Act provides for the exclusion from the definition of rule of (1) statements concerning only the internal management of an agency and not affecting private rights or

[75] ALASKA STAT. § 44.62.640(2).
[76] NEB. REV. STAT. § 84-901(2).

procedures available to the public, (2) declaratory rulings by the agency, (3) intra-agency memoranda.

A large number of states have adopted the first exclusionary provision of the Revised Model State Act, *i.e.,* statements concerning internal management and not affecting private rights or available procedures.[77]

In a few states, the exclusion applies to all statements concerning matters of internal management, with the result that it could be argued that even though the regulation actually affects private rights and procedures available to the public, nevertheless the agency could not be compelled to comply with the rule-making procedures if the regulation could be described as one relating to the internal management of the agency.[78]

Under such statutes, reliance must be placed on the courts to foreclose any tendencies that agencies might exhibit to avoid the rule-making requirements by casting regulations in terms of internal management.

Only a few states have followed the suggestion of the Revised Model State Act to exclude from the definition of rule declaratory or advisory rulings issued by the agency.[79]

In order to encourage agencies to utilize the practice of issuing declaratory advisory rulings—a practice which in many instances is of inestimable value to the parties—it would be helpful for the state legislatures to make it plain that in issuing such declaratory rulings agencies need not comply with the rule-making requirements.

---

[77] Arizona (REV. STAT. ANN. § 41-1001(3)); Georgia (CODE ANN. § 3A-101); Hawaii (SESS. LAWS 1961, Act 103, § 1(d)); Illinois (REV. STAT. ch. 127, § 264); Indiana (ANN. STAT. § 60-1503); Maine (REV. STAT. ANN. ch. 20-A, § 1-III); Maryland (ANN. CODE art. 41, § 244(b)); Massachusetts (GEN. LAWS ANN. ch. 30A, § 1(5)); Michigan (COMP. LAWS § 3.560(2)); Minnesota (STAT. § 15.0411(3)); Missouri (REV. STAT. § 536.010(2)); Nebraska (REV. STAT. § 84-901(2)); Ohio (REV. CODE ANN. § 119.01(C)); Oklahoma (STAT. tit. 75, § 301(2) (1961)); Rhode Island (GEN. LAWS ANN. § 42-35-1(g)); Texas (REV. CIV. STAT. art. 6252-13, § 1(b)); Washington (REV. CODE § 34.-04.010(2)); West Virginia (CODE ANN. § 258(1), amended by ch. 1, Acts of 1964); Wisconsin (STAT. § 227.01(5a)).

[78] Alaska (STAT. § 44.62.640(a2)); California (GOV'T CODE § 11371(b)); Connecticut (GEN. STAT. REV. § 4-41); Florida (STAT. § 120.021(2)); Iowa (CODE § 17A.1(3)); Kentucky (REV. STAT. § 13.080(2)); North Dakota (CENT. CODE § 28-32-01(2)); Vermont (STAT. ANN. tit. 3, § 701(2)); Virginia (CODE ANN. § 9-6.2(6)).

[79] Georgia (CODE ANN. § 3A-101); Hawaii (SESS. LAWS 1961, Act 103, § 1); Massachusetts (GEN. LAWS ANN. ch. 30A, § 1(5)); Oklahoma (STAT. tit. 75, § 301(2)); Rhode Island (GEN. LAWS ANN. § 42-35-1).

Likewise, only a few states[80] have adopted the suggestion of the Revised Model State Act to exclude intra-agency memoranda from the definition of rule. It may fairly be presumed, however, that agencies consider such memoranda as falling outside the ambit of the statutory definition.

(F) ADDITIONAL EXCLUSIONS FROM DEFINITION OF "RULE"

The legislatures of a number of states have found it advisable to make other specific exclusions from the definition of rule. Some of them are apparently designed merely as reassuring clarifications of the definition. Others apparently reflect successful lobbying tactics on the part of the agencies which normally seek a narrow definition of the term rule, and others reflect particular local needs.

Typical of such specific exclusions are those specifying that the term "rule" does not include forms, instructions relating to to the use of forms,[81] rules addressed to named persons and not of general application,[82] statements relating to military or naval functions,[83] regulations concerning admission to and graduation from educational institutions,[84] regulations relating to commitment to and release from state institutions,[85] emergency health rules,[86] determination of rates or tariffs,[87] regulations concerning the use of streets or highways made known by way of signs or markers,[88] activities relating to the management and develop-

---

80 Georgia (CODE ANN. § 3A-101); Hawaii (SESS. LAWS 1961, Act 103, § 1); Oklahoma (STAT. tit. 75, § 301(2)); Rhode Island (GEN. LAWS ANN. § 42-35-1 (g)).

81 Alaska (STAT. § 44.62.640(a)(2)); California (GOV'T CODE § 11371 (b)).

82 Connecticut (GEN. STAT. REV. § 4-41); Illinois (REV. STAT. ch. 127, § 264); Kentucky (REV. STAT. § 13.080(2)); Wisconsin (STAT. § 227.01(5) (c)).

83 Connecticut (GEN. STAT. REV. § 4-41); Wisconsin (STAT. § 227.01(5) (i)).

84 North Dakota (CENT. CODE § 28-32-01(2)); Wisconsin (STAT. § 227.01 (5)(f)).

85 Iowa (CODE § 17A.1); Massachusetts (GEN. LAWS ANN. ch. 30A, § 1(5)); Minnesota (STAT. § 15.0411(3)); North Dakota (CENT. CODE § 28-32-01(2)); Wisconsin (STAT. § 227.01(5)(h)).

86 Iowa (CODE § 17A.1); Michigan (COMP. LAWS § 3.560).

87 Kentucky (REV. STAT. § 13.080(2)); Michigan (COMP. LAWS § 3.560); Nebraska (REV. STAT. § 84-901(2)); Oklahoma (STAT. tit. 75, § 301(2)); Wisconsin (STAT. § 227.01(5)(n)).

88 Kentucky (REV. STAT. § 13.080(2)); Massachusetts (GEN. LAWS ANN.

ment of state property,[89] licensing activities,[90] nor informational pamphlets.[91]

(G) Court Decisions Determining What Agency Statements Are Rules

There have been but few significant court decisions interpreting the statutory definitions of rule. The litigation which has led to judicial interpretation reveals a pervasive tendency on the part of the agencies to seek to construe the statutory definition in a way which will exempt some agency statements from the application of the definition.

Typical of the agency attitude and of the judicial response is a decision of the New York Court of Appeals.[92] In that case, an automobile driver convicted of speeding raised the defense that the "order" of the state traffic commission fixing a speed limit of thirty-five miles per hour in a given zone was not enforceable because the order had not been filed as a rule. The traffic commission contended that because its requirement was issued as an "order" and not as a "rule" or "regulation," there was no necessity of complying with the filing requirements.

The court said, however, that even though the order might legitimately be denominated as such, nevertheless, regardless of what it was called, it was in effect a rule or regulation. The court declared:

> The term "rule or regulation" . . . embraces any kind of legislative or quasi-legislative norm or prescription which establishes a pattern or course of conduct for the future. The label or name employed is not important and, unquestionably, many so-called "orders" come within that term.

In other cases, it has been held that agency statements applicable only to a limited number of persons who were either named or whose identity was well established were not rules because not of "general applicability." This was the ruling in Texas with

---

ch. 30A, § 1(5)); Virginia (CODE ANN. § 9-6.2(b)); Wisconsin (STAT. § 227.-01(5)(d)).

[89] Massachusetts (GEN. LAWS ANN. ch. 30A, § 1(5)).

[90] Oklahoma (STAT. tit. 75, § 301(2)).

[91] Wisconsin (STAT. § 227.01(5)(r)).

[92] People v. Cull, 10 N.Y.2d 123, 126, 218 N.Y.S.2d 38, 176 N.E.2d 495 (1961).

respect to a declaration by the railroad commission that, pending further proceedings, motor carriers could charge oil companies intra-state rates higher than established interstate rates on certain shipments.[93] The California court held that resolutions by a toll bridge authority providing for the issuance of bonds to construct a particular bridge did not constitute a rule because not of general application.[94] On the other hand, a minimum wage order of somewhat limited application has been treated as a rule.[95]

Section 3

Adjudication

(A) Analysis of Definition Found in Model Act

While the Federal Administrative Procedure Act[96] in effect includes as adjudication every agency activity which is not embraced within the definition of rule making,[97] the Revised Model State Act employs a more precise definition. Under that Act, adjudication is equated with the determination of contested cases. This term is defined as follows:

> "Contested case" means a proceeding, including but not restricted to ratemaking [price fixing], and licensing, in which the legal rights, duties, or privileges of a party are required by law to be determined by an agency after an opportunity for hearing.[98]

A significant difference between the Federal Administrative Procedure Act and the Revised Model State Act is that rate making is classified as "rule making" under the former,[99] but as a contested case under the Model Act.

This reflects a belief on the part of the draftsmen of the Revised Model State Act that in proceedings before state public

---

[93] Sun Oil Co. v. Railroad Comm'n, 158 Tex. 292, 311 S.W.2d 235 (1958).

[94] Faulkner v. California Toll Bridge Authority, 40 Cal. 2d 317, 253 P.2d 659 (1953).

[95] Allied Theatres of New England, Inc. v. Commissioner of Labor & Industries, 338 Mass. 609, 156 N.E.2d 424 (1959).

[96] 5 U.S.C. § 1001; F.C.A. 5 § 1001.

[97] The Federal Administrative Procedure Act provides at § 2(d): "'Order' means the whole or any part of the final disposition (whether affirmative, negative, injunctive, or declaratory in form) of any agency in any matter other than rule making but including licensing. 'Adjudication' means agency process for the formulation of an order." 5 U.S.C. § 1002; F.C.A. 5 § 1002.

[98] Section 1(2).

[99] 5 U.S.C. § 1001(c); F.C.A. 5 § 1001(c).

utility commissions leading to the establishment of rates for public utility companies, the interests of respondents and consumers alike are better served if it is required that there be made available the more complete opportunities for hearing that are required in case of adjudication.

It is recognized, however, that in other types of price fixing some states may prefer to utilize less formal procedures than those set up for contested cases under the Revised Model State Act. For this reason (and the further reason that some states do not have price fixing laws), the reference to *price fixing* is bracketed in the text of the Model Act, indicating that the propriety of including the term is a question which may vary from state to state.

(B) DEFINITIONS IN STATE ACTS—IN GENERAL

Most states adopting administrative procedure laws have included a definition of "adjudication" or "contested case" similar to that found in the Model Act.

The most popular definition in existing state statutes refers to a contested case as one wherein legal rights, duties or privileges of a party are required by law or constitutional right to be determined after an opportunity for agency hearing, differing from the Revised Model State Act only by insertion of the phrase "or constitutional right".[100] The inclusion of the reference to "constitutional right" reflects the circumstance that the earlier edition of the Model Act included this phrase in the definition of contested case. In the 1961 revision of the Model Act, the draftsmen concluded that the inclusion of the reference to "constitutional right" was unnecessary, because a reference to cases where a hearing is required "by law" includes both cases where it is required by statute and also cases where it is required by constitution.[101] A few state statutes, following the language of the Revised Model State Act, define contested cases as those wherein legal rights, duties or privileges of a party are required,

[100] Arizona (REV. STAT. ANN. § 41-1001-2); Maine (REV. STAT. ANN. ch. 20-A, § 1-II); Maryland (ANN. CODE art. 41, § 244(c)); Massachusetts (GEN. LAWS ANN. ch. 30A, § 1(1)); Michigan (COMP. LAWS § 3.560); Minnesota (STAT. § 15.0411(4)); Nebraska (REV. STAT. § 84-901(3)); North Carolina (GEN. STAT. § 143-306(2)); Oregon (REV. STAT. § 183.310(1)); Washington (REV. CODE § 34.04.010(3)).

[101] *Cf.*, Wong Yang Sung v. McGrath, 339 U.S. 33, 94 L. Ed. 616, 70 Sup. Ct. 445 (1950).

"by law," without reference to constitutional requirements, to be determined after an agency hearing.[102] The 1945 Missouri statute[103] limited the definition of contested case to those proceedings in which the legal rights, duties or privileges of specific parties are required "by statute" to be determined after hearing. This raises a question whether, in cases where a statute makes no specific reference to a hearing, but a hearing is required constitutionally, the case would be deemed a contested case. Under the Federal Administrative Procedure Act,[104] it was held that the procedural provisions applicable to cases of adjudication "required by *statute* to be determined on the record after opportunity for an agency hearing" were applicable where the Constitution, rather than a statute, required a hearing. The court reached this result by saying that the statute would be construed as requiring a hearing in order to avoid a question as to the constitutionality of the statute.[105]

(C) Treatment of Licensing as Adjudication

Several state statutes provide specifically that licensing shall be considered "adjudication."[106]

Special provisions relative to licensing are included in some statutes, reflecting the circumstance that certain types of licensing activities may properly be carried on without insisting upon all the procedural formalities applicable to other cases of adjudication. Thus, it is provided in Ohio[107] that the term adjudication "does not include the issuance of a license in response to an application with respect to which no question is raised." Similarly, in Virginia the statute provides[108] for the exclusion from the category of contested case of "controversies over whether the examination was fair or whether the applicant passed the examination" in cases in which an agency issues a license, permit or

---

102 Georgia (Code Ann. § 3A-101); Hawaii (Sess. Laws 1961, Act 103, § 1(e)); Virginia (Code Ann. § 9-6.2(c)).

103 Mo. Rev. Stat. § 536.010(3). In 1957 the phrase "required by statute" was changed to "required by law."

104 5 U.S.C. § 1001; F.C.A. 5 § 1001.

105 Wong Yang Sung v. McGrath, 339 U.S. 33, 94 L. Ed. 616, 70 Sup. Ct. 445 (1950).

106 Colorado (Rev. Stat. Ann. § 3-16-1(f)); Florida (Stat. § 120.21(2)); Georgia (Code Ann. § 3A-101); Oregon (Rev. Stat. § 183.310(2)); Rhode Island (Gen. Laws Ann. § 42-35-1(b)).

107 Ohio Rev. Code Ann. § 119.01(D).

108 Va. Code Ann. § 9-6.2(c).

certificate after an examination to test the knowledge or ability of the applicant.

(D) TREATMENT OF PRICE FIXING AS ADJUDICATION

Presumably because of the omission of a specific reference to rate making and price fixing in the 1946 edition of the Model Act, few of the state statutes include such specific references. However, the Rhode Island Act adopted in 1962[109] after the promulgation of the Revised Model State Act does include such a reference, indicating that as other state legislatures adopt administrative procedure acts or amend existing statutes, these words will find general acceptance. It would seem clear, however, that even without specific reference thereto in the definition, cases of rate making and price fixing would be considered to be adjudication unless specifically excluded therefrom by statute.

(E) STATUTORY EXCLUSIONS FOR CASES OF INFORMAL ADJUDICATION

A number of state statutes contain specific exclusions, excepting from the definition of adjudication instances which might otherwise be deemed to fall within the general definition. Thus, in Indiana,[110] there is excluded from the definition of adjudication the issuance of warrants for the collection of taxes, the payment of benefits under the unemployment insurance laws, certain appellate functions of the state board of tax commissioners, determinations as to eligibility for public assistance, and the dismissal of certain public employees. This, of course, represents merely the determination that certain types of administrative proceedings, or certain agencies, should be excepted from the normal procedural provisions. This is a price which must sometimes be paid to obtain enactment of an administrative procedure act.

In Maine,[111] there appears an interesting provision that the term contested case does not include "informal meetings held by consent of the agency and all interested parties."

Massachusetts[112] likewise, by exception to the definition of "adjudicatory proceedings," exempts certain types of administra-

---

109 R.I. GEN. LAWS ANN. § 42-35-1.
110 IND. ANN. STAT. § 63-3002.
111 ME. REV. STAT. ANN. ch. 20-A, § 1-II.
112 MASS. GEN. LAWS ANN. ch. 30A, § 1(1).

tive adjudication from the procedural requirements of the Act, including (a) proceedings to determine whether the agency shall institute or recommend institution of proceedings in a court, (b) proceedings for the arbitration of labor disputes, (c) proceedings for the disposition of grievances concerning public employees, (d) proceedings to classify appointive governmental positions.

In Pennsylvania,[113] the definition excludes from "adjudication" matters involving the seizure or forfeiture of property.

In Virginia,[114] there are excluded from the definition of contested case controversies relating to the amount, the payment, or the refund of taxes; controversies relating to the issuance, denial, revocation or suspension of licenses by the Virginia Alcoholic Beverage Control Board; and controversies, in cases in which an agency issues a license, permit or certificate after an examination to test the knowledge or ability of the applicant, whether the examination was fair or whether the applicant passed the examination.

(F) States Adopting Approach of F.A.P.A.

A few states, departing from the normal state pattern, define adjudication in language more closely approximating that of the federal act.[115]

(G) Other Definitions of Adjudication

Other statutes, departing both from the pattern of the Revised Model State Act and that of the federal act, contain provisions which deserve special note. Ohio[116] defines adjudication as "the determination by the highest or ultimate authority of an agency of the rights, duties, privileges, benefits, or legal relationships of a specified person." Similarly, the Pennsylvania statute[117] defines adjudication as meaning "any final order, decree, decision, determination, or ruling by an agency affecting personal or property rights, privileges, immunities or obligations of any or all

---

113 PA. STAT. ANN. tit. 71, § 1710.2(a).

114 VA. CODE ANN. § 9-6.2(c).

115 Colorado (REV. STAT. ANN. § 3-16-1(f)); Florida (STAT. § 120.21); Oklahoma (STAT. tit. 75, § 301(6)).

116 OHIO REV. CODE ANN. § 119.01(D).

117 PA. STAT. ANN. tit. 71, § 1710.2(a).

of the parties to the proceeding." Wisconsin provides[118] that contested case means "a proceeding before an agency in which, after hearing required by law, the legal rights, duties, or privileges of any party to such proceeding are determined or directly affected by a decision or order in such proceeding and in which the assertion by one party of any such right, duty, or privilege is denied or controverted by another party to such proceeding."

(H) Judicial Tendency to Construe Definition Liberally

The importance of the statutory definition of adjudication (or contested case) lies in the fact that it is only with respect to the administrative proceedings which are included within the definition that the parties can insist, as a matter of statutory right, on observance of the procedural safeguards specified in the respective statutes. These procedural safeguards (guaranteeing adequate notice, a fair hearing in accordance with prescribed rules of evidence, a separation of prosecutory and adjudicatory responsibilities, and a decision made on a written record by responsible officials having personal familiarity with the contents of the record) are vital not only in protecting the private rights of respondents, but also in preserving the public interest that administrative determinations shall reflect fully informed decisions made on an adequate record.

Recognizing the public desirability of extending as far as possible the applicability of such procedural safeguards, the state courts have in general accorded a hospitable reception to the statutory definitions, to the end of including within their ambit the greatest possible number of administrative activities, except, of course, those which have to do primarily with rule making.

Thus, it has been held that the terms adjudication and contested case include an application for the discontinuance of trains,[119] an application for a license to conduct a harness race meeting,[120] and an application for the grant of authority to open a bank.[121] In the last-cited case, the Wisconsin court suggested

118 Wisconsin (STAT. § 227.01(2)).

119 City of Newton v. Department of Pub. Utils., 339 Mass. 535, 160 N.E.2d 108 (1959).

120 Bay State Harness Horse Racing & Breeding Ass'n, Inc. v. State Racing Comm'n, 342 Mass. 694, 175 N.E.2d 244 (1961).

121 Hall v. Banking Review Bd., 13 Wis. 2d 359, 108 N.W.2d 543 (1961);

that even though a party's interest in an administrative proceeding is so insubstantial that he would not have standing as an "aggrieved party" to seek judicial review, nonetheless if he has been permitted to appear in the administrative proceedings, it should be deemed to constitute a contested case for the purpose of determining the applicability of the prescribed procedural requirements.

(I) Where Agency Can Omit Hearing, Safeguards Do Not Apply

Cases of "informal adjudication," so-called (wherein an agency is not required to afford opportunity for hearing) are outside the normal statutory definitions of adjudication (or contested case). In a number of instances, the state courts with seeming reluctance have been compelled to hold that in such proceedings the procedural safeguards set forth in the procedural codes can be disregarded, subject only to those minimal requirements of procedural fairness required as a matter of procedural due process.

The problem is a difficult one. There are many types of informal case determination (such as allowance of application for licenses in cases where the procedure is essentially ministerial in nature—like a retailer's sales tax license or a driver's license which is issued automatically upon the passing of a prescribed test) where it would unduly burden the agency staffs to require compliance with the formal procedural requirements prescribed for the conduct of contested cases. On the other hand, there are a distressing number of instances wherein substantial personal or property rights are determined administratively, by informal adjudicatory processes, and without the requirement of a hearing. It is unfortunate that in such cases the statutes (with rare exceptions) do not require the observance of the procedural safeguards which the intrinsic importance of the issues recommends.

Thus, courts have been compelled to exclude from the statutory definitions of adjudication (or contested case) administrative proceedings which were authorized to be conducted without formal hearing, even though they involved such substantial and important issues as an application to establish a branch bank,[122]

cf., Park Bldg. Corp. v. Industrial Comm'n, 9 Wis. 2d 78, 100 N.W.2d 571 (1960).

[122] Natick Trust Co. v. Board of Bank Incorporation, 337 Mass. 615, 151 N.E. 2d 70 (1958).

an application for transfer of a liquor license,[123] an application seeking a means of access, over public property, to petitioner's own property,[124] or questions involving compliance with a building code.[125]

Another result of a decision that a particular administrative proceeding, although primarily adjudicatory in nature, is not a contested case, may be to deny an aggrieved party the right to the judicial review contemplated by the Administrative Procedure Acts.[126]

Relief should be afforded from the potentially serious results flowing from the denial of procedural safeguards and of judicial review in such cases. Three possible means of obtaining such relief may be noted.

First—and most practicable—is the exercise of vigilance on the part of the state legislatures to require that every type of administrative adjudication which may substantially affect important rights of person or property must be conditioned on the allowance of a hearing to the persons involved. If this is done, then of course the proceeding automatically comes within the definition of contested case. The procedural codes cannot accomplish this objective; it must be taken care of in the specific statutes authorizing particular agencies to take specified action. It may be noted that there exists a strong trend, in recent statutes creating administrative agencies, to require them to afford notice and an opportunity for hearing in all cases in which their determinations may substantially affect rights of person or property. As this trend becomes fully felt, the problem will in large measure disappear.

Secondly, to the extent that the state courts are able to find that constitutional requirements command notice and hearing as a condition precedent to effective administrative action, the need can be met; for if a hearing is required as a matter of constitutional right, then the case becomes a contested case within the procedural codes. As noted in Chapter V, *infra,* developing

[123] Springfield Hotel Ass'n, Inc. v. Alcoholic Beverages Control Comm'n, 338 Mass. 699, 157 N.E.2d 219 (1959).

[124] Hayeck v. Metropolitan Dist. Comm'n, 335 Mass. 372, 140 N.E.2d 210 (1957).

[125] Park Bldg. Corp. v. Industrial Comm'n, note 121 *supra.*

[126] City of Milwaukee v. Public Serv. Comm'n, 11 Wis. 2d 111, 104 N.W. 2d 167 (1960).

concepts of procedural due process afford courts ample opportunity to include within the contested case category most of the instances of informal adjudication in which the statute does not require a hearing, but in which a hearing is required as a matter of fairness.

Third, it is possible for state legislatures to follow the suggestion of the Task Force on Legal Services and Procedures of the Second Hoover Commission, and make particular provisions applicable to instances of informal adjudication where it is felt unnecessary to follow all of the rather complex procedures required in contested cases, and where some less exacting procedures are deemed sufficient to satisfy the basic need of assuring fully informed and fair administrative action. The Hoover Commission Task Force[127] proposed that in cases of informal adjudication, not required by constitution or statute to be based on a formal hearing and record (such as dispositions of public property, the granting of loans and benefits, and the administration of public contracts), the agency should be required to give the interested parties notice of the agency's proposed decision before it is formally adopted, and allow the parties opportunity to file exceptions to the proposed decision, and obtain an intra-agency review, to the end that the proposed decision would be critically reviewed by the heads of the agency in light of the objections of the protesting parties. Such procedures could wisely be made applicable to many types of proceedings within state agencies. Here again, reliance must be placed on the vigilance of the state legislatures.

(J) Preliminary Inquiries Not "Contested Cases"

Agencies frequently conduct informal preliminary inquiries to determine whether or not formal proceedings should be instituted. Even though the formal proceeding, if instituted, would be a contested case, the preliminary inquiry is not included within the scope of the statutory definition.[128]

---

[127] Commission on Organization of Executive Branch of the Government, Task Force Report on Legal Services and Procedure 170 (1955).

[128] Miller v. Alcoholic Beverages Control Comm'n, 340 Mass. 33, 162 N.E.2d 656 (1959).

Section 4

Parties

(A) Definition Same as in Federal Act

The definition of party in Section 1(5) of the Revised Model State Act is substantially the same as that found in the Federal Administrative Procedure Act.[129] It provides: "'Party' means each person or agency named or admitted as a party, or properly seeking and entitled as of right to be admitted as a party." The Revised Model State Act omits the further caveat found in the federal act recognizing the right of agencies to admit persons (or agencies) as parties for limited purposes. But this right, as noted below, has been recognized by the state courts without aid of statute; and so it may safely be concluded that with respect to the definition of party judicial interpretations of the term under the federal act may be accepted as persuasive authorities in connection with the application of the Revised Model State Act.

The first branch of the statutory definition—embracing each person named or admitted as a party—merely restates long-established legal concepts. The second branch—including within the term each person or agency properly seeking and entitled as of right to be admitted as a party—serves to protect the right of a party who is entitled to intervene to seek judicial review, or otherwise attack, an administrative order if his timely petition to intervene is denied. Although not admitted as a party, such a person possesses, by virtue of the statutory definition, all the rights he would have had if the agency had permitted him to intervene.

(B) Summary of State Legislation

Comparatively few state statutes incorporate, in their definition of party, the second branch of the definition found in the Revised Model State Act.[130] The omission of this provision from other state statutes is only a reflection of the circumstance that the earlier version of the Model Act, on which most state statutes

---

[129] 5 U.S.C. § 1001(b); F.C.A. 5 § 1001(b).

[130] Such provisions are found in the statutes of Georgia (Code Ann. § 3A-101); Hawaii (Sess. Laws 1961, Act 103, § 1(c)); Massachusetts (Gen. Laws Ann. ch. 30A, § 1(3)); New Hampshire (Rev. Stat. Ann. § 541:8); Oklahoma (Stat. tit. 75, § 301(8)); Rhode Island (Gen. Laws Ann. § 42-35-1(e)).

have been based, did not include this provision. It serves a well-defined need, and presumably will be widely adopted.

A number of the state statutes include, as part of the definition of party, noteworthy specific inclusions. Thus, Alaska[131] provides that the agency conducting the case is always to be deemed a party. The New Hampshire statute[132] declares that any person whose rights may be directly affected may appear and become a party; and provides that the courts may order the joinder of any person as a party, if justice so requires. Ohio[133] provides that any person whose interests are the subject of an adjudication by an agency shall be deemed a party.

An interesting exclusion from the statutory definition appears both in Alaska[134] and California[135] where the statutes provide that an officer or employee of the agency appearing in his official capacity shall not be deemed a party.

(C) Court Decisions as to Identity of "Parties"

The test of one's status as a party occurs most frequently when his right to seek judicial review is challenged.[136]

A number of state courts have held, that, absent a definition like that found in the Revised Model State Act, a person admitted in an agency proceeding as an intervenor does not thereby become a party entitled to seek judicial review. Thus, New Jersey has held that independent bus companies, permitted to intervene and present proofs at a public utility commission hearing held to consider a petition by a larger carrier seeking permission to increase rates, did not thereby become parties, and were not entitled to notice of the Attorney General's appeal from the administrative order.[137] Similarly, in Missouri it was held that a bank which had been permitted to intervene in hearings on an application by a group of incorporators seeking a charter for a new bank, was not entitled as an intervening interested party to obtain judicial review.[138] These decisions accomplish the same

---

131 Alaska Stat. § 44.62.640(4).
132 N.H. Rev. Stat. Ann. § 541:8.
133 Ohio Rev. Code Ann. § 119.01(G).
134 Alaska Stat. § 44.62.640(4).
135 Cal. Gov't Code § 11500(b).
136 See Ch. XVI *infra,* discussing the question of standing to appeal.
137 Public Serv. Coordinated Transp. v. State, 5 N.J. 196, 74 A.2d 580 (1950).
138 State *ex rel.* University Bank v. Blair, 365 Mo. 699, 285 S.W.2d 678 (1956).

end as the provision of the federal act[139] recognizing the right of an agency to permit a person to intervene for limited purposes only.

Where the agency has denied an applicant the right to intervene, it appears that—absent a statutory provision like that of the Revised Model State Act and a showing that his application was improperly denied—he is not to be deemed a party for purposes of judicial review.[140]

The right of an administrative officer whose decision was reversed by an appellate administrative tribunal to seek judicial review was denied, on the grounds that he was not a party, by the Missouri court.[141] New Jersey has gone one step further, holding that the very agency whose determination is appealed by the state attorney general is not a party to the appellate proceedings.[142]

The wholesome principle that one whose rights will be directly affected by administrative action is an indispensable party to the administrative proceedings appears to be well established. Thus, Connecticut has held that an individual granted permission by a zoning board to utilize his property for a non-conforming use was an indispensable party to proceedings seeking review of the administrative determination.[143]

Similarly, it was held in Illinois that taxpayers who had objected to the legality of a school tax and had paid the levy under protest were indispensable parties to mandamus proceedings instituted by the school districts to compel the county treasurer to pay them the taxes he had collected.[144]

---

139 5 U.S.C. § 1001(b); F.C.A. 5 § 1001(b), which provides that the definition of "party" as including any one properly seeking and entitled as of right to be admitted as a party, does not prevent an agency from admitting any one as a party for limited purposes.

140 J. L. Shiely Co. v. Chicago, Milwaukee, St. Paul & P.R.R., 252 Minn. 535, 91 N.W.2d 116 (1958).

141 State *ex rel.* University Bank v. Blair, note 138 *supra.*

142 Public Serv. Coordinated Transp. v. State, note 137 *supra.*

143 Shulman v. Zoning Bd. of Appeals, 143 Conn. 182, 120 A.2d 550 (1956).

144 People *ex rel.* School Dist. 118 v. Reinhardt, 21 Ill. 2d 153, 171 N.E.2d 660 (1961).

Section 5

Persons

(A) New Definition in Revised Model State Act

While the earlier version of the Model State Act contained no definition of the term "person" (nor, indeed, do most of the existing state administrative procedure laws), the Revised Model State Act, borrowing from the Federal Administrative Procedure Act[145] incorporates a definition which is principally noteworthy in its exclusion of agencies from the term "person."

The Revised Model State Act provides (Section 1(6)): " 'Person' means any individual, partnership, corporation, association, governmental subdivision, or public or private organization of any character other than an agency." This means, in net result, that while an agency is normally a party to the proceeding it is conducting, and while one agency may become a party to proceedings being conducted by another agency, still agencies are not as such entitled to the privileges which the Revised Model State Act creates for persons. This may become relevant in a number of connections. For example, Section 15 of the Revised Model State Act confers standing to claim judicial review on persons who are aggrieved by a final decision in a contested case. Basically, the concept is that there should be two categories: one for the agencies, and the other for all legal entities *dehors* the agencies.

(B) Existing Statutory Definitions

The newer state statutes generally follow, in substance, the suggestion of the Revised Model State Act, as to the definition of person.[146] The older state statutes which contain a definition of the term person incorporate, for the most part, language which makes it clear that the term includes associations, partnerships, and corporations, as well as natural persons.[147] A few also

---

[145] 5 U.S.C. § 1001(b); F.C.A. 5 § 1001(b).

[146] Colorado (REV. STAT. ANN. § 3-16-1(c)); Georgia (CODE ANN. § 3A-101); Hawaii (SESS. LAWS 1961, No. 103, § 1(b)); Oklahoma (STAT. tit. 75, § 301(a)); Rhode Island (GEN. LAWS ANN. § 42-35-1(f)).

[147] Iowa (CODE § 17A.1-2); North Dakota (CENT. CODE § 28-32-01-3); Ohio (REV. CODE ANN. § 119.01(F)).

specifically provide for the inclusion of political subdivisions as persons.[148]

(C) JUDICIAL INTERPRETATION OF TERM "PERSON"

While the question as to what persons are "aggrieved" so as to have standing to appeal is one which has proved troublesome to the courts,[149] there appears to have been little occasion for judicial construction of the term person under state administrative procedure acts. In Massachusetts, a question was raised whether a town was a person, and the court (aided by the statutory definition) held that it was.[150]

Section 6

Licensing

(A) DEFINITION IN REVISED MODEL STATE ACT

Because of widespread dissatisfaction with the performance of many state agencies in matters connected with the granting, suspension, and revocation of licenses—particularly, occupational licenses—the Revised Model State Act contains a specific section relating to the conduct of such licensing proceedings. Implementing these provisions, the Act contains the following definition: " 'License' includes the whole or part of any agency permit, certificate, approval, registration, charter, or similar form of permission required by law, but it does not include a license required solely for revenue purposes." (Section 1(3)).

Obviously, the intent of the definition is to achieve broad applicability for the Act's substantive provisions as to the conduct of licensing proceedings. The exclusion referable to licenses required solely for revenue purposes recognizes the practice in many states of issuing licenses in a purely routine, ministerial manner as an aid in the collection of sales and use taxes, and similar levies.

---

148 Indiana (ANN. STAT. § 63-3002); Massachusetts (GEN. LAWS ANN. ch. 30A, § 1(4)); Pennsylvania (STAT. ANN. tit. 71, § 1710.2(d)).

149 See Ch. XVI *infra.*

150 Natick v. Massachusetts Dep't of Pub. Welfare, 341 Mass. 618, 171 N.E. 2d 273 (1961).

(B) Definitions in Other State Statutes

While few of the existing state statutes make special provisions for licensing procedures, those which have been enacted evidence general legislative acceptance of the principle of the Model Act that the term should be given a broad application. Thus, the statutes of Colorado[151] and Florida[152] provide that the term license includes not only permits, certificates, approvals, registrations, and charters but also *memberships* and *statutory exemptions.* Indiana[153] also contains specific reference to *membership;* Massachusetts[154] refers specifically to *any authority;* and Ohio[155] includes in the definition *any commission.* The newer statutes in Oklahoma[156] and Rhode Island[157] adopt the definition found in the Revised Model State Act.

---

151 Colo. Rev. Stat. Ann. § 3-16-1(g).
152 Fla. Stat. § 120.21(5).
153 Ind. Ann. Stat. § 63-3002.
154 Mass. Gen. Laws Ann. ch. 30A, § 13.
155 Ohio Rev. Code Ann. § 119.01(B).
156 Okla. Stat. tit. 75, § 301(3).
157 R.I. Gen. Laws Ann. § 42-35-1(c); *cf.,* Ga. Code Ann. § 3A-101.

CHAPTER V

CONSTITUTIONAL REQUIREMENTS OF NOTICE AND OPPORTUNITY TO BE HEARD

Section 1

Scope Note

To an ever increasing extent, provisions are appearing in state statutes, requiring that before an administrative agency takes any action which will significantly affect private rights, the agency must give notice and afford interested parties an opportunity to be heard. This legislative trend reflects a deep-seated conviction that as a matter of sound governmental policy, parties to be affected by administrative action should have a full opportunity to present their views before any official action is taken. Thus, the Revised Model State Act requires notice in rule-making proceedings[1] as well as in contested cases,[2] and includes special provisions designed to assure the fairness of hearing procedures in cases involving the grant or denial and the revocation or suspension of licenses.[3] In many states which have not adopted the Model Act, the statutes delegating specified powers to particular agencies set forth in considerable detail the type of notice and the nature of the opportunity for hearing that must be afforded. These statutes often go much further, in requiring notice and opportunity for hearing, than is required by the courts as a matter of constitutional right.

The application and interpretation of such statutory provisions will be discussed, *infra,* in the chapters dealing with rule making and the adjudication of contested cases. The present chapter is concerned with the question: In the absence of statute,

1 Section 3.
2 Section 9.
3 Section 14.

under what circumstances will notice and opportunity for hearing be required by the courts as a matter of constitutional necessity?

Section 2

Historical Development

The question as to the constitutional necessity of notice and hearing arises, of course, only in cases where an agency asserts the right to make *ex parte* determinations. It is not in all cases that (in the absence of statutory requirements for hearings) the agencies assert such a right. In many cases, recognizing that they can better perform their functions if they act only after obtaining all the information that can be obtained from the private parties involved, agencies voluntarily, by formal or informal processes, give the parties in interest full opportunity to discuss with agency representatives the problem involved, and to explore mutually the advisability of alternative solutions to that problem. It is only in cases where the agency officials believe that such conferences would not be fruitful that a difficulty arises.

In such cases, the difficulty revolves principally around the fact that administrative agencies, although deciding cases individually (as do courts), may dispose of them on considerations of policy, acting as legislative agents. The affected party, looking at the ruling as an individual disposition of his particular case, demands a right to be heard fully; he feels he should have his "day in court." However, the agency, treating the ruling only as an incidental step in the development of a general policy, which it must determine on the basis of broad considerations that would be but little affected by the testimony of the individual as to the facts of his own case, often prefers to act legislatively on the basis of its own information and judgment, without granting a hearing.

The assessment of property for local *ad valorem* taxes affords a typical example. The taxpayer, mightily concerned with a potential increase in his tax bill, insists that he should have an opportunity to appear before the assessors, and explain why the true cash value of his property is less than the sum at which the tax officials propose to assess it. But the assessors, desiring to base their actions exclusively on their own complicated formulas, believe that to hear each taxpayer separately would be a waste of time.

Again, in the case of ordering grade separations at intersections of railroads and busy highways, the public utility commissions believe that their conclusions can best be predicated on such ascertainable data as traffic counts and crossing-accident statistics. The railroad owner, facing the possible necessity of having to spend many thousand dollars on the construction of the grade separation, is, *per contra,* outraged if he is denied the opportunity to present to the commissioners the arguments which in his opinion demonstrate the lack of necessity for a grade separation.

The fundamental legal problem involved in each such case is one as to the requirements of due process of law; and the historical development of this broad constitutional requirement has been reflected in changing theories as to the requirements that should be imposed on administrative agencies. In the eighteenth century, English courts were strongly inclined to insist on notice and court-like, adversary hearing procedures, in all administrative proceedings.[4] But as experience demonstrated that too great insistence on formality in hearing procedures interfered with the effectiveness of administrative adjudication, the courts exhibited a willingness to permit such modification as practical necessities required. Thus, the rule was early evolved in tax cases that constitutional requirements were satisfied if a hearing was given at any stage of the proceedings prior to the final non-reviewable determination and collection of the tax.

The eminently practical approach adopted in the field of taxation demonstrated the desirability of devising substitute procedures that would effectively guard the interests served by formal adversary-type hearings. But, unfortunately, for a long time the courts failed to apply in other fields the precept furnished by the practice in tax cases. By and large, the courts (until the last forty years) overlooked the development of efficient substitutes for formal notice and hearing, and were on the whole inclined to hold either that notice and hearing could be dispensed with entirely, or that a formal court-like procedure would be required. Thus, in one case[5] it was held that a statute which provided for the seizure and public sale of estrayed calves was void because

---

[4] MOTT, DUE PROCESS OF LAW 216-40 (1926).

[5] Lacey v. Lemmons, 22 N.M. 54, 159 Pac. 949 (1916).

it made no provision for notice to the owner—despite the fact that the owner was unknown and that notice and an opportunity for hearing was in fact given to the person in possession of the calves at the time they were seized.

In more recent years, the conceptual (not to say mechanical) approach of the earlier decisions has been quite generally abandoned in favor of the view that so long as procedures are devised which guard the private interests served by the constitutional guaranties, administrative action will not be held invalid because of the lack of formal, adversary proceedings before the agency.

The current view has been stated by the California Court of Appeals:

> . . . when the Legislature has determined that summary powers must be exercised by administrative bodies in order to protect the public, they may do so without prior notice or hearing provided that there may be a subsequent administrative or judicial review thereof.[6]

Thus, when an insurance company sought to enjoin the insurance commission from taking over the company's assets in a summary conservatorship proceeding, the court declined to issue the injunction on the grounds that to delay the conservatorship while determining the motives and justification of the commission would defeat the legislative purpose—the assets might be dissipated while the hearing was pending. The court said: "Although the requirements of due process often involve a prior full hearing, it has long been recognized that where public necessity requires, there can be action followed by a hearing."[7] Similarly, the California court upheld the suspension of a driver's license for failure to deposit security after an accident, since there was opportunity for adequate judicial review of the administrative determination, and the compelling public interest in getting

---

[6] Hesperia Land Dev. Co. v. Superior Court of Los Angeles County, 184 Cal. App. 2d 865, 7 Cal. Rptr. 815 (1960), approving the issuance, without formal hearing, of a temporary cease and desist order by the real estate commissioner to prevent subdividers from continuing sale of subdivision lots pending determination of the adequacy of the water supply.

[7] Financial Indem. Co. v. Superior Court, 45 Cal. 2d 395, 401, 289 P.2d 233 (1955).

financially irresponsible drivers off the road justified the summary action.[8]

The Illinois court held that a "blighted areas redevelopment act" was not invalid because of its failure to require notice to property owners prior to hearings before the state housing board, since the owners could obtain a full hearing in the condemnation proceedings which followed the determination of the housing board.[9]

In broad terms, the Missouri court stated that due process is satisfied if there is either an administrative hearing subject to judicial review or the right to have a hearing in a court which may adequately review the administrative determination.[10]

These cases represent the prevailing view. It is a view which recognizes that under some circumstances, where private rights cannot otherwise be properly protected, there must be a full hearing prior to administrative action; and that normally this is the desirable procedure; but that nevertheless, where there is a compelling public interest in summary action, administrative action may precede notice and hearing, providing that the private parties adversely affected thereby may—either in subsequent administrative proceedings or upon judicial review—obtain an adequate review of their assertions that their legal rights have been denied. It is a view which also recognizes that in some situations—for example, determining the safety of a parachute or determining whether wheat is of the highest grade—determinations based on test may be better than determinations based on the testimony of opposing experts, provided always that an opportunity is made available, on motion for rehearing, to compile a record of testimony so as to permit judicial review. Finally, it is a view which recognizes that in some situations, informal conferences may be more conducive to the goal of fully informed administrative determinations than a formal, court-type proceeding would be.

---

[8] Escobedo v. State Dep't of Motor Vehicles, 35 Cal. 2d 870, 222 P.2d 1 (1950).

[9] Ross v. Chicago Land Clearance Comm'n, 413 Ill. 377, 108 N.E.2d 776 (1952).

[10] State *ex rel.* Leggett v. Jensen, 318 S.W.2d 353 (Mo. 1958).

Section 3

Basic Considerations, In Determining Necessity of Notice and Hearing

No general formula can be relied upon to determine whether or not, in a given situation, notice and hearing must precede administrative action.

Primarily, the judicial function is that of striking a balance, in each particular situation, between the public interest in permitting summary action to obtain expeditious realization of the objectives which the agency seeks to accomplish, and the countervailing private interest that there should be full consideration of the rights and privileges of the affected parties before any official action is taken.

Secondly, account must be taken of the tradition in the particular field. Statements of principle made in a case involving one administrative function cannot safely be applied in predicting what result will be reached in a case involving a different agency performing its work in a different field.

Furthermore, not only do the courts tend to follow the accepted tradition in a particular field, but they tend also to restrict their rulings to the particular type of administrative activity with respect to which the ruling was made. Factual distinctions assume great importance. For example, the doctrine permitting summary destruction of fish nets used illegally by a fisherman[11] does not permit similar seizure of the boats which he uses to conduct his illegal fishing operations.[12] More important, the fact that the requirements of notice and hearing have become attenuated in a particular field, by a gradual process of judicial erosion, does not mean that the same flexibility of procedure will be tolerated in an analogous case where administrative supervision is an unaccustomed innovation.

But the divergent traditions obtaining in various fields of administrative activity can be rationalized, and the warp and woof of seemingly conflicting decisions can be spun into whole cloth, by reference to the underlying policy factors which (more frequently than judicial opinions indicate) motivate decision. In

---

11 Lawton v. Steele, 152 U.S. 133, 38 L. Ed. 385, 14 Sup. Ct. 499 (1894).
12 Colon v. Lisk, 153 N.Y. 188, 47 N.E. 302, 60 Am. St. 609 (1897).

reaching their decisions, courts probe into considerations lying far beneath the surface of the readily seen.

One such consideration is the importance to the private parties involved of the repercussions of a particular administrative activity, and the immediacy of the effect. Where private property of a particular person is singled out for specific action, notice and hearing are ordinarily deemed appropriate.[13] More particularly is this the case where the property interest involved is of substantial value. On the other hand, where the number of persons affected by the administrative determination is large, and where the order will not directly impinge on private rights of person or property, the necessity of notice and hearing is less persuasively indicated. This result is prompted in part by the practical difficulties involved in hearing large numbers of persons before taking action; further, the courts sense the difficulty of aligning the interests of thousands of parties and resolving many individual complaints into clear-cut issues.[14]

Closely related to this factor is another. As a result of judicial experience, courts know that in some types of inquiries, a formal hearing is less well calculated to reveal the truth than is private investigation and inspection. In such cases, notice and formal hearing will not ordinarily be required.[15]

Decision is influenced somewhat by the court's confidence in the agency. A court that views with doubts and misgivings the functioning of a given agency is naturally inclined to repress that agency's freedom of discretionary action. It can often be most efficiently repressed by insistence that the agency must proceed only on the basis of a record which is shown to contain substantial evidence to support the agency's conclusions. Coupled with this is the counter tendency (particularly in cases where it is believed administrative action is not likely to be ill-advised or, even if in error, not likely to be a cause of irreparable injury) to waive insistence upon a hearing in advance of administrative action, where there is adequate opportunity for correcting administrative mistakes upon judicial review.

---

[13] State v. Weinstein, 322 S.W.2d 778 (Mo. 1959), requiring a hearing as to relocation of privately owned pipelines; McCarthy v. Coos Head Timber Co., 208 Ore. 371, 302 P.2d 238 (1956).

[14] Sherwin v. Mackie, 364 Mich. 188, 111 N.W.2d 56 (1961).

[15] White v. State Industrial Acc. Comm'n, 227 Ore. 306, 362 P.2d 302 (1961).

The suggestion is found in some of the older cases (and in some texts) that in determining the constitutional necessity of notice and hearing, an important factor is the classification of the agency's function as legislative or judicial. The suggested rule is that a hearing is required if the agency is exercising judicial functions, and is not required if the agency is exercising legislative functions.

This supposed test cannot, however, be relied on as an actual guide to decision. While some courts do apparently give some weight to the classification of the agency's function as legislative or judicial, in deciding whether there exists a constitutional right to notice and hearing (and are more inclined to insist on the allowance thereof if the agency's function is judicial) it is believed that these labels have always played a much smaller part in actual judicial decision than in opinion writing. The labelling of a function as judicial or legislative was often the result of, rather than the basis of, the court's decision on the constitutional question. In any event, it is clear that the supposed rule has lost its popularity; and the nature of the agency's function is not often spoken of, in current decisions, as the basis for decision on the constitutional issue. In fact, hearings are required in some types of cases where the agency's function is essentially legislative in character, if the considerations outlined above dictate the advisability of insisting on a hearing.[16]

The application of the general considerations above described may be illustrated in various types of administrative activity.

Section 4

Public Safety Cases

In cases where the administrative agency acts in the interest of preserving the public safety (in such areas as abating nuisances that might imperil the public health or morals), the underlying policy factors that motivate decision come clearly to light. The courts balance the immediacy of the public danger against the

[16] State *ex rel.* Chicago, R.I. & Pac. R.R. v. Public Serv. Comm'n, 355 S.W.2d 45 (Mo. 1962); Chicago, M. & St. P. Ry. v. Board of R.R. Comm'rs, 76 Mont. 305, 247 Pac. 162 (1926); City of Passaic v. City of Clifton, 14 N.J. 136, 101 A.2d 530 (1953); *cf.* Bailey v. Council of the Div. of Planning & Dev., 22 N.J. 366, 126 A.2d 189 (1956).

substantiality of the property interest involved, in determining whether summary action, without notice and opportunity for hearing, involves a deprival of constitutional guaranties.[17]

It has long been established that in such cases as the destruction of putrid food,[18] or the quarantining of persons suffering from contagious diseases,[19] the administrative agency may proceed summarily, so long as some opportunity is afforded the private parties to establish, after the event, that the administrative determination was erroneous, and (upon such showing) obtain appropriate redress.

Similar considerations govern suspension of drivers' licenses (at least in cases where a prior conviction in criminal court affords the same sort of protection that would be afforded by a hearing in connection with the license revocation proceedings),[20] or the temporary seizure of liquor, pending judicial determination of the alleged violations of law.[21] The great public interest in avoiding bank insolvencies has been held to permit summary seizure of banks by the superintendent of banking.[22] Some courts have gone far in sustaining summary proceedings as to property legislatively declared to be a nuisance, even though there might be doubt whether the particular property seized under the statute was in fact being so used as to constitute a nuisance.[23]

---

[17] Summary action is more often permitted where the dollar value of the property involved is small. Thus, in *Lawton v. Steele,* 152 U.S. 133, 38 L. Ed. 385, 14 Sup. Ct. 499 (1894), the court, in upholding summary destruction of fish nets maintained in alleged violation of a state statute, remarked that it would be "belittling the dignity of the judiciary" to require the destruction of "property . . . of trifling value" to be "preceded by a solemn condemnation in a court of justice." Where the fisherman's boats rather than his nets were the subject of the state, it was held that notice and hearing must precede seizure, the court pointing out that the property involved might reach in value many thousands of dollars. Colon v. Lisk, 153 N.Y. 188, 47 N.E. 302, 60 Am. St. 609 (1897). In *Cox v. Cox,* 400 Ill. 291, 79 N.E.2d 497 (1948), the subject of seizure was, as in *Lawton v. Steele,* fish nets; but in the Illinois case the court held that notice and hearing were required, the court pointing out that the nets involved were of much greater value than those involved in the earlier case.

[18] North American Cold Storage Co. v. City of Chicago, 211 U.S. 306, 53 L. Ed. 195, 29 Sup. Ct. 101 (1908).

[19] *Ex parte* Lewis, 328 Mo. 843, 42 S.W.2d 21 (1931); *cf.,* Rock v. Carney, 216 Mich. 280, 185 N.W. 798, 22 A.L.R. 1178 (1921).

[20] Hough v. McCarthy, 54 Cal. 2d 273, 353 P.2d 276 (1960).

[21] People v. Diamond, 233 N.Y. 130, 135 N.E. 200 (1922).

[22] State Sav. & Commercial Bank v. Anderson, 165 Cal. 437, 132 Pac. 755 (1913), *aff'd,* 238 U.S. 611, 59 L. Ed. 1488, 35 Sup. Ct. 792 (1915).

[23] People *ex rel.* Copcutt v. Board of Health, 140 N.Y. 1, 35 N.E. 320, 23 L.R.A. 481, 37 Am. St. 522 (1893); but *cf.* City of Paducah v. Hook Amusement Co., 257 Ky. 19, 77 S.W.2d 383 (1934).

On the other hand, where it plainly appears that no overwhelming public need for speedy action exists, and where summary action might imperil substantial property rights, the courts tend to insist upon advance notice and an opportunity to be heard before administrative action is taken. Thus, seizure and sale of a car allegedly used in connection with the transportation of unstamped whisky, without notice and hearing, was held invalid.[24] Similarly, banning the public showing of a motion picture film, without hearing or opportunity to present evidence, was held to involve a deprival of constitutional rights.[25] Summary destruction of unbranded horses, without notice, was likewise held invalid in absence of a showing that speedy action was necessary.[26]

In some types of cases, where the facts can be ascertained by an objective standard, inspection by an expert offers a more reliable method than does a trial to determine the truth; and in such cases summary action is quite properly justified, where there is any substantial public interest to justify it.[27]

Section 5

Licenses

(A) Summary of Developing Trend

Cases decided during the last decade involving administrative licensing activity demonstrate an ever-increasing acceptance of the principle that notice and opportunity for hearing should be required whenever administrative rulings in licensing cases impinge significantly on individual rights or privileges. There was a time[28] when many courts, accepting a semantic distinction between "property rights" and "mere privileges" held that the grant of a license to engage in specified activities did not create any

[24] Brooks v. McCoy, 192 Tenn. 586, 241 S.W.2d 579 (1951).

[25] William Goldman Theatres, Inc. v. Dana, 405 Pa. 83, 173 A.2d 59 (1961).

[26] Bowden v. Davis, 205 Ore. 421, 289 P.2d 1100 (1955).

[27] As in the case of seizure of cattle having an infectious disease, State v. Schriber, 185 Ore. 615, 205 P.2d 149 (1949); or seizure of bees brought into the state in violation of agricultural regulations, Wyant v. Figy, 340 Mich. 602, 66 N.W.2d 240 (1954); or the detention of persons afflicted with loathsome diseases, State *ex rel.* McBride v. Superior Court, 103 Wash. 409, 174 Pac. 973 (1918); *cf.* State *ex rel.* Fuller v. Mullinax, 364 Mo. 858, 269 S.W.2d 72 (1954), requiring hearing prior to commitment to mental hospital.

[28] *E.g.*, People *ex rel.* Lodes v. Department of Health, 189 N.Y. 187, 82 N.E. 187, 13 L.R.A. (n.s.) 894 (1907).

property rights, and that therefore the license could be revoked without notice and hearing. Thus, a license to engage in a substantial business was equated (despite the considerable investment involved) with a gratuitous grant of permission by a neighbor to walk across his lawn. Both being mere "licenses," and creating no rights of "property," either could be revoked summarily by the grantor, according to this outmoded theory. Obviously, however, a license to walk across another's land does not belong in the same category as a license to conduct a business.

As the unfairness of the above-described conceptual approach became manifest, courts began to abandon it in favor of an approach which accorded greater weight to ideals of fairness of administrative procedure. One of the early points of departure involved cases concerning the revocation of a license to practice a profession. In this area, one court said as early as 1892 that:

> Whether the right to practice law or medicine is property, in the technical sense, it is a valuable franchise, and one of which a person ought not to be deprived, without being offered an opportunity, by timely notice, to defend it.[29]

In subsequent years, this trend has been gradually extended to include other types of licensed activities. Now, it can fairly be said that the courts tend to insist that notice and hearing must normally be accorded in the sphere of licensing, even in the absence of statutory requirement. Only where most compelling considerations of public necessity intervene, may notice and hearing be dispensed with.

The Revised Model State Act not only requires hearing in all cases involving revocation of licenses, but makes a number of related provisions designed to assure fairness of procedures in administrative licensing proceedings. These provisions of the Revised Model State Act, and of cognate statutory provisions in states which have adopted parallel legislation, are explored in Chapter XIV *infra*.

(B) Early Cases Not Requiring Notice and Hearing

Typical of the early cases which transferred to the field of administrative law the conveyancer's distinction between "prop-

---

[29] State v. Schultz, 11 Mont. 429, 433, 28 Pac. 643 (1892).

erty rights" and "mere licenses" is the often cited decision of the New York court in 1907, declaring (with reference to a license to sell milk):

> In other words, a license is not a contract or property, but merely a temporary permit issued in the exercise of the police powers to do that which would otherwise be prohibited. . . . the permit itself cannot be treated as property in any legal or constitutional sense, but was a mere license revocable by the power that was authorized to issue it.[30]

The same reasoning has been applied in a variety of cases, involving drivers' licenses,[31] lobster fishers,[32] and theaters.[33] In fact, candor requires recognition of the fact that, although this approach may properly be condemned as old fashioned, it has not yet entirely disappeared.[34]

Many of the decisions which held that notice and hearing would not be required in license revocation proceedings involved situations where in fact notice and hearing had been given in judicial proceedings that established a basis for revocation of the license; and the results may therefore be justified on the basis that there was no need for a second hearing to establish the licensee's guilt.[35]

---

[30] People *ex rel.* Lodes v. Department of Health, note 28 *supra,* 189 N.Y. at 192-3.

[31] Nulter v. State Road Comm'n, 119 W. Va. 312, 193 S.E. 549, 194 S.E. 270 (1937).

[32] State v. Cote, 122 Me. 450, 120 Atl. 538 (1923).

[33] Thayer Amusement Corp. v. Moulton, 63 R.I. 182, 7 A.2d 682, 124 A.L.R. 236 (1939).

[34] Richmond County v. Glanton, 209 Ga. 733, 76 S.E.2d 65 (1953); Yellow Cab Taxi Serv. v. City of Twin Falls, 68 Idaho 145, 190 P.2d 681 (1948); Michael v. Town of Logan, 247 Iowa 574, 73 N.W.2d 714 (1956); Pinzino v. Supervisor of Liquor Control, 334 S.W.2d 20 (Mo. 1960); Ledgering v. State, 385 P.2d 522 (Wash. 1963); State v. Stehlek, 262 Wis. 642, 56 N.W.2d 514 (1953).

[35] Thus, in *State ex rel. Nowotny v. City of Milwaukee,* 140 Wis. 38, 121 N.W. 658 (1909), a milk peddler's license was revoked only after he had been convicted of selling impure milk—quite likely, the administrative agency had helped prosecute the criminal proceedings. Similarly, in *People ex rel. Lodes v. Department of Health,* 189 N.Y. 187, 82 N.E. 187, 13 L.R.A. (n.s.) 894 (1907), the licensee had been convicted not once, but four times, of selling adulterated milk.

(C) THE CURRENT TREND TO REQUIRE NOTICE AND HEARING

(1) Revocation of Licenses

During the last ten years, the courts have come to hold with increasing frequency that notice and an opportunity to be heard must be afforded prior to the revocation of a license to engage in a profession,[36] or a license to engage in a business not in the "public risk" category, *e.g.,* the liquor business, or the conduct of dance halls or horse races. Thus, notice and hearing have been held necessary in connection with the revocation of a license to engage in the operation of a bus line,[37] an amusement park,[38] a school of cosmetology,[39] a second-hand car dealership,[40] an insurance business,[41] a barber college,[42] or a drive-in theater.[43]

Typical of the current approach is the language of the New York court in 1954 (contrasting strangely with the language employed by the same court in 1907 in the *Lodes* case, *supra*) in holding that revocation of a hack driver's license was void, for lack of proper notice and hearing, when the agency revoked the license on evidence of violations somewhat different from those specified in a notice which had been given the driver. Holding that the shift in the grounds for revocation, without affording adequate opportunity to the cab driver to meet the new grounds, involved a violation of due process, the court said:

> . . . petitioner had a constitutionally guaranteed right to know in advance of the hearing that that evidence would be considered. That he did not have, and that is sufficient reason to set aside the determination of the administrative body . . . Revocation of a license—even where the same rested within the discretion of an administrative official—is not a legislative act. . . . It is clearly not a merely administrative act concerned with the internal functioning of the agency

---

[36] Prouty v. Heron, 127 Colo. 168, 255 P.2d 755 (1953); Smith v. Department of Registration & Educ., 412 Ill. 332, 106 N.E.2d 722 (1952); Bechler v. Parsekian, 36 N.J. 242, 176 A.2d 470 (1961); Alpert v. Board of Governors of City Hosp., 286 App. Div. 542, 145 N.Y.S.2d 534 (1955).

[37] City of Miami v. South Miami Coach Lines, Inc., 59 So. 2d 52 (Fla. 1952).

[38] Eastwood Park Amusement Co. v. Mayor, 325 Mich. 60, 38 N.W.2d 77 (1949).

[39] Gilchrist v. Bierring, 234 Iowa 899, 14 N.W.2d 724 (1944).

[40] State *ex rel.* Ellis v. Kelly, 145 W. Va. 70, 112 S.E.2d 641 (1960).

[41] Bankers Life & Cas. Co. v. Cravey, 208 Ga. 682, 69 S.E.2d 87 (1952).

[42] Parker v. Board of Barber Examiners, 84 So. 2d 80 (La. App. 1955).

[43] Central States Theatre Corp. v. Sar, 245 Iowa 1254, 66 N.W.2d 450 (1954).

itself, but is a judicial or quasi-judicial function of the administrative body.[44]

The principle extends to other cases not involving substantial investment in a business. It extends, for example, to the revocation of drivers' licenses, for causes other than the preservation of the public safety.[45]

When the license concerns a business involving a risk to public morals or safety, the courts are less inclined to insist on notice and hearing. As noted by the California court: "On the question of the constitutional power to authorize revocation of licenses in certain business involving dangers to the public without notice and hearing there is considerable uncertainty in the cases."[46]

California has determined, on grounds which should commend themselves to administrative officials, that (except in cases where summary action is clearly necessary to protect the public safety) there must be notice and hearing before an agency may deny or revoke a license to engage even in those businesses which, because of the risk involved, the state may regulate to the point of prohibition. Thus, in a case involving an application for a license to operate games of chance, the court held that an agency should no more assume to act without hearing on a license application than would a court.[47] Similarly, insisting upon notice and hearing on an application for a beer license, the California court declared:

> It would be preposterous to concede that any judicial tribunal could be clothed with the arbitrary power of issuing licenses and regulating business subject only to its own caprice; that with or without a hearing on the merits of the application, with or without reason, or upon *ex parte* statements or rumors, with no opportunity of refuting them, the board could grant or deny a petition for license. . . . Law contemplates justice whether it is granted as a privilege or recognized as a vested right.[48]

---

[44] Hecht v. Monaghan, 307 N.Y. 461, 469, 473, 121 N.E.2d 421 (1954).

[45] Ratliff v. Lampton, 32 Cal. 2d 226, 195 P.2d 792 (1948); State v. Moseng, 254 Minn. 263, 95 N.W.2d 6 (1959); Bechler v. Parsekian, 36 N.J. 242, 176 A.2d 470 (1961); De Lynn v. MacDuff, 305 N.Y. 501, 114 N.E.2d 12 (1953); Wignall v. Fletcher, 303 N.Y. 435, 103 N.E.2d 728 (1952).

[46] Carroll v. California Horse Racing Bd., 16 Cal. 2d 164, 168, 105 P.2d 110 (1940).

[47] Fascination, Inc. v. Hoover, 39 Cal. 2d 260, 246 P.2d 656 (1952).

[48] Martin v. Board of Supervisors, 135 Cal. App. 96, 102, 26 P.2d 843 (1933). See also, Irvine v. State Bd. of Equalization, 40 Cal. App. 2d 280, 104 P.2d 847 (1940); Carroll v. California Horse Racing Bd., note 46 *supra.*

But not all state courts have followed the lead of California. A number continue to hold that where the license involves the operation of a business characterized by a high measure of risk to the public, the public interest justifies revocation without notice and hearing. Such decisions have been rendered with respect to beer or liquor licenses[49] and horse-racing.[50]

(2) Suspension of Licenses

Since the suspension of a license, as opposed to its revocation, involves merely a temporary interference with the conduct of the licensee's business, ordinarily entailing much less serious consequences than the revocation of a license (which puts him out of business altogether), it is sometimes held that a temporary suspension may be justified without opportunity for notice and hearing, where a real need for prompt action has been established.[51] In cases where an acute need for speedy action can be demonstrated, the device of temporarily suspending a license, until the licensee can give assurance that future operations will be properly conducted, affords a method of adequately protecting the public interest without undue harm to the licensee. Some agencies are developing this technique, independently of statutory provisions, as a means of meeting the difficult license revocation problem. It offers wide opportunities.

(3) Application for Licenses

When application is made to an administrative agency for the issuance of a license, there is of course no problem as to notice, and ordinarily no question is presented as to the necessity of affording a hearing. The informal procedural techniques of the agencies are well adapted to the investigation of applications for licenses. The judicial technique of a hearing is displaced by the administrative mechanics of the questionnaire and written state-

---

[49] Walker v. City of Clinton, 244 Iowa 1099, 59 N.W.2d 785 (1953); Hornstein v. Illinois Liquor Control Comm'n, 412 Ill. 365, 106 N.E.2d 354 (1952); Pinzino v. Supervisor of Liquor Control, 334 S.W.2d 20 (Mo. 1960); State *ex rel.* Camper v. Pollard, 189 Tenn. 86, 222 S.W.2d 374 (1949); Green Mountain Post No. 1, American Legion v. Liquor Control Bd., 117 Vt. 405, 94 A.2d 230 (1953).

[50] Fink v. Cole, 1 N.Y.2d 48, 150 N.Y.S.2d 175, 133 N.E.2d 691 (1956).

[51] State Bd. of Medical Examiners v. Weiner, 68 N.J. Super. 468, 172 A.2d 661 (1961); Halsey, Stuart & Co. v. Public Serv. Comm'n, 212 Wis. 184, 248 N.W. 458 (1933).

ment. Frequently, the license is granted on the basis of the application as filed. If the application is deemed insufficient to present all the desired information, or if the agency wishes to demand additional assurances from the applicant, he may be informally advised of what must be added to his application to secure favorable action. Usually, the only purpose of a hearing is to insure that the agency obtains the information and assurances that it insists upon as a prerequisite to the issuance of a license; and the license seeker, approaching the agency in propitiatory mood, willingly suits his convenience to the agency's desires.

A distinction should be noted (although it is not often the subject of discussion in court opinions) between the granting and the denial of license applications. If the outcome of the case is the granting of the license, the applicant cares little whether he has been granted a hearing or not; it is the grant of the license that is important. It is only in cases where the agency proposes to deny the license that the question as to the applicant's right to a hearing becomes acute. In such cases, the situation is closely akin to that of proceedings to revoke a license; and, at least where decision is based on a finding of fact, it seems clear that the same considerations should apply as in cases involving the revocation of licenses. And this, clearly, is the trend of the decisions. The teaching of the United States Supreme Court[52] that an applicant for a license to practice before the Board of Tax Appeals "should not have been rejected upon charges of his unfitness without giving him an opportunity by notice for hearing and answer," resting as it does on federal constitutional grounds, should be deemed controlling when this question arises in state courts. Both the California[53] and New York[54] courts recognize, as the New York court put it in the last-cited case, that an application for a license may not be refused on the grounds of the applicant's unfitness "unless the applicant has a fair opportunity to meet a challenge to his good character. . . ."[55]

---

52 Goldsmith v. United States Bd. of Tax Appeals, 270 U.S. 117, 70 L. Ed. 494, 46 Sup. Ct. 215 (1926).

53 Fascination, Inc. v. Hoover, note 47 *supra*. Martin v. Board of Supervisors, 135 Cal. App. 96, 26 P.2d 843 (1933).

54 Brown v. Murphy, 34 Misc. 2d 151, 224 N.Y.S.2d 423 (1962); Perpente v. Moss, 293 N.Y. 325, 56 N.E.2d 726 (1944).

55 See also, Application of Burke, 87 Ariz. 336, 351 P.2d 169 (1960); Appli-

In cases where the granting of a license is fundamentally a ministerial function, the administrative action is subject to control by mandamus, which proceeding offers the right to notice and hearing.

Section 6

Interference With Substantial Rights of Person or Property

When an agency is engaged in the regulation of private business (as opposed to activities which can be described as the conduct of the public business), and likewise where an agency's activities impinge directly on matters involving the personal liberties of private citizens, notice and an opportunity for hearing are quite uniformly required.

Typical of the cases in this category are those involving the fixing of rates or prices. This function has been characterized as legislative by the federal courts and by some of the state courts. It is classed as "rule-making" in the Federal Administrative Procedure Act[56] and as "adjudication" (*i.e.,* as a "contested case") in the Revised Model State Act.[57] But the diversity of classification has not affected the decision of the courts as to the necessity for notice and hearing in rate-fixing cases. The courts have not considered them simply as instances to be governed by general rules applicable to all rule-making activities (or, in the state courts characterizing rate-fixing as judicial, by any general rules applicable to all judicial activities). Thus, the rate-fixing cases demonstrate the fallacy of the ancient hornbook suggestion that notice and hearing are required in cases where agencies act judicially, but are not required in cases where agencies act legislatively. Rather, the courts have required or excused notice and hearing on the basis of far more practical considerations.

Normally, the order in a rate-fixing case affects a single company or a well-defined group of companies engaged in the sale of a particular commodity or service. As a practical matter, the

---

cation of Warren, 149 Conn. 266, 178 A.2d 528 (1962); Albert v. Public Serv. Comm'n, 209 Md. 27, 120 A.2d 346 (1956). The problem is discussed in Byse, *Opportunity to be Heard in License Issuance,* 101 U. PA. L. REV. 57 (1952).

[56] 5 U.S.C. § 1001(c); F.C.A. 5 § 1001(c).

[57] Section 1(2).

agency must refer to the records of the company in order to obtain complete and reliable information of the sort needed to permit it to make a fully informed judgment as to what rate is proper. It would be unthinkable to permit an agency to fix rates merely on the basis of guesswork when reliable information may conveniently be obtained by giving notice to the companies affected, and affording them an opportunity to be heard. Therefore, notice and hearing are required.[58]

On the other hand, where an agency is engaged in the type of price-fixing conducted by the Office of Price Administration in World War II, the justification of its order does not depend upon disputed facts which singularly concern individual parties, nor upon information which can best be obtained from them. In the O.P.A. type of case, determination is based on broad economic postulates best susceptible to investigation by the methods of skilled economists and statisticians. Accordingly, the United States Supreme Court held that there was no denial of due process in the circumstance that orders of O.P.A. fixing maximum prices became effective without the parties affected having had an opportunity to be heard.[59] It would seem that the state courts would reach a similar result.[60]

Closely related to the rate-fixing cases are those involving the imposition of liability upon employers for payment of workmen's compensation awards. Here again, the courts insist on the giving of notice and opportunity to be heard as to the amount which may properly be chargeable to a particular employer.[61]

In the field of zoning—another area in which administrative activity impinges significantly on substantial property rights—it is held that notice and hearing must precede the granting of

---

[58] Lombardo Wine Co. v. Taylor, 407 Ill. 454, 95 N.E.2d 607 (1950)—price posting; Massachusetts Medical Serv. v. Commissioner of Ins., 344 Mass. 335, 182 N.E.2d 298 (1962); Railroad & Warehouse Comm'n v. Chicago & No. W. Ry., 256 Minn. 227, 98 N.W.2d 60 (1959); Colteryahn Sanitary Dairy v. Milk Control Comm'n, 332 Pa. 15, 1 A.2d 775, 122 A.L.R. 1049 (1938); Glen Oaks Utils., Inc. v. Houston, 161 Tex. 417, 340 S.W.2d 783 (1960); McGrew v. Industrial Comm'n, 96 Utah 203, 85 P.2d 608 (1938).

[59] Bowles v. Willingham, 321 U.S. 503, 88 L. Ed. 892, 64 Sup. Ct. 641 (1944).

[60] *Cf.*, State *ex rel.* State Bd. of Milk Control v. Newark Milk Co., 118 N.J. Eq. 504, 179 Atl. 116 (1935); Spokane Hotel Co. v. Younger, 113 Wash. 359, 194 Pac. 595 (1920).

[61] Trellsite Foundry & Stamping Co. v. Enterprise Foundry, 365 Mich. 209, 112 N.W.2d 476 (1961); Pioneer Mills Co. v. Webster, 186 Okla. 616, 99 P.2d 507 (1940).

a variance from the established requirements of a zoning ordinance,[62] for the eminently practical reason that it is unfair to enter orders which might decrease the value of neighboring owners' properties without hearing their views on the matter. On the other hand, when a municipal council determines to accept or reject a zoning ordinance, there is no necessity of giving notice and hearing to all property owners in the municipality, for there is no reason to suppose that the holding of a town meeting would lead to a more fully informed decision.[63]

In cases involving personal liberty or other purely personal rights, the balance is even clearer than in cases where the administrative determination directly affects an individual's private property rights. Plainly, in the personal liberty cases, notice and hearing are required. Thus, an order of commitment to a mental institution is not valid if made without notice and an opportunity for hearing.[64] While the courts are not in full agreement, the trend of decision seems to be toward holding that in passing on applications of prisoners for parole, hearing must be afforded.[65]

An order disbarring an individual from practice before a state agency must be based on notice and hearing,[66] and the same is true of proceedings involving an alleged discrimination in employment because of race.[67]

Section 7

Taxation

There is obviously a danger of deprivation of substantial property rights if administrative proceedings for assessing and collect-

62 Protomastro v. Board of Adjustment of Hoboken, 3 N.J. 494, 70 A.2d 873 (1950).

63 Burke v. Board of Representatives of Stamford, 148 Conn. 33, 166 A.2d 849 (1961); Griggs v. Borough of Princeton, 33 N.J. 207, 162 A.2d 862 (1960).

64 Petition of O'Leary, 325 Mass. 179, 89 N.E.2d 769 (1950).

65 McGee v. Arizona State Bd. of Pardons & Paroles, 92 Ariz. 317, 376 P.2d 779 (1962); State *ex rel.* Murray v. Swenson, 196 Md. 222, 76 A.2d 150 (1950); Juliane v. Chemung County Court, 282 App. Div. 822, 123 N.Y.S.2d 610 (1953); State v. Haddock, 241 N.C. 182, 84 S.E.2d 548 (1954); City of Cleveland v. Hutcherson, 97 Ohio App. 227, 114 N.E.2d 611 (1953); *Contra: Ex parte* Anderson, 191 Ore. 409, 229 P.2d 633 (1951); *In re* Larsen, 44 Cal. 2d 642, 283 P.2d 1043 (1955); Washburn v. Utecht, 236 Minn. 31, 51 N.W.2d 657 (1952).

66 Industrial Acc. Bd. v. O'Dowd, 157 Tex. 432, 303 S.W.2d 763 (1957).

67 Lesniak v. Fair Employment Practices Comm'n, 364 Mich. 495, 111 N.W.2d 790 (1961).

ing taxes are permitted to proceed without notice and hearing. At the same time, there is an equally obvious need that the collection of the public revenues be permitted to proceed expeditiously without the interruptions and delays that might be caused by elaborate procedures for individual notice and lengthy hearings on questions of valuation. For these reasons, and as well the reason that it is one of the most ancient spheres of administrative action, the tax field is an interesting one in which to observe the interplay of competing policies.

In favor of requiring notice and an opportunity to be heard are the factors: (1) the private property of an individual is singled out for specific action; (2) the pecuniary interest of the taxpayer is ordinarily substantial; and (3) the administrative authorities have but little occasion to exercise expert discretion in fixing policies, for it is rather their duty to apply reasonably objective standards which on the whole are adaptable to judicial review. On the other hand, equally potent factors require that the assessors and tax collecting authorities be relieved of the burdens that would attend the giving of individual notice and a full hearing in each case: (1) there is the overpowering necessity for prompt collection of the necessary public revenues; (2) the large number of cases to be disposed of requires the use of summary procedures; (3) many of the issues involved, such as the question of valuation of property, can be better determined by inspection, investigation, and the exercise of the assessor's informed judgment, than by a judicial hearing at which the contradictory estimates of opposing expert witnesses on the question of valuation would be of little practical help; and (4) the fact that judicial review is usually available for issues affecting jurisdiction, construction of the statute, uniformity of the levy, and claims of fraud—that there may thus be a hearing after the event—is often thought to excuse a failure to give notice and hearing at the administrative stage.

The result has been that requirements of notice and hearing in the tax field are rather attenuated. While many decisions declare that an owner is entitled to notice of a proceeding against his property, and has a right to be heard,[68] yet it has long

[68] Universal Consol. Oil Co. v. Byram, 25 Cal. 2d 353, 153 P.2d 746 (1944); People *ex rel.* Isaacs v. Johnson, 26 Ill. 2d 268, 186 N.E.2d 346 (1962); International Salt Co. v. Herrick, 367 Mich. 160, 116 N.W.2d 328 (1962); Fifth Street Pier Corp. v. City of Hoboken, 22 N.J. 326, 126 A.2d 6 (1956).

been settled that the requirements of due process are satisfied if there is an opportunity for the owner to present his objections before a competent tribunal at any stage of the proceedings before the command to pay becomes final and irrevocable.[69]

As noted long ago in a classic text: "In general, . . . the protection afforded the taxpayer against arbitrary assessment is sporadic and uncertain."[70] So far as concerns court decisions predicated on due process concepts, this observation remains true. But there has been a tendency over the years to adopt statutory provisions giving a greater opportunity for notice and hearing than strict constitutional necessities require. Absent statute, the courts are apparently influenced by the fact that it has been customary from time immemorial to have summary procedures for the collection of taxes. Doubtless, such procedures were in existence when the concept of notice as an element of due process was first developed. As a result, courts have tended to sustain summary methods in the collection of taxes that would not be tolerated in newer fields of administrative activity. In the tax field, moreover, administrative activity is in many cases largely executive or ministerial, involving little judicial or legislative responsibility. This circumstance likewise has contributed to the attenuated requirements as to notice and hearing which exist in the tax field.

Indeed, in cases where there seems to be but little practical need for notice and hearing—where the measure of the tax is fixed by mechanical standards, as in the case of a poll tax, or an assessment measured by the size of the property—notice and hearing can apparently be dispensed with.[71]

Notice need not be formal. It is enough if the statute gives general notice that taxes will be levied,[72] or if a general notice of a meeting of the tax board is published.[73]

---

[69] Nickey v. Mississippi, 292 U.S. 393, 78 L. Ed. 1323, 54 Sup. Ct. 743 (1934); Dietman v. Hunter, 5 Ill. 2d 486, 126 N.E.2d 22 (1955).

[70] DICKINSON, ADMINISTRATIVE JUSTICE AND THE SUPREMACY OF LAW 272 (1927).

[71] Franchise Tax Board v. Superior Court, 36 Cal. 2d 538, 225 P.2d 905 (1950); People *ex rel.* Ruchty v. Saad, 411 Ill. 390, 104 N.E.2d 273 (1952); *cf.*, Oceanic Steam Nav. Co. v. Stranahan, 214 U.S. 320, 53 L. Ed. 1013, 29 Sup. Ct. 671 (1909).

[72] Merchants' & Mfr's Nat'l Bank v. Pennsylvania, 167 U.S. 461, 42 L. Ed. 236, 17 Sup. Ct. 829 (1897).

[73] Wight v. Davidson, 181 U.S. 371, 45 L. Ed. 900, 21 Sup. Ct. 616 (1901).

The taxpayer need not be heard by the administrative officials who made the assessment; he may be compelled to wait. Nor need he be granted hearings at all of the successive stages of administrative activity which precede the final levy of the tax. One hearing is sufficient to constitute due process.[74] It is enough if there is a right to a hearing before the assessing officers, or in connection with administrative appeals, or before a court, either in a suit by the government to collect the tax or a suit by the taxpayer to enjoin the collection thereof or to recover sums paid over to the collector.

Section 8

Conduct of Public Business

Where official action does not affect private rights, constitutional doctrines requiring notice and hearing have little if any application. Some types of administrative activity, concerned with executive action in the conduct of the public business, affect private rights so tangentially that (to the extent that the convenient conduct of the public business requires expeditious action) the courts have been willing to relax requirements for notice and hearing. Thus, notice and hearing are not required in connection with the decision on a request to grant a privilege which the state is free to grant or withhold, in its discretion.[75] But the line between privilege and right is a narrow one, and essentially semantic. Moved by the same considerations which have persuaded legislatures to provide hearings in connection with almost all types of administrative activity, the courts have in the last decade shown an increasing reluctance to approve complete denial of hearings even in cases involving primarily the conduct of the public business.

An illustration of the modern trend is afforded by a New Jersey decision.[76] Two cities, on separate *ex parte* applications, had obtained permission from the department of conservation to build certain structures in a river which flowed through both cities. Neither had received notice of the application of the

---

[74] Michigan Cent. R.R. v. Powers, 201 U.S. 245, 50 L. Ed. 744, 26 Sup. Ct. 459 (1906).

[75] Fortin v. Mayor of Chicopee, 325 Mass. 214, 89 N.E.2d 760 (1950).

[76] City of Passaic v. City of Clifton, 14 N.J. 136, 145, 101 A.2d 530 (1953).

other, and the court considered it doubtful that notice was required. However, the use which the city of Clifton proposed to make would result in extra costs to the city of Passaic. Urging that the city of Clifton should pay at least a share of these extra costs, the city of Passaic appealed to the administrative authorities for relief. The court noted the strong desirability of giving notice and hearing in such instances of administrative activities, even though concerned solely with the conduct of the public business, in these words:

> This case illustrates that the solution of an applicant's water problem can seriously concern other members of the public and provides cogent evidence of the wisdom of the practice which we were told by the Attorney General . . . is now ordinarily followed by the Division, of giving prior notice and hearing before action upon the application.

Traditionally, state civil service commissions were permitted to carry on their public business with little opportunity to the civil servants to be heard on the formulation and implementation of policies which substantially affected them in their means of livelihood. To a considerable extent, this is still true. Thus, the courts have in recent years upheld the actions of civil service authorities in proceeding, without notice and hearing, to cancel an examination and hold a new one,[77] or to furlough a number of employees,[78] or to compel the retirement of employees,[79] or to choose among candidates for a promotion.[80]

But a trend has been developing (based in part upon construction of the enabling acts rather than upon pure doctrines of constitutional law) to insist on the granting of an opportunity for hearing, where the court's sense of fairness suggests that the need therefor is compelling. The New Jersey court, under the leadership of Justice Vanderbilt, has been in the forefront of this significant new departure from the easy formula of former days which held that where no rights of private property were involved, there was no need for hearing. Thus, in one case,[81] it was held that where plaintiff made application to the civil service

[77] Moore v. Civil Serv. Comm'n, 333 Mass. 430, 131 N.E.2d 179 (1956).

[78] Kusza v. Maximonis, 363 Pa. 479, 70 A.2d 329 (1950).

[79] Board of Educ. of Jersey City v. Cuff, 38 N.J. 430, 185 A.2d 833 (1962).

[80] Falcey v. Civil Serv. Comm'n, 16 N.J. 117, 106 A.2d 549 (1954).

[81] Weaver v. Department of Civil Serv., 6 N.J. 553, 79 A.2d 305 (1951). *Accord,* Taylor v. Lee, 119 Utah 302, 226 P.2d 531 (1951).

commission for a hearing on the question of the legality of his dismissal from his job, he was entitled to a full hearing on his contention that his dismissal was politically inspired. In another case,[82] where a civil service commission, after first refusing a police officer a hearing on his dismissal, later reversed itself and granted a hearing, it was held to be error for the commission to have failed to give the borough which had discharged the officer an opportunity to participate in the hearing.[83]

The trend has also manifested itself in New York.[84] In a case in which a civil service commission, finding that an insufficient number of candidates had passed an examination, made an adjustment in grades on the basis of a conversion formula, the court held it was improper to do this without notice, saying:

> Such body may not, however, lawfully adjust the required passing grade for part of a written examination, unless it notifies the candidates in advance of the examination by duly promulgated rule or otherwise, that such an adjustment may be made, and discloses the method and factors to be used in determining such adjustment.

Absent statutory provisions (which, fortunately, are found in many states), the removal of school teachers without notice and hearing is ordinarily upheld, whether the removal is for cause,[85] or because of a reduction in force,[86] or because of the abolition of the job.[87]

Similarly, the clear weight of authority supports the power of the state to remove public officers from office without notice or hearing. Presumably, the decisions to this effect are motivated by the overwhelming public interest in preventing corruption or inefficiency in public office.[88]

---

82 Borough of Park Ridge v. Salimone, 36 N.J. Super. 485, 21 N.J. 28, 116 A.2d 532 (1955).

83 See also, Currigan v. Stone, 136 Colo. 326, 317 P.2d 1044 (1957); Handlon v. Town of Belleville, 4 N.J. 99, 71 A.2d 624 (1950).

84 Hymes v. Schechter, 6 N.Y.2d 352, 357, 160 N.E.2d 627 (1959).

85 Di Genova v. State Bd. of Educ., 45 Cal. 2d 255, 288 P.2d 862 (1955).

86 Hankenson v. Board of Educ., 10 Ill. 2d 560, 141 N.E.2d 5 (1957).

87 Appeal of Ritzie, 372 Pa. 588, 94 A.2d 729 (1953).

88 Howard v. State Bd. of Retirement, 325 Mass. 211, 89 N.E.2d 758 (1950).

Section 9

Rehearings

Occasionally, a question arises as to the necessity of granting an opportunity to be heard in cases where an agency is reconsidering a case, following the vacating (*e.g.,* upon judicial review) of its original order.

Where a case has been remanded because of a mere technical inadequacy in the form of order,[89] or for reconsideration of specified matters appearing in the record,[90] there is no necessity for permitting the parties to re-argue the case, or to put in further evidence.

However, if it appears that there may have occurred a change in conditions which should be considered by the agency in its reconsideration of the case, opportunity for further hearing must be afforded.[91] Similarly, if the original determination had been based upon an informal hearing, so that the reconsideration is in reality a hearing *de novo,* it is the duty of the agency to hear the parties on all issues.[92]

---

[89] State *ex rel.* Kansas City v. Public Serv. Comm'n, 360 Mo. 339, 228 S.W. 2d 738 (1950).

[90] Dittmeier v. Missouri Real Estate Comm'n, 316 S.W.2d 1 (Mo. 1958).

[91] Southern Pac. Co. v. Corporation Comm'n, 83 Ariz. 333, 321 P.2d 224 (1958).

[92] Waller v. Howard P. Foley Co., 90 Ariz. 337, 367 P.2d 795 (1961); Little v. Persun Constr. Co., 332 S.W.2d 647 (Ky. 1960).

CHAPTER VI

PUBLIC INFORMATION

Section 1

The Problem

A basic and serious shortcoming in the administrative law of most states is the lack of public information concerning the actual procedures and policies of state agencies. Absent statutory requirement (and these are unfortunately few) agencies sometimes choose to operate without the benefit of written rules, using techniques reminiscent of the Roman Emperor Caligula who, it is said, posted his laws so high that none could read them, and then beheaded those who violated his laws.

In other cases, rules are adopted, but are drafted in a manner that is essentially uninformative, covering such sterile points as a specification whether moving papers should be typewritten or mimeographed, or an announcement that the appeal period must be calculated from the day of mailing the agency's order, rather than from the date of its receipt. Statements describing the details of practice and procedure are often sketchy and incomplete, failing to reveal the whole process of administration, or the various alternative procedures which may be utilized. Sometimes through mere inertia, and more frequently perhaps through a desire to avoid commitment to any set course of procedure (for once a definite rule of procedure is established, a person appearing before the agency may justifiably complain of departures therefrom), many state agencies have been loath to adopt or publish detailed procedural rules.

Even though a reasonably detailed and workable set of regulations may be available describing the general rules of procedure, it is often difficult to ascertain the rules of decision by which cases will be decided on their merits. Frequently, agency decisions are unpublished; sometimes, it is not even possible to obtain copies from the agency. Or, if copies are available, they may prove to be written in conclusionary language which merely parrots the phraseology of the governing statute, without revealing the real *ratio decidendi.* The decisions may simply announce, for example (without an informative statement of the facts), that a claimant for unemployment compensation did (or did not) refuse suitable work without just cause, or that the public interest, convenience, and necessity does (or does not) require the granting of a license to a common carrier by motor truck.

The publication of detailed rules and of informative decisions, that disclose the reasoning which led an agency to its announced conclusion, should be viewed as mere minimal standards of public information. There is, in fact, a crying need for more. All agencies develop policies and criteria of decision to implement the statutes they administer. These policies and criteria not only serve to interpret the underlying statutes; they serve as actual rules of decision. Often they are reduced to writing (in the form of staff manuals and handbooks, field letters, bulletins, "operations" instructions, or opinions of general counsel) but, although written, they are treated as confidential documents and are not made publicly available.

The results of this lack of public information are serious. It leads to situations where those subject to an agency's jurisdiction are unable to ascertain the rules to which their conduct must conform. It leads, also, to situations where even their counsel are unable to ascertain the rules, and are thus unable to fulfill their function effectively. Counsel are unable to predict with any degree of confidence or accuracy what decision the agency would make on postulated facts; they do not know what arguments would be effective with the agency in particular case situations.

The result is, for example, that a claimant for workmen's compensation must go to a lawyer who specializes in that field and who has learned from day-by-day experience all the nuances of procedure and policy which one must know to present the claim effectively, but which a lawyer who did not specialize in that field could not ascertain. Similarly, general counsel for a corporation finding itself summoned to appear before a public service commission may well feel compelled to seek the assistance of an expert in the affairs of that agency—and preferably a lawyer who has recently served on the commission.

This need for seeking the assistance of specialists arises, in the case of many state agencies, not from the fact that the problems involved are characterized by the baffling intricacies of the sort that typify cases considered by some of the federal agencies, but merely from the lack of public information as to the rules, decisions, and policies of the agency.

This lack of information is, in general, a much more glaring fault in the case of state agencies than in the federal agencies. Section 3 of the Federal Administrative Procedure Act[1] requires (with certain troublesome exceptions relating to matters required by the public interest to be kept secret, or relating to the internal management of the agency) the publication of rules describing the agency's organization, setting forth the methods whereby the public may secure information or make submittals, describing the general course and method by which its functions are channeled, setting forth the nature and requirements of all formal and informal procedures, as well as forms and instructions, and announcing substantive rules and statements of general policy or interpretations adopted for the guidance of the public.

Despite the requirements of the federal statute, the need for making available a greater measure of information concerning the *modus operandi* of federal agencies has frequently been noted. Thus, the Task Force on Legal Services and Procedure of the Second Hoover Commission observed:

> Substantive rules, statements of policy, and interpretations are issued by agencies in many forms. Whether contained in manuals, handbooks, digests, indexes, legal opinions and interpretations, bulletins, field letters, circulars, or instructions, they should conform to the publicity requirements of section 3 of the Administrative Procedure Act if they are used by agency employees in the performance of duties which affect members of the public. It has been said that confidential treatment of many rules is permitted by the interpretation of section 3 that they are intended for the guidance of agency officials and employees and are not for the guidance of the public. To correct this, the task force recommends that the section be amended to require the publication of substantive rules and statements of policy or interpretations formulated, adopted, or used by an agency. . . .[2]

---

1 5 U.S.C. § 1002; F.C.A. 5 § 1002, which requires publication only of those statements of general policy which are adopted "for the guidance of the public."

2 Commission on Organization of Executive Branch of Government, TASK FORCE REPORT ON LEGAL SERVICES AND PROCEDURE 150 (1955).

There is a need, clearly, for adoption of legislation which would require state agencies to make publicly available the type of information which the Hoover Commission Task Force recommended as desirable in the case of the federal agencies. State agencies operate in more restricted spheres, as well as in narrower geographical areas, than do the federal agencies. The problems they consider are often simpler. There is less reason to avoid explicit announcement of the criteria of decision, in order to permit *ad hoc* temporizing and the preservation of an experimental approach (as may be true in the case of such federal agencies as the Atomic Energy Commission). The need, is rather, for explicit requirements that will necessitate the making public of such information as will enable any member of the bar properly to represent his clients before any state agency. The need can be answered only by adoption of statutory provisions like those found in the Revised Model State Act, for in the absence of statute the courts have not found it practicable to impose such requirements on the state agencies.

Section 2

Adoption of Rules

Section 2(a) of the Revised Model State Act provides that each agency shall (in addition to other rule-making requirements imposed by law):

> (1) adopt as a rule a description of its organization, stating the general course and method of its operations and the methods whereby the public may obtain information or make submissions or requests;
>
> (2) adopt rules of practice setting forth the nature and requirements of all formal and informal procedures available, including a description of all forms and instructions used by the agency;
>
> (3) make available for public inspection all rules and all other written statements of policy or interpretations formulated, adopted, or used by the agency in the discharge of its functions;
>
> (4) make available for public inspection all final orders, decisions, and opinions.

Awareness on the part of the state legislatures of the need to require the adoption of rules, and acceptance of the general principles set forth in the Revised Model State Act, are indicated by the adoption in some states of legislation containing cognate provisions.

The first requirement of the Revised Model State Act is that each agency shall adopt as a rule a description of its organization. This is important, to enable the public (and especially lawyers) to ascertain the respective functions and powers of each division and officer within the agency. Without this information, one cannot know how to gain a proper entree into the administrative maze. Within a state department of conservation, for example, there may be one official whose particular concern it is to effect a workable accommodation between the necessities of manufacturing concerns whose operations require the discharge of toxic wastes into rivers, and the desires of outdoorsmen that fishing should be protected. Once a manufacturer with such a problem establishes a contact with this official, he is on the way toward working out a solution to his problem. But if (without having learned the identity of this official and without the benefit of having advised and consulted with him) he proceeds to discharge industrial wastes into the river without first having obtained official sanction, he may face expensive litigation seeking injunctive relief and damages as well. The publication of a description of the agency's organization affords a practicable means of making it easier for the manufacturer to find the official who can help him discover a solution to his problem.

Since this is a new requirement in the Revised Model State Act, not having been included in the original Model Act of 1946, it has not yet been widely adopted. It is interesting to note, however, that at least three states which have adopted administrative procedure acts since the promulgation of the Revised Model Act in 1961,[3] have included this provision in their enactments.

The second requirement of the Revised Model State Act is that agencies must adopt rules stating the general course and method of their operations. This provision is a refinement of language which had appeared in the 1946 version of the Model Act, requiring agencies, "so far as practicable," to supplement

---

[3] Georgia (CODE ANN. § 3A-101); Oklahoma (STAT. tit. 75, § 302(a)); Rhode Island (GEN. LAWS ANN. § 42-35-2).

their rules with descriptive statements of their procedures. The earlier version had been adopted in several states.[4]

The revised requirement of the 1961 edition of the Model State Act is more rigidly definitive; it eliminates the loophole afforded by the phrase "so far as practicable," and makes it clear that the descriptive statement must set forth the general course and method of the agency's operations. This means, of course, that the rule must set forth such matters as the requirements respecting the filing of pleadings, the opportunities for informal adjustment, the details of prehearing conferences, the mechanics of noticing cases for hearing, the method of making post-hearing submissions, the responsibilities and spheres of delegated authority of the agency staff, and the like. The language of the Revised Model Act has already been adopted in some states.[5]

The third requirement of the Revised Model State Act is that agencies must adopt rules setting forth the methods whereby the public may obtain information or make submissions or requests. This provision, too, is new in the Revised Model Act. It is intended to eliminate the frustrating difficulties too often encountered, and the loss of time involved, in the absence of public information as to how requests for information or other submissions should be made, and to whom they should be addressed. Every agency, obviously, has a public responsibility to answer proper inquiries put to it concerning its policies in the administration of the statute it administers. But such requests may often go unanswered for many weeks either because they did not come to the attention of the proper official or because the agency has failed to set up any formalized method of dealing with such requests and submissions. Adoption of rules concerning the method for making such requests, and obtaining information, should go far toward eliminating these unnecessary diffi-

---

4 Maine (REV. STAT. ANN. ch. 20-A, § 2); Maryland (ANN. CODE art. 41, § 245); Michigan (COMP. LAWS § 3.560); Minnesota (STAT. § 15.0412); Nebraska (REV. STAT. § 84-909); Oregon (REV. STAT. § 183.330); Texas (REV. CIV. STAT. art. 6252-13, § 2); Washington (REV. CODE § 34.04.020). In Virginia (CODE ANN. § 9-6.3), the requirement of publishing descriptive statements appears in lieu of other requirements as to the adoption of rules. The problems created by this provision are discussed in McFarland & Boyd, *The General Administrative Agencies Act*, 46 VA. L. REV. 823 (1960).

5 Georgia (CODE ANN. § 3A-101); Oklahoma (STAT. tit. 75, § 302(a)); Rhode Island (GEN. LAWS ANN. § 42-35-2(a)).

culties. Shortly after the promulgation of the Revised Model State Act, four states incorporated this provision in their statutory law.[6]

The fourth requirement of the Revised Model State Act imposes on agencies a duty to adopt rules of practice setting forth the nature and requirements of all formal and informal procedures available. Experience has shown this requirement to be an important one, particularly with respect to the mandate to advise the public of the informal procedures that may be utilized. In many types of administrative adjudication, formal proceedings are utilized only to impose sanctions for violations of applicable legal requirements. In order to work out mutually acceptable understandings as to methods of operation that will not be officially challenged, it is necessary to resort to informal procedures. Too often, these have not been published, and are known only to the handful of specialists devoting a major part of their time and effort to the representation of clients before a particular agency. The purpose of the Revised Model State Act is to make sure that all procedural devices will be officially described and made known to the public. This purpose has recommended itself to the legislatures of many states.[7]

The fifth type of rule which all agencies are enjoined to adopt, under the Revised Model State Act, embraces a description of all forms and instructions used by the agency. Every citizen who has sent a carefully prepared application to an agency, only to have it returned because it did not comply with an unpublished requirement of the agency as to the particular form in which such an application must be prepared, will attest the desirability of this provision. Further, it saves the time and effort of agency staffs if there is general public knowledge concerning the desired format of applications and other papers filed with the agency,

[6] Georgia (CODE ANN. § 3A-101); Hawaii (SESS. LAWS 1961, Act 103, § 2 (a)); Oklahoma (STAT. tit. 75, § 302(a)); Rhode Island (GEN. LAWS ANN. § 42-35-2(a)).

[7] Hawaii (SESS. LAWS 1961, Act 103, § 2(a)); Maine (REV. STAT. ANN. ch. 20-A, § 2); Maryland (ANN. CODE art. 41, § 245); Michigan (COMP. LAWS § 3.560); Nebraska (REV. STAT. § 84-909); Oklahoma (STAT. tit. 75, § 302); Oregon (REV. STAT. § 183.330); Rhode Island (GEN. LAWS ANN. § 42-35-2); Texas (REV. CIV. STAT. art. 6252-13, § 2); Washington (REV. CODE § 34.04.020). Minnesota has a related provision, providing that agencies "may" rather than that they shall, adopt such rules (STAT. § 15.0412). The statutes in Massachusetts (GEN. LAWS ANN. ch. 30A, § 9) and Wisconsin (STAT. § 227.013) have the same general thrust, but use different phraseology.

and concerning the agency's instructions as to the preferred method of supplying information or making submissions; for with the broad dissemination of such knowledge, a much larger percentage of the papers coming to the agency staff will be in proper form, thus avoiding the necessity of re-submissions and all the unnecessary paper work thereby entailed. Statutory provisions requiring that such instructions and forms be published as rules are found in a number of states.[8]

Section 3

Availability of Rules and Orders

Of equal importance with the requirement for the adoption of rules covering the five major points above discussed, is the requirement that all written statements of policy or interpretations formulated, adopted, or used by an agency in the discharge of its functions, should be made a matter of public information. Absent such requirement, there is a persistent tendency on the part of many agencies to attach a different label to statements which for all practical purposes really amount to rules, and then (because they are not labelled as rules) to keep them confidential.[9] This secrecy serves neither the public good nor that of the agency. All such criteria of decision should be made public. The Revised Model State Act so requires. This requirement is beginning to appear in states which have adopted or amended their administrative procedure statutes subsequent to the promulgation of the Revised Model Act.[10]

---

[8] Hawaii (SESS. LAWS 1961, art. 103, § 2(a)); Maine (REV. STAT. ANN. ch. 20-A, § 2); Maryland (ANN. CODE art. 41, § 245); Michigan (COMP. LAWS § 3.560); Nebraska (REV. STAT. § 84-909); Oklahoma (STAT. tit. 75, § 302(a)); Oregon (REV. STAT. § 183.330); Rhode Island (GEN. LAWS ANN. § 42-35-2); Washington (REV. CODE § 34.04.020); West Virginia (Acts of 1964, art. 3, ch. 1, § 1). In other states, provisions for the publication of forms and instructions are placed on an optional rather than a mandatory basis: Minnesota (STAT. § 15.0412); Texas (REV. CIV. STAT. art. 6252-13, § 2).

[9] *E.g.*, REPORT OF SENATE INTERIM COMMITTEE ON ADMINISTRATIVE REGULATIONS TO THE CALIFORNIA LEGISLATURE 8-9; HEADY, ADMINISTRATIVE PROCEDURE LEGISLATION IN THE STATES 49-62 (1952).

[10] Georgia (CODE ANN. § 3A-101); Hawaii (SESS. LAWS 1961, Act 103, § 2 (a)); Oklahoma (STAT. tit. 75, § 302); Rhode Island (GEN. LAWS ANN. § 42-35-2). Oregon (REV. STAT. § 183.380) provides, *contra*, that the requirements for publication do not apply to general statements of policy or interpretive rules. This provision apparently reflects the exceptions found in the federal act, which, as noted

All orders and opinions filed by agencies should also be made publicly available, for the information obtainable from a perusal thereof is necessary both to the lawyer's function of counselling his client and to his task of advocacy when appearing before the agency. Such requirements appear, in one form or another, in the statutes of several states.[11]

A number of other states have adopted statutes providing (with variant limitations) a right to inspect the files and records of agencies.[12] While these provisions serve a useful purpose, they are clearly not as well adapted to achieve the desired end as are the provisions of the Revised Model State Act, for the goal—desirable both from the viewpoint of the public doing business with the agencies and from that of the agencies themselves—is that all the policies and criteria of decision relied on by the agency (whether reflected in formal rules, or in informal internal statements, or in opinions and orders) should be a matter of public knowledge, available to all interested parties.

Several states provide for the maintenance by state agencies of mailing lists, so that individuals and organizations desiring to have advance notice of proposed rule-making activities of the agencies may obtain individual notice by placing their names on such lists.[13] In other states, a number of agencies maintain such mailing lists informally, without statutory requirement. The information so distributed sometimes includes not only rules and policy statements, but also orders and rulings in individual cases. Since it is not commercially feasible, in the case of many agencies in most states, to publish and sell reports of the agencies' activities (in the manner of the loose-leaf services which cover many of the federal agencies) this device of distributing by mail to all interested persons a complete account of all the activities of the agency, is one which has a great deal to recommend it.

---

above, have been strongly criticized by the Task Force on Legal Services and Procedure of the Second Hoover Commission.

11 Connecticut (GEN. STAT. REV. § 4-19); Hawaii (SESS. LAWS 1961, Act 103, § 2(a)); Oklahoma (STAT. tit. 75, § 302(a)); Oregon (REV. STAT. § 183.360); Rhode Island (GEN. LAWS ANN. § 42-35-2).

12 Arkansas (STAT. ANN. § 5-502); Colorado (REV. STAT. ANN. § 3-16-2); Connecticut (GEN. STAT. REV. § 1-19); Indiana (ANN. STAT. § 57-603); Minnesota (STAT. §§ 15.0413, 15.17).

13 Alaska (STAT. § 44.62.190); California (GOV'T CODE § 11423); and Colorado (REV. STAT. ANN. § 3-16-2).

SANCTIONS

Experience with the federal agencies, with respect to which public information requirements comparable to those of the Revised Model State Act have been in effect for nearly two decades, has demonstrated that it cannot be expected that agencies will, if left to their own devices, fully comply with public information provisions that are merely directory.[14]

Viewing the situation in the federal agencies, the Hoover Commission Task Force on Legal Services and Procedure recommended that sanctions be written into the federal act, to provide that no agency order, opinion, description, statement, rule, notice, instruction, or other regulation should be valid or effective against any person or party if not made a matter of public information in accordance with the statute.[15]

While statutory requirements in the states designed to provide for the availability of public information as to agency policies and procedures have been minimal, there are indications that agencies have not fully complied with the spirit—sometimes, not even with the letter—of such modest requirements as have existed.[16]

In light of this experience, the draftsmen of the Revised Model State Act deemed it wise to provide sanctions to enforce the public information requirements. The Act provides:

> No agency rule, order, or decision is valid or effective against any person or party, nor may it be invoked by the agency for any purpose, until it has been made available for public inspection as herein

---

[14] See Commission on Organization of Executive Branch of Government, TASK FORCE REPORT ON LEGAL SERVICES AND PROCEDURE 147 et seq. (1955); Sellers, *Extent of Agency Compliance With Sec. 3,* 33 A.B.A.J. 7 (1947); *cf. Administrative Procedure in Government Agencies,* S. DOC. No. 8, 77th Cong., 1st Sess. 25-29 (1941)—the comparison indicating that the deficiencies in public information noted in 1941 had not been noticeably improved by 1955. Decisions in the lower federal courts indicate that troubles continue to arise from the failure of agencies to comply with publicity requirements, *e.g.,* United States v. Aarons, 310 F.2d 341 (2d Cir. 1962); Low v. Thomas, 163 F. Supp. 945 (E.D. Pa. 1958); G. J. Howard Co. v. Cassidy, 162 F. Supp. 568 (E.D. N.Y. 1958); T. S. C. Motor Freight Lines, Inc. v. United States, 186 F. Supp. 777 (S.D. Tex. 1960), 366 U.S. 419, 6 L. Ed. 2d 387, 81 Sup. Ct. 1356 (1961).

[15] Commission on Organization of Executive Branch of Government, TASK FORCE REPORT ON LEGAL SERVICES AND PROCEDURE 157 (1955).

[16] FIRST REPORT OF THE SENATE INTERIM COMMITTEE ON ADMINISTRATIVE REGULATIONS TO THE 1955 CALIFORNIA LEGISLATURE 8-9; HEADY, ADMINISTRATIVE PROCEDURE LEGISLATION IN THE UNITED STATES 49-62 (1952).

required. This provision is not applicable in favor of any person or party who has actual knowledge thereof.[17]

The breadth of this provision is significant. The cognate section of the federal act,[18] after stating the public information requirements, provides only, "No person shall in any manner be required to resort to organization or procedure not so published." Clearly, the Revised Model State Act contains much more effective sanctions.

During the first two years following the promulgation of the Revised Model State Act, at least three states adopted this provision, imposing sanctions to assure agency compliance with the public information requirements.[19]

There is little legislation in other states designed to provide sanctions to compel agencies to make available public information as to their procedures and policies (although, as noted in Chapter VII, *infra,* many states have statutes requiring publication as a condition of the validity of agency rules). A Colorado statute provides that no agency rule may be relied on or cited unless, in addition to publication, information concerning it has been made available to the public.[20] Virginia has decreed that no rule shall be enforceable unless copies of it are available for distribution to the public, at the agency office, for more than sixty consecutive days.[21]

The scanty case authority available indicates that the state courts will be diligent in the enforcement of statutory mandates to agencies, directing them to make their procedures and policies a matter of public information. Thus, in interpreting a statute requiring publication of tabulations of tax-exempt property, the New York court (rejecting an interpretation that would have permitted publication of a generalized statement) ruled that there must be published a detailed list of specific properties, noting that: "The Legislature appears to have been actuated in

---

17 Section 2(b).

18 5 U.S.C. § 1002; F.C.A. 5 § 1002.

19 Georgia (CODE ANN. § 3A-101); Hawaii (SESS. LAWS 1961, Act 103, § 2); Rhode Island (GEN. LAWS ANN. § 42-35-2). Oklahoma adopted an administrative procedure act in 1963, drawing in large measure upon the provisions of the Revised Model Act, but this particular section was omitted. (OKLA. STAT. tit. 75, § 302.)

20 COLO. REV. STAT. ANN. § 3-16-2(10).

21 VA. CODE ANN. § 9-6.7(c).

this instance by the policy of subjecting tax exemptions to the scrutiny of the neighbors."[22] Again, an attempt to avoid publication by calling a regulation an "order" was held to be ineffective.[23] In another case, the same court refused to enforce against a waitress an administrative rule that tips must be reported to the restaurant owner, where no provision had been made to advise waitresses of the rule except to require employers of waitresses so to advise them. Noting that restaurant owners would have a direct financial interest in neglecting this duty, the court said that it was unreasonable for the agency not to have adopted methods better designed to make sure that waitresses would have adequate opportunity to learn of the requirement.[24]

---

22 Lockport Union-Sun & Journal, Inc. v. Preisch, 8 N.Y.2d 54, 58-9, 201 N.Y.S.2d 505, 167 N.E.2d 839 (1960).

23 People v. Cull, 10 N.Y.2d 123, 218 N.Y.S.2d 38, 176 N.E.2d 495 (1961).

24 Claim of Gold, 307 N.Y. 224, 120 N.E.2d 799 (1954).

CHAPTER VII

RULE MAKING: PROCEDURES

Section 1

Functions of Rules

(A) Rules Are of Different Types

Agency rules serve three basic purposes and may accordingly be grouped into three general categories: procedural rules, interpretive rules, and legislative rules. While the categories are neither precise nor clearcut, and while some rules serve two or more of these three purposes simultaneously,[1] nevertheless the distinction is important. Judicial decisions respecting (a) the requirements that will be imposed with reference to the procedures used in adopting and promulgating the rule, and also respecting (b) the validity and legal effect of a challenged rule, reflect substantially different types of treatment for these different types of rules. These differences will be discussed at appropriate points in this chapter. At the outset, it is necessary to describe the distinctions—distinctions which the courts have not always emphasized and which are not susceptible of precise definition.

(1) Procedural Rules

As here used, the term *procedural rules* refers to those describing the methods by which the agency will carry out its appointed functions—rules which make provisions for the filing of applications, the institution of complaints, the serving of papers, the conduct of hearings, and the like.

An agency cannot very well function without rules of procedure, and it may be supposed that every agency has such rules, at least at the level of intra-office memoranda. But in too frequent

[1] For example, a rule prescribing the burden of proof in administrative hearings may serve as a statement of procedure, and at the same time evince the agency's interpretation of the governing statute. Indeed, it is conceivable that such a rule might, under some circumstances, serve the purpose of a legislative regulation.

cases, the only rules published and made generally available contain so little information as to the actual procedural steps, and as to the various alternative procedures which may be available, that a person having a case before the agency is at a loss to know how to proceed except upon seeking advice of a representative of the agency; and then, because of the partisan position necessarily assumed by the agencies in many matters, the person seeking information may entertain understandable doubts whether the advice he has received is entirely disinterested. It is for this reason that the Attorney General's Committee, more than twenty years ago,[2] strongly urged that each agency be required to make available, and to maintain current, statements describing both formal and informal procedures available in various types of cases, specifying among other things the officers and types of personnel, the various subdivisions of the agency, and the duties, functions, and general authority of all divisions of the agency in each of the several types of cases handled.

The deficiencies noted more than two decades ago still exist. Their persistence may be attributed, it seems, to a disinclination on the part of agencies to commit themselves to any fixed procedural pattern. In fact, the adoption of procedural rules involves principally the development of a working compromise between the agency's interest in unregulated fluidity of procedure, and the public's interest in being able to ascertain in advance the mechanics which will govern the disposition of cases. As every lawyer knows, the rules of procedure are not infrequently determinative of the outcome of a case.[3]

Frequently, agency statements describing the rules of practice and procedure are sketchy and incomplete, failing to reveal the whole process of administration, or the various alternative procedures which may be utilized.

(2) Interpretive Rules

As the name suggests, *interpretive rules* are, basically, those that interpret and apply the provisions of the statute under which

2 ADMINISTRATIVE PROCEDURE IN GOVERNMENT AGENCIES, S. DOC. No. 8, 77th Cong., 1st Sess. 195 (1941).

3 "Thus the procedures by which the facts of the case are determined assume an importance fully as great as the validity of the substantive rule of law to be applied." Speiser v. Randall, 357 U.S. 513, 520, 2 L. Ed. 2d 1460, 78 Sup. Ct. 1332 (1958).

the agency operates. No sanction attaches to the violation of an interpretive rule as such; the sanction attaches to the violation of the statute, which the rule merely interprets. Thus, for example, most of the regulations of the Internal Revenue Service are interpretive.

Some interpretive rules serve much the same purpose as opinions of general counsel for the agency (and, indeed, are frequently written by him). They state the interpretation of ambiguous or doubtful statutory language which will be followed by the agency unless and until the statute is otherwise authoritatively interpreted by the courts.

Other interpretive rules describe the general discretionary policies to be followed by the agency. For example, an agency given broad discretionary powers in respect to the granting of licenses may formulate a statement of the conditions which must be met in order to obtain a license. In many cases, agencies have thus worked out standards and policies which in effect control the administrative decision in a wide variety of cases.

Judicious use of the power to make interpretive rules thus offers an opportunity to correct a woeful lack of adequate public information concerning the substance of administrative policies. It having become an accepted technique of statutory draftsmanship to establish legislative standards in broad, vague, general terms, the office of interpretation has become commensurately more important.

(3) Legislative Rules

If the rule represents something more than the agency's opinion as to what the statute requires—if the legislature has delegated a measure of legislative power to the agency, and has provided a statutory sanction for violation of such rules as the agency may adopt—then the rule may properly be described as *legislative.* The distinction between interpretive and legislative rules (a distinction which courts recognize in their rulings, but which is rarely discussed in judicial opinions) is well stated by Robert Benjamin:[4] "Those that go beyond interpretation and, within limits prescribed by the governing statute, themselves enact new substantive provisions" are legislative rules. There are, thus, two

[4] BENJAMIN, ADMINISTRATIVE ADJUDICATION IN THE STATE OF NEW YORK 294 (1942).

identifying characteristics of legislative rules: (1) the statute has delegated power to the agency to adopt the rule; (2) the statute provides that the rule shall, if within the delegated power, have authoritative force.

(B) Authority to Adopt Rules

The question as to the power of an agency to adopt procedural rules is one which rarely arises. It would seem that the very delegation to an agency of power to administer a statute would carry with it the power to adopt such reasonable procedures as are necessary or useful in carrying out its administrative tasks. In any event, the well nigh universal legislative custom of providing, in any statute creating an agency, that the agency shall have power to make such rules as are necessary and proper in carrying out its delegated powers, is clearly sufficient to authorize the adoption of procedural regulations.

It is equally clear that an agency may, without specific statutory authority, make known its interpretation of the provisions of the statute it administers. Whether these be called "General Counsel Opinions" or "Interpretive Bulletins" or "rules," makes no practical difference, so far as concerns the question of authority to issue them.

Conversely, it is clear on principle that an agency may not issue legislative rules in the absence of legislative authority to do so. Sometimes the legislative delegation is clear and specific. But in other cases, the question whether inexact statutory language should be construed as granting an implied power to adopt legislative rules, causes difficulty. Thus, the New York court was called upon to decide whether delegation of power to the workmen's compensation board to prescribe, by rule, fees for "medical treatment and care" should be construed as embracing the grant of legislative power to adopt rules fixing rates for "hospital care."[5] Declaring that the board had no power to adopt such a legislative rule "unless it be given by an express statute," the court held that in light of the distinction found elsewhere in the statute between hospital services and medical services, the grant of a power to adopt legislative rules concerning rates for medical services did not encompass a power to adopt rules setting rates for hospital services.

---

5 Brooklyn Hosp. v. Donlon, 309 N.Y. 520, 524, 132 N.E.2d 489 (1956).

The Indiana court held[6] that an agency rule forbidding automobile dealers to receive "rating" refunds on insurance premiums, the cost of which had been made part of the price in the installment sales contracts covering the insured cars, was invalid without statutory authorization.

Similarly, upon a finding that a state public utilities commission had statutory authority only to make rules governing its own procedures, the Ohio court held[7] that the agency could not adopt legislative rules setting safety standards for the construction of railroad tracks.

Conversely, it was held in Alaska that very general language empowering the alcoholic beverage control board to adopt such rules as were necessary to "effectuate and carry out the purpose" of the liquor control statute should be construed as authorizing the agency to adopt legislative rules limiting the sale of liquor to specified hours.[8]

Because of the ever-present danger that an agency may adopt legislative rules which go beyond, and possibly conflict with, the legislative intent, it is desirable to insist that an asserted power to adopt legislative rules be predicated upon a specific and explicit delegation of statutory authority. Such is the view of eminent commentators.[9] However, there are not enough decisions speaking clearly on this point to justify an assertion that the law has been settled.

(C) THE CHOICE BETWEEN RULE MAKING AND ADJUDICATION

(1) Consequences of the Choice

In many cases, agencies have a choice (except as limited by judicial restraints or by statutory mandates) whether to proceed by general rule making or by *ad hoc,* case-to-case adjudication.

The consequences of this choice are significant, both from the viewpoint of the procedural methods adopted and from the

---

6 Department of Financial Institutions v. Johnson Chevrolet Co., 228 Ind. 397, 92 N.E.2d 714 (1950).

7 Akron & Barberton Belt R.R. v. Public Utils. Comm'n, 165 Ohio St. 316, 74 N.E.2d 256 (1947).

8 Boehl v. Sabre Jet Room, Inc., 349 P.2d 585 (Alaska 1960).

9 *E.g.,* Brown, *Regulations, Reenactment and the Revenue Acts,* 54 HARV. L. REV. 377 (1941); Alvord, *Treasury Regulations and the Wilshire Oil Case,* 40 COLUM. L. REV. 252 (1940).

viewpoint of the nature and degree of protection afforded the individual interests involved. The whole tenor of rule-making procedures is markedly different from those adopted in the adjudication of contested cases. The type of notice is different, the form of hearing is different, the mechanics of decision are different, and the scope of review is different.

Manifestly, these procedural differences have important ramifications in respect to the protection of the private interests of those to be affected by the administrative action. The choice beween adjudication and rule making typically controls, for example, the question whether those affected are entitled to a trial-type hearing, whether they have a right to introduce testimony and cross-examine witnesses, whether they have a right to oral argument, whether they can insist that the agency produce substantial evidence in support of findings which can be shown reasonably to justify the administrative action. Again, the scope of judicial review varies widely, as between cases of rule making and cases of adjudication.[10]

Beyond all these differences, there are others which are even more important, and which reflect various applications of the principle that rules are normally prospective in their operation, while decisions in adjudicatory matters are normally (like judicial decisions) retroactive.

For example, an insurance commission may determine to consider the reasonableness of a particular "standard clause" which dozens of insurance companies have included in their contracts with insurance agents. If the commission elects to initiate rule-making proceedings, all insurance companies are notified of the fact that the propriety of the clause has been questioned; all are given an opportunity to present their arguments as to the reasonableness of the clause; all are affected at the same time and in the same way by the provisions of the rule that is adopted; and, furthermore, the rule will normally have prospective operation—the rule may provide, for example, that by a certain date all companies must eliminate or amend the challenged clause. The result is that all companies stand in the same position. Furthermore, the rule would normally be so phrased as to safeguard

---

[10] This point was emphasized in *O'Neill v. Martori,* 69 Ariz. 270, 212 P.2d 994 (1949).

the affected companies from any retroactive application of the principles adopted as a guide for the future.

On the other hand, the consequences to all concerned would be far different if the insurance commission chose to proceed, by the contested case route, to make a determination, in a case involving a single company, whether the use of the questioned contract clause was unfair and unreasonable. If the proceedings resulted in an adverse determination, all the other insurance companies would be substantially affected by the outcome of a case in which they had been given no opportunity to participate. Conceivably, they would not have heard of the pendency of the case until the decision was announced. A number of the companies might believe that because of the manner in which this one isolated case was presented (or because there were not involved, in this particular case, circumstances which affected the question as it applied to other companies), the commission's decision had been based on a record which did not properly reflect all of the facts which the commission ought to have taken into consideration. Putting it bluntly, the other insurance companies might justifiably believe that if the commission had made known its interest in the problem, and if it had considered all the arguments that would have been presented by all the companies, it would probably have reached a different result; at least, its decision would have been more fully informed.

Thus, in situations where it appears that a large number of persons will be affected in substantially the same manner by the administrative decision, there is much to be said in favor of the utilization of rule-making techniques. Some state agencies, cognizant of these considerations, strive conscientiously to utilize rule-making procedures in such situations—even to the extent of transforming proceedings that originated as single-party adjudications into multi-party rule-making proceedings.[11] But other state agencies show an inclination to rely on techniques of *ad hoc,* case-to-case adjudication, even in cases where it can reasonably

[11] Thus, in *National Merchandising Corp. v. Public Serv. Comm'n,* 5 N.Y.2d 485, 158 N.E.2d 714 (1959), when two telephone companies filed proposed tariff amendments which would have permitted them to limit the use of advertising matter in connection with the directories they furnished their customers, the Commission—perceiving that the interests of many phone companies and many advertising agencies would be affected—on its own motion instituted proceedings leading to the adoption of a rule of general application.

be foreseen that the implications of the case extend far beyond the immediate interests of the named parties directly involved.

Conversely, where a single party (or a small, well-defined group) will bear the brunt of the administrative order, the adoption of rule-making techniques may cause hardship to the individuals affected. This is true because the adoption of such techniques operates to deprive them of the advantages of an adversary type hearing, and of the right to insist that the order be based on specific findings of fact which in turn are supported by substantial evidence, and of the right to the broader scope of judicial review available in cases involving adjudication. So severe are these consequences that the state courts have occasionally intervened, and insisted on the use of the contested-case procedure.[12]

(2) Agencies' Right to Choose

To a large degree, agencies may choose which course to pursue. While the question has been but seldom considered by the state courts, there is no reason to believe that they would not subscribe to the statement of the United States Supreme Court[13] that ". . . the choice made between proceeding by general rule or by individual *ad hoc* litigation is one that lies primarily in the informed discretion of the administrative agency."

But, it should be noted, the choice does not lie exclusively within the discretion of the agency. In the same case,[14] the Court added:

> Since the Commission, unlike a court, does have the ability to make new law prospectively through the exercise of its rule making powers,

[12] In *Polar Ice Cream & Creamery Co. v. Andrews,* 146 So. 2d 609 (Fla. 1962), the milk commission adopted a rule, denominated as a "motion," directed primarily to the pricing practices of one creamery. When the agency brought an action to determine the validity of its order as a "rule," the court held that the order must be treated as one made in a contested case, and granted a change of venue which would not have been available in the case of rule making. In *Missouri ex rel. State Highway Comm'n v. Weinstein,* 322 S.W.2d 778 (Mo. 1959), involving a determination by the state highway commission as to the relocation of the mains of a water company, the court said that while the commission exercised legislative authority and could properly invoke rule-making techniques in locating and relocating highways, still "in determining whether and where a particular pipe line should be relocated . . . the Commission is determining adjudicative facts . . . and so is making a quasi-judicial decision." Accordingly, the court held that the water company could properly claim an appeal of the type available for adjudicatory cases, under the state act.

[13] SEC v. Chenery Corp., 332 U.S. 194, 203, 91 L. Ed. 1995, 67 Sup. Ct. 1575 (1947).

[14] *Id.* at 202.

> it has less reason to rely upon *ad hoc* adjudication to formulate new standards of conduct within the framework of [the pertinent legislation]. The function of filling in the interstices of the pertinent legislation, should be performed, as much as possible, through this quasi-legislative promulgation of rules to be applied in the future.

Applying the policy so formulated by the Nation's highest court, a number of the federal Courts of Appeal have set aside administrative orders in cases where it seemed plain that, in view of the attendant consequences (as described above) the ends of justice required that rule-making procedures be employed in cases where it was foreseeable that the future actions of many persons would be affected, and where it seemed only fair that they should have some opportunity to participate in the proceedings in which the rules of conduct were determined. Thus, in a decision setting aside an NLRB order, the Court of Appeals for the Sixth Circuit recognized that the agency had in fact engaged in rule making in the course of an adjudicatory proceeding (the thrust of the agency decision being to brand illegal a hiring hall agreement of a type common to many collective bargaining agreements, affecting large numbers of companies, unions, and employees); and the court's opinion strongly suggests that retroactive application of a rule of broad significance developed in an adjudicatory proceeding should not be allowed when the agency could have followed rule-making procedures, unless the agency can show that the public interest demands that the new rule be imposed "at once and now."[15] Again, the Court of Appeals for the Ninth Circuit condemned the use of the *ad hoc* adjudication procedure because of the availability and the advisability, under the circumstances, of resort to conventional rule-making techniques.[16]

(3) The Proper Basis for the Choice

The general rule that should guide the agencies in making the choice between rule making and *ad hoc* adjudication might be formulated as follows: where an agency faces the alternative of proceeding by rule making or by adjudication, the process of rule making should be utilized except in cases where there is a

[15] NLRB v. E. & B. Brewing Co., 276 F.2d 594 (6th Cir. 1960).
[16] NLRB v. Guy F. Atkinson Co., 195 F.2d 141 (9th Cir. 1952).

danger that its utilization would frustrate the effective accomplishment of the agency's functions. Where such danger exists, *e.g.*, where the "agency may not have had sufficient experience with a particular problem to warrant rigidifying its tentative judgment into a hard and fast rule,"[17] or where the problem is so "specialized and varying in nature as to be impossible of capture within the boundaries of a general rule,"[18] the advantages to the agency of utilizing the *ad hoc* adjudication technique must be balanced against the possible deleterious public consequences resulting from the retroactive application of a new standard of general application to large numbers of parties who have had no opportunity to be heard as to what the standard should be. Unless the balance clearly preponderates in favor of the *ad hoc* adjudication method, the agency should utilize rule-making procedures.

The suggestion was well phrased in an A.B.A. committee report which recommended that:

> Administrative agencies shall (1) as a fixed policy, prefer and encourage rule making to reduce to the minimum the necessity for case-by-case administrative adjudications; and . . . (4) shall promptly formulate, incorporate in and promulgate as a rule or statement of policy any and all general principles, not otherwise published as rules or specified in statutes, enumerated in any specific case decision.[19]

More specifically, it has been well suggested that while the practice of working out policy piecemeal by *ad hoc* adjudication may be justified in the initial stages of administrative regulation of a new field, yet when time and experience have served to sharpen and focus the problems involved, then the agency should utilize rule-making procedures to lay down general rules for the future guidance of all parties affected. How this approach can work may be illustrated by the experience of the War Labor Board in World War II. At first, the national board (and its regional boards in the several states) decided applications for wage adjustments on an *ad hoc* basis. As experience was gained, general regulations and statements of policy were enunciated; and as these were tested in the course of daily case decisions, various amendments and refinements were devised; and finally

---

[17] SEC v. Chenery Corp., note 13 *supra,* at 202-203.

[18] *Ibid.*

[19] *Report of Committee on Agency Rule Making, Administrative Law Section, American Bar Association,* 12 AD. L. REV. 180, 190 (1959).

after some two years' experience, general orders were promulgated as rules which permitted some wage adjustments to be made without formal approval, and, further, laid down standards, applicable to cases where approval was required, under which it became fairly possible to ascertain in advance what the agency's ruling would be in various situations.

The advisability of utilizing rule-making procedures whenever possible as a means of laying down guides for future conduct, rather than relying on the technique of *ad hoc* adjudication, was emphasized—with particular reference to state agencies—many years ago in the well known Benjamin Report,[20] which declared:

> Where an administrative agency has power both to adjudicate and to legislate in a given field (e.g., in the interpretation, development, and application of a regulatory statute, or in the exercise of discretion within limits fixed by the statute), it must determine, with respect to any particular problem in that field, the point (if there is one) at which legislation should properly take the place of adjudication. . . . In determining what course to follow, it is important that the agency should have in mind the advantages of formulating in substantive regulations, so far as it is practicable to do so, the grounds on which the agency proposes to act. The primary advantages to outside interests are: . . . Regulations will afford to persons within the sphere of the agency's activity guidance in determining their conduct; they will afford to persons actually engaged in quasi-judicial litigation before the agency opportunity to know, so far as possible, the legal materials of decision, and opportunity to criticize and distinguish. There are other advantages, to outside interests and to the agency itself. Regulations will contribute to consistent and uniform adjudication, particularly where there is a numerous adjudicating personnel; they will avoid the burden on that personnel of considering a question anew each time it arises.

(4) State Court Decisions

While agencies must necessarily be given a large degree of discretion in deciding whether to follow the route of adjudication or that of rule making, indications are beginning to appear that in appropriate cases the state courts will hereafter, as the federal courts have begun to do, assert a power to set aside agency orders on the ground that under the particular circumstances it was an abuse of discretion for an agency to eschew the rule-making device.

---

[20] BENJAMIN, *op. cit. supra* note 4.

An informative illustration is afforded by a decision of the New Jersey court,[21] reversing an order of the division of alcoholic beverage control. The agency faced the question whether to permit or prohibit the sale of whiskey in "Mason" jars of the type commonly used in home canning—and also, apparently, in home distilling. Instead of adopting a rule announcing its policy in this regard, the agency adopted the *ad hoc* technique and wrote a letter to a particular seller of whiskey. The letter stated that he would not be permitted to sell his whiskey in Mason jars because the agency had found such practice "objectionable for a number of reasons, including the fact that 'moonshine' has been traditionally packaged in Mason jars." The court held this ruling invalid. In its opinion, the court bespoke the desirability of the publication by the director of the agency of "detailed interpretations or applications of the statute, and his regulations for the future guidance of all persons who may be affected." The court then criticized the letter-ruling on the grounds that it "amounts to *ad hoc* legislation and a simultaneous determination of violation thereof in a particular situation . . . where prior thereto the alleged transgression had not been covered or proscribed by statute or regulation." The court concluded that: "The general mandate, either statutory or administrative, must precede the specific violation."

In another case, the Wisconsin court lent its support to the proposition that agencies should favor the use of rule-making procedures, rather than relying on *ad hoc* adjudication to establish policies, by treating as a rule (within the definition in the state's Administrative Procedure Act) a decision that amounted to a "rule" in operation, even though it was not so labelled by the agency. The case involved an application for the renewal of a real estate broker license. The application was denied on the basis of a mimeographed instruction which had been issued by the agency, requiring that all members of a partnership must be licensed as real estate brokers as a condition of licensing the partnership. This mimeographed policy statement was not formulated as a rule; but the court said: "When a party files an application for a license with an administrative agency and the latter points to some announced agency policy of general application

---

[21] Boller Beverages, Inc. v. Davis, 38 N.J. 138, 142, 154-55, 183 A.2d 64 (1962).

as a reason for rejecting the application, such announced policy constitutes a rule."[22] Accordingly, the court held that the validity of this policy statement could be reviewed on application for a declaratory judgment—a procedure available only with respect to agency rules.

Section 2

Rule-Making Procedures

(A) Notice

(1) Analysis of Model Act

An increasing number of states require state agencies to do considerably more than is required of the federal agencies by the Federal Administrative Procedure Act by way of giving meaningful advance notice of proposed rule making.[23]

Many of the provisions of Section 3(a) of the Revised Model State Act, which incorporates the most thorough going requirements in this respect found in any statute in this country, are contained in existing state statutes; and the trend in new state legislation is to copy more closely the provisions of the Revised Model Act. In a number of noteworthy instances, this Model Act goes further than does the federal act,[24] in requiring the agencies to give advance notice by methods calculated to make sure that

---

22 Frankenthal v. Wisconsin Real Estate Brokers' Bd., 3 Wis. 2d 249, 257, 88 N.W.2d 352 (1958).

23 5 U.S.C. § 1003; F.C.A. 5 § 1003.

24 Section 3(a)(1) of the Revised Model State Act provides: "Prior to the adoption, amendment, or repeal of any rule, the agency shall: (1) give at least 20 days' notice of its intended action. The notice shall include a statement of either the terms or substance of the intended action or a description of the subjects and issues involved, and the time when, the place where, and the manner in which interested persons may present their views thereon. The notice shall be mailed to all persons who have made timely request of the agency for advance notice of its rule-making proceedings and shall be published in [here insert the medium of publication appropriate for the adopting state.]"

The corresponding provision of the Federal Administrative Procedure Act (5 U.S.C. § 1003; F.C.A. 5 § 1003) provides: "Except to the extent that there is involved (1) any military, naval, or foreign affairs function of the United States or (2) any matter relating to agency management or personnel or to public property, loans, grants, benefits, or contracts—(a) *Notice.*—General notice of proposed rule-making shall be published in the Federal Register (unless all persons subject thereto are named and either personally served or otherwise have actual notice thereof in accordance with law) and shall include (1) a statement of the time, place, and nature of public rule-making proceedings; (2) reference to the authority under which the rule is proposed; and (3) either the terms or substance of the

all persons having an interest in the proposed rule making will be advised of the proposed action well in advance of the institution of the rule-making proceedings. The federal act contains many exceptions, with the result that advance notice of agency rule making need not be given (1) if the rule making involves agency management or personnel, or public property, loans, grants, benefits, or contracts; (2) if the rule making involves interpretive rules, or general statements of policy, or rules of agency organization, procedure or practice; or (3) if the agency for good cause finds that notice is impracticable, unnecessary, or contrary to the public interest. There are still other exceptions.[25] But none of these exceptions appears in the Revised Model State Act. Few of them appear in the numerous state statutes which have been adopted in recent years.

The federal act is silent as to an important time element—it does not specify how long publication must precede the institution of rule-making proceedings. In the Revised Model State Act, at least twenty days' advance notice is required. The federal act makes no mandatory provision for personal notice to those having a particular interest in the subject; the Revised Model State Act does (and the statutes in many states do, likewise).

Only in respect to its requirements as to the content of the notice does the Revised Model State Act draw heavily upon the federal act. Comparable to the requirement of the federal act that the notice must include "either the terms or substance of the proposed rule or a description of the subjects and issues involved"[26] is the provision of the Revised Model State Act that the notice shall include "a statement of either the terms or substance of the intended action or a description of the subjects and issues involved." Significantly, a number of states have adopted statutes requiring that the notice which initiates rule-making proceedings must state with even greater particularity the substance of the rule which the agency proposes to adopt.

---

proposed rule or a description of the subjects and issues involved. Except where notice or hearing is required by statute, this subsection shall not apply to interpretative rules, general statements of policy, rules of agency organization, procedure, or practice, or in any situation in which the agency for good cause finds (and incorporates the finding and a brief statement of the reasons therefor in the rules issued) that notice and public procedure thereon are impracticable, unnecessary, or contrary to the public interest."

25 5 U.S.C. § 1003; F.C.A. 5 § 1003.

26 *Ibid.*

Section 3 (a) (1) of the Revised Model State Act provides:

> Prior to the adoption, amendment, or repeal of any rule, the agency shall: (1) give at least 20 days' notice of its intended action. The notice shall include a statement of either the terms or substance of the intended action or a description of the subjects and issues involved, and the time when, the place where, and the manner in which interested persons may present their views thereon. The notice shall be mailed to all persons who have made timely request of the agency for advance notice of its rule-making proceedings and shall be published in [here insert the medium of publication appropriate for the adopting state].

The critical provisions of this section are those relating to (1) the length of advance notice required; (2) the manner of publication; and (3) the contents of the notice. The significance of these provisions can be seen by an examination of the existing state statutes, in light of these three requirements of the Revised Model Act.

(2) State Legislation

Length of Advance Notice. A number of states have adopted provisions comparable to those of the Revised Model Act, requiring that notice of the proposed rule making must precede the initiation of proceedings by a specified time. The time requirements vary substantially; and a number of state legislatures have provided for more than the twenty days minimum suggested in the Revised Model State Act. The time periods specified in the various state laws are: ten days,[27] fifteen days,[28] twenty days,[29] twenty-one days,[30] and thirty days.[31]

Requirement of Publication by Printing. Most of the states which have adopted administrative procedure statutes require, as does the Revised Model Act, that notice of rule-making proce-

---

27 Indiana (ANN. STAT. § 60-1504); Nebraska (REV. STAT. § 84-907); Wisconsin (STAT. § 227.021).

28 Virginia (CODE ANN. § 9-6.4).

29 Arizona (REV. STAT. ANN. § 41-1002); Colorado (REV. STAT. ANN. § 3-16-2); Georgia (CODE ANN. § 3A-101); Hawaii (SESS. LAWS 1961, Act 103, § 3); Oklahoma (STAT. tit. 75, § 303); Rhode Island (GEN. LAWS ANN. § 42-35-3).

30 Massachusetts (GEN. LAWS ANN. ch. 30A, § 2).

31 Alaska (STAT. § 44.62.190); California (GOV'T CODE § 11423); Connecticut (GEN. STAT. REV. § 4-42); Minnesota (STAT. § 15.0412.4); Ohio (REV. CODE ANN. § 119.03); West Virginia (Acts of 1964, art. 3, ch. 1, § 2).

dures shall be published in newspapers or other generally circulated printed media.[32]

Requirement of Mailed Notice. A number of state statutes, following the suggestion of the Revised Model Act, provide in varying forms of language that an agency must give notice by mail of proposed rule making to persons who have requested that they be so notified.[33] In several of these statutes, it is further provided (for obvious reasons) that the failure of a person having made such a request to receive a copy of a particular proposed rule-making procedure, shall not afford a basis for invalidating the rule.

Other Publication Requirements. A few states require only that the notice must be filed with the secretary of state.[34] Clearly, this requirement standing alone is insufficient to assure that all interested persons will be apprised in advance of the proposed rule making. However, a requirement that the full text of the proposed rule either be filed with the secretary of state, or made available for public inspection in the offices of the agency,[35] serves a valuable purpose if made as an addition to the requirement of newspaper publication and mail service to those who had indicated their interest. A number of states have, in fact, adopted provisions in addition to the basic requirements of publication and mailing, to assure that notice of proposed agency rule making will be brought to the attention of those who presumably would have a particular interest.[36]

Contents of Rule. Coming squarely to grips with the central problem, and meeting it boldly, a number of states require that

---

[32] Alaska (STAT. § 44.62.190); California (GOV'T CODE § 11423); Connecticut (GEN. STAT. REV. § 4-42); Georgia (CODE ANN. § 3A-101); Hawaii (SESS. LAWS 1961, Act 103, § 3); Indiana (ANN. STAT. § 60-1504); Massachusetts (GEN. LAWS ANN. ch. 30A, § 2); Nebraska (REV. STAT. § 84-907); Oklahoma (STAT. tit. 75, § 303); Rhode Island (GEN. LAWS ANN. § 42-35-3); Virginia (CODE ANN. § 9-6.4); Wisconsin (STAT. § 227.021).

[33] Alaska (STAT. § 44.62.190); California (GOV'T CODE § 11423); Colorado (REV. STAT. ANN. § 3-16-2); Georgia (CODE ANN. § 3A-101); Hawaii (SESS. LAWS 1961, Act 103, § 3); Massachusetts (GEN. LAWS ANN. ch. 30A, § 2); Michigan (STAT. ANN. § 3.560); Minnesota (STAT. § 15.0412); Oklahoma (STAT. tit. 75, § 303); Rhode Island (GEN. LAWS ANN. § 42-35-3); West Virginia (Acts of 1964, art. 3, ch. 1, § 2).

[34] Arizona (REV. STAT. ANN. § 41-1002); Ohio (REV. CODE ANN. § 119.-03).

[35] *Cf.* Colorado (REV. STAT. ANN. § 3-16-2); Indiana (ANN. STAT. § 60-1504); Ohio (REV. CODE ANN. § 119.03).

[36] Alaska (STAT. § 44.62.190); California (GOV'T CODE § 11423); Wisconsin (STAT. § 227.021).

the notice shall set forth either the text of the proposed rule, or an informative summary of the proposed action. This requirement, which goes further than that of the Revised Model State Act, provides a realistic and workable answer to the key problem, viz.: how to let interested persons know, before action is taken, what rule the agency proposes to adopt. The agencies usually have in mind a definite proposal before rule-making proceedings are initiated. The public hearings are called not so much for the purpose of producing new suggestions for the agency to consider, as to test the public acceptability and the practicality of a suggestion the agency has in mind. It is therefore no handicap to the agencies that they be required to make the proposed text public. In some cases, of course, the proposed rule is so lengthy that publication of the complete text would be unduly expensive; in such cases, publication of an informative summary will suffice.[37]

Other states have adopted substantially the language of the Revised Model Act.[38] The statutes in some states look in this direction, but are less explicit in their requirements.[39]

Invitation to Present Views. To make sure that all interested parties are apprised of their privilege to participate in the rule-making proceedings, it is desirable that the notice remind all to whose attention it comes, that they have the privilege of presenting their views. It is for this purpose that the Revised Model State Act requires that the notice shall state "the time when, the place where, and the manner in which interested persons may present their views." This language has been adopted, in substance or verbatim, in a number of state statutes.[40] Other state statutes, not requiring quite so explicit an invitation to the public to participate in the formulation of the rule, provide only

---

[37] Alaska (STAT. § 44.62.200); Arizona (REV. STAT. ANN. § 41-1002); California (GOV'T CODE § 11423); Virginia (CODE ANN. § 9-6.4); Wisconsin (STAT. § 227.021).

[38] Colorado (REV. STAT. ANN. § 3-16-2); Connecticut (GEN. STAT. REV. § 4-42); Georgia (CODE ANN. § 3A-101); Hawaii (SESS. LAWS 1961, Act 103, § 3, requires publication of the substance of the proposed rule); Massachusetts (GEN. LAWS ANN. ch. 30A, § 2); Oklahoma (STAT. tit. 75, § 303); Rhode Island (GEN. LAWS ANN. § 42-35-3); Washington (REV. CODE § 34.04.020).

[39] Indiana (ANN. STAT. § 60-1504—notice shall refer to subject matter of proposed rule); Ohio (REV. CODE ANN. § 119.03—notice shall contain a synopsis of proposed rule or a general statement of the subject matter).

[40] Georgia (CODE ANN. § 3A-101); Hawaii (SESS. LAWS 1961, Act 103, § 3); Oklahoma (STAT. tit. 75, § 303); Rhode Island (GEN. LAWS ANN. § 42-35-3).

that the notice must recite the time, place, and nature of the contemplated rule-making proceedings.[41] Still others require only that the notice must state the time and place of the rule-making proceedings.[42] In several states, which adopted the language of the original Model State Act and have not yet updated their statutes, it is required only that prior to the adoption of any rule, or the amendment or repeal thereof, the adopting agency shall, so far as practicable, publish or otherwise circulate notice of its intended action and afford interested persons opportunity to submit suggestions orally or in writing.[43] Experience in those states has demonstrated that these mild and hortatory requirements are not always sufficient to induce agencies to publish the really informative, helpful notices containing the details that are made a matter of specific requirement in the Revised Model State Act.

Authority. A few states, following the suggestion of the federal act[44] require that the notice must set forth a reference to the authority under which the regulation is proposed, and a reference to the code sections which are being implemented.[45] In some cases such a requirement may be of real help; but in most instances, there is little question as to either the rule-making authority of the agency or the sections of the statute which the regulation will implement.

Escape Clauses. Perhaps the outstanding feature of the state legislation is that it is notably free of the exceptions and escape clauses which exist in the federal act[46] and which have long been a source of trouble, as pointed out in the perceptive criticisms of the Hoover Commission Task Force on Legal Services

---

41 Alaska (STAT. § 44.62.200); Arizona (REV. STAT. ANN. § 41-1002); California (GOV'T CODE § 11424); Virginia (CODE ANN. § 9-6.4); Washington (REV. CODE § 34.04.020).

42 Indiana (ANN. STAT. § 60-1504); Massachusetts (GEN. LAWS ANN. ch. 30A, § 2); Ohio (REV. CODE ANN. § 119.03); Wisconsin (STAT. § 227.021).

43 Maine (REV. STAT. ANN. ch. 20-A, § 2); Maryland (ANN. CODE art. 41, § 245); Michigan (STAT. ANN. § 3.560(21.2)); Minnesota (STAT. § 15.0412); Nebraska (REV. STAT. § 84-909); Oregon (REV. STAT. § 183.330); Texas (REV. CIV. STAT. art. 6252-13, § 2).

44 5 U.S.C. § 1003; F.C.A. 5 § 1003.

45 Alaska (STAT. § 44.62.200); Arizona (REV. STAT. ANN. § 41-1002); California (GOV'T CODE § 11424); Colorado (REV. STAT. ANN. § 3-16-2); Connecticut (GEN. STAT. REV. § 4-42); Massachusetts (GEN. LAWS ANN. ch. 30A, § 3); Virginia (CODE ANN. § 9-6.4); Washington (REV. CODE § 34.04.020); Wisconsin (STAT. § 227.021).

46 5 U.S.C. § 1003; F.C.A. 5 § 1003.

and Procedure.[47] Few of the state statutes contain such escape clauses. Their general purport is that notice must always be given (except in the case of emergency rules, discussed *infra,* where the notice requirements are substantially modified). But a few state statutes do have provisions which enable agencies to avoid the normal requirement of giving notice in special circumstances. Thus, the Massachusetts statute[48] authorizes agencies to dispense with the notice requirements if the agency finds that compliance therewith would be unnecessary, impracticable, or contrary to the public interest, and if the agency incorporates in the rule a brief statement supporting its findings in that regard. The Nebraska statute[49] authorizes the governor, for good cause shown prior to the adoption of the rule, to waive the requirements for publishing notice, in particular cases. The Washington statute[50] contains an exception for interpretive rules, general statements of policy, and rules of internal agency organization, procedure or practice.

Indicative of the cool reception accorded these escape clauses by the state courts is a decision in Massachusetts,[51] which, while upholding a determination of the agency that under the circumstances notice was not necessary, gently chided the agency for its failure to give notice, and emphasized its remarks by remanding the case to the agency, for further consideration of the matter.

(3) Court Decisions as to Sufficiency of Notice

The purposes intended to be served by state laws requiring the publication of notice, prior to the adoption of rules by state agencies, were well stated by the Connecticut court in two cases. Both involved the giving of notice in connection with applications to zoning boards. In both cases, the notice was held adequate.

In the first case, the court noted that the challenged notice referred to everything upon which the agency proposed to act

47 Commission on Organization of Executive Branch of Government, TASK FORCE REPORT ON LEGAL SERVICES AND PROCEDURE 159 (1955).

48 MASS. GEN. LAWS ANN. ch. 30A, § 3.

49 NEB. REV. STAT. § 84-907.

50 WASH. REV. CODE § 34.04.020.

51 Harris v. Board of Registration in Chiropody (Podiatry), 343 Mass. 536, 179 N.E.2d 910 (1962).

and invited the attention of the public thereto. This, the court indicated, is the basic test which must be satisfied. Finding that it was satisfied, the court said:

> No one could be misled by the notice, and all affected persons were apprised of the change sought. They were fully and fairly advised of their opportunity to be heard on specific matters; this, it might be added, is the fundamental reason for any requirement of notice.[52]

Beyond these basic purposes, it was noted in the other Connecticut decision, is the requirement of fairness. The posting of notice must be more than a mere formality, marking a waiting period which must elapse before the rule becomes effective. The agency must, in fairness, withhold final judgment as to what the rule shall be until it has heard and considered the representations made by those who will be affected by the rule. As the court put it:

> If the public hearing was had merely to comply with a statutory requirement and if the commission had theretofore resolved that, regardless of what might be developed by those in attendance, the zones were to be established as previously determined, the action of the commission might well be classified as arbitrary. The ultimate decision to effect a change in the boundaries had to await the hearing, at which the public were privileged to express themselves.[53]

The state courts have held invalid rules adopted without the statutory notice and hearing.[54] Further, if the notice given is insufficient, as judged by the statutory requirements, the rule may be set aside.[55] However, in judging the sufficiency of compliance with the statutory requirements, the state courts apply the rule of reason. A merely technical defect, which is not shown to have resulted in prejudice, will not be enough to invalidate the rule. Thus, it is not a fatal defect if the notice of a zoning hearing does not set out the exact boundaries of the proposed use zone, so long as the notice apprises interested persons of the general nature of the proposed changes.[56] Similarly, where an

---

[52] Winslow v. Zoning Bd., 143 Conn. 381, 388-89, 122 A.2d 789 (1956).

[53] Couch v. Zoning Comm'n, 141 Conn. 349, 357, 106 A.2d 173 (1954).

[54] Shellnut v. Arkansas State Game & Fish Comm'n, 222 Ark. 25, 258 S.W.2d 570 (1953); J. H. Adams v. Lee, 89 So. 2d 217 (Fla. 1956); Safeway Stores, Inc. v. Ohlsen, 192 Ore. 1, 233 P.2d 778 (1951).

[55] Treat v. Town Plan & Zoning Comm'n, 145 Conn. 136, 139 A.2d 601 (1958); State *ex rel.* Seaboard Air Line R.R. v. King, 93 So. 2d 368 (Fla. 1957).

[56] Ciaffone v. Community Shopping Corp., 195 Va. 41, 77 S.E.2d 817 (1953).

insurance commissioner published notices fully conforming to the statutory requirement in newspapers in ten cities, and published abbreviated notices in other newspapers, it was held that there was substantial compliance with the statutory requirement and that, no prejudice having been shown, the proceedings were valid.[57] In other cases, alleged technical deficiencies in the giving of the statutory notice were held to afford no basis for upsetting the rule, where it appeared that the notice as published was sufficient to accomplish the legislative purpose of giving all interested persons sufficient advance notice of the contents of the proposed rule to permit them to ascertain whether protection of their interests required them to intervene in the proceedings.[58]

(B) Requirement of Hearing

The Revised Model State Act goes further than the corresponding provisions of the Federal Administrative Procedure Act[59] in guaranteeing to interested persons an opportunity to participate in agency rule-making proceedings and to present their views as to what the rule should be.

(1) Analysis of Model Act

The Revised Model State Act provides[60] that prior to the adoption, amendment, or repeal of any rule, the agency shall:

> afford all interested persons reasonable opportunity to submit data, views, or arguments, orally or in writing. In case of substantive rules, opportunity for oral hearing must be granted if requested by 25 persons, by a governmental subdivision or agency, or by an association having not less than 25 members. The agency shall consider fully all written and oral submissions respecting the proposed rule. Upon adoption of a rule, the agency, if requested to do so by an interested person either prior to adoption or within 30 days thereafter, shall issue a concise statement of the principal reasons for and against its adoption, incorporating therein its reasons for overruling the considerations urged against its adoption.

---

57 Century Cab Inc. v. Commissioner of Ins., 327 Mass. 652, 100 N.E.2d 481 (1951).

58 Neuger v. Zoning Bd., 145 Conn. 625, 145 A.2d 738 (1958); Welsand v. Minnesota R. & Warehouse Comm'n, 251 Minn. 504, 88 N.W.2d 834 (1958); N. H. Lyons & Co. v. Corsi, 3 N.Y.2d 60, 163 N.Y.S.2d 677, 143 N.E.2d 392 (1957); Cayuga County v. McHugh, 4 N.Y.2d 609, 176 N.Y.S.2d 643, 152 N.E. 2d 73 (1958).

59 5 U.S.C. § 1003; F.C.A. 5 § 1003.

60 Section 3(a)(2).

In its requirement that oral arguments be allowed in specified cases (a requirement not found in the federal act),[61] the Revised Model State Act recognizes that an opportunity for confrontation of the agency officers who are to adopt the rule is more likely to result in full understanding of, and consideration of, the views of the interested parties than is any procedure calling merely for the filing of written statements. Such submissions are too easily skimmed over without careful study, or handed to staff assistants for their consideration, or even (it may be feared) sometimes disregarded.

But recognizing that the hearing of too many oral arguments might impose onerous burdens, the guarantee for oral hearings is limited to cases involving substantive rules. The draftsmen believed that where the rule concerned merely matters of agency procedure, with respect to which agency officials possess a high degree of discretion as well as an intimate knowledge of the problems involved, the requirement for oral argument as a matter of absolute right was not justified.

As a means of making sure that agencies will faithfully follow the statutory mandate that they "consider fully all written and oral submissions," provision is made for requiring the agencies to demonstrate the care with which they considered such submissions by issuing a statement of their reasons for overruling the points urged in those submissions which were overruled.

(2) State Legislation

Substantially all of the states which have enacted codes of administrative procedure have embraced the general principle that in adopting rules, agencies must afford reasonable opportunity to interested persons to submit their views to the agency as to the content of the proposed rule, and thus afford the public at least a minimal opportunity to participate in the rule-making procedure.[62] Some states go much further, in making sure that

---

[61] See note 59 *supra*.

[62] Alaska (STAT. § 44.62.210); Arizona (REV. STAT. ANN. § 41-1002); California (GOV'T CODE § 11425); Connecticut (GEN. STAT. REV. § 4-43); Hawaii (SESS. LAWS 1961, Act 103, § 3); Indiana (ANN. STAT. § 60-1504); Maine (REV. STAT. ANN. ch. 20-A, § 2); Maryland (ANN. CODE art. 41, § 245(c)); Massachusetts—with a proviso that the agency may dispense with such requirement when found to be unnecessary, impracticable, or contrary to the public interest (GEN. LAWS ANN. ch. 30A, § 3); Michigan (STAT. ANN. § 3.560(21.2)); Minnesota (STAT. § 15.0412); Nebraska (REV. STAT. § 84-909); Oklahoma (STAT. tit. 75,

the right to public participation in rule-making proceedings can be effectively exercised. Outstanding examples are afforded by the statutes of Ohio and Wisconsin.

The Ohio statute[63] requires the agencies, in connection with the adoption, amendment, or rescission of rules, to hold public hearings, at which any person who would be affected by the proposed rule may be heard in person, or by attorney, orally or in writing. Guaranteeing full-scale hearings, the statute provides for the examination of witnesses, and for the making of a stenographic record of the testimony.

The Wisconsin statute,[64] reflecting the long experience from which the state has benefited—Wisconsin being one of the pioneers in the adoption of statutes regulating state administrative procedure—prescribes in detail the terms and conditions under which public participation in agency rule making is to be afforded. The statute provides that agencies shall hold public hearings antecedent all rule-making activities unless the proposed rule is procedural, or is designed merely to conform a pre-existing rule with the requirements of statutory amendments or judicial decisions, or is an emergency rule. There is a further provision which is of particular interest. It ordains that if an agency publishes the proposed rule in the state "administrative register" and announces it intends to adopt the rule, then it may do so without public hearing unless within thirty days a request for a hearing is filed by twenty-five interested persons, or a municipality which will be affected, or by an association that represents a farm, labor, business, or professional group which will be affected by the rule. Thus, agencies are spared the burden of conducting public hearings in cases where there is no substantial interest, but at the same time the rights of interested persons to have a hearing are fully protected.

A number of other states have adopted statutes requiring that in specified cases opportunity for oral argument must be afforded. Sometimes this is accomplished by a statutory requirement that there must be a public hearing on the proposed rule prior to its

---

§ 3031); Oregon (REV. STAT. § 183.330); Rhode Island (GEN. LAWS ANN. § 42-35-37); Texas (REV. CIV. STAT. art. 6252-13, § 2); Virginia (CODE ANN. § 9-6.6); Washington (REV. CODE § 34.04.020).

[63] OHIO REV. CODE ANN. § 119.03.

[64] WIS. STAT. § 227.02.

adoption.[65] The Colorado statute[66] provides that there shall be an opportunity to present views orally unless the agency deems such procedure unnecessary. Similarly, the Massachusetts statute[67] provides that if the agency finds that oral presentation is unnecessary or impracticable, it may limit the parties to submission of views in writing. Oklahoma[68] and Rhode Island[69] have adopted the limited guarantee for oral hearings provided in the Revised Model State Act.

While comparatively few states have, as yet, adopted the provision of the Revised Model State Act designed to guarantee agency consideration of the submissions by requiring the agency to submit a detailed statement explaining its reasons for overruling objections,[70] many state statutes contain a general requirement—which hopefully will be self-enforcing—that in adopting the rule, the agency must give consideration to the submissions which have been made.[71]

Provisions of especial interest are found in the statutes of Indiana and Iowa. The Indiana statute[72] contains a permissive provision encouraging agencies to hold conferences and invite the submission of suggestions in advance of the drafting of the proposed rule. This provision surely deserves consideration, for both agencies and individuals may benefit from this procedure. It assures the agencies the benefit of information that might not otherwise come to the attention of agency staffs, at a time when the agency's thinking about the subject is still in a formative stage. It is of value to those outside the agency, because of the simple psychological truth that it is easier to persuade agency

[65] Minnesota (STAT. § 15.0412); Nebraska (REV. STAT. § 84-907); Ohio (REV. CODE ANN. § 119.03); Virginia (CODE ANN. § 9-6.6).

[66] COLO. REV. STAT. ANN. § 3-16-2.

[67] MASS. GEN. LAWS ANN. ch. 30A, § 3(2).

[68] OKLA. STAT. tit. 75, § 303.

[69] R.I. GEN. LAWS ANN. § 42-35-3; and see GA. CODE ANN. § 3A-101).

[70] Georgia (CODE ANN. § 3A-101) and Rhode Island (GEN. LAWS ANN. § 42-35-3) have adopted the provisions of the Revised Model State Act. Some requirements for the filing of a concise general statement of the basis and purpose of the rule are found in the statutes of Colorado (REV. STAT. ANN. § 3-16-2); Connecticut (GEN. STAT. REV. § 4-43); Hawaii (SESS. LAWS 1961, Act 103, § 3); Massachusetts (GEN. LAWS ANN. ch. 30A, § 3); and Oregon (REV. STAT. § 183.330).

[71] Alaska (STAT. § 44.62.210); California (GOV'T CODE § 11425); Colorado (REV. STAT. ANN. § 3-16-2); Connecticut (GEN. STAT. REV. § 4-43); Hawaii (SESS. LAWS 1961, Act 103, § 3); Indiana (ANN. STAT. § 60-1504); Oklahoma (H.B. 865, 1963, § 3); Oregon (REV. STAT. § 183.330).

[72] IND. ANN. STAT. § 60-1504.

staffs before their views have become crystallized through the adoption of a definitive proposed regulation. The Iowa statute[73] makes specific provision for a petition for reconsideration. It declares that any person substantially interested in an agency rule may petition the agency for a reconsideration of such rule; and he shall thereupon become entitled to a public hearing on the question.

In some states[74] there is no guarantee of public participation in the formulation of interpretive rules, general statements of policy, or rules of internal agency organization, procedure, or practice. Massachusetts[75] goes even further, authorizing agencies to dispense with the opportunities for public participation if the agency finds that such participation in a particular case is unnecessary, impracticable, or contrary to the public interest; and Nebraska[76] provides that the governor may, for good cause shown, waive compliance by an agency with the normal requirements for public participation.

(3) Practical Problems

The matter of permitting public participation in agency rule-making proceedings is an eminently practical problem.

The state statutes, either because of their explicitness (in some cases) or (in other cases) their very vagueness, have given rise to but little litigation. Few are the court cases concerned with the matter of public participation in rule-making proceedings. The Missouri court held[77] that a zoning regulation which had been adopted without observance of the required public hearing procedure was therefore invalid, thus recognizing that the statutory requirements should be construed as mandatory, and not merely directory. On the other hand, where the party raising the objection had not availed himself of the opportunity to be heard,[78] or where the protest is a merely formal one—*e.g.*, that the witnesses at the hearing were not sworn—[79] the objections will be overruled.

---

[73] IOWA CODE § 17A.13.
[74] Oregon (REV. STAT. § 183.330); Washington (REV. CODE § 34.04.020).
[75] MASS. GEN. LAWS ANN. ch. 30A, § 3.
[76] NEB. REV. STAT. § 84-907.
[77] State *ex rel.* Sims v. Eckhardt, 322 S.W.2d 903 (Mo. 1959).
[78] Treat v. Town Plan & Zoning Comm'n, note 55 *supra*.
[79] Yellow Cab Co. v. City of Chicago, 23 Ill. 2d 453, 178 N.E.2d 330 (1961).

More significant than the statutory right to present views at a formal hearing are the opportunities which may be afforded interested persons to engage in informal consultations with agency representatives before the rule is adopted. Even in cases where the statute does not require, and the agency does not voluntarily solicit, public participation in rule-making procedures, the members of an agency staff engaged in drafting the rule will almost always be found willing to receive the suggestions of interested persons as to the formulation of the rule, and to discuss informally the problems involved.

Such informal consultation may afford the most effective method for participation in rule-making proceedings. If one can discuss the problems involved with the draftsmen within the agency's staff who will write the proposed rule that the heads of the agency will consider, it is often possible to obtain a more intimate insight into the agency's views than is available in more formal public hearings.

In such discussions, furthermore, representatives of private parties are afforded an unparalleled opportunity to suggest methods whereby the agency's purposes can be achieved with least dislocation of business practices. Staff members can point out administrative objections to the proposals urged by private parties. Frequently, an area of mutually satisfactory compromise can be discovered.[80]

A device that can be employed most effectively in many instances is that of an unofficial advisory committee. Such committees have the function of working out technically acceptable solutions to problems complicated both by administrative difficulties and by emotional clashes between competing special interest groups.

An informative discussion of the operations of such advisory committees may be found in Robert M. Benjamin's discussion of the adoption of Industrial Code Rules in New York.[81] He points out:

> The usual procedure for formulating the set of rules making up a particular code project is as follows: There is a preliminary study by administrative personnel, which produces a body of factual material

80 *Cf.*, COOPER, THE LAWYER AND ADMINISTRATIVE AGENCIES 274 et seq. (1957).

81 BENJAMIN, ADMINISTRATIVE ADJUDICATION IN THE STATE OF NEW YORK 304 et seq. (1942).

> and also, normally, a first draft of the rules. The factual material and the first draft (if one has been prepared) are then submitted to an advisory committee appointed for the particular project. The advisory committee is made up in part of administrative personnel . . . , the remaining members being either persons experienced in the field or persons representing interests to be affected by the rules. . . . The advisory committee carries on its activities through meetings of the full committee and through studies by subcommittees of particular aspects of the code project—the subcommittees reporting their findings and recommendations to the full committee for its consideration. . . . Finally, on the basis of these studies . . . the advisory committee prepares what are known as "proposed rules"; these rules are submitted to the Board. . . . The next procedural step is the scheduling of public hearings by the Board.

Pointing out the advantages inherent in the use of such informal advisory committees, Mr. Benjamin observed:

> . . . it is a distinguishing characteristic of the consultative method of quasi-legislative procedure that it permits active participation in the actual formulation of regulations by those whom the regulations will affect and by others outside the administrative organization. This is a feature of great value, and one which suggests that the consultative method should be used frequently.

Mr. Benjamin also points out possible disadvantages, particularly when conflicting interests are not fairly represented; and he observes that those who participate in consultation are likely to have more influence on the final result than those who participate in the public hearings.[82]

A similar procedure has long worked well in Wisconsin, where the industrial commission has for many years had an advisory committee representing the various interests directly affected. A report of the Wisconsin Legislative Council[83] describes the procedure employed. It is much like that of New York. The secretary of the committee, prior to the committee's meeting, usually makes a rough draft of the proposed rule. But thereafter, the actual drafting process is in large measure the responsibility of the whole committee. When a draft of the rule has been completed to the satisfaction of the advisory committee, it is scheduled for public hearing.

---

[82] *Id.* at 308.

[83] II WISCONSIN LEGISLATIVE COUNCIL, 1955 REPORT, *Administrative Rule Making,* part II, at 39-40.

The use of advisory committees, and similar devices designed to facilitate the participation of informed and interested persons in the actual drafting process, deserves careful examination. It is surely the most efficient method available of permitting effective public participation in the formulation of agency rules. Its benefits redound both to the agencies and to those whom will be affected by the rules.

(C) EMERGENCY RULES

(1) Analysis of Model Act

The requirements for notice and opportunity for participation in the rule-making process, and the provisions for delayed effective dates[84] prescribed by the Revised Model State Act as limits on the exercise of discretion by agencies in their quasi-legislative activities, do unquestionably result in slowing down the administrative rule-making process. In the normal case, this is desirable. But instances do exist where a demonstrable public need for speedy action recommends that emergency rules be made temporarily effective without observance of the normal safeguards.

For these reasons, provision is made in the Revised Model State Act that:

> If an agency finds that an imminent peril to the public health, safety, or welfare requires adoption of a rule upon fewer than 20 days' notice and states in writing its reasons for that finding, it may proceed without prior notice or hearing or upon any abbreviated notice and hearing that it finds practicable, to adopt an emergency rule. The rule may be effective for a period of not longer than 120 days [renewable once for a period not exceeding — days], but the adoption of an identical rule under subsections (a) (1) and (a) (2) of this Section is not precluded.[85]

(2) State Legislation

The three fundamental limitations applicable to emergency rules relate, respectively, to (1) the conditions which must be satisfied before an emergency rule may be adopted; (2) the length of time for which an emergency rule may remain in effect; (3) whether an emergency rule may be renewed.

---

[84] See Ch. VIII, § 1(D) *infra*.
[85] Section 3(b).

Conditions. The two most important conditions precedent to the adoption of an emergency rule are (a) that the rule is necessary to the preservation of the public health, safety, or welfare, and (b) that there exists an imminent or immediate threat which necessitates prompt action. All of the states which have adopted one of these conditions have adopted the other one as well; and this is not surprising, for if the two conditions are not combined (and especially, if the requirement as to the imminence of the public peril be omitted) almost any rule could be described as an emergency rule. Most states which have enacted statutes authorizing the adoption of emergency rules require that both these conditions must be met before an emergency rule can be adopted.[86]

In order to make these limitations truly effective, it is important to provide that before adopting an emergency rule, the agency must make and file written findings demonstrating the existence of the prescribed conditions. This provision, too, has been widely adopted, although not so widely as the requirement that there must exist an imminent or immediate peril to the public health, safety, or welfare.[87]

On the other hand, a few state statutes contain a general exemption from the normal requirements of notice and hearing in the case of "emergency" rules, without specifying the conditions under which this procedure (and the consequent interference with private rights) may be invoked.[88] Such provisions create a danger that agencies may invoke asserted emergency powers, when in fact no emergency exists. This is demonstrated by the experience in Michigan, where it is provided[89] that a

---

[86] Alaska (STAT. § 44.62.250); Arizona (REV. STAT. ANN. § 41-1003); California (GOV'T CODE § 11421); Colorado (REV. STAT. ANN. § 3-16-2); Florida (STAT. § 120.041); Georgia (CODE ANN. § 3A-101); Hawaii (SESS. LAWS 1961, Act 103, § 3); Massachusetts (GEN. LAWS ANN. ch. 30A, § 2); Oklahoma (STAT. tit. 75, § 303); Rhode Island (GEN. LAWS ANN. § 42-35-3); Virginia (CODE ANN. § 9-6.5); Washington (REV. CODE § 34.04.030); West Virginia (Acts 1964, art. 3, ch. 1, § 5); Wisconsin (STAT. § 227.027).

[87] State statutes requiring the filing of written findings include Alaska (STAT. § 44.62.250); California (GOV'T CODE § 11421); Colorado (REV. STAT. ANN. § 3-16-2); Florida (STAT. § 120.041); Georgia (CODE ANN. § 3A-101); Hawaii (SESS. LAWS 1961, Act 103, § 3); Massachusetts (GEN. LAWS ANN. ch. 30A, § 2); Oklahoma (STAT. tit. 75, § 303); Rhode Island (GEN. LAWS ANN. § 42-35-3); Washington (REV. CODE § 34.04.030); West Virginia (Acts 1964, art. 3, ch. 1, § 5).

[88] Connecticut (GEN. STAT. REV. § 4-47); Minnesota (STAT. § 15.0412); *Cf.* Iowa (CODE § 17A.1).

[89] MICH. COMP. LAWS § 24.75. A similar provision applies in Ohio (REV. CODE ANN. § 119.03).

certification by the governor is enough to establish the existence of an emergency. In Michigan, it was for a long time a common practice to label almost every rule an emergency rule, and to obtain the necessary gubernatorial certification, permitting agencies to avoid the normal procedural requirements.

Duration of Rule. The state statutes show considerable variation as to the length of time that an emergency rule may remain in effect, varying from 60 to 120 days.[90] In a few states, no limit is provided on the duration of emergency rules, with the result that a rule labelled as an "emergency" measure may endure permanently even though the public had been given no opportunity to participate in its formulation.[91]

Renewal. Few state statutes contain an explicit prohibition, such as that found in the Revised Model State Act, proscribing the unlimited renewal of an emergency rule. The effect of such omission, of course, is to enable an agency to evade the normal requirements by repeated re-enactments of a rule labelled as an "emergency rule." It may be presumed that the courts might intervene if it could be demonstrated that this device were being employed in bad faith to evade the legislative mandate; but it would seem that enactment of a positive prohibition is justified.[92]

(3) Court Decisions

A Massachusetts decision[93] sustaining an emergency rule, contains the suggestion that the courts will consider, in reviewing the validity of challenged emergency rules, whether the adminis-

---

[90] The limit is 120 days in California (GOV'T CODE § 11422.1); Georgia (CODE ANN. § 3A-101); Hawaii (SESS. LAWS 1961, Act 103, § 3); Oklahoma (STAT. tit. 75, § 303); Rhode Island (GEN. LAWS ANN. § 42-35-3); Wisconsin (STAT. § 227.027). A limit of three months is provided in Colorado (REV. STAT. ANN. § 3-16-2), and Massachusetts (GEN. LAWS ANN. ch. 30A, § 2). A similar limit of 90 days is provided in Alaska (STAT. § 44.62.260); Florida (STAT. § 120.041); Washington (REV. CODE § 34.04.030); and West Virginia (Acts 1964, art. 3, ch. 1, § 5). A limit of 60 days is found in the statutes of Minnesota (STAT. § 15.0412); Ohio (REV. CODE ANN. § 119.03); and Virginia (CODE ANN. § 9-6.5).

[91] Arizona (REV. STAT. ANN. § 41-1003); Connecticut (GEN. STAT. REV. § 4-47); Michigan (COMP. LAWS § 24.75).

[92] Hawaii provides there may be no renewal of an emergency rule (SESS. LAWS 1961, Act 103, § 3). Rhode Island, following the Revised Model Act, permits one renewal (GEN. LAWS ANN. § 42-35-3). An unusual provision is found in the Minnesota statute (STAT. § 15.0412), which provides that an emergency rule "may not immediately be reissued or continued." Arguably, if the agency let one day intervene between the expiration of a rule and its renewal, the statutory mandate would be satisfied.

[93] Dacey v. Milk Control Comm'n, 340 Mass. 681, 166 N.E.2d 362 (1960).

trative finding of an emergency is "arbitrary or capricious" or an "abuse of discretion."

The results that may follow if the statutes permit adoption of emergency rules without a clear showing that specified conditions have been met, and without a specific limitation on their duration, are illustrated by an Ohio decision[94] upholding a "ninth supplemental emergency order" in circumstances where it appears that emergency orders had been in effect continuously for more than four years.

(D) Petitions for Adoption of Rules

In the state agencies, occasions for the submission by private parties of requests for the adoption, amendment, or repeal of a rule, arise more frequently than in the case of the federal agencies. There are many reasons for this. One of them is the very accessibility of the state agencies. They are comparatively small, and neighborly in point of geography (if not attitude), and characteristically informal in their operations. It is therefore easy for the parties involved to seek a solution to their problem by asking the agency to adopt a rule that will provide an acceptable solution. A more important reason, probably, is that many state agencies operate in spheres directly affecting details of peculiarly personal concern; their problems, by and large, are more simple than those of the federal agencies, and may touch many individuals more directly. For example, to ask a state insurance commission to adopt a rule concerning the payment of premiums to insurance agents is a much simpler and less formidable task than to undertake to initiate proceedings before the Federal Trade Commission for the promulgation of a nationwide industry code of fair competitive practices.

Recognizing the need, and the frequent occasions for its exercise, the draftsmen of the original Model State Administrative Procedure Act provided that:

> Any interested person may petition an agency requesting the promulgation, amendment, or repeal of any rule. Each agency shall prescribe by rule the form for such petitions and the procedure for their submission, consideration, and disposition.[95]

---

[94] Cincinnati Gas & Elec. Co. v. Public Utils. Comm'n, 157 Ohio St. 574, 106 N.E.2d 642 (1952).

[95] Section 5.

This provision found favor with the legislatures in many states, and was widely adopted.[96] However, it did not produce wholly satisfactory results. Some agencies were lax in complying with the duty to adopt such rules. Many that did adopt rules chose to cast them in form which did not impose any definite procedure to assure that careful consideration would in fact be given to such petitions. In point of fact, many such petitions, after being filed, were never heard of again. The petition would be turned over to appropriate staff assistants, and that would be the end of the matter. There would be no public hearing. There would be no opportunity to bring the matter to the attention of the agency heads in any meaningful way. Worst of all, no action would be taken.

Determined that something should be done to correct this situation, the draftsmen of the Revised Model State Act chose to draw on the provisions of the Wisconsin Act, which had been tested by experience and had proved workable and effective. The carefully considered provisions of the Wisconsin Act merit the consideration of any group engaged in drafting administrative procedure legislation for any state.

Under the leadership of such men as James J. Burke, Revisor of Statutes, and Earl Sachse, of the Wisconsin Joint Legislative Council, it was determined that some method should be devised that would avoid the difficulty of having the time of agency officials taken up with unfounded and "pestiferous" petitions, but would at the same time assure that active consideration would be given to any petition deserving serious attention. It was determined that these ends could best be achieved by making the procedure depend upon the number of persons requesting action. If a single individual files a petition, the agency may dispose of it in such manner as seems to it most appropriate; but if a group of five or more persons join in the petition (or if it is filed by a municipality) the agency is required "within a reasonable period of time" to "either deny the petition in writing or proceed with the requested rule making." The statute further provides: "If the agency denies the petition, it shall promptly give notice

---

[96] Maine (REV. STAT. ANN. ch. 20-A, § 5); Maryland (ANN. CODE art. 41, § 248); Massachusetts (GEN. LAWS ANN. ch. 30A, § 4); Michigan (STAT. ANN. § 3.560(21.3)); Minnesota (STAT. § 15.0415); Nebraska (REV. STAT. § 84-910); Oklahoma (STAT. tit. 75, § 305); Oregon (REV. STAT. § 183.890); Washington (REV. CODE § 34.04.060).

thereof to the person who filed the petition, including a brief statement of its reasons for the denial." If the agency proceeds with the requested rule making, it is directed to follow the provisions applicable to adoption of any agency rule. The Wisconsin statute further prescribes, with meticulous care, the form of such petitions. They must "state clearly and concisely: (a) the substance or nature of the rule making which is requested; and (b) the reasons for the request and the petitioners' interest in the request; and (c) references to the authority of the agency to take the action which is requested."[97]

In an effort to capture the essence of the Wisconsin provision in a briefer, simpler, more modest form, the Revised Model State Act provides:

> An interested person may petition an agency requesting the promulgation, amendment, or repeal of a rule. Each agency shall prescribe by rule the form for petitions and the procedure for their submission, consideration, and disposition. Within 30 days after submission of a petition, the agency either shall deny the petition in writing (stating its reasons for the denials) or shall initiate rule making proceedings in accordance with Section 3.[98]

Provisions substantially similar to those of the Revised Model Act have already been adopted in a number of states.[99] An Iowa statute requires an agency to grant a public hearing on petitions for adoption of rules.[100] This, of course, requires the agency to give at least a modicum of attention to the request. Other states have statutes that permit the filing of requests that rules be adopted but fail to require the agency to act upon such petitions.[101]

The Federal Administrative Procedure Act[102] provides merely that "Every agency shall accord any interested person the right to petition for issuance, amendment, or repeal of a rule." It is thus subject to the same defects that hampered the effectiveness

---

97 WIS. STAT. § 227.015.

98 Section 6.

99 Alaska (STAT. § 44.62.220); California (GOV'T CODE § 11426); Georgia (CODE ANN. § 3A-101); Hawaii (SESS. LAWS 1961, Act 103, § 6); Rhode Island (GEN. LAWS ANN. § 42-35-6).

100 IOWA CODE § 17A.13.

101 Colorado (REV. STAT. ANN. § 3-16-2); Connecticut (GEN. STAT. REV. § 4-44); Missouri (REV. STAT. § 536.040); North Dakota (CENT. CODE § 28-32-04); Virginia (CODE ANN. § 9-6.8).

102 5 U.S.C. § 1003; F.C.A. 5 § 1003.

of the original Model State Act. The Task Force on Legal Services and Procedure of the Second Hoover Commission, noted:[103]

> In some cases, public participation in rule making through petition has been hampered by the failure of the agency to provide procedures for the submission of petitions. . . . On the other hand, several agencies having experience with petitions under their rules, such as the Federal Communications Commission, the Federal Trade Commission, and the Federal Power Commission, reported to the task force that petitions are often of assistance in bringing to their attention situations in which the issuance, amendment, or repeal of rules may be desirable.

It is then, to the interest of state agencies as well as to the interest of persons subject to their authority, that legislation be adopted assuring that agencies not only provide for the filing of such petitions, but that the agencies take prompt and definitive action with respect thereto.

(E) Sanctions

Statutory provisions respecting rule-making procedures are not self-enforcing. Experience has indicated that some agencies exhibit a tendency to slight the procedural niceties prescribed by statute. Some administrators seem to believe that it is more important to get things done than to follow with meticulous care the time-consuming procedures set forth in the statutes. Because of this circumstance, and because there is some doubt whether the courts would construe the statutes as being mandatory or only directory, it is helpful to provide specific sanctions designed to assure reasonably strict compliance with the rule-making procedures provided by law.

Recognizing these necessities, the Revised Model State Act provides:

> No rule hereafter adopted is valid unless adopted in substantial compliance with this Section. A proceeding to contest any rule on the ground of non-compliance with the procedural requirements of this Section must be commenced within 2 years from the effective date of the rule.[104]

---

[103] Commission on Organization of Executive Branch of Government, Task Force Report on Legal Services and Procedure 161 (1955).

[104] Section 3(c).

This provision reflects a concern that has been expressed by many state legislatures. A large number of state statutes provide that agency rules shall be declared invalid, on appropriate petition, if the court finds that the rule was adopted without compliance with the rule-making procedures prescribed by statute.[105] The Florida statute contains somewhat stricter sanctions, providing in part: "Only rules adopted by an agency in the manner and form provided . . . shall be valid or effective, and then only if reasonably necessary to effectuate the specific authority granted to the agency. . . ."[106]

To avoid the possibility that some non-prejudicial neglect to comply with the procedural requirements may be seized upon at a later date by a defenseless defendant, and utilized as a basis to excuse non-compliance with a rule or regulation that has long been in effect, the Revised Model State Act provides a special two-year period of limitations applicable to actions contesting the validity of a rule on the grounds of non-compliance with the statutory procedural requirements.[107] It was believed by the draftsmen that any person actually prejudiced by procedural irregularities would have occasion within two years to discover that he had been harmed; and it appeared reasonable to require attacks predicated upon such grounds to be instituted promptly. Otherwise, a rule which had been in effect for many years might be upset on some technical ground, and the setting aside of a rule under such circumstances might cause substantial mischief. The two-year period of limitations does not apply, of course, to attacks based on substantive grounds; it is limited to challenges predicated upon the failure of the agency to follow the procedural requirements.

This provision was not found in the original Model State Act, and appears in few state statutes. However, it has recently been

---

105 Alaska (STAT. § 44.62.300); Arizona (REV. STAT. ANN. § 41-1007); California (GOV'T CODE § 11440); Florida (STAT. § 120.031); Hawaii (SESS. LAWS 1961, Act 103, § 7); Indiana (ANN. STAT. § 60-1505); Maryland (ANN. CODE art. 41, § 249); Minnesota (STAT. § 15.0417); Nebraska (REV. STAT. § 84-911); Ohio (REV. CODE ANN. § 119.02); Oklahoma (STAT. tit. 75, § 303); Oregon (REV. STAT. § 183.400); Rhode Island (GEN. LAWS ANN. § 42-35-3); Texas (REV. CIV. STAT. art. 6252-13, § 4); Virginia (CODE ANN. § 9-6.9); Washington (REV. CODE § 34-04.070); Wisconsin (STAT. § 227.05).

106 FLA. STAT. § 120.031.

107 Section 3(c).

adopted by some states;[108] and it may well be more widely adopted as other state legislatures consider the revision of their respective administrative procedure acts.

A few states have adopted special sanctions with respect to emergency rules, providing that an emergency rule may be set aside upon a showing, and judicial determination, that the findings and statement of emergency adopted by the agency in justification of putting the rule on an emergency footing, do not in fact constitute an emergency within the meaning of the statutory definition.[109] In view of the frequency with which some state agencies shortcut the normal procedures by declaring that an emergency justifies it, this provision deserves careful study. However, it appears clear that even without the benefit of such a statutory provision, state courts could set aside emergency rules on the grounds that their purported justification did not exist, since the situation confronting the agency was not in truth an emergency, as defined by statute.

---

108 Georgia (CODE ANN. § 3A-101); Oklahoma (STAT. tit. 75, § 303); Rhode Island (GEN. LAWS ANN. § 42-35-3).

109 Arizona (REV. STAT. ANN. § 41-1007); California (GOV'T CODE § 11440); Florida (STAT. § 120.30).

CHAPTER VIII

RULE MAKING: FILING AND PUBLICATION

Section 1

Filing

(A) General Requirement That Rules be Filed

One of the earliest responses of state legislatures to pleas that administrative regulation had become a vast uncharted wasteland, wherein the citizen could not even discover the rules to which he must conform, was to require the filing of administrative rules in some central office—usually that of the secretary of state. This was indeed a modest beginning. It meant only that by taking a trip to the state capitol, and rummaging through many file drawers of miscellaneous documents, one would eventually be able to discover the particular rule about which he wished to learn.

A typical provision in these early statutes was the requirement that all agency rules must be filed by a specified date, and that no rules which had not been filed by the deadline could thereafter be invoked or enforced against any person. It is a significant commentary upon the conditions which existed twenty years ago that in the case of many agencies, the rules were not in written form, existing only in the memory of staff employees.

(1) Analysis of Model Act

Progress has been made in the last twenty years, however. Requirements for the filing of administrative rules have become almost universal; and the agencies have long adapted themselves to such requirements. The provisions of the Revised Model State Act, requiring that: "Each agency shall file in the office of the [Secretary of State] a certified copy of each rule adopted by it, including all rules existing on the effective date of this Act,"[1] have their counterpart in most states.

(2) Provisions of State Laws

Some of the statutes simply require the filing of the rule.[2] In many states, the statutes specify that a certified copy must be filed.[3] While it is not always easy, in view of variant statutory language, to determine whether the statute in a particular state should be construed as requiring that the filed copy be "certified" (as distinguished from, for example, an "original" copy) yet the reference to certification may have some significance. The Arizona court ruled that where a copy of the rule filed with the secretary of state did not bear a proper certificate, the rule could not be enforced. The document involved was a regulation of the agricultural commission designed to eliminate insect pests. A copy signed by the state entomologist was filed with the secretary of state, but the copy filed did not bear a certification that

---

1 Section 4 of the Revised Model State Act provides: "(a) Each agency shall file in the office of the [Secretary of State] a certified copy of each rule adopted by it, including all rules existing on the effective date of this Act. The [Secretary of State] shall keep a permanent register of the rules open to public inspection. (b) Each rule hereafter adopted is effective 20 days after filing, except that: (1) if a later date is required by statute or specified in the rule, the later date is the effective date; (2) subject to applicable constitutional or statutory provisions, an emergency rule becomes effective immediately upon filing with the [Secretary of State], or at a stated date less than 20 days thereafter, if the agency finds that this effective date is necessary because of imminent peril to the public health, safety, or welfare. The agency's finding and a brief statement of the reasons therefor shall be filed with the rule. The agency shall take appropriate measures to make emergency rules known to the persons who may be affected by them."

2 Colorado (REV. STAT. ANN. § 3-16-2); Connecticut (GEN. STAT. REV. § 4-45); Georgia (CODE ANN. § 3A-101); Indiana (ANN. STAT. § 60-1505); Iowa (CODE § 17A.8); Kentucky (REV. STAT. § 13.085); Massachusetts (GEN. LAWS ANN. ch. 30A, § 5); Michigan (COMP. LAWS § 24.72); Minnesota (STAT. § 15.0412 (4)); North Carolina (GEN. STAT. § 143-195); North Dakota (CENT. CODE § 28-32-03); Oregon (REV. STAT. § 183.350); Tennessee (CODE ANN. § 4-501); Vermont (STAT. ANN. tit. 3, § 703).

3 Alaska (STAT. § 44.62.040); Arizona (REV. STAT. ANN. § 41-1004); Arkansas (STAT. ANN. § 5-501); California (GOV'T CODE § 11380); Florida (STAT. § 120.041); Georgia (CODE ANN. § 3A-101); Hawaii (SESS. LAWS 1961, Act 103, § 4(a)); Illinois (REV. STAT. ch. 127, § 266); Maine (REV. STAT. ANN. ch. 20-A, § 3-II); Maryland (ANN. CODE art. 41, § 246(a)); Missouri (REV. STAT. § 536-020-1); Nebraska (REV. STAT. § 84-902); New York (EXECUTIVE LAW § 102(1)); Ohio (REV. CODE ANN. § 119.04); Oklahoma (STAT. tit. 75, § 251); Pennsylvania (STAT. ANN. tit. 71, § 1710.21); Rhode Island (GEN. LAWS ANN. § 35-4); South Carolina (CODE ANN. § 1-11); Texas (REV. CIV. STAT. art. 6252-13, § 3(a)); Virginia (CODE ANN. § 9-6.7(a)); Washington (REV. CODE § 34.04.040(1)); West Virginia (CODE ANN. § 258(1)(3)); Wisconsin (STAT. § 227.023).

it was a true and correct copy of the rule promulgated by the commission. The court, pointing out that the statute did not specify what officer of the agency should sign the certificate, ruled that it was undoubtedly contemplated that some officer in authority, such as the chairman or secretary of the commission, should make the certification.[4]

A few states have specific exemptions from the filing requirements in such cases as (1) rules approving rates, prices, or tariffs;[5] (2) rules relating to public works, or streets and highways;[6] or (3) rules directed to a specifically named person or group, and not of general application.[7]

(3) Court Decisions

The state courts have been inclined to enforce strictly the requirements as to filing of rules, and to hold that a rule not filed is not enforceable, even though the person charged with its violation had personal knowledge of it. In a New York case, for example,[8] it was held that a regulation establishing speed limits for automobiles on a state highway could not be enforced despite the fact that motorists had been notified of the speed by the posting of highway markers. The court said that the giving of notice was not the only purpose of the filing requirement. Underlying the requirement, it was held, was a desire to have all rules and regulations affecting the public filed in one easily available central place. Therefore, rules could not become effective unless properly filed.

Strict construction of the filing requirement was approved also in Wisconsin,[9] where the court held that a directive of the department of taxation respecting the method of investigation of a taxpayer's books and records amounted to a regulation. Since the directive had not been filed as a regulation, it was held inoperative, and a taxpayer recovered the additional taxes which had been assessed as a result of the investigation. The West Virginia

---

4 State v. Wacker, 86 Ariz. 247, 344 P.2d 1004 (1959).

5 Alaska (STAT. § 44.62.040); Arizona (REV. STAT. ANN. § 41-1004); California (GOV'T CODE § 11380).

6 *Ibid.*

7 Alaska (STAT. § 44.62.040); California (GOV'T CODE § 11380).

8 People v. Cull, 10 N.Y.2d 123, 218 N.Y.S.2d 38, 176 N.E.2d 495 (1961); *cf.*, State v. Hopkins, 154 Me. 317, 147 A.2d 450 (1958).

9 Mondovi Cooperative Equity Ass'n v. State, 258 Wis. 505, 46 N.W.2d 825 (1951).

court refused to permit the board of dental examiners to apply against an applicant for a license certain rules which had not been properly filed.[10] In one case with an unusual emphasis, an agency successfully defended an attempt by a private party to invoke the agency's rule, on the ground that since the rule had not been filed and published as required by statute, it was not binding.[11]

(B) Place Where Rules Filed

The Revised Model State Act suggests that the office of the secretary of state is normally the appropriate place for the filing of administrative rules; but the reference to the "secretary of state" is set off within brackets, to indicate the desirability of giving consideration to other or alternative depositories for administrative rules.

Almost all the states which have adopted administrative procedure acts specify the office of the secretary of state as the place where rules should be filed.[12] However, a few states have chosen alternative depositories, such as the permanent files of the agency adopting the regulation,[13] the lieutenant governor,[14] the legislative research commission,[15] or the attorney general.[16] A number of states require the filing of administrative rules in other offices in addition to that of the secretary of state. The most common requirements in this connection are that the rules be filed also with each county or local governmental unit,[17] or with a legislative agency, such as a legislative drafting bureau, or the revisor of statutes, or legislative research commission, or the clerk of

---

[10] State *ex rel.* Sheppe v. West Virginia Bd. of Dental Examiners, 128 S.E.2d 620 (W. Va. 1962).

[11] Lake v. Mercer, 216 S.C. 391, 58 S.E.2d 336 (1950).

[12] See statutory references in notes 2 and 3, *supra,* for Alaska, Arizona, Arkansas, California, Connecticut, Florida, Georgia, Illinois, Indiana, Iowa, Maine, Maryland, Massachusetts, Michigan, Minnesota, Missouri, Nebraska, New York, North Carolina, Ohio, Oklahoma, Oregon, Pennsylvania, Rhode Island, South Carolina, Tennessee, Texas, Vermont, West Virginia, Wisconsin.

[13] Colorado (Rev. Stat. Ann. § 3-16-2).

[14] Hawaii (Sess. Laws 1961, Act 103, § 4(a)).

[15] Kentucky (Rev. Stat. § 13.085); Virginia (Code Ann. § 9-6.7); Washington (Rev. Code § 34.04.040).

[16] North Dakota (Cent. Code § 28-32-03).

[17] Alaska (Stat. § 44.62.090); Arkansas (Stat. Ann. § 5-501); California (Gov't Code § 11382.5); Hawaii (Sess. Laws 1961, Act 103, § 4(a)); North Carolina (Gen. Stat. § 143-198); North Dakota (Cent. Code § 28-32-03).

the legislature.[18] In a few states, still other additional filing requirements exist, it being specified that additional copies must be filed with the governor,[19] or the clerk of the court of appeals,[20] or with the state archivist.[21]

(C) Requirement of Permanent Register

The requirement of the Revised Model State Act, that a "permanent register" of all rules shall be kept open for public inspection[22] differs in significant though subtle degree from the less demanding requirement found in some states that the rules shall be kept on file for public inspection. The requirement of permanency imposes an obligation on the secretary of state to make sure that none of the rules which have been filed should ever become inaccessible.

Even though a rule has been amended or superseded, the original version should be kept intact and available for public inspection. This may be important, for sometimes the question is what rule was in effect at some prior date; and sometimes the "legislative history" of successive rules plays an important part in determining the interpretation to be given to the most recent regulation. A large number of states, following the suggestion of the Revised Model Act, require the maintenance of a permanent file or register.[23] However, the statutes in some states require in substance only that the rules be filed for inspection.[24]

---

18 Indiana (ANN. STAT. § 60-1505); Kentucky (REV. STAT. § 13.085); Maryland (ANN. CODE art. 41, § 246); Nebraska (REV. STAT. § 84-904); Virginia (CODE ANN. § 9-6.7); Washington (REV. CODE § 34.04.040); Wisconsin (STAT. § 227.023).

19 Arkansas (STAT. ANN. § 5-501).

20 Maryland (ANN. CODE art. 41, § 246).

21 Oklahoma (STAT. tit. 75, § 251).

22 Section 4(a).

23 Alaska (STAT. § 44.62.80); Arizona (REV. STAT. ANN. § 41-1004); California (GOV'T CODE § 11382); Hawaii (SESS. LAWS 1961, Act 103, § 4); Maine (REV. STAT. ANN. ch. 20-A, § 3); Maryland (ANN. CODE art. 41, § 246(a)); Minnesota (STAT. § 15.0413); Missouri (REV. STAT. § 536.020); Nebraska (REV. STAT. § 84-902); New York (EXECUTIVE LAW § 102(3)); Ohio (REV. CODE ANN. § 119.04); Oklahoma (STAT. tit. 75, § 255); Pennsylvania (STAT. ANN. tit. 71, § 1710.21a); Rhode Island (GEN. LAWS ANN. § 42-35-4); Tennessee (CODE ANN. § 4-502); Texas (REV. CIV. STAT. art. 6252-13, § 3(a)); Washington (REV. CODE § 34.04.040); Wisconsin (STAT. § 227.023(2)).

24 Arkansas (STAT. ANN. § 5-502); Colorado (REV. STAT. ANN. § 3-16-2); Illinois (REV. STAT. ch. 127, § 268); Indiana (ANN. STAT. § 57-603); Kentucky (REV. STAT. § 13.085(3)); Michigan (COMP. LAWS § 24.72); North Carolina (GEN. STAT. § 143-197); North Dakota (CENT. CODE § 28-32-03); Oregon

(D) EFFECTIVE DATE OF RULES

Because of the greater necessity for minute detail, the drafting of administrative rules and regulations presents difficulties which can often be avoided in legislative draftsmanship. There is a greater danger that some obscure but nonetheless important contingency will not be provided for; and to meet this danger, a practice has evolved of providing a deferred effective date. This gives those affected by the rule a grace period in which to adjust their affairs to meet the new requirements. Further, it provides the agency a valuable opportunity to correct any oversights which may have occurred.

While considerations of the convenience of those to whom the rule applies are most frequently urged in favor of the requirement of a deferred effective date, it is equally to the convenience of the agencies to have such a provision. Sometimes, an agency, failing to foresee the impact that the rule will have in particular situations, adopts and files a rule which has unfortunate and unintended consequences in its application to particular parties. This may occur even though opportunity had been afforded for public participation in the rule-making procedures. The parties involved in the "hardship case" situation may not have participated; or it may not have been made plain at the public hearings that a particular phraseology (perhaps one which had not been formulated and announced at the time of the public hearing) would work unintended hardship in particular situations. If these instances do not come to light until after the rule has become effective, it is much harder for the agency to make an appropriate correction than is the case where a deferred effective date provides a hiatus during which curative amendments can be adopted.

(1) Analysis of Model Act

The original Model State Act[25] provided that rules would become effective upon filing, unless a later date were required by statute or specified in the rule. However, the Revised Model State Act adopts a more realistic arrangement, making the rule

(REV. STAT. § 183.020); South Carolina (CODE ANN. § 1-11); Vermont (STAT. ANN. tit. 3, § 703); Virginia (CODE ANN. § 9-6.7); West Virginia (CODE ANN. § 258(1)).

[25] Section 3(2).

effective twenty days after filing, with two exceptions. The first exception concerns cases where a later effective date is required by statute or is specified in the rule. The second exception relates to emergency rules. As to them, it is provided that:

> Subject to applicable constitutional or statutory provisions, an emergency rule becomes effective immediately upon filing with the [Secretary of State] or at a stated date less than 20 days thereafter, if the agency finds that this effective date is necessary because of imminent peril to the public health, safety, or welfare.

In such case, it is required that "the agency's finding and a brief statement of the reasons therefor shall be filed with the rule." Further, the agencies are required to "take appropriate measures to make emergency rules known to the persons who may be affected by them."[26]

(2) Provisions of State Laws

A number of states, even before the promulgation of the Revised Model State Act, imposed requirements providing for a deferral of the effective date of administrative rules. In some states the requirements are more rigorous than those of the Revised Model Act.

One interesting approach is to make publication a prerequisite to the effectiveness of the rule. The requirement of publication is significant in two ways. First, it recognizes that the mere act of filing a rule with the secretary of state may not be effective to bring the rule to the attention of all who will be affected by it; a requirement of publication is much more likely to assure that those subject to the rule will actually learn of it. Secondly, some period of time elapses before publication is completed, and during this interim between filing and publication, "grape-vine" lines of communication (which are often at least equally as effective as official notification) are likely to circulate the news that a regulation is forthcoming; thus, the requirement of publication affords an informal method of deferring the effective date, and creating a waiting period. A number of state statutes require publication as a condition of the effectiveness of administrative

---

[26] Section 4(b).

rules,[27] although such a condition has not been included in the Revised Model State Act.

More significant, other states provide that a rule shall not become effective until a period of time—usually ten to thirty days—following publication.[28] The Virginia Code[29] contains the interesting provision that: "No rule shall be enforced or enforceable while copies of the pamphlet containing it are not available for distribution to the public at the office of the agency for more than sixty consecutive days." Wisconsin, which has a carefully drawn and elaborate statute regulating the publication of administrative rules, provides that (save in specified exceptional cases) administrative rules do not become effective until the first day of the month following publication in the state's administrative register.[30] Such provisions may come to be more widely adopted; for provisions postponing the effective dates of rules until a specified number of days following their publication provide the most thorough safeguards for the interests of the agencies and the public alike.

Other states, again going beyond the suggestion of the Revised Model State Act, provide that rules shall not become effective until thirty days (rather than twenty days, as provided in the Revised Model Act) after they have been filed in accordance with the statutory provisions.[31] A deferred effective date of twenty days after filing (the same standard as that suggested in the Revised Model State Act) has been adopted in some states which adopted administrative procedure codes subsequent to the promulgation of the Revised Model Act.[32] Provisions for a ten-day waiting period after filing are found in some states.[33]

---

[27] Connecticut (GEN. STAT. REV. § 4-46); Michigan (COMP. LAWS § 24.74); Tennessee (CODE ANN. § 4-502).

[28] Colorado—20 days after publication (REV. STAT. ANN. § 3-16-2(5)); Florida—30 days after publication (STAT. § 120.041(3)); Oregon—10 days after publication (REV. STAT. § 183.350(2)).

[29] VA. CODE ANN. § 9-6.7.

[30] WIS. STAT. § 227.026.

[31] Alaska (STAT. § 44.62.180); California (GOV'T CODE § 11422); Iowa (CODE § 17A.8); Kentucky (REV. STAT. § 13.085(1)); Texas (REV. CIV. STAT. art. 6252-13, § 3(b)); Washington (REV. CODE § 34.04.040(2)); West Virginia (CODE ANN. § 258(1)).

[32] Georgia (CODE ANN. § 3A-101); Oklahoma (STAT. tit. 75, § 304); Rhode Island (GEN. LAWS ANN. § 42-35-4).

[33] Hawaii (SESS. LAWS 1961, Act 103, § 4(b)); Illinois (REV. STAT. ch. 127, § 266); Missouri (REV. STAT. § 536.020-2 and CONST. art. 4, § 16); Ohio (REV. CODE ANN. § 119.03(D)).

In most other states, rules may become effective upon filing (although it should be noted that in some of them, requirements for approval by the attorney general before a rule can be filed, operate informally to defer the effective date, in some cases at least).[34]

Most of the state statutes providing for a deferred effective date contain certain exceptions, permitting specified types of rules to become effective immediately upon filing. The most important exception is that which concerns emergency rules. Recognizing the validity of this exception, the Revised Model State Act (as noted above) permits immediate effectiveness of emergency rules, if necessary because of imminent peril to the public health, safety, or welfare, subject to two conditions: (1) the agency's finding and a brief statement of the reasons therefor must be filed with the rule; (2) the agency must take appropriate steps to make emergency rules known to persons who may be affected by them.

A number of states have adopted, in one form of language or another, the first of these two requirements.[35] In other states, the immediate effectiveness of an emergency rule is conditioned upon certification by the governor that an emergency exists which makes it proper to give the rule immediate effect.[36] This condition, obviously, is not as well calculated to discourage the unjustified adoption of emergency rules as is the requirement of filing a formal written finding, with a statement of the supporting reasons. In cases where an agency would be hard pressed to make a persuasive or supportable statement demonstrating the need of emergency action to avoid an imminent peril (and where the agency might therefore conclude to let the rule become effective in the normal way), it is sometimes not too difficult for the

---

34 Arizona (REV. STAT. ANN. § 41-1005); Arkansas (STAT. ANN. § 5-501); Indiana (ANN. STAT. § 60-1505); Maine (REV. STAT. ANN. ch. 20-A, § 3-III); Maryland (ANN. CODE art. 41, § 246(b)); Massachusetts (GEN. LAWS ANN. ch. 30A, § 5); Minnesota (STAT. § 15.0413(2)); Nebraska (REV. STAT. § 84-906); New York (CONST. art. 4, § 8); North Carolina (GEN. STAT. § 143-196); North Dakota (CENT. CODE § 28-32-03); Pennsylvania (STAT. ANN. tit. 71, § 1710.21); South Carolina (CODE ANN. § 1-11); Vermont (STAT. ANN. tit. 3, § 703).

35 Alaska (STAT. § 44.62.180); California (GOV'T CODE § 11422); Colorado (REV. STAT. ANN. § 3-16-2(6)); Florida (STAT. § 120.041(4)); Hawaii (SESS. LAWS 1961, Act 103, § 4(b)(2)); Illinois (REV. STAT. ch. 127, § 266); Rhode Island (GEN. LAWS ANN. § 42-35-4).

36 Kentucky (REV. STAT. § 13.085); Michigan (COMP. LAWS § 3.560(11)); Ohio (REV. CODE ANN. § 119.03(F)).

agency, if it impatiently desires immediate action, to persuade the governor's office to issue the necessary piece of paper.

In still other states, it is provided that if the agency finds that an emergency exists, it may order the rule to become immediately effective. Under this type of statute, the only protection afforded the public is that which the good judgment of the agency dictates.[37]

The second requirement proposed in the Revised Model State Act—that agencies must take appropriate measures to make emergency rules generally known—is reflected in the statutes of a comparatively small number of states; but it has been adopted by the legislatures of most states which have adopted administrative procedure statutes after the promulgation of the Revised Model Act.[38]

Another exception which has found favor in some states is one permitting immediate effectiveness of rules relating to agency organization or procedure, or internal management.[39] Such an exception should have attached to it a proviso guaranteeing that procedural rules given immediate effect should be only those which do not substantially affect any private rights. Without such a safeguard, the agencies would be exposed to a temptation to let substantive rules masquerade as rules of procedure.

The Oregon statute contains a very broad exception, permitting immediate effect where the agency finds, with a recitation of its reasons, that a date earlier than the normal period (ten days after publication) is required to avoid "serious prejudice to the public interest, or the interest of the parties concerned."[40]

It would seem scarcely necessary to provide by statute that the agency may prescribe a later effective date than that which would normally be applicable; for if the rule recites that its substantive provisions do not become operative until a stated

---

37 Connecticut (GEN. STAT. REV. § 4-47—subject to approval of attorney general); Oklahoma (STAT. tit. 75, § 304—must state reasons); Virginia (CODE ANN. § 9-6.5); Washington (REV. CODE § 34.04.030).

38 Hawaii—which adds a requirement of newspaper publication (SESS. LAWS 1961, Act 103, § 4(b)(2)); Oklahoma (STAT. tit. 75, § 304); Rhode Island (GEN. LAWS ANN. § 42-35-4); Wisconsin (STAT. § 227.027).

39 Alaska (STAT. § 44.62.180); California (GOV'T CODE § 11422); Missouri (CONST. art. 4, § 16; REV. STAT. § 536.020-2); New York (CONST. art. 4, § 8); Oregon (REV. STAT. § 183.350).

40 ORE. REV. STAT. § 183.350.

period of time after the filing and technical "effective" date of the rule, the postponement would become operative by the terms of the rule itself. However, a number of state statutes provide specifically that an agency may prescribe a later effective date.[41]

Finally, a number of state laws contain recitals that if a rule is adopted pursuant to a statute which specifically states the dates when rules adopted thereunder shall become effective, the effective date so prescribed by statute shall control—a result which presumably would follow, in any event.[42]

(3) Court Decisions

While the state courts have had but little occasion to construe the statutory provisions respecting the effective dates of administrative rules, it appears that they will be strictly construed, applied, and enforced.[43] Problems have arisen in connection with attempts by agencies to give their regulations retroactive effect. Of course, the whole purpose of providing a deferred effective date would, in many situations at least, be defeated if retroactive operation of the rule were permitted. In a number of situations, the state courts have refused, in the face of a statutory provision specifying the earliest date that a rule may become effective, to permit the rule to be given retroactive application prior to such effective date. Thus, in New York, it was held that a regulation applicable to civil service examinations could not be applied to an examination held April 7, when the rule did not become effective until April 24.[44] Other cases support the same general proposition.[45]

---

[41] Arizona (REV. STAT. ANN. § 41-1005); California (GOV'T CODE § 11422); Colorado (REV. STAT. ANN. § 3-16-2(5)); Florida (STAT. § 120.041(3)); Maine (REV. STAT. ANN. ch. 20-A, § 3-IV); Maryland (ANN. CODE art. 41, § 246(b)); Massachusetts (GEN. LAWS ANN. ch. 30A, § 5); Minnesota (STAT. § 15.0413 (2)); Ohio (REV. CODE ANN. § 119.03(D)); Oklahoma (STAT. tit. 75, § 304); Rhode Island (GEN. LAWS ANN. § 42-35-4); Washington (REV. CODE § 34.04.040(2)); Wisconsin (STAT. § 227.026).

[42] Alaska (STAT. § 44.62.180); Arizona (REV. STAT. ANN. § 41-1005); California (GOV'T CODE § 11422); Georgia (CODE ANN. § 3A-101); Hawaii (SESS. LAWS 1961, Act 103, § 4(b)); Maine (REV. STAT. ANN. ch. 20-A, § 3-IV); Maryland (ANN. CODE art. 41, § 246(b)); Minnesota (STAT. § 15.0413(2)); Oklahoma (STAT. tit. 75, § 304); Rhode Island (GEN. LAWS ANN. § 42-35-4); Washington (REV. CODE § 34.04.040(2)); Wisconsin (STAT. § 227.026).

[43] *E.g.,* State Compensation Ins. Fund v. McConnell, 46 Cal. 2d 330, 294 P.2d 440 (1956).

[44] Hymes v. Schechter, 6 N.Y.2d 352, 189 N.Y.S.2d 870, 160 N.E.2d 627 (1959).

[45] Florida Livestock Bd. v. Gladden, 76 So. 2d 291 (Fla. 1954); Alamac Es-

(E) Certification by Attorney General

The suggestion is sometimes advanced that approval by the state attorney general be made a condition precedent to the filing and effectiveness of an agency rule. In theory, this suggestion possesses some merit. Presumably, the attorney general would disapprove rules which were clearly in excess of the agency's authority, or otherwise illegal; and he would presumably remand to the agency for reconsideration and possible amendment, rules whose legality was a matter of extreme doubt. Thus, members of the public would be saved the burden of being compelled to resort to litigation to void an illegal rule. The agencies would benefit also, because of the opportunity to make any necessary corrections before the rule became effective.

It is open to grave doubt, however, whether in practice these potential benefits are actually derived. Consideration of the rule by the attorney general is *ex parte;* he may not have the opportunity to learn of the nature of the arguments that would be advanced in opposition to the legality of the rule. Further, the consideration given the rule is apt to be at best merely formal, if not superficial. Counsel for the agency who drafted the rule is likely to be himself an assistant attorney general; and in practice the requirement is likely to amount to little more than one assistant attorney general obtaining the assent of another to the filing of the work-product of the first. Under these circumstances, approval is apt to be perfunctory.

Furthermore, even though the courts are quite aware of the limited consideration which has been given by the attorney general to the objections that might be urged against the validity of a rule, the mere fact that a rule has thus received official imprimatur (and, perhaps more important, that the attorney general will feel impelled to defend vigorously in court the correctness of his certification) may have the effect of creating a prima facie case for the validity of the rule, and render more difficult the task of the private party who attacks its validity in court.

A different consideration which has been urged against the requirement involves the always-present difficulty of distinguish-

---

tates, Inc. v. McGoldrick, 2 N.Y.2d 87, 156 N.Y.S.2d 853, 138 N.E.2d 231 (1956); *cf.* Wasserman v. Board of Regents, 11 N.Y.2d 173, 227 N.Y.S.2d 649, 182 N.E.2d 264 (1962).

ing between matters of legality and those of policy. If it be assumed that the attorney general does in fact give searching consideration to the requirements of the proposed rule, then the danger exists that he may be inclined to disapprove rules on grounds of impropriety rather than illegality. It is urged that if the attorney general believes the rule unwise, he will be tempted to withhold his approval. This would mean that the discretion vested by law in the agency was being exercised in fact by the attorney general.

The Revised Model State Act does not provide for obtaining the certification of the attorney general as a condition to the filing or effectiveness of a rule.

A few states do have legislation requiring that before it can be filed and made effective, an agency rule must be approved by the attorney general. In some states, he must approve it both as to form and legality;[46] in others, approval is required only as to the legality of the rule;[47] and in others, the submission must have the general "approval" of the attorney general—suggesting that he may be empowered to disapprove it on policy grounds.[48]

(F) Legislative Approval of Rules

A comparatively recent innovation in this country—labelled, inappropriately, "legislative oversight" (a phrase which implies that the legislature may overlook administrative rules, whereas in fact a process of overseeing is contemplated)—is that of requiring the submission of administrative rules to the state legislature for approval or disapproval.

Because the procedure is new and has not been sufficiently tested to permit the establishment of a firm judgment as to its merits, the draftsmen of the Revised Model State Act did not include in their recommendations any provisions for such legislative review. However, the potentialities of this device as a method of curbing unwarranted exercise of administrative discre-

---

46 Maine (Rev. Stat. Ann. ch. 20-A, § 2-IV); Michigan (Comp. Laws § 24.74); Minnesota (Stat. § 15.0412(4)).

47 Indiana—where gubernatorial approval is also required (Ann. Stat. § 60-1505); North Dakota (Cent. Code § 28-32-02); Pennsylvania—but the statute provides that failure to submit a rule for approval shall not invalidate it (Stat. Ann. tit. 71, § 1710.21); Tennessee (Code Ann. § 4-502).

48 Connecticut—where the approval may be by the attorney general's designee (Gen. Stat. Rev. § 4-46); Nebraska (Rev. Stat. § 84-905.01).

tion justifies a brief examination of the limited experience which has been had with this experiment in some eleven states.

(1) Variant Approaches

Several variant approaches are available in connection with provisions for legislative review of administrative rules.

It may be simply provided that the regulations be laid before the legislature for its information. As to such a requirement, there is little room for objection, although there is room for considerable scepticism as to the effectiveness of this procedure in encouraging legislative examination of the administrative activity; a more effective way of accomplishing this result would be to require the annual submission of detailed reports as to each agency's activities.

Sometimes, it is provided that the regulation shall be noticed for legislative review and possible amendment or annulment within a specified period. While, of course, the legislature always has this power, nevertheless such provision does have a very real effect, in that it brings the regulation before the legislative body, and facilitates the making of an attack by parties assailing the propriety or legality of the regulation.

A third type of proviso, far more stringent than the others, decrees that the regulation shall not remain in effect beyond a limited period unless within such period it is approved and ratified by the legislature. Where this requirement is adopted, no more than legislative procrastination is required to abolish a rule which might have met with overwhelming legislative approval.

(2) The English Experience

The theory of laying administrative regulations before the legislature has been far more popular in England than in this country. Because the success of the English experience has been largely responsible for suggestions that the practice be more widely adopted here (and for the further reason that the theory of the English provisions has seemingly been misunderstood by some exponents of the cause of legislative review), it is appropriate to review the provisions for legislative review as they have been administered in England.

The requirement of laying rules (or "statutory instruments" as they are called) before Parliament for its consideration originated in England in the 1830's,[49] but the practice did not become particularly popular until about 100 years ago. During the last century there have developed two general types of review.

The first is called the affirmative resolution procedure. It is not frequently used. Under this procedure, it may be provided either (a) that the rule does not become operative until approval is given by affirmative resolution of each House of Parliament, or (b) that a rule has immediate operative effect, but an affirmative resolution is required within a specified time in order for it to have continued validity. In general, the affirmative procedure has been utilized only in such cases as those where the management of public moneys is involved, or where the enabling act states the legislative policy only in broadest terms and its actual content derives from the rules, or where because of the broadness of the delegated rule-making powers and the importance of the private rights dealt with it is felt that affirmation should be required.

The second type of procedure for parliamentary review of rules, and that which is most generally used, provides for annulment by parliamentary action. This procedure relies upon the initiative of an individual member of Parliament to introduce a resolution for annulment.

In response to a vigorous criticism by the Committee on Ministers' Powers in 1932,[50] that a lack of automatic machinery for effective scrutiny of the rules laid before Parliament was a deterrent to careful review, there was created in 1944 a Select Committee on Statutory Instruments. Its purpose is to supply members of Parliament with sufficient information so that individual members will be able to vote intelligently on rules laid before them. Its duties have been described as follows:

> The duty of the Committee is to consider whether the special attention of the House should be drawn to a statutory instrument or draft on any of the following grounds: that it imposes a charge; that it excludes challenge in the Courts; that it purports (without specific authority in the parent Act) to have retrospective effect; that there has been unjustifiable delay in publication or laying before Parliament or in sending notification to the Speaker when the instrument comes into operation before it has been laid; that its form or purport calls

[49] *Subordinate Legislation,* 30 PUB. ADMIN. REV. 227, 247 (1952).
[50] REPORT OF THE COMMITTEE ON MINISTERS' POWERS 62 (1932).

for elucidation; or that it "appears to make some unusual or unexpected use of the powers conferred by the statute under which it was made." Except insofar as the last-mentioned ground permits, the Select Committee is not intended to concern itself with the merits or policy of an instrument, these being matters more properly left to be discussed in the House itself on a prayer for annulment.[51]

The Committee, it should be emphasized, does not purport to consider the merits of the rules, nor to pass on the wisdom of the policy matters involved. In this respect, its functions have been more limited than those of corresponding committees created by the state legislatures in some of the states. In fact, a proposal that the Committee hear grievances and report on the merits of the rules was rejected in England.[52] However, as charmingly pointed out by the redoubtable Sir Cecil Carr, the Committee "has often found itself peeping over the fence at questions of policy, merits, and vires."[53]

(3) Experiments in United States

The experience in the United States has been ably and exhaustively reviewed by David L. Howe.[54]

At least eleven states have experimented, in one form or another, with the device of legislative review (or overseeing) of administrative rule-making activities.

1. The Alaska statute[55] merely provides that the legislature may, by concurrent resolution, annul any agency rule if it finds that the legislative intent is not properly reflected in the rule. The significance of this device, of course, is that it is much easier to obtain adoption of a concurrent resolution than to obtain enactment (and gubernatorial approval) of a legislative bill. The Alaska statute further provides for the making of an annual review of administrative rules, and the submission thereof to the legislature.

---

51 *Subordinate Legislation,* 30 PUB. ADMIN. REV. 227, 253 (1952); Hanson *The Select Committee on Statutory Instruments, 1944-1949,* 27 PUB. ADMIN. REV. 278 (1949).

52 Hanson, *supra* note 51, at 282-83.

53 Carr, *Parliamentary Supervision in Britain,* 30 N.Y.U.L. REV. 1045, 1050 (1955).

54 Howe, *Legislative Review of Administrative Rules,* CURRENT TRENDS IN STATE LEGISLATION, 1955-56, p. 167.

55 ALASKA STAT. § 44.62.320.

2. The Connecticut statute[56] provides in greater detail that in odd-numbered years the secretary of state shall submit a certified copy of all effective regulations to the general assembly for study; and that such regulations shall be assigned to appropriate committees for consideration; and that such committees shall schedule hearings thereon. The effect of such a provision is that a person seeking to attack a particular regulation need not assume the difficult burden of persuading the legislature to initiate proceedings to review the rule. Such proceedings are automatically provided, since the requirement for committee hearings is mandatory. The statute further provides that any regulation or part thereof disapproved by the general assembly by resolution shall be void and shall not be reissued. Under this statute, the Connecticut general assembly has from time to time disapproved administrative regulations.[57]

3. In Iowa, the statute[58] creates a "legislative department rules review committee," consisting of three senators and three representatives. Agencies are required to submit proposed rules to the state attorney general and to this legislative committee. If the committee has objections to the proposed rule, it notifies the agency of its objections and of its recommendations for amendments. The agency is not required to accept the recommendations, but when it files the rule with the secretary of state, it is required to attach thereto a copy of the attorney general's opinion and a copy of the findings of the legislative rules review committee. After the rule has been filed with the secretary of state, it is referred to the appropriate committees of the state legislature; and if a committee to which a rule has been referred finds objection thereto, it may recommend to the legislature that it "proceed by law to overcome the objection."

4. In Kansas, a statutory provision for legislative overseeing of administrative rules has been in effect since 1939.[59] Apparently, it has been little used to disapprove agency rules—perhaps because there is no provision for routine submission of rules to the legislature for its consideration.[60] It provides that, with stated exceptions, administrative rules shall become effective when

[56] CONN. GEN. STAT. REV. § 4-49.
[57] Howe, *supra* note 54, at p. 207.
[58] IOWA CODE § 17A.2-17A.11.
[59] KAN. LAWS 1939, ch. 308.
[60] Howe, *supra* note 54, p. 199.

duly filed and published, and shall continue effective "until amended or revoked by the state agency, or until the legislature, by concurrent resolution duly adopted, shall disapprove or reject the same."[61]

5. The Michigan experience, which has been widely publicized, is instructive.[62] In 1945, the state legislature adopted a bill which provided that all administrative rules should be filed with the legislature and referred to appropriate committees, in the same manner as bills are referred to committees; and that all rules which were not approved by concurrent resolution before legislative adjournment should be abrogated. This meant, of course, that no rule or regulation could survive unless it received affirmative legislative approval.[63] The governor vetoed the bill.[64] However, the next session of the legislature enacted a measure providing for the reference of all new administrative rules to appropriate legislative committees and further providing that rules disapproved by concurrent resolution would be abrogated.[65] More significant, the 1947 law provided for the creation of a joint committee on legislative rules which was empowered to meet during the interim between sessions of the legislature and to suspend, until the next regular session of the legislature, any rule found to be not in conformity with the statute under which it was promulgated. By amendment adopted in 1951,[66] it was further provided that any rule suspended by the committee would continue to be suspended until the rule was reinstated by the committee or by concurrent resolution of the legislature.

This joint committee was called upon to consider a number of agency rules. It approved some, and suspended others, and was effective in working out compromises (persuading the agency to amend its rule to meet the objections pressed) in still other cases. Counsel for many private parties were enthusiastic about results obtained under the statute. The agencies were highly

---

61 KAN. GEN. STAT. ANN. § 77-410.

62 For analysis and discussion, see particularly, Howe, *supra* note 54, p. 182 et seq.; REPORT TO THE MICHIGAN JOINT LEGISLATIVE COMMITTEE ON REORGANIZATION OF STATE GOVERNMENT, Rep. No. 11 (March, 1951), reprinted in part in DAVISON & GRUNDSTEIN, ADMINISTRATIVE LAW, CASES AND READINGS 748; HEADY, ADMINISTRATIVE PROCEDURE LEGISLATION IN THE STATES 55 et seq. (1952).

63 S.J. 910, 942 (1945).

64 *Id.* at 1328.

65 MICH. COMP. LAWS § 24.71.

66 Public Acts 1951, Act No. 9.

critical of the device; and there is evidence that some agencies adopted various expedients to avoid formal promulgation of rules, so as to evade the possibility of having their determinations reviewed by the committee.[67]

In 1953,[68] the state attorney general declared the entire process of legislative review unconstitutional as a legislative encroachment on the functions of the judiciary. Notwithstanding this ruling, the committee continued in operation. It no longer asserted the power to suspend rules, but advised and consulted with the agencies about rules which were brought into question. While grave doubts persisted as to the correctness of the attorney general's opinion (a question now rendered moot as a result of the adoption of a new Constitution in Michigan in 1963, Section 37 of Article IV of which specifically authorizes the legislature by concurrent resolution to empower a joint legislative committee to suspend administrative rules promulgated in the interim between sessions of the legislature, until the end of the next legislative session), the net result was a workable compromise. Persons attacking an agency rule had an opportunity, on short notice, to bring it to the attention of a small legislative committee. If the committee believed that the rule was not in accordance with the legislative intent, it could bring considerable pressure to bear upon the agency to amend the rule; but the agency apparently had a right—if it chose—to insist upon continuing the rule until there had been formal judicial or legislative action.

6. In Nebraska, the statute[69] requires the annual filing of administrative rules with the legislature, and provides that such rules, when considered by the legislature, may be rejected, changed, altered, amended, or modified in such manner as it deems advisable.

7. Oklahoma in 1963 adopted comprehensive provisions respecting legislative overseeing of administrative rule making.[70] Its statute provides for filing of all administrative rules with the state legislature, in accordance with a stated time schedule. If the legislature by joint resolution disapproves a rule, then "the

---

67 HEADY, *op. cit. supra* note 62, at p. 61.
68 OPS. ATT'Y GEN. (Dec. 17, 1953).
69 NEB. REV. STAT. § 84-904.
70 OKLA. STAT. tit. 75, § 308.

agency shall not have authority to repromulgate such rule, except during the first 60 calendar days of a subsequent legislative session." Conversely, failure of the legislature to disapprove a rule within thirty days after submission "shall result in approval of such rule by the legislature." The law further provides that any rights, privileges, or interests gained by any person as a result of an agency rule prior to its rejection by the legislature shall not be affected by reason of subsequent rejection.

8. The South Carolina statute[71] provides that rules when duly filed shall remain effective until they are amended or repealed by the agency or by acts of the General Assembly.

9. Virginia, for several years,[72] required that rules of specified agencies could not become effective until they were approved by a "Commission on Administrative Agencies," composed of members of the Senate and House. However, in 1952, this statute was amended, and currently the Virginia statute[73] provides that any administrative rule shall become null and void upon the adoption of a resolution by either house of the General Assembly declaring it null and void. It is further provided that no rule having substantially the same object shall thereafter be adopted unless and until the General Assembly repeals the resolution. An outstanding characteristic of this Act is that instead of requiring a concurrent resolution (as is required in several other statutes) to void an agency rule, it permits that objective to be accomplished by a mere resolution of either house.

10. The Washington legislature in 1963 (Senate Bill No. 59, Chapter 186, Laws of 1963) enacted a statute providing that agency rules shall be subject to review by the legislature to determine whether the rules are within the intent and scope of the statutes purporting to authorize the adoption thereof. If the legislature finds by concurrent resolution that the rule is without the intent or scope of the enabling statute, the agency must abrogate the rule. If the legislature finds that the rule may be revised to bring it within the intent and scope of the statute, the agency may either revise the rule accordingly or abrogate it. The law also provides for the temporary suspension of rules adopted in interim periods between sessions of the legislature, upon the

[71] S.C. CODE ANN. § 1-11.
[72] Laws 1944, ch. 160.
[73] VA. CODE ANN. § 9-6.9(d).

adoption of a resolution by the legislative council finding that the rule contravenes the intent or is without the scope of the enabling legislation.

11. In 1953 Wisconsin adopted a statute[74] providing that the legislature could at any time by joint resolution disapprove any administrative rule then in effect. The Wisconsin Attorney General[75] declared that the statute was in violation of a provision in the Wisconsin Constitution which provided that "no law shall be enacted except by bill." His opinion was not tested in the courts. Instead, the statute was amended by creating a joint legislative committee for review of administrative rules, with advisory powers only.[76] The statute provides that the committee may investigate complaints with respect to rules (with power to subpoena witnesses and hold public hearings) and may recommend to the agency, "such changes in, deletions from or additions to the rules as they believe would make the rules . . . more equitable, practical, and more in conformity with the public interest." As demonstrated by the experience in Michigan, such recommendations from a committee of the legislature that controls the purse strings are not likely to be ignored, even if without coercive force.

These eleven variant approaches to the problem reflect a substantial consensus that some form of legislative overseeing of administrative rule-making activities is in the public interest. The question as to which approach is best is one that cannot be answered until greater experience has been obtained. For one thing, constitutional questions as to the validity of the more thoroughgoing devices remain unsettled by the courts.[77] Even after these questions shall have been settled, it may well prove true that differing conditions in the several states will call for a number of variants of the general plan for authorizing legislatures, or legislative committees, to proceed quickly and informally to review administrative rules and take prompt action with respect to those found to be contrary to the legislative intent or to the public interest. However, the circumstance that a number of

---

74 Laws 1953, ch. 331, § 4.

75 43 OPS. ATT'Y GEN. 350 (1954).

76 WIS. STAT. § 227.041.

77 For a comprehensive review and analysis of court decisions bearing tangentially on this question, see Howe *Legislative Review of Administrative Rules*, CURRENT TRENDS IN STATE LEGISLATION, 1955-56, pp. 167, 209-48.

states have adopted such statutes bespeaks a widespread recognition of the desirability of working out practical and expedient approaches to this goal. Among the virtues of legislative review, as pointed out by Dean Landis,[78] are these: (1) it brings the legislative branch of the government into close and constant contact with the administrative branch; (2) it attains a greater degree of administrative responsibility to the legislature; (3) it permits agencies to call upon the legislature to assume a direct responsibility in settling difficult problems of policy. As pointed out by another writer,[79] legislative review is especially desirable where the legislature has set only broad standards, leaving the substance of the policy-making function to the administrators.

Section 2
Publication of Rules

(A) General Provisions

The unavailability of administrative rules to the public charged with the duty of complying with them has long been a source of practical difficulty. So far as the federal agencies are concerned, much has been done since 1935 to ameliorate the difficulties. But in the case of state agencies, there is a widespread lack of workable statutory requirements for indexing and codifying agency rules. In a number of states, there is not even an effective requirement for printing and public distribution of rules.

As early as 1920,[80] studies began to appear in legal periodicals urging the adoption of uniform systems for publication of the rules and regulations of administrative agencies. For the ensuing fifteen years, the subject received growing attention in periodical literature.[81] Attention was directed to the contrast between the situation in this country, where it was often impossible to ascertain the provisions of the governing rule except by discovery of the original in the offices of the issuing agency, and

---

78 LANDIS, THE ADMINISTRATIVE PROCESS 77 et seq. (1938).

79 Note, *"Laying on the Table"—A Device for Legislative Control Over Delegated Powers,* 65 HARV. L. REV. 637, 644 (1952).

80 Fairlie, *Administrative Legislation,* 18 MICH. L. REV. 181 (1920).

81 See Ronald, *Publication of Federal Administrative Legislation,* 7 GEO. WASH. L. REV. 52 (1938), for a comprehensive survey of the studies which had been made up to that date.

in England, where comprehensive requirements for publication of administrative rules had been in effect since 1893.[82]

However, neither the growing literature on the subject nor the attention directed to the English situation led Congress to take any action. As late as 1933, the President rejected a suggestion by a group of government officials that a daily publication be instituted to print administrative rules, orders, and regulations.[83]

The following year, however, official interest in the problem became at last aroused when it was discovered that a hapless individual had been arrested and convicted for asserted violation of an administrative rule which had in fact been repealed prior to his arrest. The conviction was for violation of one paragraph of the N.I.R.A. Petroleum Code. The defendant seemingly had not been aware of the provisions of the paragraph; the prosecuting authorities were not aware of its repeal. The repeal was not discovered until shortly before the case was scheduled for argument before the United States Supreme Court; and thereupon the Justice Department confessed error and moved for dismissal.[84] But the ghost of the case remained to haunt the government. Upon the argument of another case at the next term of Court, involving the same Code,[85] the situation was brought to light during oral argument, and Justice Brandeis extensively interrogated government counsel. The resulting newspaper publicity is thought to have had something to do with the enactment, a few months later, of the Federal Register Act.[86]

The *Federal Register* now provides day-by-day publication of many of the rules and regulations of the federal agencies; and the Code of Federal Regulations, codifying such rules under some fifty titles, facilitates the lawyer's task of research. Because of the provisions for publication found in the Federal Register Act, the Federal Administrative Procedure Act[87] (except for some directions as to publication of notice of rule making in the

---

82 CARR, DELEGATED LEGISLATION 33 (1921).

83 Ronald, *supra* note 81, at 65.

84 United States v. Smith, 293 U.S. 633, 79 L. Ed. 717, 55 Sup. Ct. 345 (1934).

85 Panama Ref. Co. v. Ryan, 293 U.S. 388, 79 L. Ed. 446, 55 Sup. Ct. 241 (1935).

86 44 U.S.C. § 301; F.C.A. 44 § 301.

87 5 U.S.C. § 1001; F.C.A. 5 § 1001.

Federal Register) does not provide for publication of administrative rules.

Recognizing the impracticality, in most states, of requiring publication on a basis comparable to that provided in the Federal Register Act, the Revised Model State Act contains[88] the following modest requirement:

> The [Secretary of State] shall compile, index, and publish all effective rules adopted by each agency. Compilations shall be supplemented or revised as often as necessary [and at least once every 2 years]. The [Secretary of State] shall publish a [monthly] bulletin setting forth the text of all rules filed during the preceding [month] excluding rules in effect upon the adoption of this Act.

Modest though these requirements are, they go further than do the statutory provisions of most states. The shocking fact is that in 1963 about half of the states did not have even minimal provisions for the publication, by printing, of administrative rules. In those states, a possibility exists that a citizen may be prosecuted for violation of a rule the existence of which was unknown to him, and could not have been discovered except by personal inquiry at the offices of the agency or perhaps at the secretary of state's office in the state capitol.

Typical of those states having statutory enactments are requirements calling for the compilation and publication of all currently effective rules of each agency.[89] A few state statutes provide for compilation, but without making detailed provisions for publication.[90] In others, there is some requirement for publication, without a definite requirement of compilation.[91] In

---

[88] Section 5(a), (b).

[89] Alaska (STAT. § 44.62.130); California (GOV'T CODE § 11409); Connecticut (GEN. STAT. REV. § 4-50); Florida (STAT. § 120.051(1)); Georgia (CODE ANN. § 3A-101); Hawaii (SESS. LAWS 1961, Act 103, § 5(a)); Indiana (ANN. STAT. § 60-1507); Kentucky (REV. STAT. § 13.096); Maine (REV. STAT. ANN. ch. 20-A, § 4-I); Maryland (ANN. CODE art. 41, § 247(a)); Massachusetts (GEN. LAWS ANN. ch. 30A, § 6); Michigan (COMP. LAWS § 24.74); Minnesota (STAT. § 15.0413(5)); Missouri (REV. STAT. § 536.030); Nebraska (REV. STAT. § 84-905); New York (EXECUTIVE LAW § 102); Ohio (REV. CODE ANN. § 119.05); Oklahoma (STAT. tit. 75, § 255); Oregon (REV. STAT. § 183.360); Pennsylvania—limited requirement for publication (STAT. ANN. tit. 71, § 1710.21a); South Carolina (CODE ANN. § 1-16); Virginia (CODE ANN. § 9-6.7(b)); West Virginia (Acts 1964, art. 3, ch. 1, § 7); Wisconsin (STAT. § 227.025).

[90] Arizona (REV. STAT. ANN. § 41-1006); Rhode Island (GEN. LAWS ANN. § 42-35-5); Washington (REV. CODE § 34.04.050(1)).

[91] Colorado—publication by mailing to each person on agency's mailing list (REV. STAT. ANN. § 3-16-2(11)); Iowa—limited requirement for publication of certain types of rules (CODE § 17A.14).

most states, the compilation is to be done by the secretary of state, or the revisor of statutes, or a division of administrative procedure, or some like agency of the central government; but in a few states, responsibility for compiling and publishing the rules is delegated to the agencies that adopt the rules.[92]

Obviously, mere compilation and publication of agency rules is not of great assistance unless they are adequately indexed. While some sort of index is found in almost every state where publication is required, there are few states wherein the statute specifically requires that the published compilation must be indexed.[93] Codification of rules is required in even fewer instances.[94]

In cases where the statute requires that rules be published, an unpublished rule is held invalid.[95] This is true, it seems, even though the person charged with violating the rule had actual notice thereof.[96] In view of the fact that many of the statutes requiring publication do not specify precisely what publication will suffice, questions occasionally arise as to when a rule has been "published." Under most statutes, "publication" contemplates printing and general distribution.[97]

(B) Provisions for Periodical Publication

In order that publication will serve its intended purpose of keeping interested persons currently advised of all effective rules, it is necessary that provision be made for supplementation and revision of the published compilations. As noted above, the Revised Model State Act suggests revision at least every two years, supplemented by a monthly bulletin. The statutes in the

---

92 These states include (the statutory references being the same as those listed in note 89 *supra*) Hawaii, Massachusetts, Nebraska, Ohio and Virginia.

93 These states include (the statutory references again being the same as those listed in notes 89 and 90 *supra*) Florida, Hawaii, Indiana, Maine, Maryland, Michigan, Missouri, Oregon, Rhode Island, South Carolina, Washington and Wisconsin.

94 Alaska and California require codification; and limited requirements of codification appear in the laws of Indiana and Michigan. Statutory references are those listed in note 89 *supra.*

95 Todd v. State, 205 Ga. 363, 53 S.E.2d 906 (1949); City of Sherman v. Arnold, 148 Tex. 516, 226 S.W.2d 620 (1950).

96 People v. Cull, 10 N.Y.2d 123, 218 N.Y.S.2d 38, 176 N.E.2d 495 (1961).

97 In *Kelly v. Murphy,* 377 P.2d 177 (Nev. 1963), under a statute requiring "promulgation," it was said "A 'promulgation' usually connotes an official public declaration"; and it was held that an order transmitted by telephone had not been "promulgated."

several states display a considerable variety in this regard. Many are silent on this question.

Among the states making some provision for periodical publication, the required frequency varies from semi-monthly to ten years. The most frequently encountered provisions are those requiring supplementation annually or biennially. In some states, of course,[98] requirement for publication of new rules in a newspaper of general circulation as a condition of their effectiveness serves to give up-to-the-minute notice to all interested and alert readers; but newspaper publication does not serve the purposes intended by those statutes which require periodical publication of official booklets giving the most recent amendments of all administrative rules, for only the latter method serves to make conveniently available, for ready reference, current compilations of all effective rules.

Statutory provisions for publication of periodical compilations specify the following time intervals: semi-monthly;[99] monthly;[100] each three months;[101] semi-annually;[102] annually;[103] each legislative session;[104] each two years.[105]

In some states, discretion is delegated to state officials, such as the secretary of state or the director of the office of administrative procedure, to prescribe how frequently periodical compilations shall be published. A carefully drafted provision accomplishing this purpose is found in California. It provides that the State's Division of Administrative Procedure shall provide for the continuing publication, with periodic supplements, of all regulations required to be filed with the secretary of state (or of

---

98 *E.g.*, Connecticut (GEN. STAT. REV. § 4-46) requiring publication in the *Connecticut Law Journal* as a condition of effectiveness.

99 Oklahoma (STAT. tit. 75, § 255).

100 Florida (STAT. § 120.051(1)); Georgia (CODE ANN. § 3A-101); Missouri (REV. STAT. § 536.030); Washington (REV. CODE § 34.04.050); Wisconsin (STAT. § 35.93(3)).

101 Michigan (COMP. LAWS § 24.76); Rhode Island (GEN. LAWS ANN. § 42-35-5); West Virginia (Acts 1964, art. 3, ch. 1, § 7).

102 Maryland (ANN. CODE art. 41, § 247).

103 Indiana (ANN. STAT. § 60-1509); Minnesota (STAT. § 15.0413(5)).

104 Nebraska (REV. STAT. § 84-905); South Carolina (CODE ANN. § 1-16).

105 Arizona (REV. STAT. ANN. § 41-1006); Florida—in addition to the monthly bulletin (STAT. § 120.051); Maine (REV. STAT. ANN. ch. 20-A, § 4-I); Maryland—in addition to the semi-annual bulletin (ANN. CODE art. 41, § 247 (a)); Missouri—in addition to the monthly bulletin (REV. STAT. § 536.030); Oklahoma—in addition to the semi-monthly publication (STAT. tit. 75, § 256); Oregon (REV. STAT. § 183.360); Rhode Island (GEN. LAWS ANN. § 42-35-5); Washington (REV. CODE § 34.04.050).

appropriate references to any regulations the printing of which the department finds to be impractical, such as detailed schedules or forms otherwise available to the public, or which are of limited or particular application). It is further provided that the department shall prescribe regulations governing the style and form of printing and indexing, to the end that all compilations shall be published in a uniform manner and at the earliest practicable date, and that each published regulation shall be accompanied by a reference to the statutory authority pursuant to which it was adopted.[106]

In some states, good administration has resulted in the adoption of a practice of periodical publication at intervals more frequent than required by statute. In New York, for example, there was published in 1961 a revision of the *Official Compilation of Codes, Rules and Regulations,* in loose-leaf form. Supplementation is made on a monthly basis, so that by insertion of replacement pages, it is practicable for every lawyer to have on his desk an up-to-the-month statement of all currently effective administrative rules.[107] Similar practices prevail in Wisconsin, where the loose-leaf format of publication has met wide acclaim.

(C) Provisions for Omission From Publication

Recognizing that some state agencies publish rules which contain (often by means of the device of incorporating by reference some lengthy official publication, such as a code of safety regulations adopted by some national organization) extremely detailed provisions of little general interest, and otherwise obtainable, the Revised Model State Act contains a provision excusing publication in the official compilation of "any rule the publication of which would be unduly cumbersome, expensive, or otherwise inexpedient, if the rule in printed or processed form

[106] California (GOV'T CODE § 11409. A similar provision is found in Alaska (STAT. § 44.62.130). In Oregon, it is provided that the secretary of state shall publish bulletins at such intervals as he shall determine (REV. STAT. § 183.360 (2)). Pennsylvania makes a similar provision with reference to periodical indices (STAT. ANN. tit. 71, § 1710.21a). New York provides that the secretary of state may publish supplements whenever he deems it to be necessary (EXECUTIVE LAW § 103.1). Connecticut provides for publication by the legislative commissioners "from time to time." (GEN. STAT. REV. § 4-50). In Massachusetts, a somewhat different approach is adopted. That state requires each agency to keep a publication of its effective rules "currently up to date" (GEN. LAWS ANN. ch. 30A, § 6).

[107] See Schwartz, *Administrative Law,* 36 N.Y.U.L. REV. 1429 (1961).

is made available on application to the adopting agency, and if the bulletin or compilation contains a notice stating the general subject matter of the omitted rule and stating how a copy thereof may be obtained."[108]

Similar provisions authorizing omissions from the published compilations are found in a number of state statutes. Many of them follow closely the provisions of the Revised Model Act.[109] Others allow a wider measure of discretion to the publishing authority as to what omissions may be made. Typical is the provision in the California statute, authorizing omission (and substitution of an appropriate reference) of any rules the printing of which the Division of Administrative Procedure "finds to be impractical, such as detailed schedules or forms otherwise available to the public, or which are of limited or particular application."[110] In a few states, special provision is made for cases where a rule incorporates the provisions of some code—*e.g.,* an elevator safety code—adopted by a nationally recognized organization; and publication thereof is not required if copies are readily available to interested persons.[111] New York authorizes omission from the published compilation of rules which relate solely to the organization or internal management of an agency.[112]

(D) Availability of Rules

Since the habit and instinct of Americans is to obey (albeit unhappily) rather than to ignore official rules prescribed to govern their activities, it is to the interest of the agencies to make sure that all those subject to the rules of an agency be informed as to the content of its rules. If agencies took appropriate steps to make sure that all those subject to their rules were duly apprised of the contents thereof, the workload of their

---

108 Section 5(c).

109 Georgia (CODE ANN. § 3A-101); Maine (REV. STAT. ANN. ch. 20-A, § 4-II); Maryland (ANN. CODE art. 41, § 247); Minnesota (STAT. § 15.0414); Oregon (REV. STAT. § 183.360); Rhode Island (GEN. LAWS ANN. § 42-35-5); Washington (REV. CODE § 34.04.050).

110 California (GOV'T CODE § 11409). The same provision appears in Alaska (STAT. § 42.62.130). The South Carolina statute delegates a broad measure of discretion to the code commissioners with respect to omissions (CODE ANN. § 1-16).

111 Indiana (ANN. STAT. § 60-1507); Oklahoma (STAT. tit. 75, § 251); Wisconsin (STAT. § 227.024).

112 EXECUTIVE LAW § 102.

enforcement staffs could be tremendously reduced, to the benefit of all.

Mere provision for the publication of administrative rules is not enough to assure achievement of the goal that the public be informed of the contents of the rules. Something must be done to get the publication into the hands of the persons affected.

The device best calculated to achieve this result is for each agency to maintain a mailing list of all persons known to be concerned with the activities of that agency, and to mail to every name on the list copies of all rules adopted by the agency. This practice[113] is followed by a number of agencies in many states—often on an informal basis. Statutory requirement for such procedure would mark an important forward step in administrative practice legislation.

Another device occasionally employed is the publication of rules in loose-leaf form, so that as rules are amended, replacement pages can be slipped into the binder, and the subscriber will have an up-to-date volume always at hand for ready reference. New rules, of course, can similarly be inserted in the appropriate place. In most states, one or two loose-leaf volumes would accommodate all the rules of all the state agencies. Such loose-leaf publication serves an important purpose, as can be attested by anyone who has undertaken the task of checking through twenty or thirty periodical supplements to ascertain the current rules of a particular agency.

Surprisingly little has been done in the way of providing loose-leaf publication of administrative rules. However, a few states have experimented with publication in loose-leaf format; and their experiences have been so successful as to suggest that the practice may become more widely adopted. It is not necessary, of course, that there be statutory provision to authorize loose-leaf publication. New York instituted such a practice in 1961, independent of statutory requirement. However, a few statutes specifically refer to loose-leaf publication.[114]

---

[113] Occasionally, this is required by statute. *E.g.,* COLO. REV. STAT. ANN. § 3-16-2 (9).

[114] Alaska (STAT. § 44.62.170); California (GOV'T CODE § 11409). The Kentucky statute requires publication in "a manner which will accommodate changes in regulations and allow distribution of any topical or organizational part of the regulations" (REV. STAT. § 13.096(1)). Massachusetts provides for publication in "pamphlet, loose-leaf, or other appropriate form" (GEN. LAWS ANN. ch.

The Revised Model State Act contains only modest requirements for making administrative rules conveniently available. It provides that "bulletins and compilations shall be made available upon request to [agencies and officials of this State] free of charge and to other persons at prices fixed by the [Secretary of State] to cover mailing and publication costs."[115]

The minimal provision to promote ready availability of rules is that which requires distribution at a figure approximating the cost of publishing and mailing. This requirement appears in many statutes.[116] In addition, a substantial number of statutes require free distribution to designated public officials.[117]

30A, § 6). Wisconsin requires that rules shall be published in the administrative code or register in the manner prescribed by § 35.93 (STAT. § 227.025).

115 Section 5 (d).

116 Alaska (STAT. § 44.62.150); Arizona (REV. STAT. ANN. § 41-1006); California (GOV'T CODE § 11410); Colorado (REV. STAT. ANN. § 3-16-2 (9)); Florida (STAT. § 120.051); Hawaii (SESS. LAWS 1961, Act 103, § 5 (b)); Illinois (REV. STAT. ch. 127, § 268); Indiana (ANN. STAT. § 60-1507); Kentucky (REV. STAT. § 13.096 (2)); Maine (REV. STAT. ANN. ch. 20-A, § 4-III); Maryland (ANN. CODE art. 41, § 247 (d)); Massachusetts (GEN. LAWS ANN. ch. 30A, § 6); Michigan (COMP. LAWS § 24.78); Minnesota (STAT. § 15.0413 (5)); Missouri (REV. STAT. § 536.030); Nebraska (REV. STAT. § 84-905); North Carolina (GEN. STAT. § 143-197); Ohio (REV. CODE ANN. § 119.05); Oklahoma (STAT. tit. 75, § 255); Oregon (REV. STAT. § 183.370); Rhode Island (GEN. LAWS ANN. § 42-35-5); Washington (REV. CODE § 34.04.050 (4)); West Virginia (Acts 1964, art. 3, ch. 1, § 7).

117 Alaska (STAT. § 44.62.140); California (GOV'T CODE § 11409.5); Hawaii (SESS. LAWS 1961, Act 103, § 5 (b)); Indiana (ANN. STAT. § 60-1507); Iowa (CODE § 17A.12); Maine (REV. STAT. ANN. ch. 20-A, § 4-III); Maryland (ANN. CODE art. 41, § 247 (d)); Michigan (COMP. LAWS § 24.78); Missouri (REV. STAT. § 536.030); Oklahoma (STAT. tit. 75, § 255); Oregon (REV. STAT. § 183.-370); Rhode Island (GEN. LAWS ANN. § 42-35-5 (d)); Tennessee (CODE ANN. § 4-502); Virginia (CODE ANN. § 9-6.7 (b)); Washington (REV. CODE § 34.-04.050(4)).

CHAPTER IX

RULE MAKING: DETERMINING APPLICABILITY AND VALIDITY OF RULES

Section 1

Declaratory Rulings by Agencies

(A) TWO METHODS AVAILABLE

Two methods are available for obtaining advisory opinions from agencies as to the meaning of agency rules, and the applicability thereof to particular factual situations.

The method by far most commonly employed, and one that is always available—without benefit, usually, of statutory sanction—is that of informal inquiry. One may telephone counsel for an agency, or a commissioner, or an information officer, or some acquaintance on the agency staff, and ask his question. Or one may call at the agency office, and discuss informally the problem with which he is concerned. Or a letter of inquiry may be addressed to the agency.

These informal methods of inquiry are utilized even more frequently in connection with the operation of state agencies than in the case of the federal agencies. Many factors account for this. The smaller geographical jurisdiction of state agencies is one factor. The inquirer is likely to have some acquaintance on the agency staff to whom he can readily turn for advice. Too, some state agencies are characterized by a degree of provinciality which sometimes approaches neighborliness, and this renders them less austere, and more approachable, than the federal agencies. In contrast to the high degree of formality that characterizes many federal agencies, state agencies are often inclined to approach their problems with the attitude of the mediator who says "Let's work this out together." The circumstance that state agencies are often concerned with problems that are essentially local in character also contributes to the frequent use of informal rulings in state agencies. A suggestion to an apple grower as to what he must do to comply with labeling regulations, for example, is much less likely to have far-reaching and unforeseen implications than is a ruling by the Securities and Exchange Commission as to the marketing of securities. As a result, the state agencies—not being worried as to how their rulings might affect some other case—are often more ready to give informal advice (although of course some of the larger agencies in states the size of California or New York, handling a volume of work comparable to that of federal agencies, employ similarly formal operating procedures).

The second method available for obtaining information from the agency as to the meaning and applicability of an agency rule is that of making formal application for a definitive ruling. This method is available only where there exist statutory provisions therefor. The Revised Model State Act makes provision for this type of application. It has no provisions referable to the informal type of inquiry.

(B) Applications for Formal Declaratory Rulings

The need for statutory authorization for declaratory rulings by administrative agencies was noted in 1941 by the Attorney General's Committee on Administrative Procedure. It declared:[1]

> In recent years, in the Federal and state courts, the device of the declaratory judgment has been provided to furnish guidance and certainty in many private relationships where previously parties proceeded at their own risk. . . . The time is ripe for introducing into administration itself an instrument similarly devised, to achieve similar results in the administrative field. The perils of unanticipated sanctions and liabilities may be as great in the one area as in the other. They should be reduced or eliminated. A major step in that direction would be the establishment of procedures by which an individual who proposed to pursue a course which might involve him in dispute with an administrative agency, might obtain from that agency, in the latter's discretion, a binding declaration concerning the consequences of his proposed action.

To meet the need so described, Congress enacted Section 5(d) of the Federal Administrative Procedure Act,[2] providing: "The

[1] *Administrative Procedure in Government Agencies,* S. DOC. No. 8, 77th Cong., 1st Sess. 30-33 (1941).
[2] 5 U.S.C. § 1004; F.C.A. 5 § 1004.

agency is authorized in its sound discretion, with like effect as in the case of other orders, to issue a declaratory order to terminate a controversy or remove uncertainty."

This permissive provision, however, failed to achieve the hoped-for results. As noted in the Report of the Hoover Commission Task Force on Legal Services and Procedure,[3] most agencies failed to provide procedures for the issuance of declaratory orders. The Task Force concluded that while the purpose of Section 5(d) had been to remove a blind spot from the law, the blind spot still remained after a decade of experience under the federal act. Pointing out that a primary reason for the failure to utilize the remedy more frequently was the circumstance that the issuance of such orders was discretionary with the agencies (and that courts had sustained the position of some agencies that refusal to issue an order did not constitute reviewable agency action), the Task Force recommended that the act be amended to require agencies to issue such declaratory orders, on request, in justiciable controversies.

The original Model State Act, promulgated in 1946 (the same year that the federal act was enacted) adopted an approach similar to that of the federal statute. It provided:[4]

> On petition of any interested person, any agency may issue a declaratory ruling with respect to the applicability to any person, property, or state of facts of any rule or statute enforceable by it. A declaratory ruling, if issued after argument and stated to be binding, is binding between the agency and the petitioner on the state of facts alleged, unless it is altered or set aside by a court.

The Model Act further provided for judicial review of such declaratory rulings, and declared: "Each agency shall prescribe by rule the form for such petitions and the procedure for their submission, consideration, and disposition."

Statutes closely paralleling the provisions of the original act are on the books of several states.[5]

---

3 Commission on Organization of Executive Branch of Government, TASK FORCE REPORT ON LEGAL SERVICES AND PROCEDURE 187 et seq. (1955).

4 Section 7.

5 Maine (REV. STAT. ANN. ch. 20-A, § 6); Maryland (ANN. CODE art. 41, § 250); Nebraska (REV. STAT. § 84-912); Oregon (REV. STAT. § 183.410); Washington (REV. CODE § 34.04.080); West Virginia (Acts 1964, art. 4, ch. 1, § 1).

In general, experience under such state statutes was similar to that which obtained in the case of the federal agencies. The officials of most state agencies, ready though they might be to discuss informally over their desks, or over the telephone, their ideas as to the meaning and applicability of their rules, yet exhibited a great reluctance to enter formal declaratory orders, which (if adverse to the party making the request) could speedily lead the agency into litigation before the states' highest judicial tribunals.

Recognizing this situation, the draftsmen of the Revised Model State Act sought to devise an amendment which hopefully would lead to the fuller utilization of this beneficial procedure.

First, it was decided that the declaratory ruling procedure should be available with respect to "orders" as well as rules. This amendment serves two purposes. It not only avoids the necessity of making the distinction—which in many cases is a most difficult one—between "rules" and "orders"; but, more important, it means that even in cases clearly involving a pure adjudicatory function, if there is doubt as to the meaning or applicability of an agency order, the agency may be asked to rule specifically upon the doubtful questions.

Second, it was determined to eliminate the provisions that denied binding effect to declaratory rulings unless issued after argument and stated to be binding. The first condition seemed to impose undue formality: there is no reason why the agency's ruling should not be binding if based on written submissions or conference, rather than on oral argument. The second condition gave the agency an opportunity to deprive its order of any real meaning by the simple expedient of failing to include in its ruling a specific declaration that the ruling was intended to be binding.

Third, and most important, the draftsmen determined to make it more difficult for agencies to decline to issue declaratory rulings. The original version of the Model Act, of course, allowed agencies an untrammeled freedom of choice to decline to issue declaratory rulings. In fact, the operative clause—declaring that "any agency *may* issue a declaratory ruling"—seemed almost an implicit invitation to the agencies to decline to do so.

Careful consideration was given to the suggestion that agencies be required to furnish declaratory rulings, upon request by any interested person or party. It was concluded, however, that this proposal went too far. There was some danger, it was thought, that if the procedure were made mandatory, innumerable requests for rulings on slightly altered facts might be made in an effort to reach the outermost edge of legal conduct without stepping over the boundary into actual illegality. Further, it was thought that a possibility existed that some agencies might be inundated with so large a number of requests for declaratory rulings as to impede seriously the normal activities of the agency. Finally, it was believed that cases exist wherein agencies have valid reasons for declining to rule formally, and with binding effect, on a particularly difficult question which the agency wishes to avoid deciding until it has developed a fully matured opinion on the precise point.

In view of these reasons, it was decided that agencies should be required to rule upon each request for a declaratory ruling, but that they would be permitted to make their ruling that of declining to resolve the particular question. Whatever ruling the agency made, however (even a ruling declining to rule upon a particular question), would have the same status as any other final order of the agency. This would mean that, in appropriate cases, the refusal of the agency to make a ruling could be appealed to the courts. In other cases, the denial of the request would make it a matter of formal record that (for example) the agency was not prepared to say that a particular course of conduct was prohibited by the rule in question.

To achieve these ends, the draftsmen revised the section so that in the Revised Model State Act, it reads:

> Each agency shall provide by rule for the filing and prompt disposition of petitions for declaratory rulings as to the applicability of any statutory provision or of any rule or order of the agency. Rulings disposing of petitions have the same status as agency decisions or orders in contested cases.[6]

Existing statutes in some of the states indicate an acceptance by state legislatures of the principles espoused by the draftsmen of the Revised Model Act. Rhode Island has adopted the provisions of the Revised Model Act.[7] Statutes in other states are

[6] Section 8.
[7] R. I. GEN. LAWS ANN. § 42-35-8.

modelled closely upon it.[8] In Wisconsin, reflecting its long experience in this field, amendments have been adopted making detailed provisions to govern the issuance of declaratory rulings. Under the Wisconsin statute,[9] the issuance of a declaratory ruling is mandatory when a case is referred to the agency for that purpose by a court; in other cases, the issuance of the ruling is discretionary with the agency. Detailed provisions are made as to the form and content of requests for rulings; and the statute contains other specific requirements designed to assure speedy consideration and disposition of the requests. If an agency declines to issue a declaratory ruling, it must state in writing its reasons therefor.

(C) INFORMAL ADVISORY OPINIONS

Taking the nation as a whole, it could safely be estimated that literally hundreds (and probably thousands) of informal advisory opinions are issued each day respecting the interpretation or application of statutes and rules. Requests for such advice come to the agencies from both laymen and attorneys. They are answered by officials at every level within the agency —from counter clerk to general counsel or commissioners.

In some states, and with some agencies, such opinions are not considered either by the inquirer or by the answerer to have any authoritative effect. They are viewed as merely informal exchanges of information and opinion. Even when so considered, they are nevertheless of great help. If the inquirer learns that the agency has considered a problem in which he is interested, and ascertains that the agency's views coincide with his own, he obtains a degree of practical assurance, even though he knows the advice is not binding. Conversely, if he learns that the agency (or some of its representatives) entertain views at odds with his own, he is alerted to take proper measures to conform his conduct to the standards demanded by the agency, or to test the point. In some state agencies, moreover, just as in the case of some of the federal agencies,[10] by practice and precedent,

---

[8] Georgia (CODE ANN. § 3A-101); Hawaii (SESS. LAWS 1961, Act 103, § 8); Oklahoma (STAT. tit. 75, § 307).

[9] WIS. STAT. § 227.06.

[10] See Commission on Organization of Executive Branch of Government, TASK FORCE REPORT ON LEGAL SERVICES AND PROCEDURE 189 (1955).

letters of advice and staff opinions are given limited validity within the agency.

It seems clear, however, that in the absence of statute, such informal opinions are not legally binding on the agency,[11] and that the agency is free to change its opinion and insist thereafter on its new interpretation. Whether an agency should be permitted to insist upon a retroactive application of its revised interpretation is a difficult question. The answer depends in part upon the degree of formality attendant the giving of the opinion—one is much safer in relying upon a letter than upon a telephone call.[12] It depends, in part, upon the equities of the particular case, and the attendant balancing of interests.

A few federal statutes[13] protect parties relying in good faith upon advisory opinions issued by designated officials of particular agencies. The suggestion is sometimes urged that provision should be made by statute that informal opinions given by any administrative agency may be safely relied upon by the person requesting the ruling—provided, of course, that his request for the opinion fairly stated the facts involved.[14] The suggestion is intriguing. But adoption of the suggestion would involve the assumption of a grave risk that if agencies were put on notice that they would be bound to honor their informal opinions, they would simply stop issuing them.

Such was the experience with the Wage Hour and Public Contracts Division of the United States Department of Labor. Before enactment of the Portal to Portal Act,[15] which granted protection to any person who relied in good faith upon any administrative ruling or "any administrative practice or enforcement policy," it was easy for an attorney, upon letter request, to obtain an informal opinion from the Solicitor of the Department or from any of the Division's regional attorneys. Although recognized as not being authoritative or binding, they afforded a

---

[11] *E.g.*, State v. Maddox Tractor & Equip. Co., 260 Ala. 136, 69 So. 2d 426 (1953).

[12] Related problems are discussed in § 4 (D) *infra* of this chapter, and also in Ch. XV, in connection with the application of principles of res judicata to administrative adjudication.

[13] *E.g.*, Opinions of Office of Alien Property (50 U.S.C. Appx., § 5 (b) (2); F.C.A. 50 Appx. § 5 (b) (2)), and Opinions of Wage Hour and Public Contracts Division (29 U.S.C. § 259; F.C.A. 29 § 259).

[14] *E.g.*, Newman, *Should Official Advice Be Reliable?*, 53 COLUM. L. REV. 374 (1953).

[15] 29 U.S.C. § 259; F.C.A. 29 § 259.

most convenient method of ascertaining the current thinking of the Division on fine points of statutory construction. In fact, many such opinions believed to be of general interest were widely publicized, and their publication no doubt helped to crystallize the resolution of many difficult problems. But within a few days after the enactment of the Portal to Portal Act, the Division withdrew all published opinions and informal advisory rulings, and gave public notice that none of them should be relied on. Furthermore, it became much more difficult thereafter to obtain official advice. It had become so valuable that the Division apparently felt it could no longer afford to give it away. Many lawyers expressed the thought that it was better to be able to get informal opinions that were not binding, than to be unable to obtain any opinions at all.

Section 2

Declaratory Judgments in Court

Increasing attention has been given in recent years to the use of the declaratory judgment procedure for the purpose of securing judicial pronouncements, in advance, respecting the validity and applicability of administrative rules.

Many states, of course, have general declaratory judgment acts; and actions have been brought under such statutes to obtain declaratory judgments as to the applicability and validity of some administrative actions. The general declaratory judgment acts should be sufficient for this purpose,[16] and in fact declaratory judgments have often been rendered, under such general statutes, respecting the validity and applicability of statutes administered by the agencies. However, the Uniform Declaratory Judgments Act does not specifically refer to administrative rules. Section 2 of that Act provides:

> Any person interested under a deed, will, written contract or other writings constituting a contract, or whose rights, status or other legal relations are affected by a statute, municipal ordinance, contract or franchise, may have determined any question of construction or

---

[16] *Cf.*, Borchard, *Declaratory Judgments in Administrative Law,* 11 N.Y.U.L. REV. 139 (1933); *Administrative Procedure in Government Agencies,* S. DOC. No. 8, 77th Cong., 1st Sess. 81 (1941); Public Serv. Comm'n of Utah v. Wycoff Co., 344 U.S. 237, 97 L. Ed. 291, 73 Sup. Ct. 236 (1952).

validity arising under the instrument, statute, ordinance, contract or franchise and obtain a declaration of rights, status or other legal relations thereunder.

In view of the savings clause in Section 5 of that Act, providing that the enumeration in Section 2 (above quoted) should not be construed as limiting the general powers of the courts to grant declaratory relief, the omission of a specific reference to administrative rules should not be construed as limiting the power of the courts to grant declaratory judgments as to the validity of agency rules; however, the absence of a direct reference seems to have been a deterrent to such exercise of the courts' power. Further, a number of courts (both state and federal) have from time to time declined to issue declaratory judgments concerning agency matters, absent a specific statutory provision requiring them so to do, as provided in the Revised Model State Act and many state statutes. Such refusals have been predicated on several grounds.[17] Courts have refused declaratory judgments on the ground that petitioner had not exhausted his administrative remedies;[18] or on the ground that the application did not present a case or controversy;[19] or because another remedy was viewed as exclusive.[20]

To guarantee the availability of the declaratory judgment procedure for the purpose of testing the validity or applicability of administrative rules, it is therefore desirable to enact specific statutory provisions, making it clear that such petitions do present justiciable controversies, and that they may be brought on for hearing whether or not alternative remedies are available, and whether or not administrative remedies have been exhausted.

---

17 For a critical review of such decisions, see Lavery, *The Declaratory Judgment in Administrative Law,* 14 F.R.D. 479 (1953).

18 Pennsylvania R.R. Co. v. Pennsylvania Pub. Utils. Comm'n, 396 Pa. 34, 152 A.2d 422 (1959); Utah Fuel Co. v. National Bituminous Coal Comm'n, 69 App. D.C. 333, 101 F.2d 426 (1938); Bradley Lumber Co. v. NLRB (5th Cir. 1936), 84 F.2d 97, *cert. denied,* 229 U.S. 559, 81 L. Ed. 411, 57 Sup. Ct. 21.

19 Craun Transp., Inc. v. Public Utils. Comm'n, 162 Ohio St. 9, 120 N.E.2d 436 (1954)—a case to which the Ohio Administrative Procedure Act was not applicable; Ashwander v. Tennessee Valley Authority, 297 U.S. 288, 80 L. Ed. 688, 56 Sup. Ct. 466 (1936); Electric Bond & Share Co. v. SEC, 303 U.S. 419, 82 L. Ed. 936, 58 Sup. Ct. 678, 115 A.L.R. 105 (1938).

20 Howle v. Alabama State Milk Control Bd., 265 Ala. 189, 90 So. 2d 752 (1956); Haggard v. Industrial Comm'n, 71 Ariz. 91, 223 P.2d 915 (1950)—decided before the adoption of Arizona's State Administrative Procedure Act; Castle Shannon Coal Corp. v. Upper St. Clair Township, 370 Pa. 211, 88 A.2d 56 (1952).

Such provisions are incorporated in the Revised Model State Act, viz.:

> The validity or applicability of a rule may be determined in an action for declaratory judgment in the [District Court of ——— County], if it is alleged that the rule, or its threatened application, interferes with or impairs, or threatens to interfere with or impair, the legal rights or privileges of the plaintiff. The agency shall be made a party to the action. A declaratory judgment may be rendered whether or not the plaintiff has requested the agency to pass upon the validity or applicability of the rule in question.[21]

A number of states have enacted statutes designed to accomplish the major objectives of these provisions of the Revised Model Act. A few of those statutes, following the provision of the Revised Model Act, specifically provide that questions as to the applicability, as well as the validity, of an administrative rule may be tested by declaratory judgment proceedings. This is a significant addition, for often questions as to the application of a rule may be of equal importance with questions concerning its validity.[22] Other statutes refer specifically only to declarations as to the validity of a rule or the validity of its threatened application.[23]

A number of the statutes specifically provide that if it is made to appear, in declaratory judgment proceedings, that the agency failed to follow the prescribed rule-making procedures, the rule may be declared invalid for this reason.[24] In a few, it is further provided that the declaratory judgment procedure may

---

[21] Section 7.

[22] Statutes specifically authorizing declaratory judgments as to the applicability of agency rules include: Florida (STAT. § 120.30); Missouri (REV. STAT. § 536.-050); Oklahoma (STAT. tit. 75, § 306); Rhode Island (GEN. LAWS ANN. § 42-35-7); West Virginia (Acts 1964, art. 4, ch. 1, § 2).

[23] Alaska (STAT. § 44.62.300); Arizona (REV. STAT. ANN. § 41-1007-A); California (GOV'T CODE § 11440); Georgia (CODE ANN. § 3A-101); Hawaii (SESS. LAWS 1961, Act 103, § 7); Maryland (ANN. CODE art. 41, § 249); Massachusetts (GEN. LAWS ANN. ch. 30A, § 7); Minnesota (STAT. § 15.0416); Nebraska (REV. STAT. § 84-911); New Mexico (STAT. ANN. § 67-26-25); North Carolina (GEN. STAT. § 150-32); Ohio (REV. CODE ANN. § 119.11); Oregon (REV. STAT. § 183.400); Virginia (CODE ANN. § 9-6.9); Washington (REV. CODE § 34.04.070); Wisconsin (STAT. § 227.05 (1)). The Wisconsin statute provides that, with stated exceptions, petitions for declaratory judgments shall be the exclusive means of judicial review of the validity of an administrative rule.

[24] Such provisions appear in the following states, the statutory references being the same as those noted in notes 22 and 23 *supra*: Alaska, Arizona, California, Florida, Georgia, Hawaii, Maryland, Nebraska, Ohio, Oregon, Virginia, Washington. See also MINN. STAT. § 15.0417.

be used to test the propriety of the agency finding of an emergency justifying an emergency rule.[25]

The state courts have accorded such statutes a hospitable reception. Indicative of the readiness of the state courts to permit utilization of the declaratory judgment procedure is the declaration of the New Jersey court[26] that although in the case before it, reviewed proceedings should have been instituted under a specific statute, "we shall not permit this procedural issue to detain us" from determining by declaratory decree the rights of the parties. The Arizona court (which had formerly declared that it could not render a declaratory judgment respecting an administrative rule, under the state's general declaratory judgment act, since it deemed the statutory review provisions exclusive)[27] ruled, after adoption of that state's administrative procedure act, that its provisions justified the court in granting a declaratory judgment, even though other remedies could have been utilized.[28] Again, the Connecticut court has emphasized that it is proper to grant a declaratory judgment, even though the possibility of plaintiff's suffering legal wrong is contingent upon the happening of future events.[29] Of course, the statutory authorization may not be extended, and if the statute authorizes the rendering of a declaratory judgment only with respect to agency "rules," a declaration may not be made with respect to informal agency action which does not amount to the adoption of a rule.[30]

Since the statutes authorizing the rendition of declaratory judgments respecting the validity of agency rules are permissive only, the existence of such statutes does not preclude judicial review of the validity of rules pursuant to other statutory methods of appeal.[31]

Situations in which petitions for declaratory judgments have been granted with respect to the validity of agency rules in-

---

25 Alaska, Arizona, California, Florida—the statutory references being the same as those set forth in notes 22 and 23 *supra.*

26 Bechler v. Parsekian, 36 N.J. 242, 176 A.2d 470 (1961).

27 Haggard v. Industrial Comm'n, 71 Ariz. 91, 223 P.2d 915 (1950).

28 State Tax Comm'n v. Wallapai Brick & Clay Prods., Inc., 85 Ariz. 23, 330 P.2d 988 (1958).

29 Colonial House, Inc. v. Connecticut State Bd. of Labor Relations, 23 Conn. Sup. 30, 176 A.2d 381 (1961).

30 State *ex rel.* Toberman v. Cook, 365 Mo. 274, 281 S.W.2d 777 (1955).

31 Allied Theatres of New England, Inc. v. Commissioner of Labor & Industries, 338 Mass. 609, 156 N.E.2d 424 (1959).

clude: (1) questions as to the validity of the delegation of rule-making powers;[32] (2) other constitutional issues;[33] (3) questions as to the statutory authority of the agency;[34] (4) charges that the rule was so arbitrary and unreasonable as to be void;[35] (5) assertions that the rule was invalid because the agency failed to follow prescribed rule-making procedures;[36] (6) questions as to the applicability of an agency rule;[37] (7) questions whether the challenged rule was within the agency's statutory authority;[38] (8) questions whether a rule was based upon a misinterpretation of the governing statute.[39]

Section 3

Tests Applied in Determining Validity of Rules

Logically, the questions to be examined by the courts, in determining the validity of an agency rule, should depend on the type of rule involved. In the case of a legislative rule (*i.e.*, one adopted pursuant to a delegation of legislative power, the violation of which involves statutory sanctions), the queries would be: first, whether the rule related to the subject matter on which power to legislate had been delegated; second, whether the rule conformed to the standards prescribed in the delegatory statute; and third, whether the rule was invalid on constitutional grounds, such as due process. The approach would be somewhat different, from a purely logical viewpoint, when an interpretive

---

32 Porporis v. City of Warson Woods, 352 S.W.2d 605 (Mo. 1962); Lane v. Holderman, 23 N.J. 304, 129 A.2d 8 (1957); Chiropractic Ass'n of New York, Inc. v. Hilleboe, 12 N.Y.2d 109, 237 N.Y.S.2d 289, 187 N.E.2d 756 (1962).

33 Stuyvesant Town, Inc. v. Ligham, 17 N.J. 473, 111 A.2d 744 (1955); Fruhling v. Amalgamated Housing Corp., 9 N.Y.2d 541, 215 N.Y.S.2d 493, 175 N.E.2d 156 (1961).

34 Lane v. Holderman, note 32 *supra.*

35 Stadnik v. Shell's City, Inc., 140 So. 2d 871 (Fla. 1962); Michell v. Louisiana State Bd. of Optometry Examiners, 128 So. 2d 825 (La. App. 1961); Hamilton Farms, Inc. v. Hoffman, 30 N.J. 335, 152 A.2d 848 (1959); Brookchester, Inc. v. Ligham, 17 N.J. 460, 111 A.2d 737 (1955); Chiropractic Ass'n of New York, Inc. v. Hilleboe, note 32 *supra.*

36 Shell Oil Co. v. Ricciuti, 147 Conn. 277, 160 A.2d 257 (1960); Porporis v. City of Warson Woods, 352 S.W.2d 605 (Mo. 1962).

37 Shell Oil Co. v. Ricciuti, note 36 *supra.*

38 Knudsen Creamery Co. v. Brock, 37 Cal. 2d 485, 234 P.2d 26 (1951); Hamilton Farms, Inc. v. Hoffman, note 35 *supra.*

39 Connecticut Gen. Life Ins. Co. v. Superintendent of Ins., 10 N.Y.2d 42, 217 N.Y.S.2d 39, 176 N.E.2d 63 (1961).

rule is involved. In such cases, the inquiry would concern fundamentally the question whether the rule correctly interpreted the statute, and involved with this issue there might be a quesion whether the rule amounted to an attempt to exercise legislative powers which had not been delegated. If this were the case, the rule would be held invalid as going beyond the sphere of interpretation and into that of legislation.

But in a field so surcharged with delicate questions of policy, and the balancing of competing claims and divergent governmental theories, the law cannot live on logic. The approach must be realistically pragmatic. While the decisions are ordinarily couched in maxims that set forth general "tests" as to the validity of rules, yet these formal criteria often express the result of a judgment rather than describing the means by which that judgment was reached. In interpreting and evaluating the decisions, the circumstances under which the rule was issued—and as well the circumstances of the particular application of the rule in the case before the court—must be carefully appraised. The general "tests" announced by the courts cannot be taken as talismanic touchstones to decision of any particular case.

Subject to the foregoing caveat, the current attitudes of the state courts in passing upon the validity of challenged administrative rules can be examined in light of five commonly announced "tests."

(A) A Rule Is Invalid if it Exceeds the Authority Conferred

It is often said that a rule is invalid if it exceeds the authority conferred by statute. This truism affords but a limited source of guidance, for of course the difficult question, always, is the determination of the outermost limits of the delegated authority. The rule has but little independent force except in cases where a power has been delegated to make legislative rules within a plainly limited sphere and subject to defined standards, and where the rule adopted exceeds this sphere or is contrary to the standards. The test may also be applied to cases where there has been no delegation of legislative power, and where a rule issued as an administrative interpretation of the statute is found to go beyond the sphere of interpretation and into the forbidden realm of legislative regulation.

Where a question is raised whether an administrative rule exceeds the limits of conferred authority, it is sometimes urged that its validity should be presumed, as in the case when a statute is attacked. In some states, statutory provisions create such a presumption.[40] Absent statutory provision, the state courts show little inclination to indulge in any such presumption in favor of the validity of administrative rules. Their attitude can be described by the cynical remark of Justice McReynolds[41] that:

> There is an obvious difference between legislative determination and the finding of an administrative official not supported by evidence. In theory, at least, the legislature acts upon adequate knowledge after full consideration and through members who represent the entire public.

The New Jersey court held that administrative rules have in their support a rebuttable presumption of validity only if they come within the ambit of delegated authority, and said that it was for the court to decide the ambit of authority.[42] Similarly, the California court "distinctly held to be nonapplicable" to administrative rules "The 'principle which accords the great dignity of conclusiveness to determinations of the general legislature. . . .' "[43] Again, the Arizona court said that where proceedings are brought against an agency to vacate a rule, ". . . the Commission as a defendant stands in no different position than any other litigant, . . . and in its nakedness it must meet the issues of fact in the same manner as any other party litigant."[44]

If the underlying statute conditions the rule-making power of an agency upon the occurrence of certain conditions, the state courts consider it their responsibility to determine—without reference to presumptions of the validity of official acts—whether the prescribed conditions have occurred.[45]

---

40 Board of Water Eng'rs v. Colorado River Municipal Water Dist., 152 Tex. 77, 254 S.W.2d 369 (1953), citing and relying on TEX. REV. CIV. STAT. art. 7780-3c (f), providing that the burden of proof shall be on the party attacking an administrative rule, and that the rule shall be deemed prima facie valid.

41 Southern Ry. v. Virginia, 290 U.S. 190, 197, 78 L. Ed. 260, 54 Sup. Ct. 148 (1933).

42 *In re* Weston, 36 N.J. 258, 176 A.2d 479 (1961).

43 Walker v. County of Los Angeles, 55 Cal. 2d 626, 635, 361 P.2d 247 (1961).

44 O'Neill v. Martori, 69 Ariz. 270, 275, 212 P.2d 994 (1949).

45 State *ex rel.* Sights v. Edwards, 228 Ind. 13, 89 N.E.2d 443 (1950), holding invalid a rule because required gubernatorial approval had not been obtained;

Typical of the decisions striking down administrative rules on the grounds that they exceeded the delegated authority is that of the Florida court holding that a statute delegating to the state board of health authority to make regulations in certain enumerated fields did not empower it to adopt rules governing the commercial spraying of lawns and shrubbery with toxic pesticides. The court declared:

> This is not a case where the legislature has attempted to delegate its responsibilities to a board. It is simply a case where a board has decided that a field is open for regulation, has lassoed this field, and then looked for authority upon which to hold onto its prized steer. To hold that boards may invade the legislative field upon such dubious authority would, in our opinion, be another step toward government by bureaucracy and the abolition of the legislative branch.[46]

Other cases clearly involving the naked issue of the validity of a rule that allegedly exceeded the authority conferred include decisions striking down: (1) a rule which, based upon statutory authority to require "fair dealing" by licensed real estate brokers, imposed a detailed code of regulations to prevent racial discrimination by such brokers;[47] (2) a rule providing that certificates of automobile titles would be issued only on request of licensed motor vehicle dealers;[48] (3) a rule requiring the town from which an indigent had moved to continue to pay for public assistance for a stated period of time;[49] (4) a rule setting wage schedules without required prior approvals;[50] (5) a rule treating holding companies as "financial businesses";[51] (6) a rule declaring that issuance of a check by a retail liquor dealer which

Thomas v. Ramberg, 245 Minn. 474, 73 N.W.2d 195 (1955); Linehan v. Faricy, 246 Minn. 179, 74 N.W.2d 670 (1956), holding invalid rules establishing minimum wage levels on the ground that advisory boards had not been properly constituted; Hymes v. Schechter, 6 N.Y.2d 352, 189 N.Y.S.2d 870, 160 N.E.2d 627 (1959)—rule of civil service commission did not become effective until required approval of mayor had been obtained.

46 Lewis v. Florida State Bd. of Health, 143 So. 2d 867, 877 (Fla. 1962).

47 McKibben v. Michigan Corp. & Sec. Comm'n, 369 Mich. 69, 119 N.W. 2d 557 (1963).

48 Killingsworth v. West Way Motors, Inc., 87 Ariz. 74, 347 P.2d 1098 (1959).

49 Bureau of Old Age Assistance v. Commissioner of Pub. Welfare, 326 Mass. 121, 93 N.E.2d 267 (1950).

50 Corrigan v. Joseph, 304 N.Y. 172, 106 N.E.2d 593 (1952).

51 United States Steel Corp. v. Gerosa, 7 N.Y.2d 454, 199 N.Y.S.2d 475, 166 N.E.2d 489 (1960); *cf.* Old Republic Life Ins. Co. v. Wikler, 9 N.Y.2d 524, 215 N.Y.S.2d 481, 175 N.E.2d 147 (1961), finding that statutory authority did exist for a rule respecting insurance rates.

was not cleared because the drawer had insufficient funds in the bank would be prima facie evidence that he was obtaining forced credit from the wholesaler.[52]

(B) A Rule Is Invalid if it Conflicts With the Governing Statute

In many cases, the conclusion that a rule is invalid as exceeding the authority conferred on the agency by statute is premised on the finding that there is a conflict between the challenged rule and the provisions of the governing statute. Typical of cases in this category is an Alabama decision holding invalid a rule of the state board of optometry which forbade advertising by optometrists. This rule, it was found, was in conflict with a statutory provision which authorized the operation of optometric departments as part of a general merchandising business, on condition that the name of the optometrist in charge must appear in all advertisements published by such merchant with reference to his sale of glasses.[53]

Where a procedural rule attempts to limit a right of appeal granted by statute, it is void because it in effect conflicts with the statute.[54]

A proration rule was held invalid by the Texas court because it calculated allowable production retrospectively, in direct conflict with the governing statute, which clearly prescribed prospective operation for proration regulations.[55] The same court declared invalid a rule concerning a teachers' retirement plan, upon finding that the rule conflicted with the overriding statutory purpose to support retired teachers.[56]

In cases where an interpretive rule is in conflict with the court's interpretation of the statute, the conclusion of invalidity could be premised, in succinct terms, on the basis that the agen-

[52] Alcohol Beverage Control Bd. v. Hunter, 331 S.W.2d 280 (Ky. 1960).

[53] Alabama State Bd. of Optometry v. Busch Jewelry Co., 261 Ala. 479, 75 So. 2d 121 (1954); *cf.* Jordan v. City of Mobile, 260 Ala. 393, 71 So. 2d 513 (1954), which stated the test that an administrative rule is void if its effect is to subvert or abrogate the governing statute, but found on the facts that the rule did not conflict with the statute.

[54] Flanagan v. Department of Civil Serv., 29 N.J. 1, 148 A.2d 14 (1959).

[55] Rudman v. Railroad Comm'n of Texas, 162 Tex. 579, 349 S.W.2d 717 (1961).

[56] Teacher Retirement Sys. v. Duckworth, 153 Tex. 141, 264 S.W.2d 98 (1954).

cy's interpretation of the statute was wrong. Where this is so, the courts frequently say that the regulation in question is invalid as being in conflict with the statute. An illustrative example is afforded by a Wisconsin case. A state statute governing the determination of "situs" of income provided that "for the purposes of taxation income from mercantile or manufacturing business . . . shall follow the situs of the business from which derived." The department of taxation adopted a rule which applied this standard to income earned by those engaged in the business of building roads, considering this to be a "mercantile or manufacturing" business. The court ruled that this was an incorrect interpretation of the statute, and that the rule was therefore in conflict with the statute. The court remarked that "to give such interpretation to those terms is patently to distort the plain language of the statute," and concluded that the rule was therefore "out of harmony with the statute" and hence void.[57] This approach is frequently employed in cases involving administrative rules as to assessment or collection of taxes.[58] Other instances of application of the test that a rule based upon a misinterpretation of the statute will be deemed to be in conflict with the statute occur in other fields.[59]

(C) Rules Are Void if They Extend or Modify the Statute

In some cases, the conflict between the rule and the statute appears because the rule seeks to extend or modify the statute. The governing principle was long ago expressed by the United States Supreme Court in these words: "If experience shows that Congress acted under a mistaken impression, that does not authorize the Treasury Department . . . to make new laws which they imagine Congress would have made had it been properly informed."[60]

Recent state court cases involving these considerations indicate that state courts are on the whole more willing than the federal

[57] Village of Plain v. Harder, 268 Wis. 507, 68 N.W.2d 47 (1955).

[58] State v. Maddox Tractor & Equip. Co., 260 Ala. 136, 69 So. 2d 426 (1953); Federal Compress & Warehouse Co. v. Call, 221 Ark. 537, 254 S.W.2d 319 (1953); Ruby Chevrolet, Inc. v. Department of Revenue, 6 Ill. 2d 147, 126 N.E.2d 617 (1955).

[59] O'Donnell v. Board of Chosen Freeholders, 31 N.J. 434, 158 A.2d 1 (1960); Bryant v. Barber, 237 N.C. 480, 75 S.E.2d 410 (1953).

[60] Merritt v. Welsh, 104 U.S. 694, 704, 26 L. Ed. 896 (1882).

courts have been during the last twenty years to strike down administrative rules on the ground that they give effect to policies extending or expanding the policy set forth in the statute. The state courts adhere firmly to the principle stated by a California court: "An administrative officer may not make a rule or regulation that alters or enlarges the terms of a legislative enactment."[61]

A typical application of this policy is found in a Wisconsin case.[62] The statute required employers to utilize methods "reasonably adequate" to render places of employment safe for employees. However, a rule of the industrial commission placed an absolute duty on employers to prohibit employees from working on any slippery platform until it had been sprinkled with sand or otherwise made non-slippery. Noting that the rule imposed a higher standard of care than that required by the statute, the court held the rule invalid.

Licensing rules are especially subject to attack on this ground. Typical examples are furnished by cases involving the prescription of standards of conduct for opticians and optometrists. Thus, a rule prohibiting certain types of advertising not included in the statutory proscriptions was held invalid.[63] Similarly, rules imposing requirements stricter than those imposed by statute as a condition of obtaining licenses to do business have been held to be void.[64]

Attempts by state rent control administrators to extend their jurisdiction over types of housing accommodations which were not committed to their regulatory power by the applicable statute, have been held invalid in a number of cases.[65]

---

[61] County of Los Angeles v. State Dep't of Pub. Health, 158 Cal. App. 2d 425, 438, 322 P.2d 968 (1958); Hart v. Department of Revenue, 333 Mich. 248, 52 N.W.2d 685 (1952); Terry Carpenter, Inc. v. Nebraska Liquor Control Comm'n, 175 Neb. 26, 120 N.W.2d 374 (1963); Madison v. Director of Department of Employment Security, 90 R.I. 360, 158 A.2d 154 (1960); Barker v. Sunnyside Valley Irrigation Dist., 37 Wash. 2d 115, 221 P.2d 827 (1950).

[62] Wisconsin Bridge & Iron Co. v. Industrial Comm'n, 268 Wis. 314, 67 N.W.2d 378 (1954).

[63] Stone v. Harris, 6 Wis. 2d 634, 95 N.W.2d 764 (1959); *Cf.* State v. Grayson, 5 Wis. 2d 203, 92 N.W.2d 272 (1958), upholding a rule prohibiting the use of certain therapeutic devices by chiropractors which was attacked as extending the policy of the statute.

[64] State Bd. of Dispensing Opticians v. Carp, 85 Ariz. 35, 330 P.2d 996 (1958); Crawley v. Seignious, 213 Ga. 810, 102 S.E.2d 38 (1958); State *ex rel.* Rogers v. Louisiana State Bd. of Optometry, 103 So. 2d 512 (La. App. 1958); Livestock State Bank v. State Banking Comm'n, 127 N.W.2d 139 (S.D. 1964).

[65] Brookchester, Inc. v. Ligham, 17 N.J. 460, 111 A.2d 737 (1955); Stuyve-

Other rules which have been held invalid on the grounds that they attempted improperly to extend the operative effect, or enlarge the policy, of the governing statute, include: (1) a rule that manufacturers' certificates would be accepted as a basis for issuing certificates of title only when issued by a licensed in-state dealer;[66] (2) a rule limiting the size of type that could be used in mortuary advertisements, where the applicable statute prohibited only misleading advertising;[67] (3) a rule that sought to transfer to wholesalers of petroleum gas the responsibility which under the law was placed on the agency itself to see to it that retailers observed safety regulations;[68] (4) a rule which undertook to extend to grocery stores a prohibition which under the statute was applicable only to package liquor dealers, making it unlawful to take orders for beverages over the telephone.[69]

(D) Rules Having No Reasonable Relationship to Statutory Purpose Are Void

In some cases, the general policy of the rule seems unrelated to the policy of the statute, but neither direct conflict with the statute nor any clear extension of the statutory command can be shown. In such cases, if convinced that the challenged rule produces burdensome and inequitable results, the courts may set it aside as bearing no reasonable relationship to the purpose of the governing statute, and producing a result which is out of harmony with the statute and hence unreasonable.

Typical of cases in this category is the decision of the New York court involving a rule of an alcoholic beverage control board. A local board, pursuant to a rule of the state board, refused to consider a petition for an amendment to an applicant's liquor license, because he had failed to obtain permission from the state authorities to file the petition with the local board. The court held the rule invalid, on the ground that the only statutory authority for the rule was a provision empowering the board to limit the number of licenses to be issued, and the

sant Town, Inc. v. Ligham, 17 N.J. 473, 111 A.2d 744 (1955); Fruhling v. Amalgamated Housing Corp., 9 N.Y.2d 541, 275 N.Y.S.2d 493, 175 N.E.2d 156 (1961).

66 McCarrell v. Lane, 76 Ariz. 67, 258 P.2d 988 (1953).

67 Grissom v. Van Orsdel, 137 So. 2d 246 (Fla. App. 1962).

68 Linkous v. Darch, 323 S.W.2d 850 (Ky. 1959).

69 Roppel v. Shearer, 321 S.W.2d 36 (Ky. 1959).

challenged rule (the court held) did not really operate as a limitation on the number of licenses to be issued, but rather it amounted to the creation of an alternative way of granting licenses. The court said: "Although on its face rule 45 seems designed simply to limit the number of on-premises licenses, its actual thrust is to erect a new and unauthorized procedure for the granting of these licenses."[70] Thus, concluding that the rule had no reasonable relationship to the statutory purpose, the court held the rule void.

Another New York case illustrating the same principle involved a regulation of the public service commission limiting the use, in connection with telephone directories, of covers furnished by promotional advertising companies, which were using telephone book covers as advertising devices. This regulation, it was held, had no reasonable relationship to the purposes that the public service commission was intended to serve in administering the statutory rate-making procedures. The statutory purpose concerned fixing the rates that could be charged by telephone companies; the challenged regulation sought to prevent advertising companies from competing with telephone companies in non-public service areas. Hence, the regulation could not stand.[71]

On similar grounds (viz., lack of any reasonable relationship between the purpose sought to be accomplished by the underlying statute and the purpose sought to be accomplished by the rule), courts have struck down: (1) a rule adopted by a liquor control board prohibiting the use of illuminated signs that showed the trade name of alcoholic beverages—the court ruled that this was unrelated to the board's statutory purpose of policing the sale of liquor;[72] (2) a rule by an athletic commission whose function was to establish qualifications for promoters of athletic exhibitions, but which adopted a rule instead which related not to the promoters but to the participants in such exhibitions, and undertook to prohibit women from participating in wrestling exhibitions;[73] (3) a rule which required a showman to obtain a license if he wished to exhibit animals, when the authority of

---

[70] Gross v. New York City Alcoholic Beverage Control Bd., 7 N.Y.2d 531, 537-38, 200 N.Y.S.2d 12, 166 N.E.2d 818 (1960).

[71] National Merchandising Corp. v. Public Serv. Comm'n, 5 N.Y.2d 485, 186 N.Y.S.2d 47, 158 N.E.2d 714 (1959).

[72] Portwood v. Falls City Brewing Co., 318 S.W.2d 535 (Ky. 1958).

[73] Hesseltine v. State Athletic Comm'n, 6 Ill. 2d 129, 126 N.E.2d 631 (1955).

the agency adopting the rule was limited by statute to regulating the "taking, transporting, and storing" of animals;[74] (4) a rule forbidding automobile dealers from receiving refunds on insurance premiums which were in effect paid by the customers purchasing cars on installment sales.[75]

(E) Courts Will Set Aside Rules Deemed to be Unconstitutional or Arbitrary or Unreasonable

Where excess of authority cannot be predicated on the ground that a rule is in conflict with the statute, or improperly extends or modifies the statute, or has no reasonable relationship to the purpose of the statute, then a conclusion of invalidity may be premised on the bare grounds that the regulation is unreasonable and arbitrary.

In some cases, such a conclusion is planted squarely on constitutional grounds. As it is sometimes put, the rule is invalid if it goes beyond what the legislature could authorize. If the rule, had it been enacted as a statute by the legislature, would have been held unconstitutional on any of the grounds on which statutory enactments may be attacked, then the rule must fall. Thus, a rule may be held invalid on the ground that it amounts to a taking of private property without compensation.[76] Again, a rule may be held invalid on the ground that it denies the equal protection of the laws.[77] Or a rule may be held invalid because it authorizes the revocation of a license without giving opportunity for notice and hearing to the licensee.[78]

In other cases, state courts set aside rules determined to be arbitrary or plainly unreasonable, without specific reliance on constitutional doctrines. Sometimes, the decision appears to reflect primarily a difference of judgment between the agency and the court as to the fairness and reasonableness of the challenged rule. While, as noted below, the courts recognize that it is not a part of the judicial function to substitute the court's judgment

---

[74] Barrow v. Holland, 125 So. 2d 749 (Fla. 1960).

[75] Department of Financial Institutions v. Johnson Chevrolet Co., 228 Ind. 397, 92 N.E.2d 714 (1950). Other cases in which the same principle was applied include: Morgan v. State, 155 Neb. 247, 51 N.W.2d 382 (1952); Colorado State Bd. of Pub. Welfare v. Champion, 141 Colo. 375, 348 P.2d 256 (1960).

[76] Farris v. Arkansas State Game & Fish Comm'n, 228 Ark. 776, 310 S.W.2d 231 (1958).

[77] State v. Florida Real Estate Comm'n, 99 So. 2d 582 (Fla. 1957).

[78] Johnson v. City of Ripon, 259 Wis. 84, 47 N.W.2d 328 (1951).

for that of the agency, yet if the court feels that no reasonable man of sound judgment could have approved the challenged rule—if the rule shocks the conscience of the court—it may be set aside as being arbitrary, unreasonable, or capricious.[79]

Thus, in refusing to penalize a chambermaid seeking unemployment compensation because of her failure to submit a signed statement setting forth the amount of gratuities she had received, as required by agency rule, the court premised its finding that the rule was unreasonable on the basis that the agency imposed upon the employer the duty of notifying the chambermaid of the existence of the rule. This he had failed to do. Pointing out that the employer would have a direct financial interest in neglecting the duty, the court said it was unreasonable for the agency to expect that notice would in fact be given, and unfair to penalize a claimant who had not received notice.[80]

The Florida court held that a rule which prohibited advertising the name or price of any drugs which could be dispensed only by prescription was unreasonable, when the pharmacists to whom the rule applied were prohibited by statute from selling such drugs without a doctor's prescription. The rule, said the court, produced no public benefit and amounted to an unjustified intrusion on private rights.[81]

A rule providing that absence from work for three days or longer on the part of a public employee, without the consent of the employer, would create a conclusive presumption that the employee had resigned, was found by the Illinois court to be unreasonable and hence contrary to law.[82]

Again, the Wisconsin court held invalid a rule of a licensing agency on the ground that it unreasonably reversed a long-standing policy of that agency;[83] and on somewhat similar grounds the Ohio court held that a rule, although valid when made, may

---

79 The difficulty of applying these concepts is indicated by the fact that there is sometimes a notable difference of opinion between the court's majority and the dissentient judges as to the reasonableness of a rule. See *e.g.*, Shell Oil Co. v. Ricciuti, 147 Conn. 277, 160 A.2d 257 (1960); Ryan Consolidated Petroleum Corp. v. Pickens, 155 Tex. 221, 285 S.W.2d 201 (1956).

80 Claim of Gold, 307 N.Y. 224, 120 N.E.2d 799 (1954).

81 Stadnik v. Shell's City, Inc., 140 So. 2d 871 (Fla. 1962).

82 People *ex rel.* Polen v. Hoehler, 405 Ill. 322, 90 N.E.2d 729 (1950).

83 Frankenthal v. Wisconsin Real Estate Brokers' Bd., 3 Wis. 2d 249, 88 N.W. 2d 352 (1958).

become so unreasonable with the passage of time and change of conditions as to become invalid.[84]

Failure of an agency to give due consideration to all the factors that should have been considered may form a basis for striking down a rule as unreasonable.[85] Even procedural defects may render a rule unreasonable; it has been held that an agency cannot alter the effect of its duly published rules by a mere letter expressing a new policy at variance with the practice permitted under the rules.[86]

In some cases where courts strike down rules on the basis of their unreasonableness, it is not clear whether the court is relying on constitutional principles of due process or whether its decision is basically a reflection of its reaction that the rule is so unreasonable an exercise of discretion as to shock the court's sense of fairness.[87]

While the state courts are on the whole more easily persuaded than are the federal courts to hold administrative rules invalid on the ground that they are arbitrary, capricious, or unreasonable, it is probably true in the state courts as well as in the federal courts that rules attacked on this ground are more often upheld than invalidated. The general attitude of the state courts was well expressed in a New Jersey case which upheld the reasonableness of a rule of the department of conservation concerning a "hunter's choice day." In rejecting arguments directed to the merits of the rule, the court said that if it were to decide the underlying merits, it would be improperly assuming an adminis-

---

84 The Stouffer Corp. v. Board of Liquor Control, 165 Ohio St. 96, 133 N.E. 2d 325 (1956).

85 McGraw-Edison Co. v. Sewerage Comm'n, 11 Wis. 2d 46, 104 N.W.2d 161 (1960)—involving a rule which required the use of extra-heavy cast iron pipe with hot poured lead joints for all building sewers, failing to take account of the fact that in some areas soil conditions did not permit the use of such pipe.

86 Schley v. Conservation Comm'n, 329 S.W.2d 736 (Mo. 1959).

87 In *Hamilton Farms, Inc. v. Hoffman*, 30 N.J. 335, 152 A.2d 848 (1959), the court struck down a rule which made "invidious" discriminations, permitting delivery of milk on Sundays in some areas, but prohibiting it in other areas. Thereafter, the agency amended the rule to prohibit Sunday deliveries completely, and the amended rule was held valid. Hamilton Farms, Inc. v. Hoffman, 32 N.J. 258, 160 A.2d 627 (1960). See also, McMillan v. Nave, 138 So. 2d 93 (Fla. App. 1962)—rules fixing maximum working hours for barbers held invalid; Ware v. Benedikt, 225 Ark. 185, 280 S.W.2d 234 (1955)—rules restricting licensing of physicians to use public hospitals held void; Pullman Co. v. Public Serv. Comm'n, 238 S.C. 358, 120 S.E.2d 214 (1961)—rule requiring conductors on sleeping cars held unreasonable; Richardson v. Beattie, 98 N.H. 71, 95 A.2d 122 (1953)—holding void a rule that prohibited all "human activity" on a lake used as a source of water supply.

trative function which was lodged in the agency. Only when the administrative determination is plainly demonstrated to be arbitrary, said the court, can the judiciary interfere.[88]

The reluctance of the courts to premise a finding of unreasonableness merely upon arguments as to the merits of the challenged rule may be particularly noted in the case of regulations affecting the public health[89] or morals.[90] But in other fields as well, rules which seem unfair to those adversely affected are often upheld by the state courts, as not being so demonstrably without foundation in reason as to be plainly arbitrary.[91]

(F) Practical Factors Underlying Decision

The above-described general tests offer at best a basis for argument as to the validity or invalidity of the challenged rule. Does the rule conflict with the statute by altering its meaning, or does it merely interpret and clarify an ambiguous statutory phrase? This question cannot be answered on a rhetorical basis; it often involves subtle judgments on deep-seated policy questions. Does the rule "extend" the statute, or does it merely specify an application of the legislative purpose which was implicit in the general language used by the legislature? This inquiry likewise is not purely logical; the answer depends largely on a judgment as to how broad a discretion should be vested in administrative agencies to implement vague statutory language. Is there a reasonable relationship between the terms of the rule and the statutory purpose? Appraisals of reasonableness are never based on logic.

In all but the plainest cases, the application of these general tests is at best highly debatable. The general tests do little more

---

88 United Hunters Ass'n of New Jersey, Inc. v. Adams, 36 N.J. 288, 177 A.2d 33 (1962).

89 *E.g.,* Herron v. Arkansas Wholesale Grocers Ass'n, Inc., 227 Ark. 156, 296 S.W.2d 409 (1956); Chiropractic Ass'n of New York, Inc. v. Hilleboe, 12 N.Y.2d 109, 237 N.Y.S.2d 289, 187 N.E.2d 756 (1962).

90 Bland v. Windsor Audit Co., 227 Ark. 719, 301 S.W.2d 34 (1957); *In re* Tahiti Bar, Inc., 395 Pa. 355, 150 A.2d 112 (1959).

91 Winslow v. Zoning Board, 143 Conn. 381, 122 A.2d 789 (1956); West v. Egan, 142 Conn. 437, 115 A.2d 322 (1955); Vicker v. Starkey, 265 Minn. 464, 122 N.W.2d 169 (1963); Commercial Motor Freight, Inc. v. Public Utils. Comm'n, 153 Ohio St. 441, 92 N.E.2d 265 (1950); Tasco Developing & Bldg. Corp. v. Long, 368 S.W.2d 65 (Tenn. 1963); Kee v. Baber, 157 Tex. 387, 303 S.W.2d 376 (1957); Manchester Bd. & Paper Co. v. Parker, 201 Va. 328, 111 S.E.2d 453 (1959); Quesenberry v. Estep, 142 W. Va. 426, 95 S.E.2d 832 (1956).

than to define the issue which must be argued. Decision of this issue is to a large extent dependent on the particular factual details and social implications of each case.

Implicit, however, in many of the decisions cited above is a recognition of a practical doctrine of expediency, recognizing that the scope of a particular agency's regulatory power must be determined by the practical need for giving a large degree of freedom of action to the administrative authorities. Where the purpose of the statute is to vest broad discretionary powers in an agency, and where successful execution of the agency's task of administration so requires, a broad measure of autonomy will be accorded the agency; and there will be a tendency to view its rules as in harmony with the statute and reasonable. Where, on the other hand, the statute does not disclose a purpose of any such broad grant of power to the agency, and where no need can be readily seen for the extensive implementation of the statute through the medium of rules, the courts will be more ready to discover a conflict between the statute and the rule, or to hold that the rule attempts to enlarge the statute, or is unreasonable.

Another intangible factor that may influence the result concerns the repute and standing of the agency. If the agency is long-established and has won the respect of the courts, the judges are inclined to give it the benefit of the doubt on questions as to the reasonableness and statutory propriety of a challenged regulation.

Section 4

Legal Effect of Rules

Since the bulk of an administrative agency's work is normally carried on within the framework of a more or less elaborate set of agency-created rules and regulations, questions frequently arise (both within the agency itself and in connection with judicial review of the agency's proceedings) as to the significance and legal effect of such rules.

The legal effect of agency rules depends on a variety of factors. The purpose of the rule, the authority on which it was issued, the reasonableness of a proposed application or non-application of the rule, and other similar factors, are all taken into consideration by the courts. But the primary distinction is that between legislative rules and interpretive rules.

(A) Legal Effect of Legislative Rules

Probably most state courts would adopt the principle set forth by the Maryland court[92] that:

> There are several different classes of administrative rules. Some are legislative rules, which receive statutory force upon going into effect. Others are interpretative rules, which only interpret the statute to guide the administrative agency in the performance of its duties until directed otherwise by decisions of the courts.[93]

In general, it may be said that legislative rules (*i.e.,* those substantive rules adopted pursuant to delegation of legislative authority, the violation of which entails statutory sanctions) have authoritative force. Such rules, it is said "supplement" and "implement" the statute and serve thereby to "effectuate the legislative policy."[94] It has even been suggested that they may "supersede the statutory provision."[95]

It is incorrect, however, to say (as is sometimes suggested) that legislative rules have the same legal force as do statutes. As shown by the cases cited in the preceding section, courts sometimes hold rules invalid on grounds which would not be employed in invalidating statutory enactments. Further, even in cases where the court does not hold the rule invalid, it may refuse to accord it the controlling weight that is granted to statutes. Thus, in refusing to find the operator of a refuse dump to be "in contempt" for alleged violation of a rule adopted by a state air pollution control commission, the New Jersey court held that the provisions of the rule were too vague to justify enforcement in the manner proposed.[96] Again, some courts hold that in cases where violation of a statute would constitute negligence as a matter of law, violation of an administrative rule is merely evi-

---

[92] Comptroller of Treasury v. M. E. Rockhill, Inc., 205 Md. 226, 234, 107 A.2d 93 (1954).

[93] This language was adopted and approved in Sampson-Sawyer Co. v. Johnson, 156 Me. 544, 167 A.2d 1 (1960).

[94] Rufo v. Orlando, 309 N.Y. 345, 130 N.E.2d 887 (1955).

[95] West Covina Enterprises, Inc. v. Chalmers, 49 Cal. 2d 754, 322 P.2d 13 (1958).

[96] Department of Health v. Roselle, 34 N.J. 331, 169 A.2d 153 (1961).

dence of negligence.[97] Similarly, where the court finds a rule to be vague or uncertain, it may predicate its decision on the basis of the underlying statutory provisions, disregarding the rule.[98]

(B) Legal Effect of Interpretive Rules

In the case of interpretive rules (and in this category there may be included all rules other than those adopted pursuant to a delegation of legislative authority and the violation of which is made subject to statutory sanctions), the requirements of the rule are regarded as interpretations of the substantive requirements of the statute. So long as the rules represent an interpretation of the statute which is acceptable to the court, they possess (in one sense) the force of law. But they lose all force and effect if held to be an incorrect interpretation.

Sometimes, as in the cases cited *supra,*[99] the courts hold an interpretive rule void because it represents an incorrect interpretation of the statute. In other cases, the court will simply disregard the rule, placing decision on its own interpretation of the statute. Sometimes, indeed, the courts hold that the agency has incorrectly interpreted its own rule, and predicate decision on what the court decides to be the correct interpretation of the rule.[100]

The principle has been stated frequently by the federal courts that such interpretive rules are entitled to great weight as presumptively correct interpretations of the statute.[101] But the federal courts have had no difficulty in disregarding administrative interpretations with which the court disagreed.[102] Nor do state courts hesitate to set aside or disregard interpretive rules which they deem to be incorrect interpretations of the statute.

---

97 Douglas v. Edgewater Park Co., 369 Mich. 320, 119 N.W.2d 567 (1963); Schumer v. Caplin, 241 N.Y. 346, 150 N.E. 139 (1925). *Contra,* Lutz Industries, Inc. v. Dixie Home Stores, 242 N.C. 332, 88 S.E.2d 333 (1955).

98 Walters v. City of St. Louis, 364 Mo. 56, 259 S.W.2d 377 (1953).

99 See § 3 (B), "A Rule Is Invalid if it Conflicts With the Governing Statute."

100 State *ex rel.* Utilities Comm'n v. Carolina Coach Co., 254 N.C. 319, 118 S.E.2d 762 (1961). Other courts add that an agency's interpretation of its own rule will be upset only where clearly erroneous. Columbian Fuel Corp. v. Panhandle Eastern Pipe Line Co., 176 Kan. 433, 271 P.2d 773 (1954).

101 *E.g.,* Commissioner v. South Texas Lumber Co., 333 U.S. 496, 92 L. Ed. 831, 68 Sup. Ct. 695 (1948).

102 *E.g.,* Helvering v. Sabine Transp. Co., 318 U.S. 306, 87 L. Ed. 773, 63 Sup. Ct. 569 (1943).

In general, interpretive rules are considered important only where the statute itself is ambiguous. Granting the ambiguity of the statute, the weight accorded the interpretive regulation depends in large part on circumstantial indicia of trustworthiness. If the regulation is new, does not represent long administrative experience, and has not been generally acquiesced in, it may be accorded little more weight than is granted to a well written brief. On the other hand, where it appears that the agency's construction of a statute as exemplified in an interpretive rule represents expert knowledge, and where it appears that the rule is of long standing, it is accorded substantial weight. If the rule represents the "contemporaneous construction" of a statute by the officials "charged with the responsibility of setting its machinery in motion,"[103] and if the statutory command is indefinite or doubtful, the interpretive rule will not be overturned except for most cogent reasons.[104]

(C) Procedural Rules

It is commonly said that rules prescribing the methods of procedure within an agency have the effect of law, and are binding on both the agency and on parties respondent.[105] For example, the time limits prescribed for the filing of applications are normally held to be mandatory, and it is said that the agency has no jurisdiction to act, unless proper application is made within the time prescribed by agency rules.[106]

However, the state courts do not permit agency rules of procedure to prevent the courts from doing what justice requires. Thus, where the discharge of a civil service employee was found to be unlawful, reinstatement was ordered despite the fact that the aggrieved employee had not applied for reinstatement within the time required by agency rules.[107] Further, courts deem themselves competent to alter an agency's own interpretation of its

---

103 Norwegian Nitrogen Co. v. United States, 288 U.S. 294, 315, 77 L. Ed. 796, 53 Sup. Ct. 350 (1933).

104 Oliver Iron Mining Co. v. Commissioner of Taxation, 247 Minn. 6, 76 N.W.2d 107 (1956).

105 *E.g.,* George v. Arizona Corp. Comm'n, 83 Ariz. 387, 322 P.2d 369 (1958).

106 Hale's Estate v. Industrial Comm'n, 78 Ariz. 202, 277 P.2d 1014 (1954); Baker v. State Compensation Comm'r, 143 W. Va. 536, 103 S.E.2d 391 (1958).

107 Young v. Charity Hosp., 226 La. 708, 77 So. 2d 13 (1954).

procedural rules, where it is felt the ends of justice so require.[108] Procedural rules, as well as legislative or interpretive rules, will be held void if they are found to be in conflict with statutory requirements.[109]

(D) Effect of Reliance on Rules

There is growing recognition among the state courts of the healthy principle that a person who relies in good faith on an agency rule should be held harmless from loss if that rule is later held invalid, or is amended.

Some courts do not accord this protection in the case of reliance on invalid regulations. It is admittedly difficult to find legalistic justification for doing so under traditional judicial concepts, which place one who has relied on an invalid rule in substantially the same position as one who has relied on an unconstitutional statute, or an erroneous opinion of counsel. Thus, as it was put by the Alabama court,[110] a rule which erroneously interprets a statute is a nullity and no rights are vested as a result of a taxpayer's reliance thereon, since the agency's only power is to adopt rules that would carry into effect the statutory intent, and when that has been established it must be given effect. However, some state courts are beginning to shake logomachic shackles, and to devise theories upon which protection may be accorded one who has in good faith relied on a rule which is later found to be void. Thus, in a California case,[111] the state employment stabilization commission had adopted a rule providing that insurance agents paid on a commission basis would not be deemed employees. In reliance on this rule, an insurance company paid no taxes on the commissions paid such agents. Thereafter, the commission determined that it had been without power to adopt such a rule—finding its own rule invalid—and assessed tax liability. The court, however, pointing out the inequities that would be involved in exposing

[108] Ace Delivery Service, Inc. v. Boyd, 100 So. 2d 417 (Fla. 1958); Glustrom v. State, 206 Ga. 734, 58 S.E.2d 534 (1950).

[109] Star Employment Serv., Inc. v. Florida Industrial Comm'n, 109 So. 2d 608 (Fla. App. 1959).

[110] State v. Maddox Tractor & Equip. Co., 260 Ala. 136, 69 So. 2d 426 (1953).

[111] Garrison v. California Employment Stabilization Comm'n, 64 Cal. App. 2d 820, 149 P.2d 711 (1944).

the taxpayer to retroactive liabilities (inequities compounded by the practical difficulties in collecting employees' contributions and making proper allocation of costs to policyholders) ruled that the commission was estopped to deny its power to make the rule.

Absent the conceptual difficulties encountered in cases where the rule relied on was invalid, the state courts quite uniformly accord protection to parties who had relied on an administrative rule that was subsequently amended or repealed. The new rule, of course, may be enforced prospectively; but the courts do not permit it to be applied retrospectively to periods during which the old rule was in effect, if such retrospective application would be detrimental to the interests of persons who had relied on the superseded rule.

A typical decision which illustrates the general trend is that of the Wyoming court in a tax case.[112] The decision sets forth persuasively the moral and equitable basis for the principle which prohibits an agency from giving retroactive effect to a change in its rules. The case involved an attempt by the Wyoming State Board of Equalization, which administered the state sales and use taxes, to change its position retroactively with respect to the imposition of a sales tax on certain types of transactions. The Board had originally adopted a rule stating that where personal property was purchased by a retailer outside the state of Wyoming and shipped directly to the customer in that state, the receipts were not taxable under the sales tax law. Five years later, the Board amended its rule and undertook to collect taxes on transactions that had occurred before the amended rule was adopted. In holding that the amendment could not be applied retroactively, the court declared:

> . . . there is no good reason in this day and era that we can perceive why the agencies of the state—unless clearly by statute commanded to act otherwise—should not be held to the same standards of morality, equity, and fair dealing that are exacted by the established courts of the land from the citizenry of the several states. Especially is this so where such bodies have given a contemporaneous construction to a new system of taxation and which they therein have been called upon by their official oaths to inaugurate and administer. Such construction should properly carry decided weight. In the instant case,

---

[112] Hercules Powder Co. v. State Bd. of Equalization, 66 Wyo. 268, 306, 208 P.2d 1096 (1949).

> if the Powder Company had known that the Board would now undertake to succeed in this litigation upon the position it now urges and adopts, it would have been an extremely easy matter for the appellant to have altered the contracts governing the sale of its products so as to have protected itself against such an attempted retroactive change.

The impact and thrust of the present attitude of the state courts is emphasized by the fact that courts which a few years ago accorded no protection to those who had relied in good faith on agency rules have now reversed their position. For example, in 1954, the Illinois court sustained a retroactive imposition of an additional assessment of a retailers' occupation tax, consequent upon a change in the tax agency's rules. The court remarked:

> The doctrine of collateral estoppel or of contemporaneous construction cannot be urged against the State of Illinois in the case in which a rule making or administrative agency of the State, acting under a misapprehension as to the interpretation to be given the law, makes and follows to some extent erroneous rules and regulations.[113]

Only a year later, however, the court changed its position, in another case involving regulations issued under the same retailers' occupation tax. In the second case, the Department of Revenue amended its rules so as to subject railroads to tax liabilities in certain situations which had not been subject to tax under the Department's earlier rule. The court, noting that its earlier decision "strongly suggests a contrary view" refused to permit the new rule to be applied retroactively, declaring that to do so would be unreasonable and inequitable.[114]

The principle prohibiting retroactive application of amendments to administrative rules has frequent application in tax cases. A New York case involved a sales tax law. The tax authorities had issued a ruling that sellers of liquor could exclude from their computation of gross sales the amounts of federal excise taxes they had paid. Later, the rule was amended to prohibit such exclusion. The court held that while the amended rule could be enforced thereafter, "it hardly needs statement that the City is not entitled to hold the liquor dealers liable for the higher sales tax" during the period in which they had computed

---

[113] Superior Coal Co. v. Department of Revenue, 4 Ill. 2d 459, 468, 123 N.E.2d 713 (1954).

[114] Pressed Steel Car Co. v. Lyons, 7 Ill. 2d 95, 129 N.E.2d 765 (1955).

and paid the tax in accordance with the original rule.[115] In another tax case, the Wisconsin court declared that the law "recognized the right in a taxpayer to invoke the doctrine of estoppel against the State when acting in reliance upon the ruling of an administrative agency."[116]

The doctrine is not confined to tax cases, but has been applied in other fields as well, such as rules promulgated by agricultural agencies.[117]

Some state courts are inclined to prohibit the retroactive application of amended rules, even in the absence of any showing of detrimental reliance on the superseded rule.[118]

Closely related principles are involved in cases concerning the question whether, in contested cases (adjudication), an agency should be permitted to revoke retroactively its own prior order. Such cases are discussed *infra*.[119] Because of the difficulty of classifying some agency orders, which involve characteristics both of rule making and of adjudication, the decisions cited in that section may properly be noted in connection with the present discussion.

(E) May an Agency Disregard Its Own Rules?

In the case of procedural rules, it is often expeditious for an agency to ignore a certain rule in a particular case and adopt therein a different procedure than that contemplated by the agency's rules. Questions arising in this connection impose on the courts the duty of discovering a fair and workable compromise between the administrator's demand for extreme fluidity (permitting expeditious disposal of the agency's business) and the respondent's demand for static regularity (permitting him to know in advance what his rights are and how they can be asserted). By and large, the state courts tend to resolve these

---

[115] Hoffman v. City of Syracuse, 2 N.Y.2d 484, 161 N.Y.S.2d 111, 141 N.E. 2d 605 (1957). *Cf.*, Colgate-Palmolive-Peet Co. v. Joseph, 308 N.Y. 333, 125 N.E.2d 857 (1955), holding immaterial a failure formally to repeal a rule which had in effect been overruled by a series of court decisions.

[116] Libby, McNeill & Libby v. Department of Taxation, 260 Wis. 551, 560, 51 N.W.2d 796 (1952).

[117] Olive Proration Program Comm. v. Agricultural Prorate Comm'n, 17 Cal. 2d 204, 109 P.2d 918 (1941); Clubb v. DeKeyzer, 152 So. 2d 77 (La. App. 1963).

[118] Rudman v. Railroad Comm'n of Texas, 162 Tex. 579, 349 S.W.2d 717 (1961).

[119] See Ch. XV, "Res Judicata and Stare Decisis."

questions in favor of a policy which insists on adherence to the announced procedures. However, the problem is one of varied facets.

Of course, the parties may voluntarily waive compliance with procedural rules, and such waiver may be founded on acts as well as upon verbal declarations.[120]

Similarly, disregard of minutiae of procedural niceties will be tolerated, where it clearly appears no prejudice resulted.[121] Seemingly, too, if it can be shown that a particular rule was established solely for the agency's own convenience, it may be waived by the agency.[122]

At the opposite extreme, it is clear that an agency will not be permitted to adopt a special rule of procedure for the purpose of affecting the outcome of a particular case, or (with a conscious desire toward this end) wilfully to ignore a rule in a particular case.[123]

Between these two extremes there lies a broad field where there is room to debate the wisdom and fairness of the disregard of procedural rules in a particular case, and where it is somewhat a matter of conjecture whether such disregard has prejudiced private rights. In this area, the tendency of the state courts is to resolve the doubt in favor of the party complaining of the departure from procedural norms. Thus, the courts have set aside agency action (1) where an agency, in violation of its rules, decided a pending case before the completion and filing of a transcript of testimony taken before a hearing officer;[124] (2) where an agency decided a case upon remand from a reviewing court without giving one of the parties an opportunity to be present;[125] (3) where a public utility commission granted a carrier permit without hearing, over the objection of another

---

[120] State *ex rel.* Spiker v. West Virginia Racing Comm'n, 135 W. Va. 512, 63 S.E.2d 831 (1951).

[121] City of Hackensack v. Rubinstein, 37 N.J. 39, 178 A.2d 625 (1962).

[122] Colonial House, Inc. v. State Bd. of Labor Relations, 23 Conn. Sup. 30, 176 A.2d 381 (1961)—where a labor board permitted a motion to be filed late.

[123] Narramore v. Fannin's Gas & Equip. Co., 80 Ariz. 115, 293 P.2d 671 (1956)—agency permitted application for rehearing on denial of claim for death award to be filed and considered after expiration of prescribed period, over protest of employer; Day v. Department of Institutions, 231 La. 775, 93 So. 2d 1 (1957)—civil service commission in disregard of its rule requiring written discharge, accepted an oral "resignation." See also, Application of Skeedee Independent Tel. Co., 166 Neb. 49, 87 N.W.2d 715 (1958).

[124] Weekes v. O'Connell, 304 N.Y. 259, 107 N.E.2d 290 (1952).

[125] Schnatzmeyer v. Industrial Comm'n, 78 Ariz. 112, 276 P.2d 534 (1954).

carrier;[126] (4) where a port commission called a special meeting without observing the procedural rules for calling such meetings;[127] (5) where an agency undertook to amend a formal rule by the informal expedient of sending a letter.[128]

Some courts indicate a readiness to set aside agency action upon complaint that the agency disregarded its procedural rules, even though the possibility of prejudice having been suffered as a result thereof appears at best remote.[129]

But in cases where the record clearly establishes that disregard of an agency's procedural rules could not have prejudiced any party to the proceeding, the departure from prescribed procedures is not fatal.[130]

---

[126] Becker v. Yeary, 278 S.W.2d 632 (Ky. 1955).

[127] Simpson v. City of Gulfport, 239 Miss. 136, 121 So. 2d 409 (1960).

[128] Schley v. Conservation Comm'n, 329 S.W.2d 736 (Mo. 1959).

[129] Thus, some courts insist that a grant of a permit by a utilities commission is void, if the commission did not insist that the applicant comply with all the details of the application procedure. Walker v. De Concini, 86 Ariz. 143, 341 P.2d 933 (1959); Public Serv. Comm'n v. Mt. Vernon Tel. Co., 300 S.W.2d 796 (Ky. 1957). *Cf.* Star Employment Serv., Inc. v. Florida Industrial Comm'n, 109 So. 2d 608 (Fla. App. 1959)—involving an attempt by a commission to review, on its own motion, a ruling of a deputy commissioner after the expiration of the time allowed by rule to take appeals to the full commission; State *ex rel.* Mulkey v. City of Auburn, 60 Wash. 2d 728, 375 P.2d 499 (1962).

[130] Eagle Bus Lines, Inc. v. Illinois Commerce Comm'n, 3 Ill. 2d 66, 119 N.E.2d 915 (1954)—an agency may enforce or waive its rules, as it deems necessary, where no injury has been suffered by any party.

CHAPTER X

CONTESTED CASES: PROCEEDINGS BEFORE TRIAL

Section 1

Notice

By definition, under the Revised Model State Act, a contested case is one in which the agency is required by law to afford an opportunity for hearing in connection with its determination of legal rights, duties or privileges.[1] The several provisions of the Act setting forth requirements concerning such matters as the form of notice to be given, the hearing procedures, the receipt and consideration of evidence, and the preparation and form of decisions and orders, all relate to cases where a hearing is required by law. The succeeding chapters under the "Contested Cases" heading will accordingly be concerned with procedures in cases where, either because of statutory provisions or requirements imposed by the Constitution as interpreted by the courts, a hearing is required.

(A) General Requirement of Reasonable Notice

With respect to many administrative agencies in several states, there are no statutory provisions as to the giving of notice. Under such circumstances, notice is required only in cases where concepts of procedural due process require an opportunity for hearing. Where such a requirement exists, there is an implied necessity of giving reasonable notice, for obviously there cannot be a fair hearing unless reasonable notice has been accorded. The net result in those situations is that where a hearing is required as a matter of constitutional right, there must be reasonable notice.

---

[1] Section 1(2).

But because of the uncertainties, in many areas of administrative activity, whether hearings are constitutionally required[2] (and because of the widely held conviction that hearings should be granted, as a matter of sound public policy, in cases where they might not be constitutionally required), the legislatures in many states have enacted statutes requiring agencies to grant hearings in most fields of administrative activity. In connection with such requirements, some provisions as to the giving of notice are ordinarily set forth.

The Revised Model Act sets forth initially that in all contested cases, there must be "reasonable notice."[3] The effect of this requirement, which is also found in a number of state statutes,[4] is to impose in all contested cases the same minimal requirements as to the giving of notice that in other states exist only in those cases where notice is required by constitutional concepts.

In this chapter, an examination will be made initially of the meaning and content of the requirement of "reasonable notice," as disclosed in state court opinions; and thereafter there will be reviewed the statutory provisions found in the Revised Model State Act and in the statutes of several states spelling out in greater detail what particular form of notice is required.

(B) Court Decisions Concerning Reasonable Notice

(1) Effect of Failure to Give Notice

In cases where by constitutional right or by statute, reasonable notice is required, an agency order entered without the giving of such notice will be set aside by the courts. The Wisconsin court described lack of notice as a "jurisdictional defect";[5]

---

[2] See Ch. V, "Constitutional Requirements of Notice and Opportunity to be Heard."

[3] Section 9(a).

[4] Florida (STAT. § 120.23); Georgia (CODE ANN. § 3A-101); Hawaii (SESS. LAWS 1961, Act 103, § 9(a)); Maine (REV. STAT. ANN. ch. 20-A, § 8); Maryland (ANN. CODE art. 41, § 251); Michigan (STAT. ANN. § 3.560(21.4)); Minnesota (STAT. § 15.0418); Nebraska (REV. STAT. § 84-913); Oklahoma (STAT. tit. 75, § 309(a)); Oregon (REV. STAT. § 183.420); Pennsylvania (STAT. ANN. tit. 71, § 1710.31); Rhode Island (GEN. LAWS ANN. § 42-35-9(a)); Virginia (CODE ANN. § 9-6.10(b)); Washington (REV. CODE § 34.04.090); Wisconsin (STAT. § 227.07).

[5] Bartlett v. Joint County School Comm., 11 Wis. 2d 588, 106 N.W.2d 295 (1960).

and the Arkansas court, rejecting an argument that the private parties were not prejudiced by want of notice because they had not shown a meritorious defense to the claims asserted by the agency, said it was immaterial whether actual prejudice was shown. The court added by way of explanation that "the procedure followed by governmental agencies does not ordinarily involve the same safeguards that are observed in courts of law."[6]

The state courts quite uniformly insist, whether notice is required by agency rule,[7] or by constitution, or by statute, that failure to give the required reasonable notice is a ground for invalidating agency orders.[8]

(2) Proof of Notice

While case authority is sparse, it has been held in a noteworthy opinion of the Missouri court that the agency records must disclose formally the giving of notice. In that case, appellant asserted a lack of notice, and the agency proffered a carbon copy of a letter which, it was said, disclosed that notice had in fact been given appellant. The court held that since notice was necessary to the board's having jurisdiction, evidence of notice extrinsic of the formal record could not be considered.[9]

(3) Necessity of Personal Notice

Absent valid statutory provisions for notice by publication, it is insisted by the United States Supreme Court as a matter of constitutional necessity that "notice by publication is not enough with respect to a person whose name and address are known or very easily ascertainable and whose legally protected interests

---

6 Cash v. Rocket Mfg. Co., 223 Ark. 561, 563, 267 S.W.2d 318 (1954).

7 Becker v. Yeary, 278 S.W.2d 632 (Ky. 1955).

8 Boyd v. Southeastern Tel. Co., 105 So. 2d 889 (Fla. App. 1958); People v. Jennings, 3 Ill. 2d 125, 119 N.E.2d 781 (1954); Benton Harbor Malleable Indus. v. General Motors Corp., 358 Mich. 684, 101 N.W.2d 281 (1960); Furniture Capital Truck Lines, Inc. v. Public Serv. Comm'n, 340 Mich. 173, 65 N.W.2d 303 (1954); *In re* Petition of Aten, 332 Mich. 77, 50 N.W.2d 721 (1952); McMullen v. Alger, 339 Mich. 175, 63 N.W.2d 599 (1954); Richling v. Transit, Inc., 154 Neb. 108, 47 N.W.2d 413 (1951). State *ex rel.* Public Serv. Comm'n v. Northern Pac. Ry., 75 N.W.2d 129 (N.D. 1956); Carpenter v. Powel Briscoe, Inc., 380 P.2d 245 (Okla. 1963); Great Cent. Ins. Co. v. Birdwell, 273 P.2d 764 (Okla. 1954); Radick v. Zoning Bd. of Review, 83 R.I. 392, 117 A.2d 84 (1955); State *ex rel.* Red Jacket Coal Corp. v. Stokes, 142 W. Va. 126, 94 S.E.2d 634 (1956); State v. Hix, 141 W. Va. 385, 90 S.E.2d 357 (1955).

9 State *ex rel.* Wilson Chevrolet, Inc. v. Wilson, 332 S.W.2d 867 (Mo. 1960).

are directly affected by the proceedings. . . ."[10] This rule is, of course, applicable to state administrative proceedings, and presumably would be applied under the Revised Model State Act, which contains no provision concerning the manner of service of notice. Thus, the Arizona court held that where a statute does not specify the manner by which notice is to be given, personal notice is required.[11]

(4) Service of Notice

Notice must be served in accordance with applicable statutory requirements, and in a method calculated to give actual notice to the parties affected. Thus, notice served on an attorney who had represented taxpayers in other matters was held inadequate;[12] as was notice mailed to an outlying branch of a company, instead of to the company's main office.[13] Where a notice was misaddressed, and did not reach the party in time, it was ineffective.[14]

(5) Adequacy of Notice

It is usually held that the notice must comply with all applicable statutory requirements to be valid. The state courts do not approve, for example, the giving of oral notice where a written notice is required;[15] or a notice which does not comply with statutory requirements as to time.[16] However, if it is clear that the party complaining had actual personal notice in adequate time, and was not prejudiced by minor deviations from the statutory requirement, the doctrine of harmless error may be invoked.[17]

---

[10] Schroeder v. City of New York, 371 U.S. 208, 212, 9 L. Ed. 2d 255, 83 Sup. Ct. 279, 89 A.L.R.2d 1398 (1962).

[11] School Dist. No. 6 of Pima County v. Barber, 85 Ariz. 95, 332 P.2d 496 (1958). The court also ruled that in the absence of statute or custom, notice by mail is not effective until received by the one to be served. *Cf., State ex rel. Barcroft v. Stover,* 170 Ohio St. 54, 162 N.E.2d 462 (1959), holding that a rule of a civil service commission afforded constructive notice to public employees.

[12] Pond Creek Pochontas Co. v. Breathitt County, 290 S.W.2d 34 (Ky. 1956); Chapman v. Thompson, 288 P.2d 720 (Okla. 1955).

[13] Air-Way Branches, Inc. v. Board of Review, 10 N.J. 609, 92 A.2d 771 (1952).

[14] Elliott v. City of Indianapolis, 237 Ind. 287, 142 N.E.2d 911 (1957).

[15] Young v. Charity Hosp., 226 La. 708, 77 So. 2d 13 (1954).

[16] Slagle v. Zoning Bd. of Appeals, 144 Conn. 690, 137 A.2d 542 (1957); State *ex rel.* Baker Mfg. Co. v. City of Evansville, 261 Wis. 599, 53 N.W.2d 795 (1952).

[17] Arkansas Power & Light Co. v. Arkansas Pub. Serv. Comm'n, 226 Ark. 225, 289 S.W.2d 668 (1956); City of Mattoon v. Stump, 414 Ill. 319, 111 N.E.2d

Absent statutory requirement, what will be deemed adequate depends in large part on the nature of the case, and the practical factors involved. Thus, in cases involving general property taxes, affecting large numbers of taxpayers uniformly, less is required in the way of notice than in cases where an individual's property is singled out for special treatment.[18]

Ordinarily, when a case is set down for rehearing or reconsideration, new notice must be given;[19] but if a new order is issued merely to correct a technical defect in the first, it is not necessary that a second notice be given;[20] nor is it necessary that new notice be given each time a case is adjourned.[21]

(6) Who Entitled to Notice

Because administrative adjudications frequently have a substantial impact on persons not named as parties, but whose collateral interests are substantially affected, the question as to who is entitled to notice can become most troublesome. It is often said that those whose legal rights will be affected by the administrative determination, and who would be deemed "indispensable parties" in equitable proceedings in the courts, are entitled to notice.[22] But this is scarcely a rule-of-thumb test, because the question remains as to what collateral parties are indispensable.

Typical of the problems which arise are those involving applications to a public service commission on behalf of common carriers by motor truck. The granting of a special advantage to the applicant may substantially affect the business interests of competing carriers. Must the agency ascertain what carriers

551 (1953); Petition of Boyd, 332 Mich. 553, 52 N.W.2d 216 (1952); Wilson v. City of Long Branch, 27 N.J. 360, 142 A.2d 837 (1958); Cullum v. Board of Educ. of North Bergen Township, 15 N.J. 285, 104 A.2d 641 (1954); Todd Shipyards Corp. v. Texas Employment Comm'n, 153 Tex. 159, 264 S.W.2d 709 (1954).

18 People *ex rel.* Garwood v. New York Cent. R.R., 21 Ill. 2d 315, 172 N.E.2d 357 (1961); People *ex rel.* Miller v. Doe, 22 Ill. 2d 211, 174 N.E.2d 830 (1961); People *ex rel.* Lunn v. Chicago Title & Trust Co., 409 Ill. 505, 100 N.E.2d 578 (1951).

19 Knoy v. Indiana Real Estate Comm'n, 239 Ind. 379, 157 N.E.2d 825 (1959); Call v. Luten, 219 Ark. 640, 244 S.W.2d 130 (1952).

20 State *ex rel.* Kansas City v. Public Serv. Comm'n, 360 Mo. 339, 228 S.W.2d 738 (1950).

21 Village of Cobb v. Public Serv. Comm'n, 12 Wis. 2d 441, 107 N.W.2d 595 (1961).

22 Consolidated Edison Co. v. NLRB, 305 U.S. 197, 83 L. Ed. 126, 59 Sup. Ct. 206 (1938).

would be affected, and then give them all notice? If not, must it serve notice on those whom it knows would be affected? The answer apparently depends in large degree on the circumstances of the particular case; and it cannot be said that the decisions, which often depend in part on specific statutory provisions, afford any clear-cut answer.[23]

Similar difficulties inhere in the zoning field. It is commonly said that those within the "area involved" by a proposed zoning change must be notified;[24] but it is not always easy to determine exactly the periphery of the "area involved."

Frequently, in these fields, statutory provisions specify what parties must be notified. Absent statute, the courts must weigh the potential prejudice to the party complaining of lack of notice against the practical difficulties faced by the agency. Generally, it is enough if the agency serves notice on those whose direct concern should reasonably be anticipated.

(7) Waiver of Notice

Formal service of notice may, of course, be voluntarily waived; and it has been held that defects in service of notice are waived by appearing and participating in a hearing.[25]

(C) Statutory Requirements Specifying Form of Notice

(1) Time, Place, and Nature of Hearing

It seems doubtful that anything could be called a notice that did not recite at least the *time* and *place* of hearing; but in the absence of statute it is not always required that the notice state the *nature* of the hearing. It is important that respondent be advised of this, because otherwise if he is not familiar with the proceedings of the agency (and particularly, if he is not represented by counsel) he may not appreciate the nature of the

[23] *Cf.*, Metropolitan Lines, Inc. v. Brooks, 70 Ariz. 344, 220 P.2d 480 (1950); Asche v. Rosenfield, 405 Ill. 108, 89 N.E.2d 885 (1950); Department of Motor Transp. v. Eck Miller Transfer Co., 249 S.W.2d 802 (Ky. 1952); Greyhound Corp. v. Michigan Pub. Serv. Comm'n, 360 Mich. 578, 104 N.W.2d 395 (1960).

[24] Smith v. F. W. Woolworth Co., 142 Conn. 88, 111 A.2d 552 (1955); Hutchison v. Board of Zoning Appeals, 138 Conn. 247, 83 A.2d 201 (1951).

[25] Schwartz v. Illinois Commerce Comm'n, 409 Ill. 182, 98 N.E.2d 766 (1951); May Dep't Stores Co. v. State Tax Comm'n, 308 S.W.2d 748 (Mo. 1958).

proposed action that the agency is to consider. He might not even understand, for example, that as a result of the hearing, he might face suspension or revocation of a license. He might not understand that witnesses would be called to testify against him; or that if he proposed to defend himself he must appear with witnesses competent to testify of their own knowledge to the facts he wished to establish. It is commonplace, therefore, for statutes to provide that the notice must state not only the time and place of hearing, but also the nature of the hearing. Such a requirement appears in the Revised Model Act[26] and in the statutes of several states.[27] Other statutes, still following the language of the original Model Act, require that the notice must state the issues involved. This is not as satisfactory as the requirement of the Revised Act; for a mere statement of the issues does not necessarily advise respondent of the nature of the contemplated hearing.[28]

(2) Statement of Legal Authority and Jurisdiction

If there is any question as to the legal authority or jurisdiction of the agency to decide a case, it is helpful to have this jurisdictional issue clearly framed on the record at the outset of the case. For this reason, the Revised Model State Act requires[29] that the notice contain a statement of the legal authority and jurisdiction under which the hearing is being held. This new provision is already beginning to appear in the statutory laws of the states.[30]

---

26 Section 9(b)(1) provides: "The notice shall include: (1) a statement of the time, place, and nature of the hearing."

27 Colorado (REV. STAT. ANN. § 3-16-4); Florida (STAT. § 120.23); Georgia (CODE ANN. § 3A-101); Hawaii (SESS. LAWS 1961, Act 103, § 9(b)); Oklahoma (STAT. tit. 75, § 309(b)); Rhode Island (GEN. LAWS ANN. § 42-35-9(b)).

28 Statutes requiring that the notice state the issues involved include: Indiana (ANN. STAT. § 63-3006); Maine (REV. STAT. ANN. ch. 20-A, § 8); Maryland (ANN. CODE art. 41, § 251); Massachusetts (GEN. LAWS ANN. ch. 30A, § 11); Michigan (STAT. ANN. § 3.560(21.4)); Minnesota (STAT. § 15.0418); Nebraska (REV. STAT. § 84-913); Oregon (REV. STAT. § 183.420); Virginia (CODE ANN. § 9-6.10(b)); Washington (REV. CODE § 34.04.090).

29 Section 9(b)(2) provides: "The notice shall include: . . . (2) a statement of the legal authority and jurisdiction under which the hearing is to be held."

30 Colorado (REV. STAT. ANN. § 3-16-4(2)); Florida (STAT. § 120.23); Georgia (CODE ANN. § 3A-101); Hawaii (SESS. LAWS 1961, Act 103, § 9(b)); Oklahoma (STAT. tit. 75, § 309(b)); Rhode Island (GEN. LAWS ANN. § 42-35-9 (b)). See Stuck v. Board of Medical Examiners, 94 Cal. App. 2d 751, 21 P.2d 389 (1949).

(3) Reference to Particular Sections of Rules and Statutes

A respondent notified only that he is charged with having violated a statute may have little idea of the precise nature of the charge he will be called upon to meet, particularly if the statute happens to be fifteen or twenty pages in length. For this reason, the Revised Model State Act requires, in the interests of sharp clarification of the issues in all contested cases, that the notice must specify the particular sections of the statute involved. Furthermore, since the issue may turn upon a particular provision of some agency rule, it is required that the notice refer also to the particular sections of any rule involved.[31] This requirement possesses a further advantage, in that (despite statutory provisions for the publication of rules) it sometimes occurs that a respondent is not familiar with the provisions of the rules adopted by the agency to implement the statute; and fairness requires that he be apprised of the nature of any relevant rules in advance of the hearing.

In variant forms, requirements that the notice refer both to the particular statutes and to the particular rules involved appear in the statutes of several states.[32]

(4) Other Specific Requirements as to Form of Notice

The legislatures of several states, recognizing the desirability of insistence that the notice of institution of a contested case meaningfully advise respondent of the nature and scope of the proceedings, the issues involved, and his procedural rights, have adopted provisions not found in the Revised Model Act, for the purpose of further protecting the rights of private parties in this regard. Some of the more significant provisions deserve particular mention.

A number of statutes provide that notice must be served, personally or by registered mail, a specified period of time (varying from five to thirty days in different states) before the hearing.[33]

---

31 Section 9(b)(3) provides: "The notice shall include: . . . (3) a reference to the particular sections of the statutes and rules involved."

32 Alaska (STAT. § 44.62.360); California (GOV'T CODE § 11503); Georgia (CODE ANN. § 3A-101); Hawaii (SESS. LAWS 1961, Act 103, § 9(b)); Ohio (REV. CODE ANN. § 119.07); Oklahoma (STAT. tit. 75, § 309(b)); Rhode Island (GEN. LAWS ANN. § 42-35-9(b)).

33 *E.g.*, Indiana (ANN. STAT. § 63-3006); Maine (REV. STAT. ANN. ch. 20-A,

The Missouri statute[34] requires the giving of notice, initially, of the institution of proceedings; and, thereafter, a further notice of hearing. Detailed provisions are made as to the contents and service of the notices, as to keeping appropriate official records thereof, and as to the institution of class suits in appropriate cases.

Alaska and California[35] provide for service of an *accusation* in cases involving the limitation, suspension, or revocation of any right, authority, license, or privilege; and for the service of a "statement of issues" in cases involving the issuance or renewal of rights, authorities, licenses, or privileges. Detailed provisions appear as to the contents and service of these documents; and in addition the statutes prescribe a mode of pleading designed to put each party fully on notice as to the claims of the other. Somewhat comparable provisions appear in the North Dakota statute;[36] and the Massachusetts statute[37] also makes detailed and specific provisions as to the service of notice in contested cases.

(D) Requirement That Notice Set Forth Matters of Fact Asserted

(1) The Problem of Inadequate Notice

In some state agencies, there is a tendency to await the actual hearing to acquaint the opposite party with the facts of the case. The initiatory notice often asserts the nature of the claim only in the language of the statute. Provisions for bills of particulars or discovery proceedings are seldom found in state administrative law.

If the only result of this practice were that a delay occurred in discovering the facts, perhaps no great harm would be done. But the results of the practice are far more significant. It means, for one thing, that hearings are frequently disorganized, and consume much more time than would be required if both parties knew in advance exactly what factual matters were in dispute,

§ 8); New Mexico—in licensing cases (STAT. ANN. § 67-26-4); Ohio (REV. CODE ANN. § 119.07).

34 MO. REV. STAT. § 536.063.

35 ALASKA STAT. § 44.62.360, 370; CAL. GOV'T CODE §§ 11503, 11504.

36 N.D. CENT. CODE, § 28-32-05.

37 MASS. GEN. LAWS ANN. ch. 30A, § 10.

and what the position of each party was as to the critical facts. More than this, it means that (since the parties attempt, without careful advance preparation, to develop evidence upon short notice at the hearing itself) the hearing records are often obscure and unsatisfactory; and in fact there sometimes occurs a failure to develop with accuracy and precision the facts that should control decision. Sometimes, if the hearing is held in installments, this difficulty is overcome.

These defects have long been the subject of critical comment. The Attorney General's Committee in 1941 pointed out:[38]

> Yet room remains for considerable improvement in the notice practices of many agencies. . . . the crucial notice should be the formal one which precedes the hearings. Too frequently, this notice is inadequate. Particularly in cases begun by application by private persons who seek approval or a license, or similar action from an agency, which are set down for hearing, often no indication of the issues is given; as a result, the applicant is put to his proof on such broad issues as public interest, convenience, and necessity, although in fact the ground on which the agency doubts the propriety of a grant may be narrow. Similarly, in cases begun by complaint, agencies not infrequently set out their allegations in general form, perhaps in statutory terms, thus failing fully to apprise the respondents and to permit them adequately to prepare their defenses.

In answer to this criticism, the Congress provided in Section 5 (a) of the Federal Administrative Procedure Act of 1946[39] that the initiatory notice must state the matters of fact and law asserted. But, as pointed out by the Task Force on Legal Services and Procedure of the Hoover Commission,[40] this provision did not prove wholly satisfactory. Suppose the notice alleges that respondent failed to bargain in good faith, or that a stock prospectus contained material omissions. Arguably, such a notice states the matters of fact asserted; but they are not stated in sufficient detail to serve the basic purposes of pre-hearing notice. The Hoover Commission Task Force recommended that the federal act be amended to require that the notice must state the matters of fact and law asserted in accordance (to the extent practicable)

---

38 *Administrative Procedure in Government Agencies,* S. Doc. No. 8, 77th Cong., 1st Sess. 63 (1941).

39 5 U.S.C. § 1004(a); F.C.A. 5 § 1004(a).

40 Commission on Organization of Executive Branch of Government, Task Force Report on Legal Services and Procedure, p. 165 (1955).

with the practice and requirements of pleading in the United States district courts.

The draftsmen of the Revised Model State Act went somewhat further in their recommendations for specificity in the notice by which a contested case is initiated. That Act provides[41] that the notice shall include "a short and plain statement of the matters asserted. If the agency or other party is unable to state the matters in detail at the time the notice is served, the initial notice may be limited to a statement of the issues involved. Thereafter, upon application a more definite and detailed statement shall be furnished."

This provision imposes in effect a mandatory requirement for a bill of particulars if the initial notice fails to state the asserted facts in detail; and this requirement marks a significant step forward toward the goal of adequate pre-hearing notice. Until such time as pre-hearing discovery procedures become available in contested cases, the bill of particulars is the only device available to compel adequate specification of alleged facts before the hearing. The provision of the Revised Model Act recognizes that at the time of issuance of the first notice, the particulars of the case may not yet be known to the agency. But before the hearing is reached, the attorney handling the case for the agency must learn such particulars; and under the Revised Model Act, he is compelled to disclose them.

(2) Statutory Provisions in the States

The provisions of the Revised Model Act have already won legislative acceptance in some states.[42] Other state statutes contain even more explicit provisions requiring the notice to set forth the relevant facts in a meaningful way. The phraseology varies widely, but the thrust is identical—and pointed. Thus, in Alaska[43] and California,[44] it is required that the notice "shall set forth in ordinary and concise language the acts or omissions." Hawaii[45] requires "an explicit statement in plain language of

[41] Section 9(b) (4).

[42] Georgia (CODE ANN. § 3A-101); Oklahoma (STAT. tit. 75, § 309(b) (4)); Rhode Island (GEN. LAWS ANN. § 42-35-9(b)(4)); West Virginia (Acts 1964, art. 5, ch. 1, § 1).

[43] ALASKA STAT. § 44.62.360.

[44] CAL. GOV'T CODE § 11503.

[45] Session Laws 1961, Act 103, § 9(b) (4).

the issues involved and the facts alleged by the agency in support thereof." A "clear and concise statement" is required by the statutes of Maine,[46] North Dakota,[47] and Wisconsin.[48] The licensing laws of North Carolina[49] and New Mexico[50] require that the notice set forth "the general nature of the evidence."

Emphasizing the purpose of such requirements, it is provided in some states that the language of the notice shall not consist merely of charges phrased in the language of the applicable statute or rule.[51]

Other states, following the language of the federal act, require that the notice must set forth the matters of fact and law asserted.[52]

A larger number of states, recognizing the need of filing something in the nature of a bill of particulars if the facts are not fully known when the initial notice is served, provide for the service of supplemental notices, stating the facts and issues with greater precision.[53]

Other states, following the provisions of the original Model State Act, require only that the notice must specify the issues involved—and this, of course, requires some specification of the facts.[54]

(3) Court Decisions

The courts recognize that the general requirements of pleading applicable in the courts are not imposed on administrative tribunals.[55] However, it is insisted that the notice set forth the

---

46 ME. REV. STAT. ANN. ch. 20-A, § 8.

47 N.D. CENT. CODE § 28-32-05.

48 WIS. STAT. § 227.09.

49 N.C. GEN. STAT. § 150-11(b).

50 N.M. STAT. ANN. § 67-26-4.

51 Alaska (STAT. § 44.62.360); California (GOV'T CODE § 11503); Missouri (REV. STAT. § 536.063).

52 Colorado (REV. STAT. ANN. § 3-16-4(2)); Florida (STAT. § 120.23); Indiana (ANN. STAT. § 63-3006).

53 Hawaii (SESS. LAWS 1961, Act 103, § 9(b)(4)); Maine (REV. STAT. ANN. ch. 20-A, § 8); Maryland (ANN. CODE art. 41, § 251); Massachusetts (GEN. LAWS ANN. ch. 30A, § 11); Minnesota (STAT. § 15.0418); Nebraska (REV. STAT. § 84-913); Oklahoma (STAT. tit. 75, § 309(b)(4)); Oregon (REV. STAT. § 183.420); Rhode Island (GEN. LAWS ANN. § 42-35-9(b)); Virginia (CODE ANN. § 9-6.10(b)); Washington (REV. CODE § 34.04.090(1)).

54 *E.g.*, Michigan (STAT. ANN. § 3.560(21.4)).

55 Adam v. Connecticut Medical Examining Bd., 137 Conn. 535, 79 A.2d 350 (1951); State *ex rel.* Chicago, B. & Q.R.R. v. Public Serv. Comm'n, 334 S.W.2d 54 (Mo. 1960); Branch Banking & Trust Co. v. Wilson County Bd. of

facts in sufficient detail to enable respondent to prepare his defense. Thus, the Oregon court held: "The essential requirement is that the charge shall be described with reasonable certainty in order to enable defendant to prepare his defense;"[56] and the Florida court explained: "The controlling principle is the requirement for the accusation, or administrative pleading, to indicate within the standard of fairness, the things appellant must meet."[57]

Similarly, the Michigan court found a violation of a civil service commission requirement that an employee be given notice of specific reasons for discharge, where the charge that the employee had converted personal property to her own use described the property allegedly stolen in such general terms as "institutional cleaning supplies" and "miscellaneous foodstuffs," and did not specify the dates when the thefts allegedly occurred. This generality, the court held, did not give the employee an adequate opportunity to muster proofs of innocence.[58]

The same principle has frequently been applied in cases involving the revocation of licenses. The Wisconsin court has emphasized that the notice of hearing must inform the licensee of the specific nature of the charges of misconduct made against him.[59] Similarly, the Massachusetts court held that where the notice contained only a vague recital that a hearing would be held on complaints as to respondent's operation of an inn, it did not sufficiently particularize the charges she would be called on to meet.[60] In other cases, administrative determinations revoking or suspending a license have been set aside because the initiatory

---

Educ., 251 N.C. 603, 111 S.E.2d 844 (1960); Gray Well Drilling Co. v. Wisconsin State Bd. of Health, 263 Wis. 417, 58 N.W.2d 64 (1953).

[56] *In re* Buck's License, 192 Ore. 66, 93, 232 P.2d 791 (1951); 200 Ore. 488, 258 P.2d 124 (1953).

[57] Hickey v. Wells, 91 So. 2d 206, 208 (Fla. 1957). See also, J. Ehrlich Realty Co. v. City of Dover, 36 Del. Ch. 28, 124 A.2d 732 (1956); Scott v. Undercofler, 108 Ga. App. 460, 133 S.E.2d 444 (1963); Mississippi Pub. Serv. Comm'n v. Chambers, 235 Miss. 133, 108 So. 2d 550 (1959); Safeway Stores, Inc. v. Ohlsen, 192 Ore. 1, 233 P.2d 778 (1951); Mello v. Board of Review of Newport, 177 A.2d 533 (R.I. 1962); Brassard v. McCarthy, 83 R.I. 479, 120 A.2d 325 (1956).

[58] Dillon v. Lapeer State Home & Training School, 364 Mich. 1, 110 N.W.2d 588 (1961).

[59] Nolan v. Wisconsin Real Estate Brokers' Bd., 3 Wis. 2d 510, 89 N.W.2d 317 (1958).

[60] Manchester v. Selectmen of Nantucket, 335 Mass. 156, 138 N.E.2d 766 (1956)—but there, respondent's failure to request particulars was held a basis for overruling her exceptions.

notice did not clearly apprise the licensee of the precise charges against him.[61]

Frequently, too, difficulties arise because the initiatory notice indicated one factual basis for the proposed administrative action, but thereafter, in view of the facts developed at the hearing, decision was predicated on a finding of fact involving a different issue than that suggested by the original notice. Thus, where a notice of proceedings before a public service commission indicated that the issue was whether a railroad should install warning signals, but the outcome of the hearing was an order that the railroad not only install warning signals but also alter the grade at a crossing, it was held that the order could not stand because of the incompleteness of the original notice.[62] The New York court has twice set aside administrative determinations revoking a driver's license, the reversals being predicated on the fact that the decision was based on different grounds than those suggested in the original notice.[63]

Some state courts insist that a notice which sets forth only conclusions, rather than allegations of fact, is inadequate;[64] and it has been held that correspondence between the parties cannot be relied on as a statement of facts, in lieu of formal particularization in the notice.[65] The requirement that the notice must contain at least a written specification of the issues has been noted in other cases.[66]

However, despite imperfections in the notice, if respondent has been apprised of the asserted facts by some other method, and learns of them in time to permit him to meet the evidence against him, and in time to prepare his defense, the inadequacy of the original notice is not fatal.[67]

---

[61] State Bd. of Technical Registration v. McDaniel, 84 Ariz. 223, 326 P.2d 348 (1958); Lorenz v. Board of Medical Examiners, 46 Cal. 2d 684, 298 P.2d 537 (1956); Grissom v. State, 104 So. 2d 55 (Fla. App. 1958); Nelson v. Hopper, 383 P.2d 588 (Idaho 1963); Securities Comm'n v. Holovachka, 234 Ind. 135, 124 N.E.2d 380 (1955); Rhodes v. Oregon State Veterinary Medicine Examining Bd., 190 Ore. 77, 223 P.2d 804 (1950).

[62] Petition of Village Bd. of Wheatland, 77 N.D. 194, 42 N.W.2d 321 (1950).

[63] Hecht v. Monaghan, 307 N.Y. 461, 121 N.E.2d 421 (1954); Wignall v. Fletcher, 303 N.Y. 435, 103 N.E.2d 728 (1952).

[64] Wimberly v. White, 54 So. 2d 869 (La. App. 1951).

[65] Little v. Smith, 223 Ark. 601, 267 S.W.2d 511 (1954).

[66] Turner v. Gastonia City Bd. of Educ., 250 N.C. 456, 109 S.E.2d 211 (1959); Kuhn v. Public Serv. Comm'n, 76 N.W.2d 171 (N.D. 1956).

[67] Arkansas Motor Freight Lines, Inc. v. Johnson, 221 Ark. 157, 252 S.W.2d 814 (1952); Lo Russo v. Hill, 139 Conn. 554, 95 A.2d 698 (1953); Georgia

Section 2

Requirement of Opportunity for Hearing

(A) Basic Requirements

The minimal requirement that in contested cases "all parties shall be afforded an opportunity for hearing" appears in the Revised Model State Act[68] and in the statutes of many states.[69]

This basic provision adds very little to the requirements of procedural due process. Accordingly, before examining the statutory provisions found in the Revised Model Act and the statutes of the several states prescribing requirements for hearings, a brief examination will be made of decisions of the state courts (predicated largely on concepts of procedural due process) concerning the adequacy of hearing procedures.

(B) Court Decisions Concerning Opportunity for Hearing

The state courts have interpreted the requirement of a hearing as including a guaranty that parties to administrative proceedings should have an opportunity fully to develop their cases.[70] It is not enough that respondent be notified of the proposed action of the board, and informed that an opportunity for hearing will be given if requested; all the statutory procedures must be punc-

---

Pub. Serv. Comm'n v. Jones Transp., Inc., 213 Ga. 514, 100 S.E.2d 183 (1957); Jewell v. Carpentier, 22 Ill. 2d 445, 176 N.E.2d 767 (1961); Smith v. State Bd. of Accountancy, 271 S.W.2d 875 (Ky. 1954); Town of West New York v. Bock, 38 N.J. 500, 186 A.2d 97 (1962); State *ex rel.* Spiker v. Racing Comm'n, 135 W. Va. 512, 63 S.E.2d 831 (1951).

[68] Section 9(a).

[69] Florida (Stat. § 120.22); Georgia (Code Ann. § 3A-101); Hawaii (Sess. Laws 1961, Act 103, § 9(a)); Indiana (Ann. Stat. § 63-3001); Maine (Rev. Stat. Ann. ch. 20-A, § 8); Maryland (Ann. Code art. 41, § 251); Massachusetts (Gen. Laws Ann. ch. 30A, § 10); Michigan (Stat. Ann. § 3.560(21.4)); Minnesota (Stat. § 15.0418); Nebraska (Rev. Stat. § 84-913); Oklahoma (Stat. tit. 75, § 309(a)); Oregon (Rev. Stat. § 183.420); Pennsylvania (Stat. Ann. tit. 71, § 1710.31); Rhode Island (Gen. Laws Ann. § 42-35-9(a)); Virginia (Code Ann. § 9-6.10(b)); Washington (Rev. Code § 34.04.-090); West Virginia (Acts 1964, art. 5, ch. 1, § 1); Wisconsin (Stat. § 227.07).

[70] Colorado Banking Bd. v. Finnigan, 139 Colo. 92, 336 P.2d 98 (1959); Application of Trans-Northwest Gas, Inc., 72 Idaho 215, 238 P.2d 1141 (1951); Rehberg v. Board of Educ. of Melvindale, 345 Mich. 731, 77 N.W.2d 131 (1956); State *ex rel.* Chicago, R.I. & P.R.R. v. Public Serv. Comm'n, 355 S.W.2d 45 (Mo. 1962); A. K. Spalding Constr. Co. v. Walden, 268 P.2d 247 (Okla. 1954); Miles v. State Compensation Comm'r, 136 W. Va. 183, 67 S.E.2d 34 (1951).

tiliously observed.[71] Informal discussion at a conference of opposing counsel is not enough.[72] The parties to the case must be granted a reasonable opportunity to present their contentions, by adducing testimony and presenting arguments.

Even though the administrative proceeding is primarily legislative in nature, yet if it involves elements partaking of the nature of a contested case (determining private rights or duties in situations in which a hearing is required), that type of hearing should be afforded which is established by custom or statute for adjudicatory matters.[73]

It is not enough that a hearing be accorded those requesting the agency to take action; if the proposed action will substantially and specifically affect the rights of other identifiable parties, they must also be granted an opportunity for hearing.[74] However, if the putative effect of the proposed action on the legal rights of others is slight and remote, it is not required that all those having a possible interest be granted a hearing.[75]

In those rare cases in which an agency undertakes wholly to deprive a party of a hearing in a contested case, it is held that the denial of the hearing invalidates the administrative order. These cases occur most frequently in connection with the discharge or demotion of public employees,[76] or the commitment of individuals to public institutions.[77]

It is not required that opportunity for hearing be afforded in connection with a purely administrative determination whether to institute proceedings.[78]

Holding a hearing later than the date prescribed by statute is not fatal, if no prejudice has resulted.[79]

---

[71] State *ex rel.* Gordon Memorial Hosp., Inc. v. West Va. State Bd. of Examiners for Registered Nurses, 136 W. Va. 88, 66 S.E.2d 1 (1951)—the remark was a dictum, a petition for a writ of prohibition having been denied on other grounds.

[72] Blackwood v. Penwoven, Inc., 140 So. 2d 108 (Fla. 1962).

[73] State *ex rel.* State Highway Comm'n v. Weinstein, 322 S.W.2d 778 (Mo. 1959).

[74] Piona v. Alcoholic Beverages Control Comm'n, 332 Mass. 53, 123 N.E.2d 390 (1954).

[75] Moore v. Civil Serv. Comm'n, 333 Mass. 430, 131 N.E.2d 179 (1956).

[76] People *ex rel.* Polen v. Hoehler, 405 Ill. 322, 90 N.E.2d 729 (1950); Boyd v. Collins, 11 N.Y.2d 228, 228 N.Y.S.2d 228, 182 N.E.2d 610 (1962); Smith v. School Dist. of Darby, 388 Pa. 301, 130 A.2d 661 (1957).

[77] Petition of O'Leary, 325 Mass. 179, 89 N.E.2d 769 (1950).

[78] Krueger v. American Christian Mut. Life Ins. Co., 77 N.D. 436, 43 N.W.2d 676 (1950).

[79] Docherty v. City of Philadelphia, 369 Pa. 118, 85 A.2d 143 (1952).

(C) Statutory Requirements to Guarantee Adequacy of Hearing

(1) Right to Present Evidence and Argument

Just as the statutes often prescribe particular requirements as to the type of notice to be given, in order to provide further safeguards than those inherent in the naked requirement of "reasonable notice" (as described above), so it is commonplace for legislatures to make specific provisions to assure the adequacy of the hearing procedures. Many of these specific provisions relate to such matters as the appointment and qualifications of hearing examiners, guaranties against bias and prejudice, rules as to the reception of evidence, protection against *ex parte* communications, provisions as to what items shall comprise the record, and provisions designed to assure that decisions will be made solely on the basis of the record, and by individuals who know what the record contains. All of these matters are considered in detail in succeeding chapters. However, some of the more general requirements as to the adequacy of the hearing procedure may properly be noted here.

As stressed by the courts in the decisions cited above, a basic requirement of a fair hearing is that all parties have adequate opportunity to present their contentions and to support them by evidence and argument. This right is guaranteed in the Revised Model State Act, which provides: "Opportunity shall be afforded all parties to respond and present evidence and argument on all issues involved."[80]

The provision guaranteeing the right to "respond" is new in the Revised Model Act. Its significance lies in the fact that it requires, by necessary implication, that agencies proceed with due deliberation. It precludes the practice sometimes followed, under which upon rather short notice a hearing is held directed solely to the allegations of the agency's complaint or notice. This provision requires that after the notice has been served, respondent must have an opportunity to reply thereto by filing an answer or other appropriate pleading, and thus make sure that the issues to be considered at the hearing will be framed on the basis of the respective contentions of both parties, and not merely on the allegations of the prosecutor. It thus provides

80 Section 9(c).

for the consideration at the hearing of what would have been called by a common law pleader "pleas in abatement" or "pleas in confession and avoidance." This new provision of the Revised Model State Act is already being adopted by state legislatures.[81]

The right to present evidence at the hearing of a contested case is guaranteed in many state statutes.[82] Almost all of these statutes also specifically include, as a part of the hearing procedure, the right to present arguments.[83] The right to be heard should include the right to argue before the officials making the decision. Often, the evidence is heard by a staff assistant who is not empowered to make the decision; he merely reports his findings as to the facts, with perhaps his recommendations, to the agency heads, who are charged with responsibility for making the actual decision. In view of the very circumstance that their knowledge of the facts is limited and secondhand, the right to appear and argue before them is of great practical importance.[84]

Several state statutes provide specifically that the right to a hearing includes the right to cross-examine adverse witnesses.[85]

---

81 Georgia (CODE ANN. § 3A-101); Oklahoma (STAT. tit. 75, § 309(c)); Rhode Island (GEN. LAWS ANN. § 42-35-9(c)).

82 Alaska (STAT. § 44.62.460); California (GOV'T CODE § 11513); Colorado (REV. STAT. ANN. § 3-16-4(7)); Florida (STAT. § 120.26); Hawaii (SESS. LAWS 1961, Act 103, § 9(c)); Indiana (ANN. STAT. § 63-3001); Maine (REV. STAT. ANN. ch. 20-A, § 8); Maryland (ANN. CODE art. 41, § 251); Massachusetts (GEN. LAWS ANN. ch. 30A, § 11); Michigan (STAT. ANN. § 3.560(21.4)); Minnesota (STAT. § 15.0418); Missouri (REV. STAT. § 536.063); Nebraska (REV. STAT. § 84-913); North Dakota (CENT. CODE § 28-32-05); Ohio (REV. CODE ANN. § 119.07); Oklahoma (STAT. tit. 75, § 309(c)); Oregon (REV. STAT. § 183.420); Pennsylvania (STAT. ANN. tit. 71, § 1710.3); Rhode Island (GEN. LAWS ANN. § 42-35-9(c)); Virginia (CODE ANN. § 9-6.10(b)); Washington (REV. CODE § 34.04.090(1)).

83 Among the state statutes listed in note 82 *supra,* Florida, Indiana and Missouri do not explicitly provide for the right to argument.

84 Related problems attendant the institutional decision process are discussed in detail in Ch. XIII.

85 Such provisions appear in the statutes of Florida (STAT. § 120.26); Hawaii (SESS. LAWS 1961, Act 103, § 10(c)); Indiana (ANN. STAT. § 63-3008); Maine (REV. STAT. ANN. ch. 20-A, § 10-III); Maryland (ANN. CODE art. 41, § 252); Massachusetts (GEN. LAWS ANN. ch. 30A, § 11(3)); Michigan (STAT. ANN. § 3.560(21.5)(3)); Minnesota (STAT. § 15.0419(3)); Missouri (REV. STAT. § 536.070(2)); Nebraska (REV. STAT. § 84-914(4)); North Dakota (CENT. CODE § 28-32-05(2)); Ohio (REV. CODE ANN. § 119.07); Oklahoma (STAT. tit. 75, § 310(3)); Oregon (REV. STAT. § 183.450(3)); Pennsylvania (STAT. ANN. tit. 71, § 1710.32); Rhode Island (GEN. LAWS ANN. § 42-35-10(c)); Virginia (CODE ANN. § 9-6.11(c)); Washington (REV. CODE § 34.04.100(3)). Questions as to the extent of the right of cross-examination are discussed in Ch. XII, § 2. The Missouri statute (REV. STAT. § 536.070(2)) is of particular interest because of its provision that the parties shall have the right to cross-examine

The right of cross-examination assumes particular importance in cases where an agency introduces statistical charts or staff reports or like documentary material as part of the record. Questions as to the reliability of such documents cannot be fully explored unless the other parties to the case have the right to insist that the individuals who prepared such studies be available for cross-examination.

In some states, statutes have been adopted making other specific provisions to assure the adequacy of the administrative hearing procedures in contested cases. Among the statutes of particular and general interest are those of California and Alaska (the latter apparently copied from the former).[86] They provide that the notice served on respondent must contain the following information, which not only assures the adequacy of the hearing procedure but makes sure that the respondent knows of his rights at the hearing:

> You may be present at the hearing, may be, but need not be represented by counsel, may present any relevant evidence, and will be given full opportunity to cross examine all witnesses testifying against you. You may have subpoenas issued to compel the attendance of witnesses and the production of books, documents or other things. . . ."

The Florida statute[87] provides that parties to contested cases shall have the right to present their cases by oral and documentary evidence, to submit rebuttal evidence, to conduct such cross-examination as may be required for a full and true disclosure of the facts, to submit proposed findings of fact and conclusions of law, to submit exceptions, and to be represented by counsel.

In general, then, it may be concluded that by and large the state legislatures have accepted the suggestion of Mr. Robert M. Benjamin, who urged in 1942:[88]

> . . . [T]he most satisfactory procedure may call for more than due process alone would require. . . . Fairness will generally require that, to the greatest practicable extent, there should be accorded to a party an opportunity to know the reasons for proposed administrative

opposing witnesses on any matter relevant to the issues, even though the matter was not the subject of the direct examination.

86 ALASKA STAT. § 44.62.420; CAL. GOV'T CODE § 11509.

87 FLA. STAT. § 120.26.

88 BENJAMIN, ADMINISTRATIVE ADJUDICATION IN THE STATE OF NEW YORK 85 et seq. (1942).

action and the assumed facts that support those reasons, an opportunity to test and to controvert those reasons and those facts, and an opportunity to present and explain his own position before action is taken. . . . The presentation of evidence and argument by the parties and the testing of contrary evidence and argument have advantage beyond the advantage of satisfying the legitimate feelings of the parties. Procedure of this kind will go far towards assuring informed and correct administrative action, to the benefit alike of the parties and of the administrator.

(2) Provisions for Informal Settlements

While statistics are not available, the probability is that the percentage of cases concluded by negotiation of an informal settlement is as high in the state agencies as in the federal agencies. It is therefore evident that provisions to facilitate fair settlements are an essential part of any complete code of hearing procedure. The importance of this was noted as long ago as 1941 by the Attorney General's Committee;[89] the Hoover Commission Task Force on Legal Services and Procedure in 1955 reemphasized the point, and suggested revisions in the Federal Administrative Procedure Act[90] to facilitate the closing of cases by settlement agreements.[91]

The Revised Model State Act seeks to implement these suggestions by providing that: "Unless precluded by law, informal disposition may be made of any contested case by stipulation, agreed settlement, consent order, or default."[92] The breadth of this language, hopefully, may help to discourage any tendency on the part of agencies to insist that as a condition of settlement the respondent must admit a violation of law. It is wise to discourage any such tendency. Often, the respondent in good faith asserts his complete innocence of the charge (and is unwilling to admit a violation, because of possible collateral consequences —such as unfavorable publicity or the threat of civil litigation) but is willing to submit to the entry of a stipulation requiring a specified course of future conduct. Such a stipulation is often all that the public interest requires. The agencies should permit

89 *Administrative Procedure in Government Agencies,* S. Doc. No. 8, 77th Cong., 1st Sess. 35-42 (1941).

90 5 U.S.C. § 1004(b); F.C.A. 5 § 1004(b).

91 Commission on Organization of Executive Branch of Government, Task Force Report on Legal Services and Procedure 166 (1955).

92 Section 9(d).

the termination of cases by stipulation, or consent order, without admission of guilt.

The difficulty that is inevitably present in the situation where an automobile driver undertakes to bargain with a traffic policeman on the question whether a violation "ticket" will be issued is also present, in a greater or less degree, in most cases where negotiations are undertaken between representatives of an administrative agency and a respondent in the hope of discovering a means of disposing of the case by consent. But in many types of cases there is room for bargaining, without any sacrifice to the public interest which the agency must uphold and enforce.[93]

The device of a stipulation or consent order has particular usefulness in cases where the parties informally consult with the agency before any formal complaint is issued. An important utility of the informal procedure in such cases is the possibility it affords of avoiding concomitant hardships that follow the issuance of a formal complaint.

Statutes providing specific authority for such informal settlement, cast in language similar to that of the Revised Model State Act, are found in many states.[94] The Florida statute[95] is designed to encourage informal settlements by authorizing hearing officers to hold conferences seeking such settlements.[96]

(3) Other Statutory Provisions as to Adequacy of Hearings

A variety of statutory provisions exhibit the concern felt by state legislatures to assure that hearing procedures shall be in all respects fair. Thus, in California and in Alaska,[97] the statutes require that the notice of hearing advise respondent in detail of the various alternatives open to him with respect to the

---

[93] Settlements are common in workmen's compensation cases. See, *e.g.*, Wisconsin Axle Div. v. Industrial Comm'n, 263 Wis. 529, 57 N.W.2d 696 (1953).

[94] Georgia (CODE ANN. § 3A-101); Hawaii (SESS. LAWS 1961, Act 103, § 9(d)); Indiana (ANN. STAT. § 63-3004); Maine (REV. STAT. ANN. ch. 20-A § 8); Maryland (ANN. CODE art. 41, § 251); Massachusetts (GEN. LAWS ANN. ch. 30A § 10); Michigan (STAT. ANN. § 3.560(21.4)(4)); Minnesota (STAT. § 15.0418); Missouri (REV. STAT. § 536.060); Nebraska (REV. STAT. § 84-913); Oklahoma (STAT. tit. 75, § 309(d)); Oregon (REV. STAT. § 183.420); Rhode Island (GEN. LAWS ANN. § 42-35-9(d)); Washington (REV. CODE § 34.04.090 (1)); Wisconsin (STAT. § 227.07).

[95] FLA. STAT. § 120.25.

[96] Similar provisions are found in New Mexico, in licensing cases. N.M. STAT. ANN. § 67-26-9.

[97] ALASKA STAT. § 44.62.390; CAL. GOV'T CODE § 11506.

hearing, including, *inter alia,* the right to file objections amounting to a demurrer, or to object on the ground that the accusation is so indefinite and uncertain that he cannot identify the transaction or prepare his defense, and the right to present new matter by way of defense, and be heard thereon. The Missouri statute[98] and the Ohio statute[99] prescribe the procedures and mechanics of administrative hearings in meticulous detail.

Section 3

Agencies' Rights To Secure Information

The need of compulsory process to obtain information is ordinarily not so great in the case of the state administrative agencies as in the case of the federal agencies. Many state agencies do not carry on the intensive programs of investigation which federal agencies do; nor do state agencies often have the task (which several federal agencies face) of seeking to compel obedience to a statutorily prescribed code of conduct against respondents who, on jurisdictional grounds, deny the applicability of the statute and assail the validity of the agency regulations as applied to them. On the contrary, most state agencies operate in a more informal environment, and one in which the needed information is most often available without resort to compulsory process. In workmen's compensation and unemployment compensation cases, for example, ordinarily the only information needed by the agency is that which is furnished by the adversary parties. In licensing activities, the mere threat of an adverse decision is usually all that is needed to secure the information desired. Similarly, in most public utility commission proceedings, no difficulty is experienced in obtaining information. But, nevertheless, questions as to the right of a state agency to issue and obtain enforcement of subpoenas do arise; and they are troublesome.

(A) Agency Subpoenas

There is comparatively little judicial precedent available. Most of the contested cases are resolved at the trial court level in unreported opinions, and few cases involving administrative

[98] Mo. Rev. Stat. § 536.063.
[99] Ohio Rev. Code Ann. § 119.07.

subpoenas reach the appellate courts of the states. As a result, there is widespread uncertainty as to the rights of the parties with respect to administrative subpoenas. This very uncertainty is a persuasive recommendation for the enactment of legislation prescribing the powers of administrative agencies to issue subpoenas, setting forth the conditions under which they may be issued, and providing an expeditious method for judicial resolution of disputes as to the propriety of such subpoenas. There should be a simple and effective procedure for compelling the attendance of witnesses and the production of relevant documentary evidence, at the instance of either the agency or the respondent.[100]

(1) Necessity of Statutory Authority

An administrative agency possesses no inherent power to issue subpoenas. It may do so only as authorized by statute.[101] Usually, the authority to issue subpoenas (if such authority is granted) is contained in the statute creating the particular agency; and frequently there is great variation as between the several agencies in a particular state concerning their respective powers to issue subpoenas. Most of the state acts prescribing general codes of administrative procedure are silent as to the issuance of subpoenas, and the Revised Model State Act does not include any provision on this point. This omission reflects a view that provisions respecting the issuance of subpoenas are better left to particularized treatment, since the needs of the agencies differ; and the legislatures might well deem it wise to grant broader powers to some agencies than to others.

However, a few states do make general provisions for the issuance and enforcement of agency subpoenas. Thus, in New York, the Civil Practice Act authorizes the issuance by administrative officers of subpoenas to compel the attendance of witnesses, and the production of documentary evidence, at the hearing of contested cases.[102] Some other states have general provisions authorizing their agencies to issue subpoenas.[103]

---

100 *Cf.* BENJAMIN, *op. cit. supra* note 88, at 147.

101 *In re* Di Brizzi, 303 N.Y. 206, 101 N.E.2d 464 (1951); Commonwealth *ex rel.* Margiotti v. Orsini, 368 Pa. 259, 81 A.2d 891 (1951).

102 N.Y. CIV. PRAC. Act § 406.

103 *E.g.*, Iowa (CODE § 622.81); Nebraska (REV. STAT. § 81-119); Pennsylvania (STAT. ANN. tit. 71, § 200); Wisconsin (STAT. § 325.01(4)).

Alaska and California have espoused the approach that subpoenas should be as readily available in agency adjudication as in the case of proceedings in the courts. Their statutes[104] make it mandatory for agencies to issue subpoenas at the request of any party, before the hearing has commenced, in accordance with the state's code of civil procedure; and further provide that after the hearing has opened, the hearing officer has discretion whether or not to authorize the issuance of subpoenas. Other states provide that the agency or the officer conducting the hearing shall, upon request of any party, require by subpoena the attendance and testimony of witnesses and the production of documents.[105] In most states, however, there is no uniformly applicable statutory provision respecting the power of agencies to obtain information by compulsory process.

If the legislature sees fit to grant such power, it may (in general) make the grant as broad as is deemed desirable. It has been held in a number of cases that legislatures may validly grant powers to state agencies to compel production of information for general purposes of investigation, whether or not it is sought in connection with the hearing of a particular contested case, and whether or not the information is sought on the basis that there exists probable cause to believe that the law has been violated.[106] But, on the other hand, a statute which merely grants agencies power to issue subpoenas to require attendance

---

[104] ALASKA STAT. § 44.62.430; CAL. GOV'T CODE § 11510.

[105] Maine (REV. STAT. ANN. ch. 20-A, § 11); Massachusetts (GEN. LAWS ANN. ch. 30A § 12(3)); Missouri (REV. STAT. § 536.077); New Mexico—as to licensing (STAT. ANN. § 67-26-8); North Carolina—as to licensing (GEN. STAT. § 150-15); North Dakota (CENT. CODE § 28-32-09); Ohio (REV. CODE ANN. § 119.09); Oklahoma (STAT. tit. 75, § 315(2)); Virginia (CODE ANN. § 9-6.10(d)). Indiana provides for the issuance of subpoenas upon request, and of subpoenas duces tecum upon a showing of general relevancy of the evidence sought to be produced (ANN. STAT. § 63-3021). Oregon—upon showing of general relevancy and reasonable scope of the proposed evidence (REV. STAT. § 183.440). *Cf.*, West Virginia (Acts 1964, art. 5, ch. 1, § 1).

[106] *In re* Petition of Graham, 104 So. 2d 16 (Fla. 1958); Vissering Mercantile Co. v. Annunzio, 1 Ill. 2d 108, 115 N.E.2d 306 (1953); Smith v. State Bd. of Accountancy, 271 S.W.2d 875 (Ky. 1954); Warren v. Board of Appeals, 226 Md. 1, 172 A.2d 124 (1961); State *ex rel.* Railroad & Warehouse Comm'n v. Mees, 235 Minn. 42, 49 N.W.2d 386 (1951); Pope & Talbot, Inc. v. Smith, 216 Ore. 605, 340 P.2d 960 (1959); In the Matter of Buoncuore, 39 N.J. 20, 186 A.2d 673 (1962); *In re* Di Brizzi, 303 N.Y. 206, 101 N.E.2d 464 (1951); Leahy v. City of Knoxville, 193 Tenn. 242, 245 S.W.2d 772 (1952); Humble Oil & Ref. Co. v. Daniel, 259 S.W.2d 580 (Tex. Civ. App. 1953); Mayers v. Bronson, 100 Utah 279, 114 P.2d 213, 136 A.L.R. 698 (1941).

at administrative hearings has been held not to authorize the issuance of subpoenas in connection with investigations.[107]

(2) Methods of Enforcement

The usual method of enforcement of administrative subpoenas in the states, as in the federal government, is by means of application to a trial court of general jurisdiction for an order directing the witness to respond to the subpoena.[108] If the court order is not obeyed, the witness is subject to contempt penalties.

Aside from constitutional doubts, most state legislatures have evinced the belief that the advantages that would be gained, in the way of prompt and speedy enforcement, by granting contempt power to administrative agencies, are exceeded by the hazards involved. There appears a deep-seated reluctance to grant to nonjudicial officers, bent on prosecuting their own cases, power to imprison a witness who refuses to aid them in their task. As Justice Frankfurter said in his dissenting opinion in *Penfield Company v. Securities Exchange Commission,*[109] the fact that "Congress should so consistently have withheld powers of testimonial compulsion from administrative agencies discloses a policy that speaks with impressive significance."

Several state courts have held unconstitutional statutes which undertook to invest agencies with power to invoke contempt penalties in case of refusal to comply with an administrative subpoena.[110]

However, the question of constitutional power has not been settled. A few state courts have upheld statutes granting contempt powers to agencies,[111] or have assumed that agencies have

---

[107] Commonwealth *ex rel.* Margiotti v. Orsini, 368 Pa. 259, 81 A.2d 891 (1951).

[108] In *Interstate Commerce Comm'n v. Brimson,* 154 U.S. 447, 38 L. Ed. 1047, 14 Sup. Ct. 1125 (1894), the Court remarked that Congress could not constitutionally grant to administrative agencies power to punish for contempt, in case of refusal to obey a subpoena.

[109] 330 U.S. 585, 604, 91 L. Ed. 1117, 67 Sup. Ct. 918, 928 (1947).

[110] People v. Swena, 88 Colo. 337, 296 Pac. 271 (1931); Langenberg v. Decker, 131 Ind. 471, 31 N.E. 190, 16 L.R.A. 108 (1892); *In re* Sims, 54 Kan. 1, 37 Pac. 135, 25 L.R.A. 110, 45 Am. St. Rep. 261 (1894); Roberts v. Hackney, 109 Ky. 265, 58 S.W. 810, 22 Ky. L. Rep. 975 (1900); *In re* Whitcomb's Case, 120 Mass. 118, 21 Am. Rep. 502 (1876).

[111] Southern Pac. Co. v. State, 19 Ariz. 20, 165 Pac. 303 (1917); Plunkett v. Hamilton, 136 Ga. 72, 70 S.E. 781, 35 A.L.R.(N.S.) 583 (1911); Vogel v. Corporation Comm'n, 190 Okla. 156, 121 P.2d 586 (1942).

inherent power to punish for contempt.[112] Also, a few state constitutions contain provisions empowering named agencies to punish for contempt.[113]

Nothing has appeared to indicate the likelihood of any reversal of the long-standing tendency of the state legislatures to deny contempt powers to administrative agencies.[114] It will apparently continue to be the responsibility of the state courts to decide when refusal to obey a subpoena will be deemed justifiable, and to determine the terms on which (and the extent to which) compliance will be insisted on.

In an interesting and significant case,[115] the New York court faced the problem whether a witness could be held in contempt for giving answers that the agency deemed "incredible" and "unworthy of belief." A state commission held public hearings to investigate the "Appalachin Meeting" of suspected hoodlums. Witnesses who refused to answer questions were jailed by the court. After a short period of incarceration, they sought leave to purge themselves of contempt by testifying. The commission (and this may be indicative of the dangers that would be encountered if contempt powers were granted to agencies) urged that since their answers were inherently "incredible" they should be remanded to jail as continuing contemptors. But the court said that since the answers were clear and unequivocal, they must be deemed to have purged themselves of contempt (pointing out that under the agency's theory a witness might spend his life in jail if the answers he gave were not satisfactory to the agency); and it was held that a perjury proceeding offered the only remedy available to the agency.

Occasionally, informal sanctions (such as denial of statutory benefits) can be utilized by agencies as a means of securing the information they want from recalcitrant witnesses.[116]

---

[112] *Ex parte* Sanford, 236 Mo. 665, 139 S.W. 376 (1911); *In re* Hayes, 200 N.C. 133, 156 S.E. 791, 73 A.L.R. 1179 (1931).

[113] CAL. CONST. art. XII, § 22; LA. CONST. art. VI, § 4; OKLA. CONST. art. IX, § 19; VA. CONST. art. XII, § 156(c).

[114] See Sherwood, *The Enforcement of Administrative Subpoenas,* 44 COLUM. L. REV. 531 (1944); *The Power of Administrative Agencies to Commit for Contempt,* 35 COLUM. L. REV. (1935).

[115] People *ex rel.* Valenti v. McCloskey, 6 N.Y.2d 390, 189 N.Y.S.2d 898, 160 N.E.2d 647 (1959).

[116] State *ex rel.* Fulton Foundry & Mach. Co. v. Industrial Comm'n, 168 Ohio St. 410, 155 N.E.2d 898 (1959).

(3) General Tests Used by Courts in Determining Whether To Enforce Administrative Subpoenas

The general rule is that when application is made to a court for assistance in enforcing compliance with an administrative subpoena, the court will sustain the subpoena to the extent that it is found to be in accordance with law.[117] But when is a subpoena deemed to be "in accordance with law"? While there are few explicit answers to this question to be found in the opinions of the state courts, such decisions as can be found indicate that the state courts are coming to accept the statement of the United States Supreme Court in *Oklahoma Press Publishing Company v. Walling,*[118] that the three basic tests by which to determine whether the subpoena is "in accordance with law" are (1) whether the inquiry is one the demanding agency is authorized by law to make; (2) whether the materials specified are relevant to an authorized inquiry; (3) whether the disclosure sought is reasonable.[119] Thus, the Minnesota court declared: "So long as the investigation is for a lawfully authorized purpose and the information sought relevant and material to the investigation, we cannot see where due process is offended by requiring any person possessed of that information to testify."[120] Similarly, the California court, after interjecting the pointed observation that "the power to make administrative inquiry . . . is more analogous to the power of a grand jury" than to the judicial function, ruled that if the inquiry is one the agency is authorized to make, if the demand is not too indefinite, and if the information sought is reasonably relevant, then the administrative subpoena should be enforced.[121]

A fuller understanding of the meaning and application of these three basic tests may be obtained by an examination of the

---

[117] This is the phrase found in the Federal Administrative Procedure Act, 5 U.S.C. § 1005(c); F.C.A. 5 § 1005(c).

[118] 327 U.S. 186, 90 L. Ed. 614, 66 Sup. Ct. 494, 166 Am. L. Rep. 531 (1946).

[119] A review of the decisions of the lower federal courts applying these tests, covering the period 1948-1960, is found in Cooper, "Federal Agency Investigations: Requirements for the Production of Documents," 60 *Mich. L. Rev.* 187 (1961).

[120] State *ex rel.* Railroad & Warehouse Comm'n v. Mees, 235 Minn. 42, 53, 49 N.W.2d 386, 393 (1951).

[121] Brovelli v. Superior Court, 56 Cal. 2d 524, 364 P.2d 462, 15 Cal. Rptr. 630 (1961). (But order held invalid because lower court had not obtained jurisdiction.)

decisions holding whether or not particular applications for enforcement of subpoenas were justified in light of these tests and of certain subsidiary principles stated below.

(4) Determining Whether Demand Is Authorized by Law

When enforcement of an administrative subpoena is resisted, the court first looks to the statute creating the agency to determine whether it authorizes the issuance of the subpoena. In making this determination, the task of the court is not the barren legalistic one of rhetorical construction of the statutory provision. The courts do not make a fortress of the dictionary, nor deem their task one which can be accomplished by dispassionate, disinterested construction of the language found in the statute. Rather, they consider the consequences of alternate constructions; and the court's judgment as to the desirability of broadening or restricting the agency's investigatory powers often controls the construction adopted.

Decisions finding the subpoena to be within the breadth of the agency's authority emphasize the necessity of broad investigatory powers to enable the agency effectively to accomplish its purposes.[122] Conversely, opinions declaring a subpoena to be without statutory authority often indicate that the decision reflected the court's judgment that, in the circumstances involved, the individual's right to privacy and to freedom from officious intermeddling weighed heavier in the scales of justice than did the agency's asserted need for the information.[123]

(5) The Requirement of Relevancy

It is not possible to derive from the few state court opinions discussing the requirement of relevancy (nor from the many decisions of the lower federal courts discussing this requirement)[124] any convenient hornbook rule as to what showing of relevancy the agency must make to secure judicial enforcement of its subpoena for the production of documents. The difficulty faced by

---

[122] *In re* Hawkins, 49 Del. 544, 121 A.2d 486 (1956); In the Matter of Waterfront Comm'n of New York Harbor, 35 N.J. 62, 171 A.2d 295 (1961); *In re* Di Brizzi, 303 N.Y. 206, 101 N.E.2d 464 (1951).

[123] *Cf.*, Board of Review v. Williams, 195 Miss. 618, 15 So. 2d 48 (1943); *In re* Kaplan, 8 N.Y.2d 214, 203 N.Y.S.2d 836, 168 N.E.2d 660 (1960); Commonwealth *ex rel.* Margiotti v. Orsini, 368 Pa. 259, 81 A.2d 891 (1951).

[124] 60 MICH. L. REV. 187, 191 (1961).

the courts in attempting to formulate workable tests arises fundamentally from the fact that the court is asked to determine the relevancy of unknown documents to unspecified issues—a rather difficult feat for even the most agile judges. The agency has not seen the documents it is demanding; not knowing what the documents might reveal, it is difficult for counsel for the agency to establish their relevancy. Counsel for respondent has a different problem. He does not wish to reveal the documents, for to do so would be to defeat his purpose of keeping them undiscovered; and it is, to say the least, difficult to establish the irrelevancy of a document whose contents one does not wish to disclose. Further, when the issue of relevancy is argued, the actual issues involved in the administrative proceedings may not yet have been crystallized.

Faced with this practical difficulty, the courts are inclined to say that the agency has discharged whatever initial burden may be imposed on it as moving party, if it accompanies the application with a formal statement setting forth the reasons which lead the agency to believe that the subpoenaed material will be of substantial aid to the agency.[125]

Most courts rule that if the agency has made an initial showing that the desired information may be reasonably relevant, the burden shifts to the respondent to disprove its relevancy; and the courts are generally inclined to overrule a defense of irrelevancy unless the party resisting the subpoena makes it appear plainly to the court that the documents in question are clearly irrelevant, or that they have no potential relevancy. In general, a heavy burden of persuasion is placed on defendant if he is to convince the court that production of the information should be denied for reasons of irrelevancy alone.

However, the burden is not insurmountable. In one New Jersey case, for example,[126] the decision quashing a subpoena duces tecum was predicated primarily on the "patent irrelevancy and immateriality" of the evidence sought. The court added that in case of "demonstrated irrelevancy," the courts should not compel obedience to a subpoena duces tecum.

[125] It is important that the agency make such a showing. Many judges exhibit a much less hospitable attitude when an agency demands enforcement of its subpoena without thus explaining its need for the information. *In re* Davies, 168 N.Y. 89, 61 N.E. 118, 56 L.R.A. 855 (1901).

[126] Schlossberg v. Jersey City Sewerage Authority, 15 N.J. 360, 104 A.2d 662 (1954).

If the argument of irrelevancy is buttressed by a showing that compliance with the demands of the subpoena would cause undue burden, involving an unreasonable interference with protected rights of privacy, the objections are more likely to succeed. Thus, when a special legislative commission appointed to investigate gambling subpoenaed all the records of a number of persons which would show their connection with fifty-two named corporations involved in the dissemination of sporting news, the defense of irrelevancy was successful. The court ruled that a subpoena duces tecum "could not properly be issued to have brought in a mass of books and papers in order that there might be a search through them to gather evidence."[127]

But where the objection is based solely on respondent's assertions of irrelevancy, the objection is not often upheld. Thus, in another case involving an investigation by a commission appointed to investigate gambling in connection with horse racing, wherein the parties served with subpoenas objected to producing all their documents showing their investments in certain associations engaged in conducting horse race meets, the New York court overruled their objections, remarking: "In its investigation pursuant to these subpoenas, the commission will, of course, be restricted to such material as is relevant to the subject of the inquiry, but is not obliged to take petitioners' word for what is or is not relevant.[128]

The New Jersey court has imposed a further obstacle in the path of witnesses who rely solely on asserted irrelevancy, by holding that this objection may be raised only in connection with specific questions or specific documents.[129]

(6) Defense of Undue Burden

The Supreme Court in the *Oklahoma Press* case[130] did not define the "unreasonable disclosure" that is proscribed as being oppressive and unduly burdensome, except to say: "The gist of the protection is in the requirement, expressed in terms, that the

---

[127] Annenberg v. Roberts, 333 Pa. 203, 214, 2 A.2d 612, 618 (1938).

[128] Alexander v. New York State Comm'n, 306 N.Y. 421, 426, 118 N.E.2d 588, 589 (1954). Another decision permitting a broad investigation and overruling objections of relevancy, is *Humble Oil & Refining Co. v. Daniel,* 259 S.W.2d 580 (Tex. Civ. App. 1953).

[129] Application of Waterfront Comm'n of New York Harbor, 32 N.J. 323, 160 A.2d 832 (1960).

[130] *Supra,* note 118.

disclosure sought shall not be unreasonable."[131] The test appears to contemplate that if the difficulty of complying with the subpoena is plainly out of all proportion to the end sought, the courts can justifiably deny their aid when application is made to enforce the subpoena.

But the mere circumstance that compliance with the requirements of the subpoena will be expensive and inconvenient—or that it will interfere with the normal conduct of respondent's business—does not in itself ordinarily afford a basis for refusal to enforce the subpoena.[132]

However, in some decisions recognition may be found of the principle that if, under all the circumstances, the demands of the subpoena are unreasonable and oppressive, the defense of undue burden will furnish a basis for quashing the subpoena. In one New Jersey case,[133] the court, while predicating its decision primarily upon the "demonstrated irrelevancy" of the materials sought, accorded at least a limited recognition to the proposition that compliance with a subpoena should not be enforced where to do so would impose an undue burden and interfere with the witness's rights of privacy. The court said:

> . . . . Except as he may be relieved from compliance with the subpoena *duces tecum* upon appropriate motion under R.R. 4:46-2 because the subpoena is "unreasonable and oppressive," or is excused from compliance because he would be incriminated thereby or because the matter is otherwise privileged, the duty owed by every witness to the State to aid in the quest for truth in the administration of justice makes it compulsory that he appear and produce documentary evidence in his possession and, if required, to testify concerning it . . . .

Here, as in other aspects of the problem of judicial enforcement of agency subpoenas, a broad measure of discretion is vested in the trial courts; and their decisions are not often appealed to the state supreme courts.

A succinct phrase of Judge Hutcheson[134] suggests the attitude which is characteristic of the state courts as well as the

[131] *Id.* at 208.

[132] Vissering Mercantile Co. v. Annunzio, 1 Ill. 2d 108, 115 N.E.2d 306 (1953); Pope & Talbot, Inc. v. Smith, 216 Ore. 605, 340 P.2d 960 (1959).

[133] Schlossberg v. Jersey City Sewerage Authority, 15 N.J. 360, 372, 104 A.2d 662 (1954).

[134] Winn & Lovett Grocery Co. v. NLRB, 213 F.2d 785, 786 (5th Cir. 1954).

federal courts in considering contentions that a subpoena is unduly burdensome. He suggested that if it appears to the court on the whole record that the purpose of the subpoena is to "annoy and embarrass" rather than to "discover and reveal," the court may deny enforcement. It is noteworthy that in most of the cases where a court has relied on the undue burden imposed by a subpoena in declining application for enforcement, there is a strong suggestion that the subpoena was issued for improper purposes.[135]

(7) Defense That Agency Does Not Have Jurisdiction

The defense that an administrative subpoena should not be enforced because of asserted lack of jurisdiction in the agency, arises in an entirely different context in the state courts than in the federal courts.

In cases involving the federal agencies, the defense typically involves the assertion that a respondent against whom the agency is proceeding because of alleged violation of a federal regulatory statute, is not subject to the act which the agency is seeking to enforce. The typical example is that where respondent asserts he is not engaged in interstate commerce and is therefore not subject to federal regulation.

In the federal courts, it remains a troublesome and unsettled question whether, in a case where an agency asserts jurisdiction, the court should, before enforcing the agency's subpoena, make an independent inquiry as to whether the agency does in fact possess the asserted jurisdiction. The lower federal courts for years believed it proper to make at least a preliminary investigation of the alleged lack of agency jurisdiction. The question appears not to have been considered by the Supreme Court prior to its decision in *Endicott Johnson Corporation v. Perkins.*[136] That decision did not dispose of the problem; for it appeared to be limited principally to cases involving government contractors; and, indeed, it was far from clear that any actual question of lack of jurisdiction was involved. But, a few years later, in *Oklahoma Press Publishing Company v. Walling,*[137] the Supreme

---

135 60 MICH. L. REV. 187, 198 (1961).

136 317 U.S. 501, 87 L. Ed. 424, 63 Sup.Ct. 339 (1943).

137 327 U.S. 186, 90 L. Ed. 614, 66 Sup. Ct. 494, 166 Am. L. Rep. 531 (1946).

Court strongly hinted that the issue of lack of jurisdiction could not be raised as a defense on application for enforcement of a subpoena, that being a question to be determined, at least in the first instance, by the agency itself. The case was decided in February, 1946, three months before the enactment of the Federal Administrative Procedure Act,[138] and the decision apparently was not considered by Congress in adopting that statute.[139]

Although the federal act was enacted after the *Oklahoma Press* decision, and could well have been construed as overruling it (for it could plausibly be argued that an agency subpoena has not been issued "in accordance with law" if the agency has no jurisdiction over the respondent against whom it is proceeding),[140] the suggestion of the *Oklahoma Press* case—that the question as to the agency's jurisdiction is, at least initially, for the agency to determine—appears to have survived the enactment of the statute.[141]

Unfortunately, it is not clear just what the *Oklahoma Press* case stands for. It seemingly does not prevent a court from denying enforcement of a subpoena if it appears clear that the respondent is not subject to the agency's jurisdiction. But if the issue is doubtful, most of the federal courts now feel obliged to enforce the subpoena. Amelioration of the uncertain and unsatisfactory state of affairs now existing in this area can appar-

---

138 5 U.S.C. §§ 1001-1011; F.C.A. 5 §§ 1001-1011.

139 As one commentator put it: "Although the draftsmen of the Act undoubtedly believed that private parties should be allowed to raise the defense of lack of agency jurisdiction in a subpoena enforcement proceeding, they did not include an express provision to that effect, because they deemed it unnecessary." [The act providing only that a subpoena should not be enforced "except as authorized by law." 5 U.S.C. § 1005(b); F.C.A. 5 § 1005(b)] Schwartz, *The Administrative Procedure Act in Operation,* 29 N.Y.U.L. REV. 1173 (1954).

140 The Hoover Commission Task Force on Legal Services and Procedure was of the view that a court should consider the jurisdictional question in any proceedings for the enforcement of a subpoena. TASK FORCE REPORT ON LEGAL SERVICES AND PROCEDURE, p. 174 (1955). The legislative history of the federal act is not clear on this point. While the Senate Judiciary Committee Report and the floor explanation delivered by the chairman of the House Subcommittee indicate a purpose to require some judicial scrutiny of the agency's jurisdiction, they conflict as to the scope of this authority. The Senate Report indicated that it would be enough if the court were satisfied that the agency could possibly have jurisdiction. S. REP. No. 752, 79th Cong., 1st Sess. 20 (1945). The House Report indicated that the phrase "in accordance with law" meant that the subpoena should be enforced only if the facts demonstrated that the persons and subject matter to which the subpoena was directed were within the jurisdiction of the agency. H.R. REP. NO. 1980, 79th Cong., 2d Sess. 32-33 (1946).

141 Tobin v. Banks & Rumbaugh, 201 F.2d 223 (5th Cir. 1953); D.G. Bland Lumber Co. v. NLRB, 177 F.2d 555 (5th Cir. 1949).

ently be attained only by legislative enactment. The Hoover Commission Task Force on Legal Services and Procedure concluded that the jurisdictional question should be considered by the courts in proceedings to enforce subpoenas to a limited extent, viz.: "The court shall quash the subpoena . . . to the extent that it finds the same . . . beyond the probable jurisdiction of the agency. . . ."[142]

Occasionally, a question somewhat similar to that which has plagued the federal courts arises in the state courts, when a respondent against whom the agency is proceeding asserts that the act which the agency enforces does not apply to him. But, despite the similarity, this question is really somewhat different than that involved in the federal cases, because the respondent does not (as in the federal cases) dispute the power of the government to regulate respondent's activities; the claim is the narrower one that the state government has not chosen to do so. Because of this distinction, it is easier for the state courts to hold that a state agency need not prove the applicability of the act to respondent as a condition of obtaining judicial enforcement of the agency's subpoena directed to the respondent; and several state courts have so held.[143] But this view is not universally accepted.[144]

Most state cases involve simply the question whether, in order to obtain information against a company subject to a regulatory statute, the agency may subpoena a witness who is not claimed to be subject to the act. As to this question, the prevailing view is that witnesses may be subpoenaed to produce information, regardless of the applicability of the regulatory act to the witness so summoned. A leading case is *State v. Mees,*[145] and it is suggested in an *American Law Reports* annotation on this decision that the "correctness of the result . . . can hardly be doubted, since a contrary rule would make it impossible for an adminis-

---

142 Commission on Organization of Executive Branch of Government, TASK FORCE REPORT ON LEGAL SERVICES AND PROCEDURE, PROPOSED ADMINISTRATIVE CODE § 204(b), p. 368 (1955).

143 Hill v. Brisbane, 66 Cal. App. 2d 15, 151 P.2d 578 (1944); *In re* Iowa State Commerce Comm'n, 252 Iowa 1237, 110 N.W.2d 390 (1961); Warren v. Board of Appeals, 226 Md. 1, 172 A.2d 124 (1961).

144 See Board of Review v. Williams, 195 Miss. 618, 15 So. 2d 48 (1943).

145 235 Minn. 42, 49 N.W.2d 386 (1951).

trative agency effectively to carry out its investigatory duties."[146] Several other decisions are in accord.[147]

(8) Objection That Agency Is Engaged in "Fishing Expedition"

Whether an agency may utilize the process of subpoena to engage in what are commonly called "fishing expeditions"—general inquiries undertaken in the hope that the search may disclose some information of potential value—is a question that does not permit any categorical answer.

A division of opinion is reflected in the comparatively few appellate decisions of state courts that speak directly to the problem. Twenty years ago, the state courts quite uniformly followed the view, which then prevailed in the federal courts, that agencies would not be permitted to use compulsory process to engage in "fishing expeditions." Typical of the attitudes of that day are the comments of the Mississippi court, in denying an application by the unemployment compensation commission for an order directing a corporation to produce certain records, where it appeared that the purpose of the request was to ascertain whether an individual was employed by the corporation, so as to be eligible for unemployment benefits. The court said:

> The law is well settled on the question. It is within the sound discretion of the court whether it will grant an order for the issuance of a subpoena *duces tecum*. . . . The order will not issue unless the books and papers are pertinent, relevant, and material to the issues then being tried, and the application or petition must show these facts. . . . The writ will not be granted as a fishing expedition nor where the purpose is for mere inquiry or to discover whether there is any evidence in them that will be useful to the applicant, or for a general inquisitorial examination.[148]

Similarly, in 1938, the Pennsylvania court declared: "a subpoena duces tecum could not properly be issued to have brought

---

[146] 27 A.L.R.2d 1208, 1211 (1953).

[147] Redding Pine Mills, Inc. v. State Bd. of Equalization, 157 Cal. App. 2d 40, 320 P.2d 25 (1958); Application of Waterfront Comm'n of New York Harbor, 32 N.J. 323, 160 A.2d 832 (1960); Syracuse Cooperative Milk Distributors' Bargaining Agency, Inc. v. Attorney General, 13 Misc. 2d 26, 177 N.Y.S.2d 107 (1958); Pope & Talbot, Inc. v. Smith, 216 Ore. 605, 340 P.2d 960 (1959).

[148] Board of Review v. Williams, *supra* note 144, at 629.

in a mass of books and papers in order that there might be a search through them to gather evidence."[149]

While some state courts continue to entertain these views, others are coming in more recent years to follow the trend in current federal cases, where the proscription against "fishing expeditions" has been notably relaxed. The Oregon court, for example, sustained as against a contention that the agency was engaged in a fishing expedition, a subpoena calling for production of all records "showing the names and addresses of all loggers and other individuals and corporations from whom logs, pilings, pulpwood and other forest products were purchased in the year 1954, together with the number of board feet or other units purchased from each," where the apparent purpose of the investigation was to ascertain whether any of the sellers of such products owed taxes.[150]

Doubtless, there is a similar division of opinion among the trial judges in the state courts, whose decisions on applications for enforcement of subpoenas are not often appealed.[151]

This disagreement reflects a difference of opinion noted in debates concerning the propriety of "fishing expeditions" on the part of the federal agencies.

The older federal cases strongly condemned such roving inquiries. In *Harriman v. Interstate Commerce Commission,*[152] denying the asserted right of the Commission to examine witnesses as to various matters on which the Commission sought information that might influence its recommendations to Congress for new legislation, the court referred in outraged tones to the "enormous scope" of the claimed power to require disclosure of any facts "no matter how private," and declared that no such unlimited authority had ever been given to any commission or court. As recently as 1936,[153] the United States Supreme Court declared that a roving inquisitorial investigation was unknown to the Constitution and would constitute an intolerable tyranny.

Apparently similar views were entertained by the Congress that enacted the Federal Administrative Procedure Act of

149 Annenberg v. Roberts, 333 Pa. 203, 214, 2 A.2d 612, 618 (1938).

150 Pope & Talbot, Inc. v. Smith, note 147 *supra. Cf., In re* Iowa State Commerce Comm'n, note 143 *supra.*

151 In some states, they are not appealable. *In re* Appeal of Pennsylania R.R., 20 N.J. 398, 120 A.2d 94 (1956).

152 211 U.S. 407, 53 L. Ed. 253, 29 Sup. Ct. 115 (1908).

153 Jones v. SEC, 298 U.S. 1, 80 L. Ed. 1015, 56 Sup. Ct. 654 (1936).

1946.[154] The Senate Committee declared that its provisions, particularly Section 6, which forbids any investigative act "in any manner or for any purpose except as authorized by law,"[155] were "designed to preclude 'fishing expeditions.' "[156] The House Committee asserted in similar terms that under the provisions of the federal act: "Investigations may not disturb or disrupt personal privacy, or unreasonably interfere with private occupation or enterprise."[157]

Four years later, however, the Supreme Court declared in *United States v. Morton Salt Company*:[158] "Even if one were to regard the request for information in this case as caused by nothing more than official curiosity, nevertheless law-enforcing agencies have a legitimate right to satisfy themselves that corporate behavior is consistent with the law and the public interest."

The Court's decision in the *Morton Salt* case was undoubtedly influenced by the fact that the Federal Trade Commission (the agency involved) wanted to learn whether respondent was in compliance with the requirements of an order previously entered against it. It may be doubted whether an inquiry as broad as that there permitted would have been sustained if addressed to one who had not previously been found to have engaged in illegal practices.

It is suggested that, so far as many state courts are concerned, there is no longer any doctrine which prohibits "fishing expeditions" as such. Rather, where an agency is proceeding to drag the nets of inquiry, in the hope that a tasty fish may be caught, the court will test the legality of the demand in terms of statutory authorization, the potential relevancy and significance of the information sought, and the degree of burden imposed on the witness.

As a matter of policy, there is room for debate. There have been indications both from Congress and from unofficial organizations that it would be better on the whole if such broad inquiries were discouraged. The congressional declarations that accompanied the enactment of the federal act are noted above. In similar language, the Hoover Commission Task Force on

---

[154] 5 U.S.C. §§ 1001-1011; F.C.A. 5 §§ 1001-1011.
[155] 5 U.S.C. § 1005(b); F.C.A. 5 § 1005(b).
[156] S. Doc. No. 248, 79th Cong., 2d Sess. 205 (1946).
[157] *Id.* at p. 264.
[158] 338 U.S. 632, 652, 94 L. Ed. 401, 70 Sup. Ct. 357 (1950).

Legal Services and Procedure urged that "fishing expeditions" should not be permitted which unduly "impinge on the rights of the citizen." It added: "Because of the extent to which the investigatory power may impinge upon the privacy of the citizen, it is important that its scope be reasonably restricted. 'Fishing expeditions' are contrary to sound administrative practice, as well as to law."[159]

Such considerations of policy are in large part the responsibility of legislative bodies. In view of the uncertainty as to the extent to which a trend may develop in the state courts to reverse the rules formerly prevailing and to permit "fishing expeditions," legislatures considering the adoption of administrative procedure acts would be well advised to consider whether it is consistent with sound public policy to permit agencies to utilize compulsory process to carry on general inquiries instituted in the hope that an intensive search of a mass of books and papers may disclose some information of potential value to the agency.

(9) Requirement That Documents be Specifically Described

The courts continue to pay at least lip service to the doctrine that the documents demanded pursuant to subpoena must be "specifically described"; but in actual application of this requirement, the courts are satisfied if the documents are "appropriately described." Any description is deemed appropriate and sufficiently specific if it enables respondent to identify the documents which the agency desires to see. The requirement, therefore, can readily be met in most cases. For example, a demand that all correspondence relating to specified topics (or all documents relevant to a specified inquiry) be produced, is generally deemed to be a sufficiently precise description. In this, the state courts follow the federal courts.[160]

(10) Privileged Information

It is clear, on principle, that evidence which is privileged in civil proceedings before the courts should also be privileged in proceedings before administrative agencies, whether the pro-

[159] Commission on Organization of Executive Branch of Government, TASK FORCE REPORT ON LEGAL SERVICES AND PROCEDURE 60, 175 (1955).

[160] Brown v. United States, 276 U.S. 134, 72 L. Ed. 500, 48 Sup. Ct. 288 (1928); Consolidated Mines of California v. SEC, 97 F.2d 704 (9th Cir. 1938); Pope & Talbot, Inc. v. Smith, 216 Ore. 605, 340 P.2d 960 (1959).

ceedings are adjudicatory or investigatory.[161] The New York court has so held with respect to the assertion of the attorney-client privilege in an administrative investigatory proceeding.[162] It would no doubt be so held with respect to the other privileges recognized in the courts.

The privilege against self-incrimination is applicable to the same extent as in the case of the federal agencies, and subject to the same limitations. It cannot be asserted on behalf of a corporation.[163] It may be cut off by enactment of an immunity statute providing that the witness must answer the questions put to him, but cannot be prosecuted on account of the transactions covered by his testimony.[164] The state courts are in agreement with the federal courts that where such a statute has been enacted, the testimony can be compelled even though it exposes the witness to disgrace. Thus, the Illinois court declared of its constitutional provision for compulsory testimony: "It is not the purpose of this constitutional provision to save a witness from embarrassment, disgrace, or opprobrium arising out of the exposure of a crime, and the fact that his answers may tend to degrade him does not permit him to refuse to testify."[165] It was formerly held that the fact that the statute of the state did not undertake to confer immunity from prosecution in the federal courts did not excuse a failure to produce incriminating evidence; but these decisions must be deemed to have been modified by the 1964 decisions of the United States Supreme Court in *Murphy v. Waterfront Commission,* holding that witnesses immune from prosecution under state law cannot be prosecuted under federal law.[166]

(B) Inspection of Premises

It is true in administrative adjudication, just as it is in the case of litigation in the courts, that the decision-maker may view the

---

161 8 WIGMORE, EVIDENCE §§ 2300(a), 2285 (McNaughton rev. 1961).

162 *In re* Kaplan, 8 N.Y.2d 214, 168 N.E.2d 660 (1960).

163 Hale v. Henkel, 201 U.S. 43, 50 L. Ed. 652, 26 Sup. Ct. 370 (1906); Leahy v. City of Knoxville, 193 Tenn. 242, 245 S.W.2d 772 (1952).

164 McLain v. Superior Court, 99 Cal. App. 2d 109, 221 P.2d 300 (1950); Halpin v. Scotti, 415 Ill. 104, 112 N.E.2d 91 (1953); Application of Waterfront Comm'n of New York Harbor, 39 N.J. 436, 189 A.2d 36 (1963).

165 Halpin v. Scotti, 415 Ill. 104, 108, 112 N.E.2d 91, 93 (1953).

166 Murphy v. Waterfront Comm'n of New York Harbor, 378 U.S. 52, 12 L. Ed. 2d 678, 84 Sup. Ct. 1594 (1964); Cabot v. Corcoran, 332 Mass. 44, 123 N.E.2d 221 (1954).

premises involved, in order to obtain a better understanding of the testimony relating to those premises. It is probably more true of administrative officers than of trial judges in the state courts that when they view the premises with this announced purpose, they in fact may rely on their impressions of what they see as a substitute for testimony.[167]

In cases where there is no requirement that the administrative decision be based on a hearing, and no provision for judicial review to determine whether the administrative decision was based on substantial evidence, the agencies are free to predicate decision on their own impressions of the facts as gleaned from their inspection of the premises.[168]

But where the administrative decision must be based on a hearing, or where there is opportunity for judicial review to test the substantiality of the evidence on which the administrative decision was based, it is sometimes held that agencies are not entitled to consider as evidence in the case the impressions obtained from their examination of the premises; and if it can be shown that they did so, the administrative order may be reversed.[169]

(C) Requiring Reports

Agencies may not, without statutory authority, require persons subject to their jurisdiction to file reports for the purpose of advising the agency concerning matters about which the agency

---

[167] In one case, well known in the uncommon and unreported law of Michigan, the state supreme court reversed a lower court decision because the trial judge, dissatisfied with the testimony he had heard as to the operation of a traffic control light at a street intersection, visited the intersection and based his decision on his own observation. One of the supreme court judges reportedly told his friends that he had been about to file a vigorous dissent, but decided to concur in the result because, while the case was under submission to the supreme court, he had had occasion to drive by the intersection in question; and noted that the observations of the trial judge had been quite erroneous.

[168] State *ex rel.* Public Utils. Comm'n v. Atchison, T. & S.F. Ry., 115 Kan. 3, 221 Pac. 259 (1923); Balch v. Glenn, 85 Kan. 735, 119 Pac. 67 (1911); People *ex rel.* Copcutt v. Board of Health, 140 N.Y. 1, 35 N.E. 320, 23 L.R.A. 481, 37 Am. St. 522 (1893).

[169] Farmers' Elevator Co. v. Chicago, R.I. & P. Ry., 266 Ill. 567, 107 N.E. 841 (1915); Monon R.R. v. Public Serv. Comm'n, 241 Ind. 142, 170 N.E.2d 441 (1960); Koplar v. State Tax Comm'n, 321 S.W.2d 686 (Mo. 1959); Forrest v. Evershed, 7 N.Y.2d 256, 164 N.E.2d 841 (1959); *Cf.*, Sultan Turkish Bath, Inc. v. Board of Police Comm'rs of City of Los Angeles, 169 Cal. App. 2d 188, 337 P.2d 203 (1959) for remark that examiner's view of premises, with consent of counsel, "is evidence in the case."

desires to obtain information. In practice, of course, many agencies do undertake, by means of questionnaires and similar inquiries, to persuade those subject to the agency's jurisdiction voluntarily to submit reports of various types. Such requests are honored in a high percentage of the cases, either because of the willingness of the parties to cooperate with the agency, or because of a fear that refusal to cooperate might result in formal investigatory proceedings and the issuance of subpoenas.

Where the statute does authorize an agency to require the filing of reports, the state courts show no hesitation in granting their aid to compel compliance.[170]

(D) Prescribing Accounting Systems

A few statutes authorize public utility commissions to prescribe uniform methods of accounting for the utilities subject to their jurisdiction. Such statutory requirements have been upheld by the courts. However, the state courts are more willing than are the federal courts to set aside accounting requirements believed by the court to be unreasonable.[171] It has been held, also, that an agency may not utilize its statutory power to prescribe a uniform system of accounts as a method of regulating the transactions which will be reflected in the accounts—as by prescribing the terms of contracts.[172]

Section 4

Respondents' Rights To Secure Information

In the case of a number of agencies in some states, respondents are left to their own devices to obtain the information needed to present their cases. This result is unfortunate, from the viewpoint both of the interest of the respondent in having a fair trial at which the odds between the contesting parties will be even, and also the interest of the state in assuring fully informed administrative decisions.

170 Dundalk Liquor Co. v. Tawes, 201 Md. 58, 92 A.2d 560 (1953); Atchison, T. & S.F. Ry. v. State, 72 Okla. 271, 180 Pac. 849 (1919).

171 Matter of New York Edison Co. v. Maltbie, 244 App. Div. 685, 281 N.Y.S. 223, *aff'd.*, 271 N.Y. 103, 2 N.E.2d 277 (1936); *cf.* American Tel. & Tel. Co. v. United States, 299 U.S. 232, 81 L. Ed. 142, 57 Sup. Ct. 170 (1936).

172 Pacific Tel. & Tel. Co. v. Public Utils. Comm'n, 34 Cal. 2d 822, 215 P.2d 441 (1950).

In a few states, statutes specifically assure respondent the right of compulsory process. Especially interesting is the provision in the California statute[173] that the notice initiating administrative action contain the following provision: "You are entitled to the issuance of subpoenas to compel the attendance of witnesses and the production of books, documents, or other things by applying to (here insert appropriate office of agency)." By making sure that all respondents know of the availability for their use of compulsory process, this provision tends to insure the utilization of the statutory provision. Other statutes provide simply that the agency or the officer conducting the hearing shall, upon request of any party, require by subpoena the attendance and testimony of witnesses and the production of documents.[174] Predictably, more state legislatures will in future years see fit to adopt such provisions. As the sphere of administrative adjudication expands, the need for providing means to secure compulsory attendance of witnesses at the behest of respondent becomes more important.

Absent provisions specifically requiring agencies to issue subpoenas at the request of respondents, a question sometimes arises whether an agency which is given a general power to issue subpoenas may be compelled to make subpoenas as readily available to counsel for respondents as to counsel for the agency. Provisions assuring equal availability of subpoenas to all parties are clearly desirable, for it is important to avoid not only unfairness but even the appearance of unfairness. This has been noted both by commentators[175] and by the courts. As the Kentucky court put it, in holding that counsel for the employer in a workmen's compensation case should be granted a subpoena to compel the production for their examination of X-rays of claimant's decedent:

> The adversary nature of our practice sometimes leads us to forget that a trial is not a game, but is a quiet search for the truth. There can be no justification for playing hide-and-seek with records that may be of assistance in that process. Upon remand of this case, and on proper motion, the board may issue such orders and subpoenas as

---

[173] CAL. GOV'T CODE § 11509. The provision has been copied in the Alaska statute. ALASKA STAT. § 44.62.420.

[174] See statutes cited in note 105 *supra*.

[175] BENJAMIN, ADMINISTRATIVE ADJUDICATION IN THE STATE OF NEW YORK 147 (1942).

> are appropriate in order to enable medical witnesses of the company's choosing to examine the X-ray films. . . .[176]

Indeed, no persuasive reason has been advanced why administrative subpoenas should not be issuable as a matter of course by a clerk in the agency's office—just as they are issued upon request by clerks of court in judicial proceedings.

A number of state courts have recognized that it is a deprival of procedural due process to impose unreasonable conditions on the issuance of subpoenas to respondents. In a New York case, counsel for respondent requested the Division of Milk Control to issue twenty subpoenas. The agency declined to issue them unless respondent stated the names of the witnesses whom he wished to subpoena and the character of the testimony he proposed to adduce. Counsel for respondent refused to reveal this information; and the agency accordingly refused to issue the subpoenas. Holding this to be error, the court remarked:

> The privilege of a litigant to enforce the attendance of witnesses is an ancient right and should not be denied by prejudging the materiality of the testimony which may be given. . . . The issuance of a subpoena for witnesses during the progress of a cause at the request of a party is a matter of right.[177]

In reversing an administrative decision removing a public employee, the New Jersey court opined that the respondent was entitled to the same kind of discovery processes as in an ordinary civil trial, and that means should have been made available to him to get specified data to establish his defense.[178] A California court, construing the provision in its statute[179] that after the hearing has opened, issuance of a subpoena is discretionary with the hearing officer, said that it would be an abuse of discretion to refuse a request if a proper showing of materiality were made.[180]

A problem which has troubled the state courts is whether respondent should be entitled to a subpoena to obtain access to

---

[176] Cox v. Peabody Coal Co., 357 S.W.2d 878, 879 (Ky. 1962).

[177] Coney Island Dairy Prods. Corp. v. Baldwin, 243 App. Div. 178, 180, 276 N.Y.S. 682 (1935).

[178] Russo v. Meyner, 22 N.J. 156, 123 A.2d 482 (1956).

[179] CAL. GOV'T CODE § 11510(a).

[180] National Automobile & Cas. Ins. Co. v. Garrison, 76 Cal. App. 2d 415, 173 P.2d 67 (1946).

data in agency files that have been labelled as confidential by the agency. Quite frequently, such requests have been denied—for example, with respect to a request to examine a death certificate containing a confidential medical report;[181] a request to examine "field investigation notes" of a planning commission;[182] and a request for leave to examine members of an agency as to the extent of their examination of the record.[183] On the other hand, the New Jersey court held respondents entitled to receive a copy of the transcript of proceedings had before an agency, even though the agency had by rule made the transcript confidential.[184]

Occasionally, a question is presented whether, where an agency lacks power to issue a subpoena, the fact that respondent accordingly does not have the benefit of compulsory process amounts to a deprival of procedural due process. The Kansas court[185] held that where respondent failed to establish that he had actually been prejudiced by the lack of compulsory process, he was not entitled to have the administrative order set aside. However, an Ohio decision[186] held that a statute was invalid as not affording due process of law, because it provided no means by which a doctor faced with proceedings for the revocation of his license to practice could compel the attendance of witnesses on his behalf.

Section 5

Pre-hearing Procedures

(A) Importance of Pre-Trial Hearings

The importance of pre-trial hearings in administrative adjudication has long been recognized, and many recommendations have been made that agencies—following the lead of the courts—adopt more widely the practice of holding pre-trial hearings in appropriate cases.

---

181 *In re* Bakers Mut. Ins. Co. of New York, 301 N.Y. 21, 92 N.E.2d 49 (1950).

182 Wiley v. Woods, 393 Pa. 341, 141 A.2d 844 (1958).

183 Wright v. Industrial Comm'n, 10 Wis. 2d 653, 103 N.W.2d 531 (1960).

184 State v. Murphy, 36 N.J. 172, 175 A.2d 622 (1961).

185 Brinkley v. Hassig, 130 Kan. 874, 289 Pac. 64 (1930).

186 Jewell v. McCann, 95 Ohio St. 191, 116 N.E. 42 (1917).

In 1941, the Attorney General's Committee declared: ". . . perhaps the most fruitful possibilities for expediting and simplifying formal administrative proceedings lie in the field of pre-hearing techniques."[187] After pointing out the desirability of disposing of contested matters by settlement or stipulation, without initiation of formal proceedings, the Committee continued: "But even after notice has been issued and formal decisive action is begun, there is scope for further pre-hearing methods to dispose of the case, narrow its issues, or simplify the subsequent methods of proof;" and the Committee pointed out the successes which had been attained in a few federal agencies which made diligent use of the device of pre-trial hearings.[188]

Fourteen years later, the President's Conference on Administrative Procedure[189] recommended that agencies adopt rules providing:

> In any proceeding the agency or its designated hearing officer upon its or his own motion, or upon the motion of one of the parties or their qualified representatives, may in its or his discretion direct the parties or their qualified representatives to appear at a specified time and place for a conference to consider: (a) the simplification of the issues; (b) the necessity of amendments to the pleadings; (c) the possibility of obtaining stipulations, admissions of facts and of documents; (d) the limitation of the number of expert witnesses; (e) such other matters as may aid in the disposition of the proceeding.

The recommendation further provided that a formal order be entered at the conclusion of the pre-trial hearing, to control the subsequent course of the proceeding.

Still more recently, Judge Irving R. Kaufman declared: "It is my firm conviction that the administrative agencies, as the courts, will find in the pretrial conference their most important procedural weapon."[190]

---

187 *Administrative Procedure in Government Agencies,* S. DOC. No. 8, 77th Cong., 1st Sess. 64 (1941).

188 *Id.* at pp. 64-65.

189 FINAL REPORT OF THE PRESIDENT'S CONFERENCE ON ADMINISTRATIVE PROCEDURE 37 (1955).

190 Kaufman, *Have Administrative Agencies Kept Pace With Modern Court-Developed Techniques Against Delay?—A Judge's View* 12 AD. L. BULL. 103, 111 (1959-1960).

(B) Advantages to Agencies

From the viewpoint of the agency, pre-trial hearings in pending cases offer many advantages.[191] First and foremost, it is only by the use of such informal procedures that the agencies can keep abreast of their heavy case loads. Many agencies dispose of nine-tenths or more of all matters instituted before them without trial. The agencies would be compelled to neglect many cases deserving of attention if they were required to go through formal trial-type hearings in all cases. Imbued as they are by a desire to fulfill what they deem to be their broad social missions, the agencies find many reasons for preferring the comparatively informal procedures available through pre-trial techniques. They can sometimes persuade a party to adopt a course of action which he perhaps could not be compelled to adopt if he resisted formal proceedings directed to such end, or they can obtain agreements that something be done which it would be beyond their powers to compel.

(C) Advantages to Respondents

From the viewpoint of the private parties concerned, pre-trial hearings are important for other reasons. The respondent faces a practical necessity of discussing his case informally with the agency in order that he may learn exactly what is involved. Such discussion is often the only practical means of learning, in advance of the hearing, the actual claims of the agency and the true issues involved. Similarly, consultation and conferences are frequently the only methods of ascertaining the existence and content of various unpublished rulings and general counsel opinions which may be determinative of the administrative ruling. The respondent can thus advantageously utilize pre-trial proceedings as an effective means of trial preparation.

Other advantages are offered the respondent. Consultation and conference with agency representatives offer him an opportunity to convince the agency of the fairness of his position; and if this can be done his worries are very nearly at an end. Furthermore, negotiation with agency attorneys often serves to disclose alternative bases of settlement; counsel for respondent can

---

191 Cooper, Administrative Agencies and the Courts 114 et seq. (1951).

learn of various formulas, stipulations, or agreements which the agency will sometimes consent to as a means of disposing of the case. Such alternative solutions often afford, so far as the respondent is concerned, an easy way out. Sometimes the agency will be satisfied with a concession which the respondent is entirely willing to make. These possibilities can be fully explored only by diligent use of pre-hearing techniques, for the agency rules do not ordinarily disclose all these alternative possibilities, and agency representatives are likely at the outset to suggest only such modes of settlement as are most favorable to the agency, rather than those which are most favorable to the respondent.

(D) Objectives of Pre-Hearing Conference

A pre-hearing conference in administrative proceedings serves much the same purposes as its counterpart in court trials.[192]

By permitting the parties to ascertain the real areas of disagreement, and the basis of such disagreement, the pre-hearing conference serves to clarify and simplify the issues. In cases, for example, where the agency simply announces in its initial notice that it will hold a hearing to determine what action should be taken, or where an agency complaint alleges a violation in terms as broadly all-inclusive as those of the governing statute, the parties have little idea as to what issues will become of controlling importance until the proofs are received. Such uncertainties may be eliminated early in the course of the proceedings by utilization of pre-hearing conferences.

One important corollary effect of the pre-hearing conference is that it sometimes improves the quality and usefulness of the pleadings. When the parties, through the give-and-take of oral colloquy, have discovered the true posture of the case and the identity of the really contested issues, it often appears desirable to one or both sides to amend the pleadings, so that the lines of battle will be more clearly drawn.

Probably the most important single objective of the pre-hearing conference is to limit the proofs and thereby shorten the record. This aim is accomplished in several ways:

Ordinarily, most of the documentary evidence that the parties desire to introduce can be agreed on and exchanged. This inter-

---

192 *Cf.* Cooper, The Lawyer and Administrative Agencies 168 et seq. (1957).

change eliminates the necessity of proving the authenticity of the exhibits, and gives each party adequate opportunity to study his opponent's documentary evidence. In appropriate cases, agreements can be reached as to the admissibility of statistical summaries and tabulations.

When each of the parties has the opportunity of previewing the other's proofs (especially where expert testimony is involved), counsel can prepare in advance for cross-examination, thereby producing not only shorter cross-examination, but cross-examination that is more penetrating.

Discussion of the areas of agreement and disagreement on the factual aspects of the case may lead to formal admissions as to certain facts, or even to comprehensive stipulations of facts.

While settlements are not necessarily one of the direct objectives of the pre-trial hearing, they are sometimes a beneficial by-product thereof.

Finally, the pre-trial hearing sets up a plan for the hearing, covering such important details as hearing dates, order of proofs, whether there should be separate hearings on separable issues, or whether there should be advance determination of controlling questions of law before the proofs are taken.

(E) Statutory Authority Is Essential

It is doubtful, however, despite their potentialities for good, whether formal pre-trial hearings (as distinguished from informal pre-hearing conferences) will be successfully utilized to any great extent in most state agencies unless they are provided for by statute.

This conclusion is predicated on the reluctance of counsel to participate wholeheartedly (because of their disinclination to reveal to their opponents in advance the most telling points of their case), and the lack of enthusiasm on the part of agency officials (who find that the process involves difficulties in connection with the scheduling of cases and the assignment of hearing officers to conduct them), and on the circumstance that there is grave doubt as to the power of an agency to enforce a pre-trial order without statutory sanctions.

In a Florida case, where the deputy commissioner of the workmen's compensation commission called a conference of opposing counsel to discuss a pending claim and entered an order awarding certain medical expenses, the reviewing court set the order aside. It held that since the workmen's compensation statute included no provision for pre-trial proceedings, such hearings could not be made the basis for determining the rights of the parties unless the parties so stipulated or clearly waived their rights to a hearing.[193]

The federal act[194] provides that hearing officers may hold conferences for the settlement or simplification of the issues by consent of the parties; and in a few of the federal agencies pre-trial procedures have been successfully employed.[195]

The Revised Model State Act makes no provision for pre-trial hearings; and as yet very few state legislatures have made appropriate provision for this need.[196]

---

193 Blackwood v. Penwoven, Inc., 140 So. 2d 108 (Fla. 1962). The court did add that pre-trial hearings may be useful.

194 5 U.S.C. § 1006(b); F.C.A. 5 § 1006(b).

195 Bond, *The Use of Pre-Trial Technique in Administrative Hearings*, 13 FED. COM. B.J. 55 (1953).

196 The Florida statute provides that hearing officers shall have power, subject to the agency's published rules, to hold conferences for the settlement or simplification of the issues, by consent of the parties. FLA. STAT. § 120.25; *Cf.* COLO. REV. STAT. ANN. § 3-16-4(4).

CHAPTER XI

CONTESTED CASES: ANCILLARY MATTERS

During the course of trial preparations, in the interval between the service of the initial notice and the opening of the hearing, questions may arise as to a number of matters ancillary to the hearing itself. Several such questions are discussed in this chapter.

Section 1
Necessary Parties

Traditional court-made rules respecting joinder of parties play but little part in administrative adjudication. Ordinarily, the only indispensable parties are those who, as a matter of due process or because of specific statutory requirements, must be given notice of contemplated action and an opportunity to be heard thereon.[1] Parties with dissimilar or even conflicting and competing interests may be joined in a single proceeding, or the proceeding may continue without joinder of parties who might appropriately be brought into the proceeding, and parties may be dropped or new parties added, as administrative convenience suggests, ordinarily subject to no restriction except occasional statutory provision or agency rules,[2] and the requirements of procedural due process, mentioned below.

If it is required that notice be served on specified parties at the time administrative proceedings are initiated, they are necessary parties to the hearing procedure, and failure to join them as parties affords a basis for setting aside the administrative determination.[3]

---

[1] See Ch. X, § 1(A)(6) "Who Entitled to Notice."

[2] See Oberst *Parties to Administrative Proceedings,* 40 MICH. L. REV. 378 (1942).

[3] Burkhardt v. State, 77 N.D. 232, 42 N.W.2d 670 (1950); Greyhound Corp. v. Michigan Public Serv. Comm'n, 360 Mich. 578, 104 N.W.2d 395 (1960);

Further, in cases where it is clearly apparent that the administrative order may substantially prejudice a party who is not specified as one on whom notice must be served, several state courts hold that failure to join him as a party is error. The principle may be illustrated by a decison of the New Jersey court[4] involving a claim for unemployment benefits. The claimants, after going out on strike, obtained temporary jobs, and the primary question was whether this served to cancel the applicability of the labor dispute disqualification in the state unemployment compensation law, which disqualified for benefits those whose unemployment was the result of their having gone on strike. The administrative agency refused to consider the appeal of the protesting employer, on the ground that, under the applicable statute, if benefits were allowed they would be initially chargeable only to other employers. The court, pointing out that if benefits were allowed, and if the amount of benefits eventually collected exceeded the amount chargeable to the other employers, the excess would be chargeable to the protesting employer, held that the agency erred in failing to consider his appeal.

In another case, the New Jersey court pointed out the untoward results that sometimes flow from the practice of acting on applications for licenses without joining as parties to the proceedings others whose interests would be affected by the grant of the license.[5]

The Mississippi court faced a similar problem in a case where, after the public service commission had approved the transfer of a certificate of convenience and necessity, it instituted further proceedings to determine whether its order approving the transfer should be set aside, but failed to make the original holder of the certificate a party to the subsequent proceedings. The court held that he was a necessary party to the subsequent proceedings, because an invalidation of the transfer would substantially affect his rights.[6]

Trellsite Foundry & Stamping Co. v. Enterprise Foundry, 365 Mich. 209, 112 N.W.2d 476 (1961).

[4] The New Jersey Zinc Co. v. Board of Review, 25 N.J. 235, 135 A.2d 496 (1957).

[5] City of Passaic v. City of Clifton, 14 N.J. 136, 101 A.2d 530 (1953).

[6] Mississippi Pub. Serv. Comm'n v. Chambers, 235 Miss. 133, 108 So. 2d 550 (1959).

When an administrative order confers rights on a party, he is an indispensable party in proceedings to review the administrative determination.[7]

Section 2

Right of Intervention

Frequently one who is not a necessary party desires to intervene in administrative proceedings the outcome of which may indirectly or collaterally affect his interests. Thus, in proceedings before workmen's compensation commissions or unemployment compensation commissions, if a particular case involves a question of statutory construction which will control the result in many pending and future cases, other employers or trade associations representing employers, or labor unions whose members will be affected, may desire to intervene, in order to offer proof and argument that they hope will persuade the agency to decide the question in their favor. Similarly, in proceedings before public utility commissions, carriers not directly involved in the proceeding often wish to intervene, because the grant of a license to the carrier whose application is being considered may affect the profitability of operation of other carriers.

Allowance or denial of petitions to intervene usually rests in administrative discretion. The Revised Model State Act makes no provision with respect to the right to intervene. A number of state statutes make provisions with respect to intervention in particular proceedings (such provisions are almost always found in the statute creating the particular agency involved); but the statutes are, quite uniformly, merely permissive, with the result that applications to intervene are normally decided on the basis of the rules and practices and discretion of the agency involved.

The agencies, motivated by a desire to exclude potential troublemakers, often deny such petitions. The attitude of the agencies is understandable. They fear that if the number of intervenors becomes substantial—if, for example, counsel for ten or twelve intervening parties each calls his own witnesses and in turn

[7] Shulman v. Zoning Bd. of Appeals, 143 Conn. 182, 120 A.2d 550 (1956), where a zoning board had granted an owner permission to make a nonconforming use of certain property, and other property owners, in bringing proceedings to review the determination, named the zoning board as the only defendant.

cross-examines all of the witnesses called by counsel for each of the parties—the hearing record would be extended to unmanageable proportions. They fear, too, that the technique of multi-party intervention might be employed purposefully as a stalling tactic, to delay the administrative disposition of the case.

But the denial of petitions to intervene may lead to unfortunate results. Denial of such petitions may mean that important issues are ignored. The result may be that interested parties, whose interests may be substantially affected by the outcome of the proceeding, are deprived of the opportunity to play their part in shaping the course of administrative determination.

Occasionally, denial of a petition to intervene is held to constitute an abuse of discretion. Thus, the Wisconsin court held that where two groups of employees had diverse interests in an issue that was the subject of a grievance, and the case was decided on the record of a hearing in which only one of the two groups was heard—the other group being denied an opportunity to be heard—there was a denial of fair play which constituted an abuse of discretion.[8] Again, in a case where the denial of a continuance had the effect of depriving county tax officials of the right to intervene and present evidence in connection with an appeal by a taxpayer contesting the assessment of his property for *ad valorem* tax purposes, the Missouri court held that administrative discretion had been abused.[9]

Ordinarily, however, the courts do not upset the administrative agency's decision on the propriety of a proposed intervention. Thus, where the Missouri public service commission denied an individual consumer leave to intervene in a rate proceeding, on the ground that his interest was no different from that of the general public, the denial was upheld;[10] and when in another case the same commission, relaxing its own rules, permitted a consumer to intervene in a different rate proceeding, even though his interest was no different from that of the general public, the commission's decision was again upheld.[11]

The Missouri court has suggested that generally the same degree of interest is required for intervention as of right as

[8] Clark v. Hein-Werner Corp., 8 Wis. 2d 264, 99 N.W.2d 132 (1959).
[9] *In re* St. Joseph Lead Co., 352 S.W.2d 656 (Mo. 1961).
[10] Smith v. Public Serv. Comm'n, 336 S.W.2d 491 (Mo. 1960).
[11] State *ex rel.* Dyer v. Public Serv. Comm'n, 341 S.W.2d 795 (Mo. 1960).

would be required for becoming a complainant.[12] If one has such a direct interest in a matter that he would be entitled to file a complaint himself, his request to intervene may be treated as in effect the filing of a complaint coupled with a request that the two proceedings be consolidated. Absent such direct interest, denial of petitions to intervene has been sustained in a wide variety of cases as being within the limits of permissible administrative discretion.[13]

An interesting question is whether a person who has standing as an aggrieved party to appeal an agency determination to the courts, is entitled as of right to intervene. In a well-reasoned opinion, the Court of Appeals for the Second Circuit[14] held that the Federal Communications Commission could not deny intervention to a party who had the right to seek judicial review. The court pointed out that intervention might well be necessary in order to make the right to review effective—a point which will strike a sympathetic response from all lawyers who have had the experience of taking an appeal on a record not of their own making, and which fails to develop adequately the particular points which counsel thinks would have been dispositive of the case had they been properly brought out at the hearing.

Hopefully, this decision would be followed by the state courts.

On the other hand, allowance of a petition to intervene does not necessarily confer standing to appeal.[15]

Decisions go both ways on the right of a competitor to intervene, the result usually being to uphold the administrative decision.[16]

---

12 State *ex rel.* Consumers Pub. Serv. Co. v. Public Serv. Comm'n, 352 Mo. 905, 180 S.W.2d 40 (1944).

13 Pittsburgh v. Pennsylvania Pub. Util. Comm'n, 153 Pa. Super. 83, 33 A.2d 641 (1943)—a city denied permission to intervene in a rate proceeding; M. W. Smith Lumber Co. v. Alabama Pub. Serv. Comm'n, 247 Ala. 318, 24 So. 2d 409 (1946)—an industrial consumer denied permission to intervene in a rate proceeding involving residential consumers; Stuyvesant Town Corp. v. Impellitteri, 280 App. Div. 788, 113 N.Y.S.2d 593 (1952)—tenants denied right to intervene in a rent-fixing proceeding.

14 American Communications Ass'n v. United States, 298 F.2d 648, (2d Cir. 1962); *Cf.* National Coal Ass'n v. Federal Power Comm'n, 191 F.2d 462 (App. D.C. 1951).

15 State *ex rel.* Rouveyrol v. Donnelly, 365 Mo. 686, 285 S.W.2d 669 (1956).

16 Cases upholding the allowance of intervention include Kirkby v. Michigan Pub. Serv. Comm'n, 320 Mich. 608, 32 N.W.2d 1 (1948); W. J. Dillner Transfer Co. v. Pennsylvania Pub. Util. Comm'n, 175 Pa. Super. 461, 107 A.2d 159 (1954). Cases upholding denial of petitions to intervene include Asche v.

Not infrequently, administrative agencies permit limited participation in a case by one who is not allowed to intervene as a party. Sometimes his status is substantially like that of an *amicus curiae* in judicial proceedings, his participation being limited to filing a brief. Conversely, he may sometimes be permitted to introduce testimony and cross-examine witnesses even though he has not been formally made a party to the case. Between these two extremes, many intermediate solutions may be worked out as a means of enabling the agency to have the benefit of the views of collaterally interested persons.

These devices offer wide opportunities in the way of permitting effective participation in administrative proceedings by collaterally interested parties—thus securing valuable contributions, making for better informed administrative action, without involving the difficulties that sometimes attend formal intervention, such as the prolonging of hearings and the undue enlargement of the record or the introduction of extraneous issues.

Section 3

Right to Counsel

The Revised Model State Act does not contain a provision comparable to that found in Section 6 of the Federal Administrative Procedure Act[17] declaring that every party shall be accorded the right to appear in person or by or with counsel in any agency proceeding, and further providing that any person compelled to appear in person before any agency or representative thereof shall be accorded the right to be accompanied, represented, and advised by counsel.

The draftsmen deemed it unnecessary to include such a provision in the Revised Model State Act, in view of the widespread recognition by the state courts of the principle that the right to be represented by counsel is an inherent right of a citizen involved in any contested case before an administrative agency. The state courts subscribe to the principle stated by the United

Rosenfield, 405 Ill. 108, 89 N.E.2d 885 (1950); Application of Dairymen's League Co-op Ass'n, Inc., 282 App. Div. 69, 121 N.Y.S.2d 857 (1953).

[17] 5 U.S.C. § 1005(a); F.C.A. 5 § 1005(a).

States Supreme Court in *Powell v. Alabama*[18] that a hearing "has always included the right to the aid of counsel when desired" because "the right to be heard would be, in many cases, of little avail if it did not comprehend the right to be heard by counsel."

Strong affirmation of these principles may be found in an opinion of the New York court,[19] holding that civil service employees had been denied their right to counsel in dismissal proceedings when an informer (a fellow employee who had pretended to participate in the wrongful acts alleged, and who was named as a codefendant in the notice instituting dismissal proceedings) was present at their consultation with their counsel. Despite the fact that no prejudice was shown to have resulted (the agency having obtained no information from its informer as a result of his having participated, as a pretended codefendant, in conferences with counsel), the court held that the right of representation by counsel included the right to private consultation free from the presence of an informer.[20]

Other state courts have recognized that respondents in administrative proceedings are entitled to consult with and be represented by counsel.[21] The Arizona court has gone so far as to hold that if counsel for a claimant in a workmen's compensation case does not properly present his client's case, and as a result compensation is denied, the case will be remanded for further hearings; thus holding, in effect, that individuals are entitled not only to representation by counsel, but to competent and effective representation.[22]

---

18 287 U.S. 45, 68, 77 L. Ed. 158, 53 Sup. Ct. 55, 84 A.L.R. 527 (1932).

19 Fusco v. Moses, 304 N.Y. 424, 107 N.E.2d 581 (1952).

20 *Cf.* Finocchairo v. Kelly, 11 N.Y.2d 58, 226 N.Y.S.2d 403, 181 N.E.2d 427 (1962), where it was held that proof as to the denial of a request by a person arrested on charges of driving while drunk who sought to telephone his attorney was not relevant to a subsequent revocation of his driver's license on the ground that he had refused to take a blood test. The court pointed out that the criminal proceedings had resulted in an acquittal, and that there was no showing that respondent had been denied the right to counsel in connection with the subsequent independent proceeding to revoke his license.

21 People *ex rel.* Rea v. Nokomis Coal Co., 308 Ill. 45, 139 N.E. 41 (1923); Bancroft v. Board of Governors of Registered Dentists, 202 Okla. 108, 210 P.2d 666 (1949); People *ex rel.* Ellett v. Flood, 64 App. Div. 209, 71 N.Y.S. 1067 (1901). *Contra,* State *ex rel.* Charles v. Port Comm'rs, 159 La. 69, 105 So. 228 (1925). The Kentucky court held unconstitutional a statute which required the employer to pay half the claimant's attorney fees in a workmen's compensation case. Burns v. Shepherd, 264 S.W.2d 685 (Ky. 1953).

22 Orosco v. Poarch, 70 Ariz. 432, 222 P.2d 805 (1950).

The right to representation does not always embrace an absolute right to be represented by a particular attorney; and when an adjournment of a hearing is requested on the ground that the attorney representing respondent has other engagements which preclude his attendance at the hearing, the agency has discretion as to whether to grant a continuance.[23]

While the right to representation by counsel is vigorously insisted on by the state courts in contested cases, it is doubtful that the right to representation by counsel extends to cases where the agency is not engaged in the determination of a judicial question, but is merely conducting an investigation or taking testimony to aid it in reaching a purely executive decision. Thus, the Minnesota court held that an advisory board, created to make recommendations to the state industrial commission as to minimum wage scales, need not afford interested persons the right of representation by counsel at its investigatory public hearings.[24]

While state agencies do not often undertake to deny respondent the right of counsel in contested cases, they sometimes do seek to discourage individuals from securing legal representation in pending matters. Disapproving this practice, the legislatures of a few states (and, predictably, more may follow) have enacted statutes designed to assure that the right of representation by counsel be freely availed of. Thus, the California statute[25] requires that the notice initiating proceedings in a contested case must advise respondent specifically that: "You may be present at the hearing, may be but need not be represented by counsel, may present any relevant evidence, and will be given full opportunity to cross examine all witnesses testifying against you." The Ohio statute also provides that the initial notice must inform respondent that he may appear in person or by attorney.[26] The Florida statute[27] requires that "the agency shall afford all parties authorized by law to participate in an agency proceeding the right . . . to be accompanied, represented, and advised by counsel or to represent himself." The Oregon statute[28] likewise provides

[23] Givens v. Department of Alcoholic Beverage Control, 176 Cal. App. 2d 529, 1 Cal. Rptr. 446 (1959).

[24] Haaland v. Pomush, 263 Minn. 506, 117 N.W.2d 194 (1962).

[25] CAL. GOV'T CODE § 11509. The same provision appears in ALASKA STAT. § 44.62.420.

[26] OHIO REV. CODE ANN. § 119.07.

[27] FLA. STAT. § 120.26.

[28] ORE. REV. STAT. § 183.420.

that at the hearing of a contested case, each party shall have the right to be represented by counsel.

Section 4

Hearing Officers

(A) A Problem With Many Facets

Because of the bewildering heterogeneity of the functions and responsibilities of hearing officers in state agencies—vast differences appearing both as between different agencies in the same state and as between different states—the draftsmen of the Revised Model State Act did not undertake to make any uniform provision to prescribe the functions, duties, and powers of hearing officers.

In some state agencies—typically public utility commissions and tax commissions—the agency members undertake to participate personally in the hearing of every case, eschewing the assistance of hearing officers (but sometimes relying on the submissions of staff assistants). In other agencies—notably workmen's compensation commissions and unemployment compensation commissions—the function of decision making is often delegated to "referees" or "deputy commissioners," whose decisions are sometimes subject to review by an appellate administrative tribunal quite separate from and independent of the principal agency. In still other cases—such as liquor control commissions and conservation commissions—hearing officers are utilized on an informal basis whenever the press of business demands such assistance, and on such occasions a staff employee who can be spared from his regular duties will be assigned to preside at the hearing. Sometimes, he is given authority to do no more than to act as an official monitor; sometimes, on the other hand, he is empowered to write a proposed decision which, if approved by the agency members, becomes the decision of the agency. There are other instances in which hearing officers function generally in the manner described in the Federal Administrative Procedure Act,[29] making a record and drafting a report for the assistance of the agency staff which in turn will draft a decision for the consideration of agency members.

[29] 5 U.S.C. § 1006; F.C.A. 5 § 1006.

The hearing officer may be an individual without legal training, unskilled in the techniques of conducting a hearing and ignorant of the rules of evidence or even of basic principles of procedure. On the contrary, he may be an experienced judicial officer exhibiting a level of professional competence comparable to that of a trial judge.

Few are the general principles that emerge from this phantasmagoric pattern. While there can be no question but that the use of hearing officers creates problems about which something should be done, the problems are not susceptible of solution by any across-the-board measures. They must be tackled state by state, and perhaps agency by agency.

(B) The California Approach

A shining example of what a state can do in creating a corps of competent hearing officers and giving them appropriate functions and a proper scope of authority is afforded by the California statute and its efficient administration by the Office of Administrative Procedure.

Under the California statute, to be eligible for appointment as a hearing officer, the applicant must have been admitted to the practice of law in California for at least five years, and must possess such additional qualifications as may be established by the State Personnel Board.[30] The executive officer of the State Office of Administrative Procedure appoints a staff of hearing officers to serve the several state agencies.[31]

The statute provides two methods of holding hearings. Under the first method, the hearing officer hears the case alone. He prepares a proposed decision which is filed with the agency and served on the other parties to the case. The agency may adopt the decision of the hearing officer or may, after giving the parties opportunity to be heard, itself decide the case upon the record.[32]

Under the second method, the case is heard by the agency with the active assistance of the hearing officer, who presides at the hearing, rules on the admission and exclusion of evidence, and advises the agency on matters of law. He is present during

---

30 Cal. Gov't Code § 11502.
31 Cal. Gov't Code § 11370.3.
32 Cal. Gov't Code §§ 11512, 11517.

the consideration of the case by the agency and, upon request, assists and advises the agency in its consideration of the case.[33]

The objectives of this system[34] were described by the California Court of Appeals in a decision holding that where the hearing officer sits alone the agency may, by adopting his proposed decision, delegate to him the power to decide.[35] The court said:

> One of the primary purposes of the Legislature in passing . . . the legislation was to remedy the evils in connection with hearings before administrative boards frequently composed of laymen, untrained in procedure. To this end there was created the position of hearing officer. Such officer is a civil service employee and must be an experienced lawyer. . . . If the case is heard by the hearing officer and the agency, the agency decides the case with the assistance and advice of the hearing officer . . .; where the hearing officer alone hears the case, the agency has the power of adjudicating, but in so deciding the case, if it is satisfied with the proposed decision of the hearing officer, it may adopt the decision of the hearing officer without first reading the record but, if not satisfied with such decision, before a contrary decision may be rendered, it must give the parties a chance to argue and must read the record. In other words, in cases where the hearing officer sits alone, the administrative agency may, by adopting his proposed decision, in legal effect, and with statutory permission, delegate the power to decide to the hearing officer. But, if dissatisfied with such proposed opinion, the administrative agency may, in legal effect, grant a hearing and decide the case anew on record and argument.[36]

Thus, the essence of the California approach is to assure professional competence on the part of the hearing officer, to give him duties and responsibilities which impute stature to the position, and to make sure that every administrative hearing is conducted before and under the supervision of such a hearing officer.[37] The California provisions have worked well and deserve careful consideration in other states.

Many provisions of the California statute have been copied in Alaska.[38] A few other states have statutes which create a

33 *Ibid.*

34 The California hearing officer system and its operation are described in a symposium appearing in 44 *Cal. L. Rev.* 189-320 (1956).

35 Hohreiter v. Garrison, 81 Cal. App. 2d 384, 184 P.2d 323 (1947).

36 *Id.* at 394.

37 It has been held that it is an excess of jurisdiction for an agency to hear evidence and argument at a hearing not presided over by a statutory hearing officer. Moyer v. State Bd. of Equalization, 140 Cal. App. 2d 651, 295 P.2d 583 (1956).

38 ALASKA STAT. § 44.62.350.

properly independent status for the hearing officer, and accord him substantial powers. The Maine statute[39] provides for appointment of hearing officers for four year terms by the governor of the state. The officers serve a number of agencies, enumerated in the statute, and the decisions of the hearing officers are reviewable directly by the courts. The Ohio statute[40] provides that agencies may appoint referees or examiners to conduct hearings in certain cases, and that they shall have the same powers and authority in conducting the hearing as are granted by law to the agency, but the reports of such officers are subject to review by the appointing agency.

(C) Lessons To Be Learned From the Federal Experience

The experience of the federal agencies persuasively indicates the wisdom of adopting a statute which, as the California statute does, confers upon the position of hearing officer power and prestige and a substantial measure of independence.

As long ago as 1941, the Attorney General's Committee urged the desirability of increasing the significance of the hearing officer's work in the decisional process. It was recommended that his decision be accorded the same effect as that of the trial court; and the Committee continued:

> In general, the relationship on appeal between the hearing commissioners and the agency ought to a considerable extent be that of trial court to appellate court. Conclusions, interpretations, law, and policy should, of course, be open to full review. On the other hand, on matters which the hearing commissioner, having heard the evidence and seen the witnesses, is best qualified to decide, the agency should be reluctant to disturb his findings unless error is clearly shown.[41]

When Congress enacted the Federal Administrative Procedure Act[42] in 1946, however, it did not give full effect to these recommendations. While that Act gave agencies the choice between making the initial decisions themselves, or having the

---

[39] ME. REV. STAT. ANN. ch. 20-A, § 6.

[40] OHIO REV. CODE ANN. § 119.09.

[41] *Administrative Procedure in Government Agencies,* S. DOC. No. 8, 77th Cong., 1st Sess. 51 (1941).

[42] 5 U.S.C. § 1007; F.C.A. 5 § 1007.

initial decisions made by the hearing officer, it denigrated this provision by the further proviso that upon appeal to the agency from the initial decision of the hearing officer, the agency should have all the powers it would have had if it had made the initial decision.[43] This severe limitation on the powers and responsibilities of the hearing officer, coupled with an unfortunate series of contretemps in connection with the appointment of hearing examiners[44] led to results that satisfied no one. The Hoover Commission Task Force on Legal Services and Procedure recommended in 1955 that the hearing officers should be given status comparable to that of trial judges, with power to make the initial decision in each case; and further recommended that upon review of the initial decision of the hearing officer, the agency should (except for questions of policy delegated to the agency by Congress) have only those powers of review that a court has upon judicial review of agency decisions.[45]

Predictably, this may be the path of future developments. The main thrust of the Reorganization plans proposed by President Kennedy in 1961 was in this direction. Where those became effective—as in the case of the Federal Trade Commission—the status of the hearing officer has been substantially enhanced. Agency officials have become in recent years increasingly articulate in their criticism of the process of institutional decision, under which the role of the hearing examiner is in some senses subordinated to that of the staff, whose members—working in inaccessible anonymity on "the dark side of the moon" (to adopt Donald C. Beelar's phrase)—give the hearing examiner's report only such consideration as they choose, in their work of hammering out a proposed agency decision.[46] The Administrative Conference of the United States proposed[47] a system of limited agency review of examiners' initial decisions.

---

43 *Ibid.*

44 See Fuchs, *The Hearing Officer Problem, Symptom and Symbol,* 40 CORNELL L.Q. 281 (1954); Fuchs, *The Hearing Examiner Fiasco Under the Administrative Procedure Act,* 63 HARV. L. REV. 737 (1950); Thomas, *The Selection of Federal Hearing Examiners,* 59 YALE L.J. 431 (1949).

45 Commission on Organization of Executive Branch of Government, TASK FORCE REPORT ON LEGAL SERVICES AND PROCEDURE 203 (1955).

46 See, *e.g.,* Kintner, *Federal Administrative Law in the Decade of the Sixties,* 47 A.B.A.J. 269, 271 (1961).

47 Recommendation No. 9 of its Final Report (1962).

The lessons to be derived from the federal experience, and the example afforded by the California system, indicate a path that may be followed by state legislatures in devising methods appropriate to their own conditions whereby the status, responsibility, and powers of hearing examiners are increased. This need has been noted judicially. The Kentucky court, for example, after reviewing the rulings of a referee in an unemployment compensation case, remarked wistfully: "The procedure before the referee and the Commission illustrates the need for a uniform code of administrative procedures with trained and truly impartial referees or examiners who are independent of the various administrative bodies for which hearings are conducted."[48]

(D) EXTENT TO WHICH HEARING OFFICER SHOULD PARTICIPATE IN HEARING

The delicacy and difficulty of the hearing officer's task is emphasized by the responsibilities placed on him. He must, without deviating from an attitude of impartiality, see to it that there are fully developed on the record all the facts necessary to enable the agency to make a fully informed decision. As the Arizona court said, the hearing officer is "neither a protagonist nor an antagonist of the applicant. . . . It is his bounden duty in conducting these hearings to cause to be developed . . . by proper questions or other means then available to him, all the facts relating to applicant's claim. . . ."[49]

But the hearing officer is not to assume the duties of counsel for either party appearing before him;[50] and it has been suggested that he should avoid participating too actively in the hearing, because of the danger that he may develop an improper partisan attitude.[51] Indeed, it has been held that the hearing officer may not properly undertake to decide an issue injected on his own motion and in support of which he takes part in procuring evidence.[52]

---

48 Brown Hotel Co. v. Edwards, 365 S.W.2d 299, 301 (Ky. 1962).

49 Orosco v. Poarch, 70 Ariz. 432, 437, 222 P.2d 805 (1950), setting aside a denial of an application for workmen's compensation because the hearing officer had failed to develop facts to support applicant's case.

50 Griswold v. Department of Alcoholic Beverage Control, 141 Cal. App. 2d 807, 297 P.2d 762 (1956).

51 BENJAMIN, ADMINISTRATIVE ADJUDICATION IN THE STATE OF NEW YORK 111 (1942).

52 Deadwyler v. Consolidated Paper Co., 260 Mich. 130, 244 N.W. 484

(E) Effect of Injudicious Conduct by Hearing Officer

In an extreme case, injudicious conduct on the part of a hearing officer—if it is such as to intimidate witnesses and interfere with the proper presentation of evidence—may afford a basis for rehearing.[53] But it is rarely that charges of such misconduct are found to be sustained.[54]

Further, it appears that the state courts generally recognize the so-called "rule of necessity"—the doctrine that if the only officer competent to hear the case harbors a bias and prejudice which would ordinarily be disqualifying, he will still be allowed to hear the case, because of the necessity of having it heard to avoid a failure of justice.[55]

(F) Agency Not Bound by Findings of Hearing Officer

It is true in many state agencies, as in the federal agencies, that the hearing officer occupies an inferior position; and that the agency, acting through its staff employees, may redetermine *de novo* the facts found by the hearing officer, and rewrite his proposed decision.[56]

Some agencies, indeed, do not even permit the parties to see the hearing officer's report—it being considered a confidential document produced for the benefit of the agency and its staff.[57]

(1932). *Cf.* Lappinen v. Union Ore Co., 224 Minn. 395, 29 N.W.2d 8 (1947), holding that where proofs fail to support claimant's theory of recovery, but do support recovery on a different theory, it is the duty of the agency to proceed on the new theory. See also National Auto & Cas. Ins. Co. v. Downey, 98 Cal. App. 2d 586, 220 P.2d 962 (1950), and *In re* Erie R.R. Sys., 19 N.J. 110, 115 A.2d 89 (1955), both dealing with an asserted lack of proper participation.

[53] Jones v. State Dep't of Pub. Health & Welfare, 354 S.W.2d (Mo. App. 1962); *Cf.* Inland Steel Co. v. NLRB, 109 F.2d 9 (7th Cir. 1940).

[54] Kendall v. Board of Osteopathic Examiners, 105 Cal. App. 2d 239, 233 P.2d 107 (1951); West Coast Home Improvement Co. v. Contractors' State License Bd., 72 Cal. App. 2d 287, 164 P.2d 811 (1945).

[55] Scannell v. Wolff, 86 Cal. App. 2d 489, 195 P.2d 536 (1948); Caminetti v. Pacific Mut. Life Ins. Co., 22 Cal. 2d 344, 139 P.2d 908 (1943); Mayor of City of Everett v. Superior Court, 324 Mass. 144, 85 N.E.2d 214 (1949).

[56] Fort Pond Inn Co. v. Director of Div. of Employment Security, 324 Mass. 281, 86 N.E.2d 56 (1949); Schmoll v. J. W. Craig Co., 228 Minn. 429, 37 N.W.2d 539 (1949); Edmonds v. Skelly Oil Co., 204 Okla. 471, 231 P.2d 360 (1951); Kenny v. Esslinger's Brewery, 161 Pa. Super. 451, 55 A.2d 554 (1947).

[57] Greyhound Corp. v. Michigan Pub. Serv. Comm'n, 360 Mich. 578, 104 N.W.2d 395 (1960).

But a strong opinion by the New York court holds that the report of the hearing officer must be made available to the parties. That court explained the reasons for its decision by stating:

> The status and legal effect of the hearing officer's report are a reflection of the character of the hearing and the power of the officer himself. And, although the report would obviously carry no legal consequence without subsequent Authority action, the fact is that the procedure prescribed by the Authority constitutes its subsequent determination a form of administrative review of the hearing officer's findings rather than a primary determination.[58]

Section 5

Bias and Prejudice of Agency Members

(A) General Principles

It is frequently said that the complete impartiality of the tribunal which hears and decides the case is one of the prerequisites of a fair trial. Indeed, the United States Supreme Court has declared that an administrative agency exercising quasi-judicial powers "must, from the very nature of its duties, act with entire impartiality"[59] because "judgment ceases to be judicial if there is condemnation in advance of trial."[60] But this requirement of impartiality should not be taken as meaning that the agency must be indifferent to the result. So far as constitutional requirements are concerned, an agency may approach a hearing with a strong hope that a record may be built up which will permit the agency to enter an order, the desirability of which is to the agency a matter of predetermined conviction. The courts make a distinction between this type of emotional predisposition (which is not disqualifying) and a bias which results from personal animosities or personal interest.

This distinction is elusive and difficult. The difficulty is inherent in the very nature of administrative tribunals. Charged as they are with responsibility for the advancement of a particular public policy, their desire to enforce that policy renders it diffi-

---

[58] Matter of Sorrentino v. State Liquor Authority, 10 N.Y.2d 143, 149, 218 N.Y.S.2d 635, 176 N.E.2d 563 (1961).

[59] Humphrey's Ex'r v. United States, 295 U.S. 602, 624, 79 L. Ed. 1611, 55 Sup. Ct. 869 (1935).

[60] Escoe v. Zerbst, 295 U.S. 490, 494, 79 L. Ed. 1566, 55 Sup. Ct. 818 (1935).

cult for them to appraise with impassive objectivity the evidence adduced at the hearing. Their special experience and conviction may lead them to find claims clearly established on a record which would leave a disinterested judge in doubt.[61]

Ideally, the administrator should concern himself with his public duty to further broad statutory policies only when formulating regulations and general interpretive rulings, and should drop this attitude in favor of a strictly impartial, disinterested judicial approach in weighing the evidence presented at the hearing of a particular case.[62] But this idealism is rarely found. Administrative officers may strive for it, but in practice it is not easy to lay aside the role of the legislator for that of the judge when walking from the committee room to the hearing room.

(B) Bias Indicated by Combination of Functions of Prosecuting and Adjudicating

As noted in Chapter II,[63] the combination of prosecutory and adjudicatory functions in a single agency is not considered to be a violation of due process guarantees. However, a court may find a deprival of procedural due process if the circumstances of a particular case indicate that an excess of prosecutory zeal made it impossible for an agency to act impartially in judging the case it was prosecuting.

An instance is afforded by a decision of the West Virginia court[64] involving the revocation of a license to deal in used cars. It appeared that the commissioner of motor vehicles visited respondent's place of business and inspected his records. As a result of this inspection, he concluded that respondent was not complying with certain applicable statutory requirements. A hearing was noticed, and at the hearing, which was conducted before a deputy commissioner appointed by and responsible to the commissioner, the commissioner testified as to his investiga-

---

61 *Cf.*, Jaffe, *Invective and Investigation in Administrative Law,* 52 HARV. L. REV. 1201 (1939). It is true in the courts also, of course, that the views of particular judges on social and economic issues may predispose them to approach a particular question in different ways.

Cf., BENJAMIN, ADMINISTRATIVE ADJUDICATION IN THE STATE OF NEW YORK 22 (1942).

63 Section 2 (B).

64 State *ex rel.* Ellis v Kelly, 145 W. Va. 70, 75, 112 S.E.2d 641 (1960).

tion. On the basis of his testimony, the order of revocation was entered.

Noting that due process requires a fair hearing before an unbiased tribunal, the court said:

> It can hardly be contended that the commissioner, in the making of the investigation and in testifying before the deputy commissioner appointed by him and responsible to him, beyond any reasonable probability, did not become biased and prejudiced in the matter being heard. It would seem to be beyond human experience and expectation for impartiality to result where the officer is the investigator, prosecutor, witness, and trier of facts . . . the deputy commissioner could not have acted with impartiality in the consideration of relator's rights. His actions were for the commissioner, and could not be expected to be free and independent of his influence.

In holding that a combination of factors (including the receipt in evidence of the transcript of a prior informal investigation at which unsworn hearsay testimony had been received and which respondent had not been invited to attend) compelled the conclusion that there had been a denial of a fair trial, the Wisconsin court found objectionable the conduct of a member of the Board of Regents of State Colleges in acting at a hearing as both counsel and judge, where there was no necessity for assuming such a dual function.[65] The Pennsylvania court remarked that an attorney was deprived in disbarment proceedings of the fair hearing required by due process of law when a committee on offenses of a county bar association filed a complaint, and then appointed counsel to prosecute the complaint before its own subcommittee.[66]

However, in the absence of aggravated circumstances, the mere combination of prosecuting and adjudicatory functions is not considered to be productive of disqualifying bias. In a New Jersey case[67] involving the discharge of the business manager of a board of education, complaint was made of the fact that two members of the board who had been appointed by the board's president to make an investigation into the conduct of the busi-

---

[65] State *ex rel.* Ball v. McPhee, 6 Wis. 2d 190, 94 N.W.2d 711 (1959); *Cf.*, Reynolds v. Kirkland Police Comm'n, 62 Wash. 2d 720, 384 P.2d 819 (1963).

[66] Schlesinger Appeal, 404 Pa. 584, 172 A.2d 835 (1961). The court also found other defects in the hearing procedure, and held that in any event the testimony taken was insufficient as a matter of law to convict respondent on the charges brought against him.

[67] Mackler v. Board of Educ. of City of Camden, 16 N.J. 362, 108 A.2d 854 (1954).

ness manager, and who later signed a formal complaint against him, thereafter sat as members of the board in the hearing. The court held that their participation in the prosecution of the case did not disqualify them in the absence of a showing of malice or ill will, or any private interest in the outcome of the case. In a Kentucky case involving the revocation of a certificate of a CPA, the court answered charges that respondent had been denied a fair trial because the licensing board "acted as prosecutor, trier of facts, and judge of the controversy," by pointing out that the agency was authorized to initiate proceedings, and remarking that it must obviously make an investigation before deciding whether to file charges.[68]

In these cases where complaint is predicated on the combination of prosecutory and adjudicatory functions, the basic objection is that the agency officials responsible for the decision had made up their minds before the hearing. Exhibiting an attitude somewhat different from that of the federal courts,[69] some of the state courts indicate that if such charges can be established, the administrative order will be set aside.

The point may be illustrated by two Connecticut decisions involving a charge that the members of a zoning board had in fact concluded what their ruling would be, before hearings were held on proposed zoning changes. In one case[70] the court said:

> If the public hearing was had merely to comply with the statutory requirement and if the commission had theretofore resolved that, regardless of what might be developed by those in attendance, the zones were to be established as previously determined, the action of the commission might well be classified as arbitrary. The ultimate decision to effect a change in boundaries had to await the hearing, at which the public were privileged to express themselves.

The court found, however, that the charges had not been proved.

---

[68] Smith v. State Bd. of Accountancy, 271 S.W.2d 875 (Ky. 1954).

[69] *Cf.* Federal Trade Comm'n v. Cement Institute, 333 U.S. 683, 92 L. Ed. 1010, 68 Sup. Ct. 793 (1948).

[70] Couch v. Zoning Comm'n, 141 Conn. 349, 357, 106 A.2d 173 (1954); and see Lage v. Zoning Bd. of Appeals, 148 Conn. 597, 172 A.2d 911 (1961), holding that agency member should have disqualified himself because of previously expressed opinion. *Accord,* Barbara Realty Co. v. Zoning Bd. of Review, 85 R.I. 152, 128 A.2d 342 (1957).

This problem of proof was again considered in the second case[71] in which the court was divided as to whether appellants had sustained their burden of proving that the commission had in fact determined what its decision would be prior to the public hearing. The majority of the court sustained the finding of the trial court that the charges had not been proved.

The mere fact that the members of an agency entertained an opinion that probable cause exists for believing respondent guilty of a violation is not disqualifying.[72]

Suppose only one member of the agency has made up his mind, before the hearing, as to the merits of the case. Should he be required to disqualify himself, leaving it to the other members of the agency to rule on the case? It would seem that, on simple grounds of fairness, the answer should be *yes.* But if the recused member refuses to disqualify himself, it appears that—in the absence of appropriate statutory provision—the agency may be powerless to compel his disqualification. In a case where the chairman of a state public utility commission had issued press releases which were said to indicate strongly that he had already made up his mind about a pending case, and where respondent asked the other members of the commission to disqualify the chairman from sitting in the case, the Ohio court said that the commission had no power to disqualify one of its members, absent statutory authority.[73]

In general, it would appear that (absent a specific showing of facts clearly indicating that a fair trial was denied) the mere circumstance that an agency's interest in implementing predetermined policies may dictate the result in particular cases—and dictate, in such cases, a different result than would be reached on the same facts by a judge who was completely disinterested in the result—does not constitute the type of bias and prejudice which invalidates an administrative determination. But such invalidating bias is found to exist where it is established that the agency or a responsible official thereof has a personal or pecuniary

---

[71] Pecora v. Zoning Comm'n, 145 Conn. 435, 144 A.2d 48 (1958). It could be argued that because of factual differences, the Connecticut decisions are not necessarily inconsistent with the *Cement Institute* case, note 69 *supra.*

[72] Flannery Appeal, 406 Pa. 515, 178 A.2d 751 (1962).

[73] Ohio Transp. Inc. v. Public Utils. Comm'n, 164 Ohio St. 98, 128 N.E.2d 22 (1955). The opinion indicates that the court was not convinced that personal prejudice existed.

interest in a particular case, or where there exists a personal prejudice against a particular respondent, or where there has been such an interference with the presentation of evidence as to make it impossible for respondent fairly to present his case.

(C) Personal or Pecuniary Interest

Where a representative of an agency has a direct personal or pecuniary interest in the outcome of a case pending before the agency, he is of course disqualified to participate in the decision of the case. Where his interest is indirect, the same principle applies, but considerations of *de minimis* may be invoked where a collateral interest is so unsubstantial that it seems unlikely it would affect his decision.

Cases involving a direct pecuniary interest are not often encountered—presumably for the reason that instances seldom occur where an agency member stands to profit directly as a result of the agency's decision. In such cases, it has been acknowledged for many years that the officer must disqualify himself. In 1898, for example, the Illinois court held invalid an arrangement whereby tax assessors were paid a percentage of the amount collected—with the result that "the larger the assessment, the more compensation he would receive."[74]

More frequently encountered, and more difficult, are cases where the agency member's interest is indirect. On the whole, the state courts have exhibited diligence in disqualifying agency members even for an indirect interest, where it appears to be sufficiently substantial as to likely affect their determinations. An illustrative decision is that of the New Jersey court, holding that where Princeton University held a controlling interest in a municipal improvement corporation which owned property in a blighted area, the University was necessarily interested in the action taken with respect to rehabilitation of that area; and that consequently where two employees of the University sat as members of the municipal council before which the case was pending, and their vote was necessary for a quorum to designate the area as blighted, this circumstance was sufficient to disqualify them from acting in the matter.[75]

---

[74] Chase v. City of Evanston, 172 Ill. 403, 50 N.E. 241 (1898).
[75] Griggs v. Borough of Princeton, 33 N.J. 207, 162 A.2d 862 (1960).

Other cases in which an indirect financial interest has been held sufficient to require disqualification include: (a) two members of a town planning board who owned land zoned as industrial, and who consequently had an economic interest in denying such classification to appellant's lands, held disqualified;[76] (b) a member of a county board who would benefit from the establishment of a ditch held disqualified from participating even in preliminary proceedings looking to the establishment of the ditch;[77] (c) officer of a corporation with land for sale should not participate in proceedings to approve condemnation of property;[78] (d) member of zoning board held disqualified to vote for resolution which would benefit his property;[79] (e) agency member held disqualified where corporation employing him stood to benefit from agency action.[80]

In other cases, the courts have found the asserted interest to be so remote and contingent as not to work a disqualification.[81]

(D) Personal Bias or Prejudice

If an officer participating in the decision has a bias resulting from a predisposition for or against a particular party founded on purely personal affection or distrust, he is likewise disqualified. While the principle is clear, its application involves the same difficulties as those which plague the courts in cases involving recused judges.

Determining whether such a personal bias is involved is not easy. In one Connecticut case,[82] in setting aside an order of a zoning board because some of the members of the board were disqualified, the court said: "Public office is a trust conferred

[76] S & L Associates, Inc. v. Township of Washington, 35 N.J. 224, 172 A.2d 657 (1961); and see opinion of lower court, 61 N.J. Super. 312, 160 A.2d 635 (1960).

[77] *In re* Petition of Jacobson, 234 Minn. 296, 48 N.W.2d 441 (1951).

[78] Eways v. Reading Parking Authority, 385 Pa. 592, 124 A.2d 92 (1956) dictum; *Cf.* Application of Penny Hill Corp., 154 A.2d 888 (Del. 1959).

[79] Piggot v. Borough of Hopewell, 22 N.J. Super. 106, 91 A.2d 667 (1952).

[80] Aldom v. Borough of Roseland, 42 N.J. Super. 495, 127 A.2d 190 (1956); Pyatt v. Mayor & Council, 9 N.J. 548, 89 A.2d 1 (1952); *cf.*, Driscoll v. Burlington-Bristol Bridge Co., 8 N.J. 433, 86 A.2d 201 (1952); Lake De Smet Reservoir Co. v. Kaufmann, 75 Wyo. 87, 292 P.2d 482 (1956).

[81] Alford v. J. A. Jones Constr. Co., 313 S.W.2d 867 (Ky. 1958); Wilson v. City of Long Branch, 27 N.J. 360, 142 A.2d 837 (1958); Matthews v. Carolina Standard Corp., 232 N.C. 229, 60 S.E.2d 93 (1950).

[82] Mills v. Town Plan & Zoning Comm'n, 144 Conn. 493, 498, 134 A.2d 250 (1957).

by public authority for a public purpose. The status of each member of the commission forbids him from placing himself in a position where private interests conflict with his public duty." But in another zoning case, distinguishable on its facts, the court after carefully weighing the evidence, decided that bias had not been established.[83]

Such a disqualifying personal bias or prejudice has been found to exist in the following cases, many of which involved informal local bodies: (a) where a committee of doctors who recommended the revocation of the license of a physician who used the "Koch treatment" for cancer was composed of officers of the American Medical Association, which was waging a vigorous campaign against this form of treatment;[84] (b) a member of a zoning commission was held disqualified from voting on his wife's application;[85] (c) similarly, a member of a liquor license committee was disqualified to vote on an application filed by his brother;[86] (d) prior public statements of position may in some circumstances work a disqualification;[87] (e) an architect who was a member of a planning board which recommended an ordinance to a board of commissioners was disqualified from participating in the deliberations of the latter board;[88] (f) disqualification was found to exist where two out of the four board members sitting in a proceeding to remove a police officer (the fifth member being out of town) were also complaining witnesses.[89]

Sometimes a state agency is composed of businessmen who are themselves engaged in the very line of business which is subject to regulation by the agency. This practice necessarily gives rise to difficult and delicate problems. Concededly, the members of the agency have a very real interest in the decisions reached by the agency, for the decisions will directly affect each one of them in the conduct of his own daily business. If the regu-

---

[83] Isdale v. Town Plan & Zoning Comm'n, 141 Conn. 509, 107 A.2d 267 (1954).

[84] Smith v. Department of Registration & Educ., 412 Ill. 332, 106 N.E.2d 722 (1952).

[85] Low v. Town of Madison, 135 Conn. 1, 60 A.2d 774 (1948).

[86] Township Comm. v. Gelber, 26 N.J. Super. 388, 98 A.2d 63 (1953).

[87] Saks & Co. v. City of Beverly Hills, 107 Cal. App. 260, 237 P.2d 32 (1951).

[88] Bracey v. Long Branch, 73 N.J. Super. 91, 179 A.2d 63 (1962).

[89] Royal v. Police & Fire Comm'n of Ecorse, 345 Mich. 214, 75 N.W.2d 841 (1956).

lations to be adopted by such an agency will affect all companies engaged in that line of business in the same way, it seems to be assumed that the interest is not disqualifying; for in such case in protecting their own interests the members of the agency are at the same time protecting the similar interests of all their competitors.[90] But where a ruling which would be helpful to the members of the agency would be detrimental to other companies engaged in the same line of business, it is questionable whether the ruling should be sustained. The courts of California[91] and Michigan[92] have held invalid the delegation of price-fixing powers to industry boards under such circumstances. But the Florida court,[93] in a case where there was some representation of the public, upheld somewhat similar provisions.

Closely related to the problem posed by the industry-board cases discussed in the preceding paragraph is that encountered where adjudicatory responsibilities are vested in a so-called tri-partite commission, typically composed of one representative of management, one of labor, and one of the public. It is usually considered that the votes of two members of such an agency are committed before the case is heard; although perhaps this assumption is unjustified. But inevitably the basic idea of a tri-partite board is that it affords an opportunity for members representing opposed interests to negotiate mutually acceptable compromises; and this whole concept is at odds with the theory that administrative adjudication should be conducted on the same high level of impartiality as that on which the courts operate.[94] The Minnesota court has spoken rather vigorously in criticism of such tri-partite tribunals.[95]

---

90 *E.g.*, People v. Murphy, 364 Mich. 363, 110 N.W.2d 805 (1961).

91 State Bd. of Dry Cleaners v. Thrift-D-Lux Cleaners, 40 Cal. 2d 436, 254 P.2d 29 (1953).

92 Michigan Milk Marketing Bd. v. Johnson, 295 Mich. 644, 295 N.W. 346 (1940).

93 Miami Laundry Co. v. Florida Dry Cleaning & Laundry Bd., 134 Fla. 1, 183 So. 759, 119 A.L.R. 956 (1938).

94 See Board of Supervisors v. State Milk Comm'n, 191 Va. 1, 60 S.E.2d 35 (1950).

95 Johnson v. Village of Cohasset, 263 Minn. 425, 116 N.W.2d 692 (1962). In one interesting lower court case, the Ohio Common Pleas Court found that a rule of a state unemployment compensation commission, providing that no member of the appeal board should participate in the decision of an appeal "in which he has an interest which might prevent him from being impartial in the decision," was in conflict with the provisions of the statute, which provided that the appeal board should consist of one representative of employer interests, one of employee

(E) INTERFERENCE WITH PRESENTATION OF EVIDENCE

As the United States Supreme Court has pointed out,[96] the process of presenting evidence in hearings before administrative tribunals must be kept free from forces generating bias or intimidation. There is obviously a violation of this mandate if at the hearing the members of the agency adopt so partisan a manner or exhibit so obvious an attitude of bias as to interfere unduly with the presentation of evidence, to the end that the record does not fairly reflect the true factual situation. Such interference may take the form of interrogating witnesses in a manner so hostile as to intimidate them, or interrupting the examination of a witness so frequently as to interfere with the orderly presentation of his testimony, or interfering unduly with the cross-examination of witnesses, or exhibiting an abusive attitude toward witnesses or counsel or both, or sometimes, indeed, ordering the exclusion from the record of colloquies which show the general tone and character of the proceeding.

Of course, if such conduct can be shown to have affected the result, the objection of bias and prejudice is well taken. But ordinarily, the effect cannot be precisely measured, nor can it be demonstrated that actual harm resulted. At best, there is an inference, tenuous or persuasive in the particular case, that the result might have been otherwise if the hearing had been properly conducted. The question always is: How far must the respondent go in establishing that he has been harmed?

The prevailing view of the state courts is that unless the inference of probable injury is so strained as to be completely unimpressive, a rehearing should be ordered.

Thus, in one Missouri case, where the chairman of the industrial commission remarked to respondent's attorney at the hearing that he was losing his case (and where it appeared to the court that the agency's rulings on evidentiary offers had made it apparent that the commission had made up its mind on the matter before all the evidence was received), the court found that the ends of justice required remanding the case.[97]

---

interests, and one of public interests. Columbus Green Cabs, Inc. v. Board of Review, 184 N.E.2d 257 (Ohio 1961).

[96] NLRB v. Indiana & Michigan Elec. Co., 318 U.S. 9, 87 L. Ed. 579, 63 Sup. Ct. 394 (1943).

[97] City of Joplin v. Industrial Comm'n, 329 S.W.2d 687 (Mo. 1959).

Where agency members remarked that because police officers involved in suspension proceedings had refused to take lie detector tests, it could be assumed that they were lying, the Florida court found they had been denied a fair trial.[98]

A zoning board decision was reversed by the Michigan court upon a finding that the board's denial of a petition to erect a factory was influenced by the hostile reactions of observers at the hearing. The court said:

> It is apparent to us from this record that plaintiff-appellant never had other than a cursory (even though formally courteous) hearing before the township board. It appears to us that the fact issues were largely determined by the board under the impact of a completely committed audience reaction, and that plaintiff was denied its right under the zoning ordinance for a review of this decision by the zoning board of appeals.[99]

Where the member of a licensing board commented, near the close of the hearing, that the licensee's attorney "must believe his client is guilty as hell," the court noted that such a vehement expression reflected a biased attitude of mind and cast serious doubt on the impartiality of the hearing. Relying upon this and other factors, the court set aside the order.[100]

(F) Rule of Necessity

Where some or all of the members of an administrative agency[101] are disqualified by reason of prejudice from proceeding to hear and determine a pending case, a situation sometimes ensues where an alleged lawbreaker must be permitted to escape standing trial unless the agency is allowed to proceed notwithstanding its bias. The great majority of the state court decisions sustain the proposition that in such cases what has been called

---

98 City of Miami v. Jervis, 139 So. 2d 513 (Fla. 1962).

99 Certain-Teed Prods. Corp. v. Paris Township, 351 Mich. 434, 448, 88 N.W.2d 705 (1958).

100 Harris v. Board of Registration in Chiropody (Podiatry), 343 Mass. 536, 179 N.E.2d 910 (1962).

101 The cases are not in agreement as to the effect of the participation in a decision by disqualified members, if there remain a quorum of members who are not disqualified. *Cf.* Thompson v. City of Long Beach, 41 Cal. 2d 235, 259 P.2d 649 (1953); Low v. Town of Madison, 135 Conn. 1, 60 A.2d 774 (1948); Pyatt v. Mayor & Council, note 80 *supra.*

"the stern rule of necessity" requires the agency to act.[102] A few early cases reach a contrary result.[103]

Inasmuch as the doctrine disqualifying a tribunal for prejudice is based on the mere likelihood of an erroneous determination, the majority rule seems clearly proper. It does not necessarily follow that a biased tribunal will decide a case incorrectly. The officers may be presumed to make an honest effort to carry out their sworn obligation to decide the case fairly.

Further, where the doctrine of necessity is invoked, the reviewing court will examine the decision with particular care and diligence, for the courts exercise an inherent judicial power to vary the scope of review to meet the necessities of the situation, considering "appropriate for judicial review" every question of fact or law on which it seems best that the court should pass. The reviewing court can thus, in many cases, correct any miscarriage of justice that might otherwise have resulted. This may be seen in a pair of decisions of the New Jersey court. After first refusing to enjoin the conduct of administrative proceedings in which an allegedly biased officer would participate (basing its refusal on the doctrine of necessity), the court thereafter reviewed the resulting administrative order and reversed it on the ground that the evidence did not support the agency's findings.[104]

The opportunity for utilizing the process of judicial review to correct unjust results that may flow from the application of the doctrine of necessity was pointed out by the Wisconsin court.[105] After noting that "it appears quite clearly that the Commission was heading toward a predetermined conclusion," the court said that it would therefore scrutinize the agency's determination with especial care, noting that under "such circumstances the evidence necessary clearly and satisfactorily to

---

[102] Bridges v. McCorvey, 254 Ala. 677, 49 So. 2d 546 (1950); Caminetti v. Pacific Mut. Life Ins. Co., 22 Cal. 2d 344, 139 P.2d 908 (1943); Bourgeois v. Orleans Parish School Bd., 219 La. 512, 53 So. 2d 251 (1951); Board of Medical Examiners v. Steward, 203 Md. 574, 102 A.2d 248 (1954); Borough of Fanwood v. Rocco, 33 N.J. 404, 165 A.2d 183 (1960); Emerson v. Hughes, 117 Vt. 270, 90 A.2d 910 (1952); Evans v. Charles, 133 W. Va. 463, 56 S.E.2d 880 (1949).

[103] State *ex rel.* Miller v. Aldridge, 212 Ala. 660, 103 So. 835 (1925); Abrams v. Jones, 35 Idaho 532, 207 Pac. 724 (1922).

[104] Rinaldi v. Mongiello, 6 N.J. Super. 387, 71 A.2d 404 (1950); 4 N.J. Super. 7, 66 A.2d 182 (1949); 7 N.J. Super. 410, 71 A.2d 398 (1949).

[105] Wisconsin Tel. Co. v. Public Serv. Comm'n, 232 Wis. 274, 324, 329, 287 N.W. 593 (1939).

establish the fact that the findings of the Commission were wrong is much less than it would otherwise be. . . ."

Of course, if there is anyone else who can act in the place of the disqualified officers, such substitution of personnel should be required.[106]

Another device which is open to the agencies, to avoid the appearances of unfairness that are concomitant with the application of the doctrine of necessity, is to appoint a special hearing officer or panel to receive the evidence and make recommendations to the members of the agency as to the proper disposition of the case. By utilizing such procedure in cases where some of the members of the agency are prejudiced, it is possible to afford the respondent the opportunity of presenting his evidence and arguing his case before individuals who do not share this prejudice. Their recommendations to the agency members who must decide would be unaffected by any improper interest; and by relying on such recommendations the members of the agency can more easily overcome the effect of their personal prejudices.

One aspect of the doctrine of necessity has to do with the question whether, when a court reverses an administrative decision and remands the case to the agency for further consideration, the members of the agency should be disqualified from reconsidering the case in situations where some prejudice might arguably be inferred from the circumstance that they had already committed themselves publicly to a position which the reviewing court had found to be erroneous. The cases seem to be agreed that this circumstance does not disqualify the agency from reconsidering the case on remand.[107]

(G) Requirements as to Time, Place, and Manner of Holding the Hearing

Requirements as to the time of holding a hearing are ordinarily a subject for the rules of the agency. Those rules, in the case of most state agencies, leave it to the agency's discretion as to

---

[106] Smith v. Department of Registration & Educ., 412 Ill. 332, 106 N.E.2d 722 (1952).

[107] Aluisi v. County of Fresno, 178 Cal. App. 2d 443, 2 Cal. Rptr. 779 (1960); Board of Medical Examiners v. Steward, 203 Md. 574, 102 A.2d 248 (1954); Plainfield-Union Water Co. v. Borough of Mountainside, 14 N.J. 296, 102 A.2d 1 (1954); Borough of Vandergrift v. Polito, 407 Pa. 286, 180 A.2d 215 (1962).

when the hearing shall be had; and it is infrequently that an abuse of discretion is found to exist.

It is required, however, that respondent be given sufficient advance notice of the time of hearing in order to enable him properly to prepare his case.[108] Where an agency dismissed a complaint seeking the revocation of a dentist's license, but thereafter without notice to the dentist granted an *ex parte* request to reopen the hearing, and then revoked his license on the basis of the testimony of a surprise witness, it was held that the *ex parte* reopening of the proceedings without notice as to the nature of the additional evidence to be considered made it an unfair hearing.[109]

If the hearing is set for an earlier date than respondent desires, and his request for an adjournment of the hearing is denied, and as a result the case is heard before he is fully prepared, he cannot expect relief from the courts except in a clear case of abuse of discretion.[110]

Sometimes, *per contra,* respondent complains of assertedly unreasonable delays on the part of the agency in calling the case for hearing. Here again, great deference is paid to the agency's discretion;[111] but the state courts follow the federal courts[112] in holding that if an agency's unreasonable delay in bringing a case to hearing results in a continuing confiscation of respondent's rights of property, there is a deprival of procedural due process.[113] In one California decision,[114] an agency was held to be in error in dismissing a case because of the opposite party's delay in seeking a hearing on his petition.

Connected with the problem of fixing the time of the hearing is that of consolidating a number of separate cases for joint

---

108 Related questions are discussed in Ch. X.

109 Bruce v. Department of Registration & Educ., 26 Ill. 2d 612, 187 N.E.2d 711 (1963).

110 Meneley v. Carpenter, 129 N.E.2d 516 (Ohio App. 1954); State Bd. of Medical Educ. & Licensure v. Williams, 172 Pa. Super. 448, 94 A.2d 61 (1953)—both upholding denial of continuances; *cf.* Emerson v. Hughes, 117 Vt. 270, 90 A.2d 910 (1952).

111 Texas State Highway Dep't v. Pritchett, 155 Tex. 383, 287 S.W.2d 938 (1956).

112 Smith v. Illinois Bell Tel. Co., 270 U.S. 587, 70 L. Ed. 747, 46 Sup. Ct. 408 (1926).

113 Iowa-Illinois Gas & Elec. Co. v. Perrine, 351 Ill. App. 195, 114 N.E.2d 572 (1953) (dictum).

114 Pearson v. County of Los Angeles, 49 Cal. 2d 523, 319 P.2d 624 (1957).

hearings. Where the issues are similar, and it is convenient for the agency to hold a consolidated hearing, its discretion in so doing will not be disturbed in the absence of a clear showing of irreparable harm to the parties opposing the consolidation.[115] But the courts stand ready to remedy an abuse of discretion. In a North Dakota case[116] a railroad petitioned the state public service commission for permission to curtail a branch line service; and at the same time an affiliated company sought permission to inaugurate a substitute truck-bus service. The two petitioners requested that the petitions be heard together, alleging that the net result of granting both petitions would be to afford better service to the public. The agency, however, refused to grant a consolidated hearing. It then proceeded to deny the application of the railroad because there was a need for service to the area served by the branch lines. Thereafter, it denied the petition of the transport company because there was already adequate service provided by the railroad. The court held this to constitute an abuse of discretion, pointing out that the agency by considering the related applications without reference to each other was begging the real question involved.[117]

Problems as to the place of the hearing do not frequently arise in the case of state agencies. The agency usually holds the hearing at such place as will be most convenient for the majority of the witnesses and will afford most convenient access to the records which the agency desires to examine; and distances within a state are not ordinarily so great that the holding of a hearing in one city rather than another would deprive a party of a reasonable opportunity to present his case. Presumably, if it were made to appear that the selection of the place of hearing was motivated by a desire to handicap respondent, the state courts would doubtless follow the federal courts[118] in holding that such procedures, if they in fact deprived respondent of

---

[115] Application of Chicago, B. & Q. R.R., 154 Neb. 281, 47 N.W.2d 577 (1951); Alamo Express, Inc. v. Union City Transfer, 158 Tex. 234, 309 S.W.2d 815 (1958).

[116] Northern Pac. R. v. Anderson, 95 N.W.2d 582 (N.D. 1959).

[117] *Cf.* Armstrong v. Commercial Carriers, Inc., 341 Mich. 45, 67 N.W.2d 194 (1954).

[118] *E.g.,* NLRB v. Prettyman, 117 F.2d 786 (6th Cir. 1941); Jeffries v. Olesen, 121 F.Supp. 463 (S. D. Cal. 1954); *But cf.,* NLRB v. Southwestern Greyhound Lines, Inc., 126 F.2d 883 (8th Cir. 1942).

a fair trial, would be a basis for setting aside the administrative action.[119]

Normally, administrative hearings are open to the public; and it is ordinarily desirable that this be so, for public observation of open hearings offers some assurance that those hearings will be conducted in a manner satisfactory to the public and to the parties.[120]

Occasionally, however, a question arises whether an agency may order a private hearing over the protests of respondent, who desires that his case be tried in public. It would seem that an agency should have the same measure of discretion as that reposed in a trial court in ordering the exclusion of the public on any proper ground (*e.g.*, where scandalous matters will be aired); but the question cannot be said to be settled.[121]

Contrariwise, situations may arise where the due protection of the interests of respondent requires that publicity be avoided (as where public knowledge of the pendency of a proceeding might in itself be damaging to reputation or business, or where the hearing concerns personal or financial matters or business secrets that respondent would not wish to have publicly disclosed). In such cases, may insistence by the agency upon a public hearing deprive respondent of a fair trial? It would seem that such a possibility exists; and presumably the state courts would insist that in such cases it is the duty of the agency to protect the respondent's privilege of privacy by some method appropriate to the particular case.[122]

---

119 *Cf.*, Dierks Lumber & Coal Co. v. Holmes, 201 Okla. 545, 207 P.2d 935 (1949), where the agency's selection of a place of hearing inconvenient to respondent reflected a desire to avoid exhausting its travel expense fund; the agency action was upheld.

120 BENJAMIN, ADMINISTRATIVE ADJUDICATION IN THE STATE OF NEW YORK 126 (1942).

121 There are of course, limits on the power of a court to exclude the public from a trial, over the protests of the party being tried. People v. Jelke, 308 N.Y. 56, 123 N.E.2d 769 (1954). In *State Tax Comm'n v. El Paso Natural Gas Co.*, 73 Ariz. 43, 236 P.2d 1026 (1951), it was held that an agency erred in deciding a case on the basis of an informal conference, where the statute provided for a public hearing.

122 *Cf.* two federal cases, which are not really dispositive of the problem but have a significant bearing: American Sumatra Tobacco Corp. v. SEC, 93 F.2d 236 (App. D.C. 1937); E. Griffiths Hughes, Inc. v. Federal Trade Comm'n, 61 App. D.C. 386, 63 F.2d 362 (1933).

CHAPTER XII

CONTESTED CASES: THE HEARING

Section 1

Presumptions and Burden of Proof

(A) Burden of Proof

Neither the original nor the Revised Model State Act contains a provision like that of Section 7(c) of the Federal Administrative Procedure Act,[1] setting forth specifically that "except as statutes otherwise provide, the proponent of a rule or order shall have the burden of proof." In most states, therefore (except as statutes creating named agencies make specific provisions as to the burden of proof in proceedings before such agencies), it is for the courts to decide whether administrative agencies must be governed by the same rules respecting the burden of proof as apply in court proceedings.

The state courts quite uniformly impose on agencies the customary common-law rule that the moving party has the burden of proof, including not only the burden of going forward but also the burden of persuasion. This means, of course, that when an applicant appears before an agency seeking to establish a claim or obtain a license, the burden is on him.[2] Conversely, when the agency is the moving party, the burden is on it.[3]

These principles have been applied by the state courts in a wide variety of situations. In zoning cases, for example, the person seeking a variance from the requirements of the applicable

1 5 U.S.C. § 1006(c); F.C.A. 5 § 1006(c).

2 Martin v. Alcoholic Beverage Control Appeals Bd., 52 Cal. 2d 259, 341 P.2d 291 (1959); Southern California Jockey Club, Inc. v. California Horse Racing Bd., 36 Cal. 2d 167, 223 P.2d 1 (1950); Crossroads Recreation, Inc. v. Broz, 4 N.Y.2d 39, 172 N.Y.S.2d 129, 149 N.E.2d 65 (1958); *e.g.*, State *ex rel.* Utilities Comm'n v. Carolina Power & Light Co., 250 N.C. 421, 109 S.E.2d 253 (1959); Cupps v. City of Toledo, 172 Ohio St. 536, 179 N.E.2d 70 (1961).

3 *E.g.*, Cornell v. Reilly, 127 Cal. App. 2d 178, 273 P.2d 572 (1954); Pennsylvania Labor Relations Bd. v. Sansom House Enterprises, Inc., 378 Pa. 385, 106 A.2d 404 (1954).

ordinance has the burden of establishing that the application of the ordinance would impose upon him an unnecessary hardship.[4] In rate cases before a state public utilities commission, the burden of justifying a rate increase is on the utility seeking it.[5] A public employee protesting a discharge or demotion has the burden of proving that the action of his employer was arbitrary or discriminatory.[6]

An important question is: Do the courts or the agencies decide whether the moving party has met the burden of proof thus imposed? If, in a case where the burden is on the agency, the power were given it to decide conclusively whether it had sustained the burden of proof imposed on it, it would not be surprising if its own proofs of what it alleged would satisfy the agency as to the existence of facts that it believed to be true even before the hearing opened. Thus, the agency, by finding that any showing its counsel might make was sufficient to establish at least a prima facie case, could in effect shift the burden of proof to respondent. Indeed, counsel for respondents often complain that agencies in fact do this; and that the respondent, if he hopes to win his case, must assume the burden of introducing proof sufficient to convince the agency that its original appraisal of the facts was in error.

The state courts, however, seek to alleviate this danger by insisting that whether the burden of proof has been met is a question for the courts to determine. True, they ordinarily accept the decision of the agency as to whether the party charged with the burden of proof has sustained it.[7] However, the courts quite frequently exercise their prerogative of determining for themselves whether the proponent has satisfied the burden of proof, and reverse the agency's finding on this point if it appears clearly erroneous. Thus, where a real estate commission had imposed a disciplinary order against a broker without having undertaken to prove an essential element of the charge (that the broker's associate was not registered) the Florida court set

---

[4] Crossroads Recreation, Inc. v. Broz, note 2 *supra;* Nicholson v. Zoning Bd. of Adjustment, 392 Pa. 278, 140 A.2d 604 (1958); *In re* Volpe's Appeal, 384 Pa. 374, 121 A.2d 97 (1956).

[5] Central R.R. of New Jersey v. Department of Pub. Utils., 7 N.J. 247, 81 A.2d 162 (1951).

[6] Smith v. School Dist. of Darby, 388 Pa. 301, 130 A.2d 661 (1957).

[7] Massachusetts Bonding & Ins. Co. v. Industrial Comm'n, 8 Wis. 2d 606, 99 N.W.2d 809 (1959).

aside the order on the ground that the commission had not discharged its burden of proof. In so holding, the court overruled the agency's assertion that it could take notice of its own records to establish this asserted fact.[8] Similarly, the Tennessee court set aside an administrative order for the forfeiture of an automobile because of unstamped whiskey found in the car, since the agency had failed to satisfy its burden of proving that the whiskey was in the car for distribution, gift, or sale.[9] Again, the Pennsylvania court reversed an order of the state labor relations board finding that an employer had committed an unfair labor practice, the court ruling that the board had not satisfied the burden of proof imposed on it.[10] Such decisions are of especial significance. They demonstrate that in some instances, at least, agencies do—as any party in interest might be expected to do—exhibit a tendency to find without adequate justification that they have satisfied the burden of proof imposed on them, thus shifting the burden to the private party, who is in effect presumed guilty until he establishes his innocence. Insistence upon the right of the courts to review agency decisions as to the fulfillment of the proponent's burden of proof is therefore a matter of substantial importance.

In several types of cases, the courts have reversed agency determinations to the effect that a party appearing before the agency in a contested case involving two private parties had satisfied the burden of proof imposed on him as proponent. Thus, the courts have reversed agency decisions that applicants for workmen's compensation had satisfied the burden of proof imposed on them to support their claims for compensation.[11] Similarly, the courts have reversed findings that the petitioner in a matter before a public utilities commission had satisfied the burden imposed on him as proponent of an order.[12] Similar rulings have been made in unemployment compensation cases.[13]

---

[8] Thorn v. Florida Real Estate Comm'n, 146 So. 2d 907 (Fla. 1962).

[9] MacFarland v. Wofford, 211 Tenn. 309, 364 S.W.2d 914 (1962).

[10] Pennsylvania Labor Relations Bd. v. Elk Motor Sales Co., 388 Pa. 173, 130 A.2d 501 (1957).

[11] Larsen Co. v. Industrial Comm'n, 9 Wis. 2d 386, 101 N.W.2d 129 (1960); Turner v. State Compensation Comm'r, 126 S.E.2d 379 (W. Va. 1962).

[12] Boyd v. Arkansas Motor Freight Lines, Inc., 222 Ark. 599, 262 S.W.2d 282 (1953); Berner v. Pennsylvania Pub. Util. Comm'n, 382 Pa. 622, 116 A.2d 738 (1955).

[13] *E.g.,* Producers Produce Co. v. Industrial Comm'n, 365 Mo. 996, 291 S.W. 2d 166 (1956).

In a few instances, a party whose claim is denied on the basis that he failed to satisfy his burden of proof, has appealed on the unusual ground that there is no substantial evidence to support the finding of the agency denying his claim. In such cases, of course, there is no need for the agency to point to substantial evidence supporting its finding denying the claim. Since the burden rests on the claimant, it is enough that he has failed to establish the existence of the facts he must prove.[14]

The question as to whether proponent has satisfied the burden of proof is often involved in workmen's compensation cases. It appears to be well settled that the burden is on the claimant to establish the facts which entitle him to compensation,[15] and also the amount of compensation to which he is entitled.[16] However, the burden of establishing affirmative defenses, such as the claim that the injury resulted from intoxication or from wilful violation of safety rules, is on the employer.[17]

The same principles prevail in unemployment compensation cases. The claimant must bear the burden of proving his eligibility and availability for work,[18] and the employer has the burden of proving the existence of disqualifying circumstances.[19] Because of the vagueness of the labor dispute disqualification in many state statutes (resulting from wholesale adoption of draft language early suggested by the federal social security agency, which can most charitably be described as ambivalent), it is almost impossible to ascertain from the statutory language on

---

[14] May Dep't Stores Co. v. State Tax Comm'n, 308 S.W.2d 748 (Mo. 1958); Copeland v. Oklahoma Employment Security Comm'n, 197 Okla. 429, 172 P.2d 420 (1946).

[15] Duke v. Pekin Wood Prods. Co., 223 Ark. 182, 264 S.W.2d 834 (1954); Collier v. Wright, 340 S.W.2d 597 (Ky. 1960); Nielsen v. Industrial Comm'n, 14 Wis. 2d 112, 109 N.W.2d 483 (1961).

[16] Warner v. Industrial Comm'n, 85 Ariz. 150, 333 P.2d 733 (1958); Gallagher v. Industrial Comm'n, 9 Wis. 2d 361, 101 N.W.2d 72 (1960).

[17] Massachusetts Bonding & Ins. Co. v. Industrial Comm'n, note 7 *supra;* M. W. Martin, Inc. v. Industrial Comm'n, 13 Wis. 2d 574, 109 N.W.2d 92 (1961).

[18] Ashford v. Appeal Board of Michigan Unemployment Compensation Comm'n, 328 Mich. 428, 43 N.W.2d 918 (1950); Brown Hotel Co. v. Edwards, 365 S.W.2d 299 (Ky. 1962).

[19] Ault v. Unemployment Compensation Bd. of Review, 398 Pa. 250, 157 A.2d 375 (1960); Michigan Tool Co. v. Employment Security Comm'n, 346 Mich. 673, 78 N.W.2d 571 (1956).

whom the burden of proof is placed in such cases. The problem has troubled several courts.[20]

When a party on whom is placed the primary burden of proof has made a prima facie case, it is usually held that the burden of going forward with the proofs shifts to the opposite party (although the burden of ultimate persuasion does not); and the opposite party must introduce proofs to counter the prima facie case made by the proponent.[21] The courts decide whether such a prima facie case has been established,[22] and whether it has been overcome.[23]

(B) Presumptions

In many administrative proceedings, the burden of proof is affected by presumptions of various types, including statutory presumptions, presumptions as to the validity of official action, and presumptions based on inferences from circumstantial evidence.

Typical of statutory presumptions are those found in the workmen's compensation acts of several states creating a presumption in favor of the claimant. The early approach of some of the state courts was to conveniently ignore such presumption statutes, giving them no effect in shifting the burden of proof.[24] However, a significant change was wrought by the decision of the United States Supreme Court in *Del Vecchio v. Bowers,*[25] wherein the court held that the presumption created by such a statute is sufficient to carry claimant's burden of proof, in the complete absence of evidence; but that it does not have the quality of affirmative evidence, and that once evidence is introduced to rebut the statutory presumption, the presumption falls out of the case, which must then be decided entirely upon the basis of the evidence in the record and the inferences which the agency derives

---

[20] See, *e.g.,* Cennamo v. Adm'r, 22 Conn. Sup. 302, 170 A.2d 739 (1961); Michigan Tool Co. v. Employment Security Comm'n, note 19 *supra;* Little Rock Furniture Mfg. Co. v. Commissioner of Labor, 227 Ark. 288, 298 S.W.2d 56 (1957).

[21] Coleman v. Watts, 81 So. 2d 650 (Fla. 1955).

[22] Walker v. Lebanon Stone Co., 312 Ky. 625, 229 S.W.2d 163 (1950).

[23] Miller v. Department of Revenue, 408 Ill. 574, 97 N.E.2d 788 (1951).

[24] *E.g.,* Joseph v. United Kimono Co., 194 App. Div. 568, 185 N.Y.S. 700 (1921).

[25] 296 U.S. 280, 80 L. Ed. 229, 56 Sup. Ct. 190 (1935).

therefrom. This is now apparently the prevailing view in the state courts.[26]

The same approach is followed in the case of presumptions based on the assumed correctness of official action. Thus, the Missouri court held that a presumption of validity attaches to a tax assessment, and a taxpayer alleging over-assessment or discrimination must present substantial evidence in order to overcome that presumption of regularity.[27] But when such evidence is introduced, then the burden shifts to the agency. Thus, in a case involving the presumed correctness of a tax assessment, the Illinois court held that when the presumption was overcome by evidence submitted by the taxpayer, the taxing officials had the burden of proving their case by a preponderance of substantial evidence.[28]

Where the evidence introduced on behalf of proponent is merely circumstantial, it is often said that the inference derived therefrom gives rise to a rebuttable presumption of fact. If no substantial evidence is introduced to rebut the presumption, an award may be based thereon.[29] But when evidence is introduced to rebut the presumption, the burden of persuasion reverts to the proponent.[30]

In cases where the circumstantial evidence is equally balanced, so that an inference imposing liability and a countervailing inference which would negate liability are equally persuasive, a question sometimes arises whether the agency is free to choose which inference it will make.

Early decisions[31] indicated that in such cases it was the duty of the agency to choose the inference which resulted in a negation of liability. In cases where the record is substantially barren of evidence, and there is no really substantial basis for any inference, this result still obtains.[32] But where testimony is offered by each party which affords a reasonable circumstantial

---

[26] *E.g.,* Cellurale's Case, 333 Mass. 37, 127 N.E.2d 787 (1955).
[27] Cupples Hesse Corp. v. State Tax Comm'n, 329 S.W.2d 696 (Mo. 1959).
[28] Goldfarb v. Department of Revenue, 411 Ill. 573, 104 N.E.2d 606 (1952).
[29] Martin v. Industrial Comm'n, 73 Ariz. 401, 242 P.2d 286 (1952).
[30] Meade v. State Compensation Comm'r, 125 S.E.2d 771 (W. Va. 1962).
[31] Such as Joseph v. United Kimono Co., note 24 *supra.*
[32] Fries v. Kalamazoo Stove & Furnace Co., 338 Mich. 65, 61 N.W.2d 87 (1953); Wiltse v. Borden's Farm Prods. Co., 328 Mich. 257, 43 N.W.2d 842 (1950).

basis for a conclusion favoring that party, probably most state courts would hold that, as the United States Supreme Court put it, if the evidence "permits an inference either way upon the question . . . the . . . Commissioner and he alone is empowered to draw the inference."[33] In other words, the problem is avoided by leaving it to the agency to determine whether the inferences are in fact equally balanced.[34] The problem does not often become important; in most cases there is substantial evidence in the record which would support a decision either way; and then the question becomes whether the findings of the agency are supported by substantial evidence.

Section 2

Respondent's Right To Meet Agency's Case

(A) General Principles

One of the indispensable requisites of a fair hearing is that the course of the proceeding shall be such that the party appearing before the agency "shall have an opportunity to be heard and cross examine the witnesses against him and shall have time and opportunity at a convenient place, after the evidence against him is produced and known to him, to produce evidence and witnesses to refute the charges."[35] This general requirement was well described in an opinion of the Kentucky court, which (citing decisions from several states) observed that the right to a hearing embraces not only the right to give evidence, but also the right to know the charges seasonably, so as to be able to meet them with competent evidence, and the right to be heard in argument as to the probative force of the evidence.[36] Similarly, the Arizona court declared:

> The function of the Commission . . . is judicial in its nature and is governed by the same general principles as the judgments of the courts. . . . One of these principles is that every person is entitled

---

[33] Del Vecchio v. Bowers, note 25 *supra*.

[34] St. Joseph's Hosp. v. Wisconsin Employment Relations Bd., 264 Wis. 396, 59 N.W.2d 448 (1953); Enderby v. Industrial Comm'n, 12 Wis. 2d 91, 106 N.W.2d 315 (1960).

[35] NLRB v. Prettyman, 117 F.2d 786, 790 (6th Cir. 1941).

[36] Mayfield Gas Co. v. Public Serv. Comm'n, 259 S.W.2d 8 (Ky. 1953).

to his day in court, and the opportunity to present one's case fully and freely at least once before an impartial tribunal.[37]

(B) Right to Know Theory of Agency's Case

Obviously, respondent cannot properly meet the agency's case against him unless he is advised of the theory on which the agency is proceeding. It is not enough that respondent be served with a complaint setting forth the charge in language as broad as that of the statute under which the proceedings are brought. If respondent needs more information, so as to be able to understand the real thrust of the agency's case (in order to prepare his own proofs in opposition) he is entitled to have such information, and to have it in ample time to permit him to prepare for the hearing.

These principles have been recognized in many state court cases. Thus, where a teacher was notified that the board of education proposed to cancel her contract because her services had been "unsatisfactory and incompetent," and she protested that this information was too vague to permit her properly to marshal her proofs for the hearing, the order of dismissal was set aside.[38] Again, when a committee of a state board of law examiners, investigating the moral fitness of an applicant, summoned him to appear "for interrogation," but declined to advise him of the information on the basis of which it doubted his moral character, in sufficient detail to enable him adequately to present his defense, the Florida court held he had been denied a fair hearing.[39] Similar principles were applied by the Louisiana appellate court in an unemployment compensation case. Claimant's right to benefits had been challenged on the ground that he had been discharged for misconduct in connection with his work, specifically, violation of a rule as to the use of automobiles. He came to the hearing prepared to defend this charge, and in fact established a defense. But at the hearing it was urged that he had also been guilty of other instances of misconduct, including failure to follow instructions. He was not

---

[37] Martin v. Industrial Comm'n, 88 Ariz. 14, 19, 352 P.2d 352 (1960); Rodriquez v. Utilities Engineering & Constr. Co., 281 P.2d 946 (Okla. 1955).

[38] County Bd. of Educ. v. Oliver, 270 Ala. 107, 116 So. 2d 566 (1959). The decision was based in part on a statute which required that the teacher be furnished a detailed statement of the reasons for discharge.

[39] Coleman v. Watts, 81 So. 2d 650 (Fla. 1955).

prepared to meet this new theory, and lost his case. The court held this amounted to a denial of a fair hearing.[40] The California court summarized the requirement by saying: "The action of such an administrative board exercising adjudicatory functions when based upon information of which the parties were not apprised and which they had no opportunity to controvert amounts to a denial of a hearing."[41]

(C) Right to Examine Opposed Evidence

Not only is respondent entitled to timely advice of the theory of the case against him, but he has a right to examine the opposing evidence. He may insist that the agency advise him, by specific reference, of those parts of its files and records and reports on which it intends to rely in reaching a decision in the particular adversary proceeding with which he is concerned. While he does not have a right to delve and pry into all the records of the agency, or to examine secret reports of the agency's investigators, still all the material upon which the agency proposes to rely as establishing facts in the pending case should be open for his inspection.

The California court set forth the principle in these words:

> Administrative tribunals exercising quasi-judicial powers which are required to make a determination after a hearing cannot act on their own information. Nothing may be treated as evidence which has not been introduced as such, inasmuch as a hearing requires that the party be apprised of the evidence against him in order that he may refute, test and explain it.[42]

Application of these principles may be seen in a decision of the New Jersey court.[43] In a case involving objections by municipal assessing officers to a tax equalization schedule adopted by the county board of taxation, the county board failed to disclose to the municipal assessors the data which had been used to determine average assessment ratios, and failed to afford the municipal assessors a fair opportunity to study such data in order

---

[40] King v. Brown, 115 So. 2d 405 (La. App. 1959).

[41] English v. City of Long Beach, 35 Cal. 2d 155, 158, 217 P.2d 22 (1950).

[42] La Prade v. Department of Water & Power, 27 Cal. 2d 47, 51, 162 P.2d 13 (1945).

[43] Borough of Little Ferry v. Bergen County Bd. of Taxation, 18 N.J. 400, 113 A.2d 768 (1955).

to determine how they could best seek to refute it. Because of this deprival of the right to examine the opposing evidence under circumstances which would permit them to prepare their own proofs, the court set aside the equalization schedules, and ordered that new ones be prepared.

A violation of respondent's right to examine the opposing evidence may occur in cases where the agency relies on information furnished it *ex parte,* or information found in its own files. Thus, in a New Jersey case involving a contested application for permission to open a branch office of a savings and loan association, the court held that appellant had been improperly deprived of the right to know the evidence against it, where the agency relied in part on information furnished it *ex parte,* and on data in its own files, and on staff investigation reports which had not been made a part of the record at the hearing.[44] Other New Jersey cases further illustrate the point. Where a conservation commission heard testimony on an application concerning the creation of a municipal water supply system, and thereafter referred the matter to its engineering staff, which made a report containing assertions of many facts which had not been testified to at the hearing, it was held that the resulting denial of appellant's right to examine the evidence opposing its application required a reversal of the agency order.[45] Similarly, in a case involving the adoption of safety rules by a public utilities commission, the court held it error (although it was held to be nonprejudicial error, under the particular circumstances) for the agency to rely on information obtained as a result of investigations in related cases, without incorporating such information into the record and giving the interested parties an opportunity to examine it, and explain or refute it.[46]

It is noteworthy that the two last cited cases involved matters in which the agency's function was essentially legislative. This

---

[44] Elizabeth Fed. Sav. & Loan Ass'n v. Howell, 24 N.J. 488, 132 A.2d 779 (1957) — an opinion noteworthy not only for its excellence but also because it is one of the last opinions written by Justice Arthur Vanderbilt, whose contributions to the formulation of a sound body of state administrative law are exceeded by those of no one else. The opinion was delivered less than a week before Justice Vanderbilt's death.

[45] Application of Plainfield-Union Water Co., 11 N.J. 382, 94 A.2d 673 (1953).

[46] Pennsylvania R.R. v. Department of Pub. Utils., 14 N.J. 411, 102 A.2d 618 (1954).

principle entitling a party respondent to examine the evidence on which the agency proposes to rely in making a determination affecting that party's rights, is one which applies in all contested cases—whether the function involved is basically legislative or judicial.[47]

A case which illustrates how completely a state agency may ignore this well-settled principle was decided by the Illinois court.[48] A savings and loan association applied to the state director of financial institutions for permission to move its office. Other associations objected to the allowance of the application, and a hearing was held before a hearing officer who filed a report with the agency. When the agency considered this report, it decided that further evidence was needed. A request for further information was sent to the applicant, but the objecting companies were not even notified of the fact that further evidence was being sought. The applicant furnished a long report to the agency, but failed to send copies of it to the other parties in interest. On the basis of the additional information thus furnished by the applicant, the agency granted the application. Thereafter, the objecting institutions, whose counsel learned of the new evidence only after the decision was rendered, asked that the hearings be reopened, so that they could refute the evidence secretly supplied to the agency. Their request was refused. Only after the objectors took the matter to the state supreme court did they finally win vindication of their right to learn of the evidence on which the agency proposed to reply in opposition to their claims, and to learn of it in sufficient time to undertake to rebut it at the hearing.

Such difficulties are avoided in states which have adopted statutes based upon Sections 9 (c) and 9 (g) of the Revised Model State Act, which require that in every contested case, "opportunity shall be afforded all parties to respond and present evidence and argument on issues involved" (Section 9 (c)) and

---

[47] Cayuga County v. McHugh, 4 N.Y.2d 609, 176 N.Y.S.2d 643, 152 N.E.2d 73 (1958), which contains a dictum to the effect that the right to examine the opposing testimony is not applicable in quasi-legislative proceedings, really turns on the fact that the subordinate governmental unit, which was complaining of the action of the state commission of corrections, had no standing to complain of the action taken.

[48] North Fed. Savings & Loan Ass'n v. Becker, 24 Ill. 2d 514, 182 N.E.2d 155 (1962).

that "findings of fact shall be based exclusively on the evidence and on matters officially noticed." (Section 9 (g).)

(D) Reasonable Opportunity to Prepare Defense

Information as to the theory on which the case against respondent will be presented, and an opportunity to learn the nature of the evidence that will be offered in support thereof, must be made available in time to afford respondent an adequate opportunity to present his defense.

Ordinarily, this requirement is not a source of great practical difficulty. It is not unusual for a hearing to be held in two or more installments. At the first meeting, the agency puts in its case, thus letting respondent know the real thrust of the agency's claims, and giving him an opportunity to examine the opposing evidence. After a suitable adjournment, while respondent prepares his case, the hearing is reconvened to permit respondent to put in his proofs. In this easy way, respondent's rights can be protected and both parties can introduce their evidence "in an orderly manner and in an atmosphere of calm."[49] But where the agency requires respondent to proceed without interruption of the hearing, depriving him of ample opportunity to prepare his case, the courts are sometimes required to intercede.

A typical example involved an appeal by a mining company to a state tax commission, seeking a reduction in the assessed valuation of its mining properties, which local assessors had valued at $12,000,000. Apparently the mining company was one of the largest taxpayers in the county, and a reduction in its assessment would seriously affect the financing of the operation of the local units of county government. On the first day of the hearing, counsel for the county sought a continuance, which was denied, despite the plea that the county wished to present testimony of an expert appraiser in support of the original assessment, and such appraiser required ninety days to complete his study and prepare his report. As a result, the only witnesses to testify at the hearing were those who appeared on behalf of the mining company. Counsel for the county sought to cross-examine them, but were not in a position to do so effectively. In the words of the court, "they were all but defenseless

---

[49] King v. Brown, note 40 *supra*.

and necessarily groped." So effective was the testimony of the mining company's experts that the state tax commission cut the valuation in half, reducing it from $12,000,000 to $6,-000,000. The court held that denial of the continuance, depriving counsel for the county of an opportunity to prepare their defense, constituted an abuse of discretion, remarking:

> . . . [I]f the case is to be tried and the valuation of the company's property for the purposes of taxation determined by compurgation of expert appraisers, fairness would certainly demand that respondents be given an equal and reasonable opportunity to present such a witness and their theory of valuation.[50]

In a California case, the court overruled a contention that the setting of a case for hearing less than three weeks after the proceedings were initiated, had the effect of depriving respondent of a reasonable opportunity to present his defense.[51]

(E) Right to Introduce Evidence

The right to a full hearing includes the privilege of introducing all evidence which is competent, material, and relevant to the issues, and which respondent desires to offer. The state courts have applied this principle in a wide variety of situations.

Respondent may be denied his right to introduce evidence because of the adoption by the agency of some informal substitute for a testimonial hearing. Thus, in one Texas case, applicants for licenses as motor carriers were permitted to "make a record" in support of their applications by the simple expedient of "adopting" a transcript of testimony that had been taken previously in a similar case. The effect of this was to deprive a competitor, who wished to object to the allowance of the applications, of the right to introduce evidence in opposition. This, the court held, was error.[52]

In a workmen's compensation case, where controverted medical issues were submitted to a panel of physicians for hearing

---

[50] *In re* St. Joseph Lead Co., 352 S.W.2d 656, 664 (Mo. 1961).

[51] Raab v. Department of Alcoholic Beverage Control, 177 Cal. App. 2d 333, 2 Cal. Rptr. 26 (1960); *cf.*, Buckley v. Savage, 184 Cal. App. 2d 18, 7 Cal. Rptr. 328 (1960), holding that two years was ample time for respondent to prepare his defense.

[52] Railroad Comm'n v. Alamo Express, Inc., 158 Tex. 68, 308 S.W.2d 843 (1958).

and determination, it was held that the parties were deprived of a right to introduce evidence when the physicians reached their decision upon an examination of the documents (including medical reports) in the file, without giving the parties in interest an opportunity to appear and present testimony and argument.[53] The Arizona State Tax Commission was held to have deprived interested parties of their right to introduce testimony, when the decision was based on a mere informal conference. An auditor for the commission, believing that a natural gas company owed additional sales taxes, invited the company to send representatives to the commission's office for a conference. Counsel for the company then met with two members of the commission, but failed to reach any agreement as to the asserted tax liability. Thereafter, the commission notified the company that an assessment of tax had been made. Counsel for the company made a timely request for a hearing, but it was then denied them on the ground that the informal discussion with the company's counsel had afforded ample opportunity for hearing. In setting aside the assessment, the court pointed out that a hearing includes the right to introduce evidence, to hear and examine opposing witnesses, and to have an order based on the evidence presented.[54]

Again, the public service commission of Kentucky was reversed because of its denial of the right to introduce evidence. A hearing was opened on the question whether the rates charged by a gas utility company should be reduced. After some testimony had been presented, counsel for the company asked for and obtained a continuance. Then, before the date set for the continued hearing, the agency adopted an "interim order" compelling a temporary reduction in rates pending the final disposition of the case. The court granted an injunction to restrain the enforcement of this interim order, it having been made before the company had completed the introduction of its evidence.[55] Similarly, where a beer permit was revoked before the completion of the hearing, the order was ruled invalid.[56]

The California court held that an attempt by an agency to deprive a party of a hearing and the right to introduce evidence,

---

[53] Unora v. Glen Alden Coal Co., 377 Pa. 7, 104 A.2d 104 (1954).

[54] State Tax Comm'n v. El Paso Natural Gas Co., 73 Ariz. 43, 236 P.2d 1026 (1951).

[55] Mayfield Gas Co. v. Public Serv. Comm'n, note 36 *supra*.

[56] Chanaberry v. Gordy, 200 Tenn. 220, 292 S.W.2d 18 (1956).

on the ground that he had assertedly waited too long to request the hearing, was an abuse of discretion.[57]

Again, when an agency in reconsidering a case upon remand from a reviewing court refused to let the parties put in additional evidence, and limited the rehearing to a re-argument on the record previously made, it was held by the Arizona court that the parties had been deprived of their right to introduce testimony.[58]

In a Michigan case, application was made for an injunction to restrain the continued prosecution of a license revocation proceeding on the ground that the agency had threatened to deprive plaintiff of the opportunity to present certain evidence on which plaintiff relied. The court indicated that the complaint, if proved, would be meritorious; but dismissed the application for an injunction on the basis that plaintiff had an adequate remedy at law.[59]

In a substantial number of cases, the conclusion that respondent had been improperly denied his right to introduce testimony was based upon the agency's exclusion of evidence which plaintiff sought to introduce and which, the court held, should have been received and considered by the agency. On this basis, administrative orders were set aside because of the failure of the agency to receive and consider: (a) medical testimony offered on behalf of an employer in a workmen's compensation case as to claimant's earning capacity;[60] (b) testimony that a claimant for workmen's compensation had applied for and received unemployment compensation benefits, the receipt of which would disqualify him from receiving workmen's compensation;[61] (c) circumstantial evidence tending to establish that claimant was the wife of a deceased employee;[62] (d) evidence by a public utility in rate-fixing proceedings concerning the present value of its properties;[63] (e) medical opinion testimony, necessary as a link in proving causality between the strain of work and a

---

57 Pearson v. County of Los Angeles, 49 Cal. 2d 523, 319 P.2d 624 (1957).
58 Schnatzmeyer v. Industrial Comm'n, 78 Ariz. 112, 276 P.2d 534 (1954).
59 Norman v. Board of Examiners of Barbers, 364 Mich. 360, 111 N.W.2d 48 (1961).
60 Prince v. Industrial Comm'n, 89 Ariz. 314, 361 P.2d 929 (1961).
61 Gallant's Case, 326 Mass. 507, 95 N.E.2d 536 (1950).
62 Smith v. Smith, 361 Mo. 894, 237 S.W.2d 84 (1951).
63 New York Tel. Co. v. Public Serv. Comm'n, 309 N.Y. 569, 132 N.E.2d 847 (1956).

heart attack;[64] (f) evidence of sales prices of realty, in proceedings to fix maximum rental rates.[65]

The right to introduce testimony, it has been held by several courts, includes the right to present rebuttal testimony; and denial of a request to offer rebuttal evidence affords grounds for setting aside an agency determination.[66] Further, respondent must be given a fair opportunity to explain apparently damaging evidence, in an effort to withdraw its sting. Thus, where it was brought out, in connection with proceedings for the dismissal of public school teachers, that they had pleaded the Fifth Amendment in order to avoid answering questions in another proceeding, the court held that they must be given an opportunity to explain the circumstances in which they had so pleaded.[67]

Occasionally, an agency, while permitting certain evidence to be made a part of the record, announces that it will give no effect to such evidence in reaching its decision. If the reviewing court finds that the evidence should have been considered and given appropriate weight, the agency order is of course set aside. Thus, the Arkansas court held it was error for a workmen's compensation commission to refuse to consider a physician's answer to a hypothetical question.[68] Conversely, when the commission in another case refused to consider any evidence other than medical evidence, the court again reversed.[69] In one case, the California court made this interesting and significant remark: "Under certain conditions, the failure of the board to consider a proper defense . . . might constitute a failure to proceed 'in the manner required by law' and therefore an abuse of discretion."[70]

If respondent realizes only after the administrative hearing has been completed that he has failed to incorporate in the record evidence on which he relies, the appropriate course is to

---

[64] Owens v. McGovern, 309 N.Y. 449, 131 N.E.2d 729 (1956).

[65] Realty Agency, Inc. v. Weaver, 7 N.Y.2d 249, 196 N.Y.S.2d 953, 164 N.E.2d 837 (1959).

[66] Olive Proration Program Comm. v. Agricultural Prorate Comm'n, 17 Cal. 2d 204, 109 P.2d 918 (1941); Fairley v. Harry Bennett Constr. Co., 241 Miss. 707, 133 So. 2d 15 (1961); Wells-Lamont Corp. v. Watkins, 151 So. 2d 600 (Miss. 1963).

[67] Laba v. Board of Educ., 23 N.J. 364, 129 A.2d 273 (1957).

[68] Johnson v. Bear Brand Roofing, Inc., 233 Ark. 639, 346 S.W.2d 472 (1961).

[69] Glass v. Edens, 233 Ark. 786, 346 S.W.2d 685 (1961).

[70] Boren v. State Personnel Bd., 37 Cal. 2d 634, 640, 234 P.2d 981 (1951).

make application to re-open the hearing, or for a rehearing. In a proper case, the courts will require the agency to grant such relief.[71]

Some courts have held—and doubtless most others would agree—that the right to introduce testimony comprehends the right to be heard as to its significance, either by oral argument or written briefs.[72]

While ordinarily the denial of the right to introduce testimony constitutes ground for setting aside the administrative determination, there are a few cases where this result does not follow. Thus, where appellant would have had an opportunity to introduce the testimony in the course of a *de novo* hearing held as the first step in judicial review proceedings, but failed to take advantage of this opportunity, it was held that the failure to hear the testimony in the original administrative hearing was harmless.[73] In another case, where witnesses who had been subpoenaed failed to appear but respondent neglected to take appropriate steps to have the hearing postponed, it was found that there had been a waiver of the right to introduce the evidence.[74] Where respondent had the opportunity to present its testimony in a proceeding, but failed to do so, the refusal of the agency to grant it a separate hearing for the purpose of later presenting the testimony, was held to be justified.[75]

(F) Right to Cross-Examine

The right to cross-examine opposing witnesses is a substantial part of the guaranty of a fair trial. Where a witness is called to testify *vive voce,* the respondent must have an opportunity to cross-examine that witness. Nor can this right be defeated merely by permitting a witness to put his testimony in writing in advance of trial, and introducing his affidavit or report in lieu of calling him to the stand.

---

71 Martin v. Industrial Comm'n, 88 Ariz. 14, 352 P.2d 352 (1960); *cf.*, Gale v. Zaban's Mattress & Box Spring Co., 191 Va. 610, 62 S.E.2d 19 (1950).

72 Mayfield Gas Co. v. Public Serv. Comm'n, 259 S.W.2d 8 (Ky. 1953); Khachadoorian's Case, 329 Mass. 625, 110 N.E.2d 115 (1953); Railroad & Warehouse Comm'n v. Chicago & Northwestern Ry., 256 Minn. 227, 98 N.W.2d 60 (1959).

73 Appeal of Albert, 372 Pa. 13, 92 A.2d 663 (1952).

74 Walker v. Burr, 73 Ariz. 129, 238 P.2d 950 (1951).

75 Virginia Gas Distribution Corp. v. Washington Gas Light Co., 201 Va. 370, 111 S.E.2d 439 (1959).

But, on the other hand, the respondent has no right to insist (absent explicit statutory provision) that every bit of information on which the agency relies must be proved by testimony of witnesses subject to cross-examination. Were the requirement pushed so far, it would obviously collide with the principle that enables agencies to receive hearsay proof under appropriate circumstances, and would interfere unnecessarily with the efficient conduct of the work of many agencies.

It is at this point that the difference between courts and administrative agencies in respect to fact-finding techniques produces a real difficulty in setting standards to determine whether a party's right to a fair trial has been infringed. The general theory is clear—the agency is not to be permitted to base its ruling on evidence which is devoid of evidential value, and the respondent must be given a fair opportunity to demonstrate the unreliability of the proffered proof. In some cases, the only adequate way to undertake such a demonstration is by oral cross-examination of the party who is the author of the statement; but in other cases, an opportunity to rebut the accuracy of the statement, or to demonstrate that it does not rest on reliable sources of information, is sufficient.

The Federal Administrative Procedure Act[76] and the Revised Model State Act[77] adopt the same phrase to suggest the test which should guide the courts in determining whether deprival of the right to cross-examine has deprived a party of a fair trial. The federal act provides: "Every party shall have the right . . . to conduct such cross examination as may be required for a full and true disclosure of the facts." The Revised Model State Act provides: "[a] party may conduct cross examinations required for a full and true disclosure of the facts."

(1) Provisions of State Statutes

State legislation guaranteeing the right of cross-examination in administrative adjudication presents a variegated pattern. Several states follow the general theory of the Revised Model Act. A number, however, provide broader guaranties of the right of cross-examination.

---

[76] 5 U.S.C. § 1006(c); F.C.A. 5 § 1006(c).
[77] Section 10(3).

The same phrase as that found in the Revised Model Act appears in several state statutes.[78] The Pennsylvania statute[79] provides that "reasonable examination and cross examination shall be permitted." An interesting and unique provision appears in the Virginia statute,[80] which provides that hearsay evidence may be received only if the declarant is not readily available, and further requires that in deciding whether a witness is readily available the agency shall balance the importance of the evidence against the difficulty of obtaining it. Further, the statute declares that "the more important the evidence is the more effort should be made to produce the eyewitness." Subject to these provisions, the statute declares that every party shall have the right to cross-examine adverse witnesses, and to cross-examine any inspector or subordinate of the agency whose report is in evidence.

All of these statutes reflect the same general theory as that embraced in the Revised Model State Act—suggesting that while cross-examination is desirable and should ordinarily be insisted upon, yet it may be waived in cases where it is not necessary to a full disclosure of the facts.

The statutes of several states go further in guaranteeing the right of cross-examination. Some states provide generally, and without limitation, that every party in agency proceedings shall have the right of cross-examination.[81] In other states, the statutory provision guarantees parties the right to cross-examine witnesses who testify.[82] Still other statutes provide that every party shall have the right to cross-examine opposing witnesses on any matter relevant to the issues even though that matter was not covered in the direct examination.[83]

---

[78] Colorado (REV. STAT. ANN. § 3-16-4); Florida (STAT. § 120.26); Georgia (CODE ANN. § 3A-101); Hawaii (SESS. LAWS 1961, Act 103, § 10); Oklahoma (STAT. tit. 75, § 310); Rhode Island (GEN. LAWS ANN. § 42-35-10).

[79] PA. STAT. ANN. tit. 71, § 1710.32.

[80] VA. CODE ANN. § 9-6.11.

[81] Indiana (ANN. STAT. § 63-3008); Michigan (STAT. ANN. § 3.560(21.5)(3)); North Dakota (CENT. CODE § 28-32-05); Ohio (REV. CODE ANN. § 119.07—requiring the initial notice to inform the party that at the hearing he may examine witnesses appearing against him); West Virginia (Acts 1964, art. 5, ch. 1, § 2).

[82] Maine (REV. STAT. ANN. ch. 20-A, § 10); Maryland (ANN. CODE art. 41, § 252); Massachusetts (GEN. LAWS ANN. ch. 30A, § 11); Minnesota (STAT. § 15.0419 (3)); Nebraska (REV. STAT. § 84-914); Oregon (REV. STAT. § 183.-450); Washington (REV. CODE § 34.04.100). These statutes may not guarantee the right of cross-examination in cases where an agency relies on documents or records in support of the charge.

[83] Alaska (STAT. § 44.62.460); California (GOV'T CODE § 11513); Missouri

(2) Court Decisions

In cases where a court is asked to determine whether there has been a denial of the right of cross-examination, a great deal depends on the court's judgment as to what constitutes, in the context of the case, a reasonable substitute or equivalent for the typical judicial cross-examination procedure; and it is not surprising that courts exhibit some difference of opinion in specific case situations. However, the general tendency in state court decisions is to insist that the right of cross-examination be afforded wherever there is substantial reason to believe that denial thereof might impede the discovery of truth.

Where a witness is sworn and testifies at the agency hearing, he is of course subject to cross-examination. This was emphasized by the Arizona court in a case involving the dismissal of a public school teacher, who was denied the right at the dismissal hearing to cross-examine adverse witnesses. The agency argued that its procedure was justified because the statute did not guarantee the right to cross-examine; but the court said that the statute would be unconstitutional if construed to deny the right of cross-examination; and remarked that since an administrative agency is not limited by strict rules as to the admissibility of evidence, the obligation to preserve the essential evidentiary rules by which rights are asserted or defended is all the more imperative.[84]

In a careful and perceptive study of the right of cross-examination in administrative proceedings in New York State,[85] Robert M. Benjamin observed: "It is safe to conclude that, in the ordinary quasi-judicial hearing prescribed by statute, an opportunity must be afforded to cross examine witnesses who testify."[86] Decisions in other states are in accord.[87]

(REV. STAT. § 536.070); New Mexico (STAT. ANN. § 67-26-8—uniform licensing act); North Carolina (GEN. STAT. § 150-15—uniform licensing act).

84 Forman v. Creighton School Dist. No. 14, 87 Ariz. 329, 351 P.2d 165 (1960).

85 BENJAMIN, ADMINISTRATIVE ADJUDICATION IN THE STATE OF NEW YORK 196 (1942).

86 The author cites People *ex rel.* Packwood v. Riley, 232 N.Y. 283, 133 N.E. 891 (1922), and People *ex rel.* The Mayor v. Nichols, 79 N.Y. 582 (1880).

87 *E.g.,* Gonzales v. Industrial Acc. Comm'n, 50 Cal. 2d 360, 325 P.2d 993 (1958)—upholding the right to cross-examine an expert witness; Carey v. Bryan & Rollins, 48 Del. 395, 105 A.2d 201 (1954); Bereda Mfg. Co. v. Industrial Bd., 275 Ill. 514, 114 N.E. 275 (1916); Bristow v. State Industrial Comm'n, 317 P.2d 237 (Okla. 1957); State *ex rel.* Baker Mfg. Co. v. City of Evansville, 261 Wis. 599, 53 N.W.2d 795(1952).

The real difficulty arises where an agency receives in evidence a document, such as a letter, an affidavit, or a report, whose author is not called as a witness. To insist upon an absolute and unqualified right of cross-examination would be to deprive agencies of the right to receive such documentary evidence, contrary to the normal practices of the agencies and to the general doctrine permitting agencies to receive hearsay under certain circumstances. On the other hand, to permit agencies to predicate decision on mere reports whose accuracy is challenged, without giving the adverse party an opportunity to demonstrate by cross-examination the unreliability and inaccuracy of the report, would clearly be to deprive the party of his right to a fair trial. The courts have been compelled to choose a path, between these two equally unacceptable extremes, that will lead to the agreed desideratum—guaranteeing such measure of cross-examination as is necessary for a full and true disclosure of the facts.

The problem is well stated, and an interesting solution offered, in the discussion in Mr. Benjamin's last-cited book.[88] He observed:

> . . . [I]n some circumstances the denial of an opportunity to cross examine the author of a hearsay statement may vitiate a quasi-judicial determination. What those circumstances will be it is impossible to forecast with certainty. Wisely, I think, the courts have refrained from generalization. . . . While generalization from the decided cases is thus impossible, it seems to me reasonable to expect that a quasi-judicial determination will be reversed on this ground only if it appears that production for cross-examination of the author of a hearsay statement would have been reasonably practicable, and that in all the circumstances the refusal to produce him, or to allow a reasonable opportunity for the party adversely affected to subpoena him, was clearly unfair, and, probably, only if it appears further that the hearsay statement in question has played a substantial part in the quasi-judicial determination.

After discussing a number of New York cases[89] he concludes:

> . . . [T]he normal practice should be for the agency to produce for cross examination, at least upon request, the author of a report,

[88] BENJAMIN, *op. cit. supra* note 85, at 198 et seq.

[89] Including Heaney v. McGoldrick, 286 N.Y. 38, 35 N.E.2d 641 (1941); *In re* Magna, 258 N.Y. 82, 179 N.E. 266 (1932); *In re* Greenebaum, 201 N.Y. 343, 94 N.E. 853 (1911); People *ex rel.* Yates v. Mulrooney, 245 App. Div. 146, 281 N.Y.S. 216 (1935); People *ex rel.* Albrecht v. Harnett, 221 App. Div. 487, 224 N.Y.S. 97 (1927).

certificate, or other written statement received in evidence; and this whether or not the statement in question is legally competent within the exception to the hearsay rule.[90]

In deciding whether the admission of hearsay has infringed upon rights of cross-examination, the courts have recognized a number of general propositions.

If a letter, affidavit, or other written report is offered as a substitute for the oral testimony of an individual witness as to what he has seen, or believes, or concludes, the other party (at least if the contents of the writing are of any substantial importance) must be given an opportunity to cross-examine the author. Thus, where a civil service commission received a confidential letter from the chief of police, in proceedings for the removal of a police officer, the Pennsylvania court reversed an order of dismissal because the police officer was denied the right of cross-examination, even though it appeared that other evidence in the case afforded a sufficient basis for removal.[91] The court remarked:

> And while the commission is an administrative body, and even where it acts in a quasi-judicial capacity is not limited by the strict rules as to the admissibility of evidence which prevail in suits between private parties, the more imperative it is to preserve the essential rules of evidence by which rights are asserted or defended.

In a California case, where it was agreed at the close of the administrative hearing that two physicians might submit their reports in writing, it was held nonetheless a denial of due process to deny one of the parties the right to cross-examine the physicians.[92]

Where the testimony relates to a specific factual dispute at issue in a particular case, cross-examination is more vigorously insisted upon than in cases where the testimony relates to matters of general information. Thus, in a zoning case, involving the location of a steam generating plant of a public utility, where the area of disagreement did not involve specific factual issues but rather judgments and opinions as to the desirability of a proposed location from the viewpoint of esthetics, effect on neighborhood property values, and the like, the Connecticut court observed

[90] BENJAMIN, *op. cit. supra* note 85, at 202.

[91] Civil Serv. Comm'n v. Polito, 397 Pa. 538, 542, 156 A.2d 99 (1959).

[92] Langendorf United Bakeries, Inc. v. Industrial Acc. Comm'n, 87 Cal. App. 2d 103, 195 P.2d 887 (1948).

that a limited degree of cross-examination was sufficient to protect the rights of the parties. It said:

> We have examined this transcript with care. The plaintiffs were ably and vigorously represented. Proper cross examination must be relevant. Its limits are within the reasonable discretion of the trier. No unreasonable limitations were placed by the commission upon the right of cross examination.[93]

The most difficult case is that where an agency desires to rely on information gathered in the course of a general investigation, or on data revealed by hundreds of reports filed by disinterested parties. In some cases, where a clear showing is made of the reliability of such data[94] the court may conclude that the rights intended to be guaranteed by cross-examination can be safeguarded so long as the affected party is given full opportunity to rebut the showing made by the reports. The impracticability of calling a large number of witnesses for cross-examination as to a variety of issues related only collaterally to the specific question before the agency, coupled with the apparent unlikelihood that such cross-examination would affect the statements or reports in question, may persuade a court that it would be unwise to insist upon a literal application of the general right of cross-examination.

Thus, in a Missouri case[95] it was held that the consideration by a public service commission of data furnished by its own engineers, in connection with its approval of a rate schedule, did not prejudice appellants, even though they had no opportunity to cross-examine the engineers in order to test the accuracy of their reports. The circumstances were these: The utility offered evidence as to the estimated value of plant additions that were in the course of construction, and as to their effect on earnings. The protestants then suggested that the commission's staff make an independent study and that they have an opportunity to examine the studies before the record was closed. The commission's staff did make the studies, but did so after the record was closed, with the result that the protestants had no opportunity

---

93 Jennings v. Connecticut Light & Power Co., 140 Conn. 650, 675, 103 A.2d 535 (1954).

94 *Cf.* Opp Cotton Mills v. Administrator of Wage & Hour Div., 312 U.S. 126, 85 L. Ed. 624, 61 Sup. Ct. 524 (1941).

95 State *ex rel.* Hotel Continental v. Burton, 334 S.W.2d 75 (Mo. 1960).

to examine the studies. They protested the denial of the right to examine the studies, and to cross-examine the authors. The court remarked that the practice followed by the commission was not to be recommended, but declined to reverse because the studies were merely confirmatory of the utility's evidence, and therefore the lack of opportunity to cross-examine did not prejudice protestants.

The decision therefore suggests that if there is little real controversy as to the factual question involved, and if the administrative decision can be adequately supported by reliance on other evidence, the denial of cross-examination may be harmless.

However, in cases where reliance on information gathered in the course of a general investigation, or on statistical data, would foreclose an adversely affected party of the right to cross-examine on a seriously contested and important factual issue, the agency may be prohibited from relying on such data. Thus, the New Jersey court reversed an agency because of its failure to allow cross-examination of materials supplied by the agency's engineering staff.[96] The federal courts likewise have held that reliance on statistical data as a basis for finding critical facts may violate the adverse party's right to cross-examination.[97] The right of cross-examination is all the more likely to be insisted on where the investigational report or statistical tabulation was prepared by the agency's staff specifically for use in the particular case; under such circumstances, such reports come close to being merely a written substitute for oral testimony of a particular witness.[98]

While the state courts generally go far in insisting on the right of cross-examination wherever the denial thereof seems likely to have prejudiced substantial rights, they tolerate the deprival of the right to cross-examine where it seems that no harm could possibly have resulted. Thus, in a workmen's compensation case where the death of the workman prevented the completion of his cross-examination, the Michigan court found that no prejudice had resulted because the major portion of his

---

[96] Application of Plainfield-Union Water Co., 11 N.J. 382, 94 A.2d 673 (1953).

[97] Powhatan Mining Co. v. Ickes, 118 F.2d 105 (6th Cir. 1941).

[98] Snyder Mines, Inc. v. Industrial Comm'n, 117 Utah 471, 217 P.2d 560 (1950); *cf.*, BENJAMIN, ADMINISTRATIVE ADJUDICATION IN THE STATE OF NEW YORK 202 (1942).

testimony had been elicited under cross-examination, and no harm to the employer's case could be perceived.[99] Agencies may, within reason, limit the extent of cross-examination;[100] and may deny the right of cross-examination to an intervenor who is permitted to participate only to a limited degree.[101] The right of cross-examination may be waived.[102]

Section 3

Application of Rules of Evidence in Agency Hearings

(A) The Problem

Half a century ago, when the proposition that administrative agencies need not be bound by the rules of evidence first began to gain popularity, the state agencies were quite different from their modern counterparts. Their composition was different; their functions were different; their modes of operation were different.

Fifty years ago, the typical state agencies would include, perhaps, rural township supervisors who as members of local boards of assessors would estimate the value of their neighbors' farms, and statehouse politicians who as a railroad commission would bargain with railroad attorneys concerning the granting of franchises and the fixing of rates, and insurance commissioners who would watch with a wary eye the premiums charged by fire insurance companies (they couldn't be entrusted with such responsibilities as the supervision or prescription of forms of policies—for that would amount to an unconstitutional delegation of power),[103] and—in the more progressive states—"committees of arbitration"[104] who would informally arbitrate compensation claims of workers injured in industrial accidents under the newfangled workmen's compensation laws.

---

99 Wilson v. Doehler-Jarvis Div. of Nat'l Lead Co., 353 Mich. 363, 91 N.W. 2d 538 (1958).

100 Conley v. Board of Educ., 143 Conn. 488, 123 A.2d 747 (1956); State *ex rel.* Gregersen v. Board of Review, 5 Wis. 2d 28, 92 N.W.2d 236 (1958).

101 Smith v. Public Serv. Comm'n, 336 S.W.2d 491 (Mo. 1960).

102 Severn v. City of Baltimore, 230 Md. 160, 186 A.2d 199 (1962).

103 See, *e.g.*, Dowling v. Lancashire Ins. Co., 92 Wis. 63, 65 N.W. 738, 31 L.R.A. 112 (1896).

104 See Reck v. Whittlesberger, 181 Mich. 463, 148 N.W. 247, 52 L.R.A. (n.s.) 930 (1914).

In that far-off day, the state agencies had little occasion to concern themselves with the law of evidence. Their functions were essentially political and administrative, rather than judicial. The courts saw no necessity for the application of the rules of evidence to their deliberations. On the contrary, there was perhaps a good reason for refraining from imposing on them a necessity of following the rules of evidence, for in those days it was often true that neither the agency members nor those arguing before them had any familiarity with the rules of evidence that were followed in the courts.

It was in this context that there was born the principle that administrative agencies need not concern themselves with the rules of evidence, but may hear and consider any testimonial offer which is made.

The rule has survived, although the reasons for its survival have been but little probed, and are far from clear. In part, no doubt, its survival may be attributed to the circumstance that the rule has been popular with the agency heads, who have long preached that damnation would be the consequence of requiring agencies to decide contested cases solely on the basis of competent evidence. Further, the oft-noted and developing trend toward relaxation of the exclusionary rules in court cases has no doubt been a contributing factor.[105] Finally, lethargy on the part of state legislatures may be in part responsible.

Whatever the reason, the rule is tolerably clear that only in rare cases, which are discussed *infra,*[106] is it considered reversible error for an agency to receive evidence that would not be admissible under the exclusionary tests. If the rule is to be changed, it must—for all practical purposes—be changed by legislation. The principal problem, therefore, is whether the developments of the last fifty years (including not only the developments in the character and functions of the agencies, but also developments in the rules of evidence themselves) suggest the wisdom of changing the rule, to the end that hereafter agencies will be required to follow the rules of evidence to about the same extent

---

105 See, for example, American Law Institute, MODEL CODE OF EVIDENCE, 223-24 (1942); Uniform Rules of Evidence prepared by the National Conference of Commissioners on Uniform State Laws: 1953 HANDBOOK OF NATIONAL CONFERENCE 164 et seq.

106 Subsection (D) of this chapter, *infra.*

and in about the same way as judges do when trying cases without juries.

Several developments suggest that such a change is overdue. Among the most significant developments pointing in this direction are the practices of the agencies themselves. Many agencies have voluntarily adopted the practice of following rules of evidence; and a number of agency officials of long experience have advocated the wisdom of this practice.[107]

In a number of state agencies (as is true in some major federal agencies, as well) the nature of the proof-taking procedure is in practice almost indistinguishable from the taking of proofs in non-jury cases in the courts. Objections are made, arguments are heard thereon, and sometimes the objections are sustained. In administrative trials, as in court trials, some lawyers object with greater vigor than judgment; and others appreciate that it is sometimes wiser to waive an objection than to press it. Some hearing officers (although not many, concededly) are more strict in their evidentiary rulings than are some judges.

There are probably many reasons for this trend. Perhaps it may be attributed in large measure to the simple circumstance that administrative cases are to an ever increasing extent being tried by lawyers before competent, legally trained hearing officers. Perhaps (so far at least as respondents' counsel are concerned) it merely reflects a realization of the fact that the hearing officer may in his discretion invoke the exclusionary rules, and as a matter of safe trial tactics counsel must be prepared to prove his case by legally competent evidence, so as not to be caught unprepared if the hearing officer decides to invoke the rules of evidence.[108] Perhaps the trend toward adoption, in the trial of contested cases before agencies, of at least the basic principles of relevancy, materiality, and probative force reflects a recognition of the innate wisdom of the evidentiary rules as applied in non-jury cases in the courts.[109]

---

[107] *E.g.,* the article by J. Earl Cox, a Federal Trade Commission examiner appointed by law and informed by long and distinguished experience, whose reasons for applying the rules of evidence in administrative proceedings appear in "Adherence to the Rules of Evidence and Federal Rules of Civil Procedure as a Means of Expediting Proceedings," 12 *Ad. L. Bull.* 51 (1959).

[108] See, *e.g.,* NLRB v. Fairchild Engine & Airplane Corp., 145 F.2d 214 (4th Cir. 1944); Riker (Station KFQU) v. Federal Radio Comm'n, 60 App. D.C. 372, 55 F.2d 535 (1931).

[109] Wigmore found a "general and instinctive use" of the common-law rules

Whatever the reasons for this current trend, its pervasiveness may be illustrated by the rules which a number of the federal agencies have voluntarily adopted. Thus, the rules of the Interstate Commerce Commission[110] and of the Federal Communications Commission[111] provide that, with stated exceptions, formal hearings shall be governed by the rules of evidence governing civil proceedings in matters not involving trial by jury in the federal courts. The rules of the Federal Trade Commission[112] require the exclusion of irrelevant, immaterial, unreliable, and unduly repetitious evidence. The Commission long ago announced that in practice it has "intended to receive only legally competent evidence."[113] The typical approach of both federal and state agencies indicates, at the very least, an acceptance of the principles stated in the "code of standards of fair administrative procedure" proposed in the separate statement of Messrs. McFarland, Stason, and Vanderbilt as members of the Attorney General's Committee.[114] It declared that the basic principles of relevancy, materiality, and probative force (as recognized in federal judicial proceedings of an equitable nature) should govern the proof of all questions of fact, except that such principles should be: (1) broadly interpreted in such manner as to make effective the adjudicative powers of administrative agencies, (2) adapted to the legislative policy under which adjudications are made, and (3) so applied as to assure that as a practical matter testimony of reasonable probative value should not be excluded.

The more significant study groups which have considered the problem have concluded that this trend is in the correct direction, and that legislation should be adopted to accentuate it. Several reasons have been given for these conclusions. It has been suggested, for example, that administrators need more guidance than do judges; and that statutes should provide them with adequate standards to guide them in the evaluation of evidence

---

of evidence in contested cases deemed important. 1 WIGMORE, EVIDENCE § 4*c* (3d ed. 1940). See Stephan, *The Extent to Which Fact-Finding Boards Should Be Bound by Rules of Evidence,* 24 A.B.A.J. 630 (1938).

110 49 C.F.R. § 1.75.

111 47 C.F.R. § 1.351.

112 16 C.F.R. § 3.14.

113 STEPHENS, ADMINISTRATIVE TRIBUNALS AND THE RULES OF EVIDENCE 82 (1933).

114 S. DOC. No. 8, 77th Cong., 1st Sess. 241 (1941).

and the rights of the parties in the matter of proof.[115] It has been pointed out, too, that it assists the agencies in their work if they are given the benefit of statutory guidance in this area. The further suggestion has been made that the relaxation of the degree of vigilance with which the exclusionary rules are enforced in the courts should lead to a common standard of proof, applicable alike to courts and to administrative tribunals.[116] While the reasons have varied, the suggestions have shown a remarkable consistency.

Back in 1941, the majority statement of the Attorney General's Committee observed:

> Abuses in admitting remote hearsay and irrelevant or unreliable evidence there surely have been; but the Committee, within the limits of its resources, has found no general pattern of departure from the basic principles of evidence among administrative agencies. The ultimate test of admissibility must be whether the proffered evidence is reliable, probative and relevant. The question in each case must be whether the probability of error justifies the burden of stricter methods of proof. Discretion must be allowed to hearing commissioners just as it is to judges in equity proceedings; the latter are largely governed by principles of common sense and fairness. That strict adherence to standards of relevance and probative value should be observed needs no underscoring.[117]

As noted above, the additional statement of Messrs. McFarland, Stason, and Vanderbilt, whose views in general found a greater acceptance in subsequent congressional legislation than did those expressed in the majority report, went somewhat further.

The Task Force on Legal Services and Procedure of the Second Hoover Commission recommended that it should be required by statute that in the hearing of contested cases the same rules

---

[115] Harris, *Administrative Practice and Procedure: Comparative State Legislation,* 6 OKLA. L. REV. 29 (1953).

[116] The House of Delegates of the American Bar Association in 1953 approved the Uniform Rules of Evidence prepared by the Commissioners on Uniform State Laws. 39 A.B.A.J. 1029 (1953). One of the comments appended to those rules points out "there is no good reason why the same rules should not be employed in administrative tribunals as in the courts." HANDBOOK OF NATIONAL CONFERENCE OF COMMISSIONERS ON UNIFORM STATE LAWS 166 (1953). Related is the interesting suggestion of Judge Wyzanski in United States v. United Shoe Machinery Corp., 89 F. Supp. 349 (D.C. Mass. 1950).

[117] *Administrative Procedure in Government Agencies,* S. DOC. No. 8, 77th Cong., 1st Sess. 70-71.

of evidence and requirements of proof should apply, to the extent practicable, as in civil non-jury cases in the United States District Courts.[118]

Congress had already adopted this test for the National Labor Relations Board—which, perhaps more than any other agency, had championed the theory that rules of evidence could properly be ignored—by providing in the Labor-Management Relations Act, 1947, that contested cases before that agency "shall, so far as practicable, be conducted in accordance with the rules of evidence applicable in the district courts of the United States under the rules of civil procedure. . . ."[119]

The provisions of the Revised Model State Act are a reflection of this long developing trend.

(B) Basic Theory of Revised Model State Act

The key to the approach adopted by the National Conference of Commissioners on Uniform State Laws, in connection with the problem of whether to require agencies to follow the basic principles of proof embodied in the exclusionary rules of evidence, is found in the initial portion of Section 10 (1) of the Revised Model State Act, which provides that in contested cases:

> Irrelevant, immaterial, or unduly repetitious evidence shall be excluded. The rules of evidence as applied in [non-jury] civil cases in the [District Courts of this State] shall be followed. When necessary to ascertain facts not reasonably susceptible of proof under those rules, evidence not admissible thereunder may be admitted (except where precluded by statute) if it is of a type commonly relied upon by reasonably prudent men in the conduct of their affairs.

No section of the Revised Model State Act received more painstaking attention than did these words. After three years of careful study and frequent revision at the hands of the drafting committee, the report was fully debated on the floor at two sessions of the full Conference. A number of amendments were offered and discussed—some of them urging the simplification of the section to the end that it would provide, without exception, that the rules of evidence must be followed by the agencies as they are applied in non-jury civil cases; others (at the oppo-

---

[118] Commission on Organization of Executive Branch of Government, Task Force Report on Legal Services and Procedure 199 (1955).

[119] 29 U.S.C. § 160(b); F.C.A. 29 § 160(b).

site extreme) urging that agencies should be permitted under any circumstances to receive any evidence which the hearing officer deemed to be of a type that would be relied upon by reasonably prudent men in the conduct of their affairs. In the end, the committee proposal was accepted by an overwhelming majority. It is suggested that every phrase of it is important; and it should be analyzed phrase by phrase so that the significance of each provision will become apparent.

The first caveat is that irrelevant, immaterial, or unduly repetitious evidence shall be excluded. This is a mandate which applies in all cases. It means, in effect, that the basic principles of relevancy, materiality, and probative force, may not under any circumstances be ignored.

Then comes the second basic test. It is first stated affirmatively, as a guiding principle that normally applies; and thereafter, the applicable exceptions are noted. The second basic principle is that the rules of evidence as applied in non-jury civil cases shall be followed. This language is of especial importance. It does not require that proceedings before state administrative agencies shall be conducted as in the case of jury trials. Rather, it directs the agencies to follow the rules of evidence "as applied in non-jury civil cases."

This directive does not deny the proposition urged by some distinguished students that the same rules of evidence govern jury and non-jury cases. Rather, it assumes that the rules are much the same. But it is clear—as every trial lawyer knows—that even though the rules may be the same they are differently applied in jury and in non-jury cases. If the question of admissibility is a close one, the judge may likely exclude the evidence if a jury is present; but if there is no jury, he will likely receive it for what it is worth. Agencies are permitted to do the same. They may not completely ignore the rules, and receive any evidence on which they may wish to rely; but they are authorized to apply the rules in a liberal way in favor of admitting evidence of doubtful competency.

The phrase "non-jury" was bracketed, as explained in the official Commentary published by the Commissioners, because in some states it is difficult to differentiate between the rules followed in jury and non-jury cases. This means that if a state legislature concludes that the judges in that state do relax the evidentiary rules to the same extent in the trial of civil cases before a jury as in cases where a jury is waived, the word "non-jury" may be dropped. The result then is that the same rules shall be applied in administrative proceedings as are applied in all civil trials in the courts. In most states, of course, there is a noticeable differentiation in the vigor with which the rules are applied, as between jury and non-jury cases.

The basic theory of this second requirement is that a hearing officer should not be free to receive any testimonial offer that he considers worthy of reliance. That is the net result of the test which permits the hearing officer to receive, in any case, evidence of a type on which reasonably prudent men would rely in the conduct of their affairs. Every hearing officer considers himself a reasonably prudent man—and the hearing which he is conducting is ineluctably his affair—and so, under this rule, the hearing officer is free to accept whatever he may wish to rely on. By this test, a hearing officer may receive in evidence such items as newspaper clippings, anonymous letters, affidavits drafted by counsel and signed without having been read by the affiant, statistical computations prepared by an unknown person who is not subject to cross-examination, and many other types of testimonial offer which can readily be utilized to confound the record and distort the truth.

There are other cogent reasons which support the conclusion that agencies should be required to follow the basic exclusionary rules. First, a state agency is often prosecutor as well as judge—and it is tempting human nature too far to say that anything should be received in evidence which the prosecutor, in the heat of trial, considers reliable (sometimes the hearing is before the agency members themselves, rather than before a hearing officer). Second, many agencies in many states are subject to political appointments and political pressures which result in unfortunate tendencies that can best be checked—so far as the hearing stage is concerned—by insisting on scrupulous fairness in the taking of proofs. Such ends are not best to be attained by permitting the agency or hearing officer to receive in evidence anything on which he (as a "reasonable person") may wish to rely.

But the Revised Model State Act contains more, in its provisions respecting the taking of proofs, than the above-described first two basic postulates. After stating the basic tests, it prescribes carefully defined exceptions, which recognize that in some unusual circumstances application of the civil-trial rules (even as applied in non-jury cases) might operate to make it unduly difficult to discover the truth. Accordingly, the Revised Model Act further provides that evidence which would not be admissible under the rules applicable to civil cases in the courts may nevertheless be received, when to do so is necessary to ascertain facts not reasonably susceptible of proof under those rules (except, of course, in cases where statutes specifically provide—as a number of statutes applicable to named agencies in several states do provide—that the agency must proceed strictly in accordance with the court-established rules of evidence). Under this test, an agency is always enabled, if it cannot adduce witnesses competent to testify to the facts which the agency wishes to prove, to establish such facts by any evidence which reasonably prudent men would rely on in the conduct of their affairs.

Thus, in the final analysis, the Revised Model State Act represents a compromise between the view that agencies should be required to follow the rules of evidence, and the view that they should be permitted to disregard the rules. It bespeaks this ideal: the general practice in administrative proceedings should be to follow the rules of evidence (withal applying them in the liberal way that judges do when no jury is present). At the same time, the Revised Model Act avoids any possibility that truth may be kept from the record, by permitting departure from the general rule where such departure is necessary. This compromise should go far toward eliminating any practice of basing findings on distortions and half-truths—a danger which is always inherent in relying on letters and affidavits, and which unhappily is sometimes encountered.

(C) Exclusion of Irrelevant, Immaterial, or Unduly Repetitious Evidence

A number of state statutes contain provisions which are in accord with the initial command of the Revised Model State Act, requiring without exception the exclusion of irrelevant, immaterial, or unduly repetitious evidence. Some states have already adopted the language of the Revised Model Act.[120]

[120] Georgia (Code Ann. § 3A-101); Rhode Island (Gen. Laws Ann. § 42-

Other statutes, omitting the word "immaterial," provide that irrelevant and unduly repetitious evidence shall be excluded.[121] The most popular version, derived from the original Model State Act, provides that agencies may (but are not required to) exclude any evidence which is incompetent, as well as that which is irrelevant, immaterial, or unduly repetitious.[122] Still other states, adopting the language of the Federal Administrative Procedure Act,[123] provide that agencies shall as a matter of policy provide for the exclusion of irrelevant, immaterial, or unduly repetitious evidence.[124] The Massachusetts statute[125] provides that agencies may exclude unduly repetitious evidence.

Even in the absence of statutory provision, the Pennsylvania court has expressed its disapproval of the admission, by agencies, of irrelevant or immaterial evidence. In one case,[126] the court said that there must be excluded from consideration, on an application for a certificate of public convenience, evidence of service illegally rendered by the applicant in prior years. In another case,[127] it was held that, in a hearing in the court of common pleas on appeal of a condemnation proceeding, it was prejudicial error to permit the cross-examination of condemnor's expert as to fees received by him from the condemnor, since this had no relevancy to the issues involved. In Wisconsin (where, as above noted, the statute requires the exclusion of irrelevant, immaterial, and unduly repetitious evidence), the court has criticized an agency for admitting evidence without probative value.[128]

35-10); West Virginia (Acts 1964, art. 5, ch. 1, § 2); Wisconsin (STAT. § 227.10).

121 Alaska (STAT. § 44.62.460); California (GOV'T CODE § 11513); Missouri (REV. STAT. § 536.070).

122 Maine (REV. STAT. ANN. ch. 20-A, § 10); Maryland (ANN. CODE art. 41, § 252); Michigan (STAT. ANN. § 3.560(21.5) (1)); Minnesota (STAT. § 15.0419); Nebraska (REV. STAT. § 84-914); New Mexico (STAT. ANN. § 67-26-11—licensing act); North Carolina (GEN. STAT. § 150-18—licensing act); Oklahoma (STAT. tit. 75, § 310); Washington (REV. CODE § 34.04.100).

123 5 U.S.C. § 1006(c); F.C.A. 5 § 1006(c).

124 Hawaii (SESS. LAWS 1961, Act 103, § 10); Indiana (ANN. STAT. § 63-3008); Oregon (REV. STAT. § 183.450).

125 MASS. GEN. LAWS ANN. ch. 30A, § 11.

126 D. F. Bast, Inc. v. Pennsylvania Pub. Util. Comm'n, 397 Pa. 246, 154 A.2d 505 (1959).

127 Zamsky v. Public Parking Authority, 378 Pa. 38, 105 A.2d 335 (1954).

128 Department of Taxation v. O. H. Kindt Mfg. Co., 13 Wis. 2d 258, 108 N.W.2d 535 (1961).

(D) Application of Exclusionary Rules

Most of the states having statutes permitting the receipt, in administrative proceedings, of evidence that would not be judicially admissible, follow the pattern of the original Model State Act, providing that agencies may admit and give probative effect to evidence which possesses probative value commonly accepted by reasonably prudent men in the conduct of their affairs.[129] However, adoption of the phraseology of the Revised Model Act has already begun;[130] and statutes adopted in other states in recent years (but before the promulgation of the Revised Model Act) indicate a trend in the same direction. Thus, the Colorado statute[131] requires the agencies to conform, to the extent practicable, with the rules of evidence and requirements of proof applicable in civil non-jury actions in the district courts. The Michigan statute[132] provides that agencies shall so far as practicable follow the rules of evidence applicable to proceedings in chancery cases, but may in their discretion admit and give probative effect to any evidence which possesses probative value commonly accepted by reasonably prudent men in the conduct of their affairs. The North Dakota statute[133] provides that the admissibility of evidence in any proceeding before an administrative agency shall be determined, insofar as circumstances will permit, in accordance with the practice in the district courts.

The most commonly voiced objection to the proof-taking practices in the state agencies concerns the inclination of many agencies to rely on hearsay evidence as a basis for making findings of fact. Of course, in states where the legal residuum rule obtains[134] unsupported hearsay cannot support a finding; but a number of states have adopted legislation specifically referring to hearsay evidence. Thus, the Oregon statute[135] provides that

---

129 Maine (Rev. Stat. Ann. ch. 20-A, § 10); Maryland (Ann. Code art. 41, § 252); Minnesota (Stat. § 15.0419); Nebraska (Rev. Stat. § 84-914); New Mexico (Stat. Ann. § 67-26-11—licensing act); North Carolina (Gen. Stat. § 150-18—licensing act); Oklahoma (Stat. tit. 75, § 310); Washington (Rev. Code § 34.04.100).

130 Georgia (Code Ann. § 3A-101); Rhode Island (Gen. Laws Ann. § 42-35-10); West Virginia (Acts 1964, art. 5, ch. 1, § 2).

131 Colo. Rev. Stat. Ann. § 3-16-4.

132 Mich. Stat. Ann. § 3.560(21.5)(5).

133 N.D. Cent. Code § 28-32-06.

134 See § 4(B) *infra.*

135 Ore. Rev. Stat. § 183.450.

hearsay evidence shall not be admissible over an objection based on lack of opportunity to cross-examine. The Virginia statute[136] permits hearsay to be received only if the declarant is not readily available as a witness. The statutes in Alaska[137] and California[138] ordain that hearsay evidence may be used for the purpose of supplementing or explaining direct evidence, but shall not be sufficient in itself to support a finding unless it would be admissible over objection in a civil action.[139]

An interesting approach has been adopted in Florida, where the statute[140] provides that the agency may give probative effect to evidence which would be admissible in civil proceedings in the courts, but contains a caveat that due regard shall be given to the technical and highly complicated subject matter agencies must handle, and that the exclusionary rules shall not be used to prevent the receipt of evidence having substantial probative effect. Special interest attaches, too, to the Wisconsin statute[141] which permits agencies to admit all testimony having reasonable probative value, but requires that basic principles of relevancy, materiality, and probative force, as recognized in equitable proceedings, shall govern the proof of all questions of fact. Such statutes suggest that perhaps there should be different rules for different types of cases. In enforcement cases involving credibility of witnesses who are testifying to past events, the exclusionary rules serve an important function; but in complicated economic litigation necessarily involving matters of policy and opinion, the exclusionary rules may properly be relaxed, as they are in the courts.

Aside from the cases, cited in connection with the discussion of the legal residuum rule,[142] holding that hearsay may not be relied on as sole support for a finding of fact, there are comparatively few appellate state court cases discussing the propriety of the receipt of hearsay or other incompetent evidence in administrative proceedings. This is not surprising, for questions of this type are not often critical in cases appealed to state

---

136 VA. CODE ANN. § 9-6.11.
137 ALASKA STAT. § 44.62.460.
138 CAL. GOV'T CODE § 11513.
139 Another California statute authorizes reliance on hearsay in workmen's compensation cases. CAL. LABOR CODE § 5708.
140 FLA. STAT. § 120.27.
141 WIS. STAT. § 227.10.
142 See § 4(B) of this chapter.

supreme courts. Further, in states where the statutes either permit or prohibit the reception of hearsay, there is no occasion for the courts to review the question.

There are cases, however, indicating considerable judicial disapproval of the receipt of hearsay evidence. In an Arizona case, where an investigator of the state industrial commission had interviewed a claimant through an unsworn interpreter and was permitted to testify as to what the interpreter said the claimant had said (and was contradicted by the interpreter) the court set aside the award of compensation, declaring that the investigator's testimony should not have been admitted.[143] The Virginia court[144] affirmed a public utility commission in its refusal to permit a railroad to introduce, in support of its application for permission to discontinue train service, a statistical tabulation which had been prepared by persons other than the witness presenting the tabulation. Other courts have declared that in workmen's compensation proceedings, a physician who has examined a claimant in order to prepare himself to testify may not relate statements made to him by the claimant. The Connecticut court explained this result[145] by saying that ordinarily, when a patient consults a physician for treatment, he will state the facts as they are; but, unfortunately, when he does so preparatory to the trial of his case, his statements are not always reliable. The Kentucky court is in agreement.[146]

The California statute above cited, permitting hearsay to be used only to explain or supplement direct evidence, has been frequently construed.[147]

Some courts appear to consider that the hearsay rules applicable in court cases must be followed in administrative adjudication[148] even to the point of requiring reversal because incompetent evidence was received.[149]

---

143 Gomez v. Industrial Comm'n, 72 Ariz. 265, 233 P.2d 827 (1951).

144 Southern Ry. v. Commonwealth, 193 Va. 291, 68 S.E.2d 552 (1952).

145 Zawisza v. Quality Name Plate, Inc., 149 Conn. 115, 176 A.2d 578 (1961).

146 Mary Helen Coal Corp. v. Bigelow, 265 S.W.2d 69 (Ky. 1954).

147 *E.g.*, Manning v. Watson, 108 Cal. App. 2d 705, 239 P.2d 688 (1952); Nishkian v. City of Long Beach, 103 Cal. App. 2d 749, 230 P.2d 156 (1951).

148 Chicago & N.W. Ry. v. Illinois Commerce Comm'n, 326 Ill. 625, 158 N.E. 376, 55 A.L.R. 654 (1927); Spiegel's House Furnishing Co. v. Industrial Comm'n, 288 Ill. 422, 123 N.E. 606, 6 A.L.R. 540 (1919); Chiordi v. Jernigan, 46 N.M. 396, 129 P.2d 640 (1942).

149 *In re* Trustees of Village of Westminster, 108 Vt. 352, 187 Atl. 519 (1936).

A number of cases, in holding that particular evidence was properly received in administrative proceedings, appear to assume that the propriety of its admission was to be judged by the same rules which apply in judicial proceedings.[150]

Occasionally, a situation arises wherein the admission of evidence which is not technically inadmissible under the legal rules but which is without probative value and prejudicial in effect is held to violate the fundamental requirements of a fair hearing.[151] There are other cases, furthermore, where although this extreme situation was not presented, state courts have declared it to be reversible error for an agency to admit incompetent testimony. The Arkansas court held it reversible error for a workmen's compensation commission to admit evidence of a medical expert who in answering a hypothetical question assumed facts contrary to or in addition to the admitted facts.[152] The Illinois court declared it error for an agency to refuse to expunge the testimony of a witness who, the court held, should not have been permitted to testify.[153] In California, it was held that no weight could be given to letters submitted in opposition to a petition seeking permission to open a race track.[154] The Missouri court ruled that conclusions reached by tax assessors in connection with their viewing of the premises could not be considered as evidence;[155] and has ruled that in some types of cases hearings must be governed by the rules of evidence as applied in civil cases.[156]

While it would be stretching a point to assert that these decisions point to any general consensus on the part of the state

---

[150] Fagan v. City of Newark, 78 N.J. Super. 294, 188 A.2d 427 (1963); Bober v. Independent Plating Corp., 28 N.J. 160, 145 A.2d 463 (1958); 860 Fifth Avenue Corp. v. Tax Comm'n, 8 N.Y.2d 29, 200 N.Y.S.2d 817, 167 N.E.2d 455 (1960).

[151] People *ex rel.* Moynihan v. Greene, 179 N.Y. 253, 72 N.E. 99 (1904); People *ex rel.* Shiels v. Greene, 179 N.Y. 195, 71 N.E. 777 (1904); *cf.* Bridges v. Wixon, 326 U.S. 135, 89 L. Ed. 2103, 65 Sup. Ct. 1443 (1945).

[152] Hulsizer v. Johnson-Brennan Constr. Co., 232 Ark. 571, 339 S.W.2d 116 (1960).

[153] Bruce v. Department of Registration & Educ., 26 Ill. 2d 612, 187 N.E.2d 711 (1963).

[154] Desert Turf Club v. Board of Supervisors, 141 Cal. App. 2d 446, 296 P.2d 882 (1956).

[155] Koplar v. State Tax Comm'n, 321 S.W.2d 686 (Mo. 1959); *cf.* Stephens v. A. L. Wright & Co., 194 Va. 404, 73 S.E.2d 399 (1952), holding that personal examination by the commissioners of a workmen's compensation claimant did support a finding that there was no compensable disfigurement.

[156] Ellis v. State Dep't of Pub. Health & Welfare, 365 Mo. 614, 285 S.W.2d 634 (1955).

courts with respect to the propriety of the application of the exclusionary rules in administrative proceedings, it can fairly be said that there is wide-spread judicial recognition of the harsh truth that in many types of cases a policy in favor of unrestricted admission of hearsay impedes the discovery of the truth and may even serve as an invitation to perjury.

(E) PERMITTING DEPARTURE FROM THE RULES OF EVIDENCE IN EXCEPTIONAL CASES

The provisions of the Revised Model State Act, allowing incompetent evidence to be considered by agencies when to do so is necessary to ascertain facts not reasonably susceptible of proof under the rules of evidence as applied in non-jury civil cases (provided that it is of a type commonly relied upon by reasonably prudent men in the conduct of their affairs) are reflected in a number of state statutes. Some states, which have adopted the exclusionary rule of the Revised Model Act, have also adopted the exception there suggested.[157] Colorado, where the normal requirement is that the agencies observe the rules of evidence in civil non-jury cases in the district courts, permits relaxation of this requirement in cases where it is not practicable to comply with those requirements.[158] The Michigan statute, which requires agencies so far as practicable to follow the rules of evidence applicable to proceedings in chancery cases, provides that agencies "may in their discretion admit and give probative effect to any evidence which possesses probative value commonly accepted by reasonably prudent men in the conduct of their affairs."[159] In North Dakota, where the normal rule is that admissibility of evidence shall be determined, insofar as circumstances will permit, in accordance with the practice in the district courts, authorizes agencies to waive the usual common-law or statutory rules of evidence if such waiver is necessary to ascertain the substantial rights of the parties (but a caveat is added that only evidence of probative value shall be received).[160] In Virginia, where the statute provides that hearsay may be received only if the declarant is not readily available as a witness, and that secondary evidence

157 Georgia (CODE ANN. § 3A-101); Rhode Island (GEN. LAWS ANN. § 42-35-10); West Virginia (Acts 1964, art. 5, ch. 1, § 2).
158 COLO. REV. STAT. ANN. § 3-16-4.
159 MICH. STAT. ANN. § 3.560(21.5)(1).
160 N.D. CENT. CODE § 28-32-06.

of the contents of a document shall be received only if the original is not readily available, the agencies are admonished:

> In deciding whether a witness or a document is readily available the agency shall balance the importance of the evidence against the difficulty of obtaining it, and the more important the evidence is the more effort should be made to produce the eyewitness or the original document.[161]

In states where agencies operate under the precept that they may receive "the kind of evidence on which responsible persons are accustomed to rely in serious affairs,"[162] the courts indicate that agencies should be mindful of the warning stated by Judge Hand in the last-cited case, that mere rumor is not enough, and that hearsay should be relied on only if better evidence is not conveniently available. In many of the cases where state courts have approved the relaxation of normal evidentiary rules, the opinions describe the circumstances which convinced the court that the relaxation was reasonable under the circumstances.

The net results are not too far opposed to those reached under statutory provisions like those in the Revised Model Act, permitting waiver of the rules of evidence where to do so is necessary to ascertain facts not reasonably susceptible of proof under such rules. An example is afforded by a decision of the Wisconsin court,[163] permitting a labor relations board to receive, without formal proof of the authenticity of the copies, collective bargaining contracts in effect at other dairies, in connection with its determination of the appropriate bargaining unit at a particular dairy. It was obviously relevant to ascertain what bargaining units were customary in the industry; but it would scarcely have been practicable—nor would any good purpose have been served—to subpoena witnesses from every other dairy for the sole purpose of testifying to the authenticity of the copy of the union contract. It would be an unusual judge who would not have received unauthenticated printed copies for the same limited purpose, in a non-jury case. Similar considerations explain decisions approving the receipt of oral testimony as to the con-

---

[161] VA. CODE ANN. § 9-6.11.

[162] The phrase is that of Judge Learned Hand in NLRB v. Remington-Rand, Inc., 94 F.2d 862 (2d Cir. 1938).

[163] Dairy Employees Independent Union v. Wisconsin Employment Relations Bd., 262 Wis. 280, 55 N.W.2d 3 (1952).

tents of medical records kept in the ordinary course of business;[164] or the affidavits of a large group of doctors graduated by a named medical school in a certain year, certifying that a practitioner who asserted that he had been graduated from that school in that year was not in fact a member of the class;[165] or a statement of facts made by counsel for one group of property owners in a zoning case, the statement having been made in the presence of counsel for opposed property owners and without objection from their counsel.[166]

Again, no significant departure from the practices commonly followed by judges in non-jury cases may be seen in cases permitting a labor relations board to hear statements by employees as to the employer's attitude in collective bargaining matters, his attitude being relevant to the issues before the agency;[167] or permitting a public service commission to receive and consider a company's financial statement, without requiring proof of all the underlying books on which it was based—there apparently being no real issue as to the authenticity of the financial statement.[168]

In cases permitting agencies to go somewhat further than most judges would, even in non-jury trials—such as considering the results of lie-detector tests,[169] or receiving evidence of a telephone conversation with an individual whose voice the witness could not identify[170]—the courts justify departure from the normal rules on the grounds that under the circumstances of the particular case it was a necessary means of discovering the truth.

There is often a substantial justification for receiving opinion evidence in administrative proceedings. For example, where the question concerns the desirability of licensing a restaurant to sell liquor in a small town, or the desirability of permitting a railroad to curtail train service, the agency can be substantially aided in its task by letting the citizens affected state their views

---

164 Manfredi v. United Aircraft Corp., 138 Conn. 23, 81 A.2d 448 (1951).

165 Bockman v. Arkansas State Medical Bd., 229 Ark. 143, 313 S.W.2d 826 (1958).

166 Parsons v. Board of Zoning Appeals, 140 Conn. 290, 99 A.2d 149 (1953).

167 Bennett's Restaurant Inc. v. Industrial Comm'n, 127 Colo. 271, 256 P.2d 891 (1953).

168 Indianapolis & Southern Motor Express, Inc. v. Public Serv. Comm'n, 232 Ind. 377, 112 N.E.2d 864 (1953).

169 *Ex parte* Morris, 263 Ala. 664, 83 So. 2d 717 (1955).

170 International Brotherhood of Electrical Workers, Local 35 v. Commission on Civil Rights, 140 Conn. 537, 102 A.2d 366 (1953).

as to what is desirable—and this can be done without offending ideals of fairness; and might be permitted in the courts.[171] But a number of state courts show a tendency to restrict the agencies to much the same rules as those followed in the courts, so far as concerns the admission of opinion testimony.[172]

The state courts appear to be in agreement with the observation of the United States Supreme Court[173] that where evidence is received without objection, "it is to be considered and must be accorded 'its natural probative effect as if it were in law admissible.'" In a number of state court cases, approval of the action of an agency in receiving and considering hearsay evidence was predicated on the circumstance that it had been received without objection.[174]

On the whole, the attitude of most state courts is sympathetic to the standards proposed by the Revised Model State Act to govern the proof-taking activities of the agencies. The state courts do not, however, any more than does the Revised Model Act, insist that agencies be concerned with such purely technical procedural requirements as to whether evidence should have been introduced as a part of the case in chief, rather than on rebuttal.[175]

(F) Exclusion of Privileged Testimony

The provision of the Revised Model State Act[176] that "agencies shall give effect to the rules of privilege recognized by law" is echoed in the statutory enactments of a number of states.[177] The

---

[171] *Cf.* BENJAMIN, ADMINISTRATIVE ADJUDICATION IN THE STATE OF NEW YORK 176 (1942).

[172] *E.g.*, Swider v. Pillsbury Mills, 231 Minn. 210, 42 N.W.2d 560 (1950); *In re* Trustees of Village of Westminster, 108 Vt. 352, 187 Atl. 519 (1936).

[173] Opp Cotton Mills v. Administrator of Wage & Hour Div., 312 U.S. 126, 155, 85 L. Ed. 624, 61 Sup. Ct. 524 (1941).

[174] Napuche v. Liquor Control Comm'n, 336 Mich. 398, 58 N.W.2d 118 (1953); Mitchell Land Co. v. Planning & Zoning Bd. of Appeals, 140 Conn. 527, 102 A.2d 316 (1953); Modern Motor Express, Inc. v. Public Utils. Comm'n, 154 Ohio St. 271, 95 N.E.2d 764 (1950).

[175] International Harvester Co. v. Brown, 286 S.W.2d 920 (Ky. 1956).

[176] Section 10(1).

[177] Substantially similar provisions appear in the statutes of Alaska (STAT. § 44.62.460); California (GOV'T CODE § 11513); Georgia (CODE ANN. § 3A-101); Hawaii (SESS. LAWS 1961, Act 103, § 10); Maine (REV. STAT. ANN. ch. 20-A, § 10); Maryland (ANN. CODE art. 41, § 252); Massachusetts (GEN. LAWS ANN. ch. 30A, § 11); Michigan (STAT. ANN. § 3.560(21.5)(1)); Minnesota (STAT. § 15.0419); Missouri (REV. STAT. § 536.070); Nebraska (REV. STAT. § 84-914(1)); New Mexico (STAT. ANN. § 67-26-11—licensing act);

Oklahoma statute, reflecting the distinguished scholarship of Professor Maurice H. Merrill, spells out in detail what privileges shall be recognized. It requires agencies to give effect to the rules of privilege recognized by law in respect to self-incrimination; confidential communications between husband and wife during the subsistence of the marriage relation; communications between attorney and client, made in that relation; confessions made to a clergyman or priest in his professional capacity in the course of discipline enjoined by the church to which he belongs; communications made by a patient to a licensed practitioner of one of the healing arts with reference to any physical or supposed physical disease or of knowledge gained by such practitioner through a physical examination of a patient made in a professional capacity; records and files of any official or agency of any state of the United States which, by any statute of such state or of the United States, are made confidential and privileged.[178]

Without reference to statute, the attitude of the state courts appears to be that of giving effect to the recognized testimonial privileges in contested cases before administrative agencies. The question arises most frequently in connection with applications for the enforcement of agency subpoenas. Its application in that connection has been discussed in connection with the section on subpoenas.[179] Mr. Benjamin observes:

> . . . [T]he legal rules that exclude certain testimony on the ground of privilege (whether for the benefit of the witness himself or of some person who has made a privileged confidential communication to the witness) are apparently applicable to quasi-judicial proceedings.[180]

(G) Objections and Effect Thereof

The Revised Model State Act provides[181] that "objections to evidentiary offers may be made and shall be noted in the record." The Act does not state specifically whether or not the hearing

---

North Carolina (GEN. STAT. § 150-18—licensing act); Oregon (REV. STAT. § 183.450); Rhode Island (GEN. LAWS ANN. § 42-35-10); Virginia (CODE ANN. § 9-6.11); Washington (REV. CODE § 34.04.100); Wisconsin (STAT. § 227.10); West Virginia (Acts 1964, art. 5, ch. 1, § 2).

178 OKLA. STAT. tit. 75, § 310.

179 See ch. X, § 3(A)(10).

180 BENJAMIN, *op. cit. supra* note 171, at 172, citing New York City Council v. Goldwater, 284 N.Y. 296, 31 N.E.2d 31, 133 A.L.R. 728 (1940).

181 Section 10(1).

officer shall have power to rule upon objections, and exclude testimony if the objection is sustained. It was deemed inexpedient to make any provision with respect to this point, in view of the wide variety of practices in the various agencies of the several states respecting the status, functions, and powers of hearing officers. In some agencies in some states, the hearing officer is given powers approaching those of a trial judge, and in those states it could appropriately be provided that he may rule on objections. But in other states, the functions of the hearing officer are essentially equivalent to those of a notary public before whom a deposition is taken; and in such cases, the most practicable course is merely to note the objection in the hearing record, for the subsequent consideration of the agency officials who make the decision.

The statutes of some states contemplate that the normal procedure shall be that testimony to which objection has been taken shall, even if the objection is sustained by the hearing officer, nevertheless be preserved in some form in the hearing record. Thus, the Missouri statute[182] provides that evidence to which an objection is sustained shall, at the request of the party seeking to introduce the same, nevertheless be heard and preserved in the record, together with any cross-examination with respect thereto and any rebuttal thereof, unless it is wholly irrelevant, repetitious, privileged, or unduly long. Similarly, the Ohio statute[183] provides that the agency shall pass upon the admissibility of evidence, but a party may at the time make objection to the rulings of the agency thereon, and if the agency refuses to admit the evidence, the party offering the same shall make a proffer thereof, and such proffer shall be made a part of the record of such hearing. Other states have adopted the language of the Revised Model State Act.[184]

(H) Receiving Evidence in Written Form

In many types of administrative proceedings, the utilization of written evidence, as a substitute for oral examination of witnesses, is effective to expedite the consideration of cases. A typical

---

182 Mo. Rev. Stat. § 536.070.

183 Ohio Rev. Code Ann. § 119.09.

184 Georgia (Code Ann. § 3A-101); Oklahoma (Stat. tit. 75, § 310); Rhode Island (Gen. Laws Ann. § 42-35-10); West Virginia (Acts 1964, art. 5, ch. 1, § 2).

example involves rate proceedings before state public utility commissions. In such cases, it is common practice for expert witnesses on each side to submit their testimony in written form for the examination of the agency and of counsel for other parties, who then—to the extent they deem it desirable to do so—cross-examine the witnesses with respect to their written submissions. This procedure saves time, shortens records, and makes for more effective cross-examination. For many years, a similar so-called "shortened procedure" has been made available in Interstate Commerce Commission proceedings. When this procedure is adopted by the consent of the affected parties, the case may be decided upon stipulations, depositions, and briefs.[185]

Because of the circumstance that in a substantial number of cases before state agencies there is but little argument over the facts, which are often chiefly statistical in nature (the argument being as to the significance or proper interpretation of a technical and complex factual situation), there is every indication that similar procedures could well be adopted more generally.

The Revised Model State Act makes appropriate provision for such procedure. It declares that, subject to the general requirements set forth in the Act as to the reception of evidence, "when a hearing will be expedited and the interests of the parties will not be prejudiced substantially, any part of the evidence may be received in written form."[186] This provision is beginning to appear in state statutes.[187]

In other states, the legislatures have adopted a wide variety of statutory provisions serving, to a greater or less degree, the same general purpose. Of especial interest is the comprehensive statute in Missouri.[188] In addition to providing for the introduction of business entries, it provides (subject to stated limitations and restrictions) that the results of statistical studies or the results of surveys involving interviews with a large number of persons shall be admissible in evidence if the person under whose supervision such studies were made testifies as to the accuracy of the surveys and is made available for cross-examination. The

---

185 Monograph No. 11 of Attorney General's Committee on Administrative Procedure, S. DOC. No. 10, 77th Cong., 1st Sess. 23 (1941).

186 Section 10(1).

187 Colorado (REV. STAT. ANN. § 3-16-4); Georgia (CODE ANN. § 3A-101); Oklahoma (STAT. tit. 75, § 310(1)); Rhode Island (GEN. LAWS ANN. § 42-35-10).

188 MO. REV. STAT. §§ 536.070-536.073.

Missouri statute also provides (as noted below) for the introduction of affidavits in lieu of oral testimony under stated circumstances, and for the taking of depositions.

Not quite so ambitious as the Missouri statute are enactments found in some states providing for the utilization of affidavits, by consent of the parties, in lieu of oral testimony. The Alaska and California statutes[189] provide that at any time ten or more days prior to a hearing, any party may serve on an opposing party a copy of any affidavit he proposes to introduce in evidence; and that unless the opposing party serves notice of a request to cross-examine the affiant, the affidavit may be introduced in evidence and given the same effect as if the affiant had testified orally. The statutes of these two states further provide that if the request for cross-examination is not honored, the affidavit may nonetheless be introduced, but shall be given only the same effect as other hearsay evidence. The Missouri statute above noted[190] is similar, but contains a further provision that if the opposing party objects to the use of the affidavit or to designated portions thereof, the affidavit may not be used except in ways that would be permissible without reference to the statute.

Other states have statutory provisions that go part way toward the goal of permitting a case to be determined on the basis of written submissions, by making provisions for the taking of depositions of witnesses, and the introduction thereof in evidence, subject generally to the same conditions as attach to the use of depositions in proceedings in the courts.[191]

Even without the benefit of statutory provisions, it is sometimes possible, by informal cooperation between attorneys for the agency and for the respondent, to approximate the result contemplated by the Revised Model State Act. Often an agency assigns a case for hearing before its staff members have become familiar with the factual details involved; and the submission by respondent's attorney of a carefully prepared statement covering the significant facts of the case may become the basis for a stipulation of facts, on which the case may be disposed of.

---

[189] ALASKA STAT. § 44.62.470; CAL. GOV'T CODE § 11514.

[190] MO. REV. STAT. § 536.070(12).

[191] Alaska (STAT. § 44.62.440); California (GOV'T CODE § 11511); Florida (STAT. § 120.25); Indiana (ANN. STAT. § 63-3007); Missouri (GEN. LAWS ANN. § 536.070); Ohio (REV. CODE ANN. § 119.09); Virginia (CODE ANN. § 9-6.10).

Utilization of this informal device is often advantageous both for the respondent and for the agency.

(I) SPECIAL PROVISIONS FOR DOCUMENTARY EVIDENCE

Because the statutes and court decisions of some states impose strict (not to say archaic) restrictions on the use of copies of documentary evidence in court proceedings, the draftsmen of the Revised Model State Act proposed language which it was believed could appropriately be adopted in those states in order to avoid unnecessary difficulties in connection with the use of copies of documents in administrative proceedings, where the introduction of large quantities of documentary evidence is commonplace. The Revised Model Act provides:[192] "[(2) documentary evidence may be received in the form of copies or excerpts, if the original is not readily available. Upon request, parties shall be given an opportunity to compare the copy with the original;]". The sentence was put within brackets, as pointed out in the Commentary published by the National Conference of Commissioners on Uniform State Laws, to indicate that it is intended for states where the rules of evidence applied in court proceedings impose stricter limits on the use of copies of documentary evidence.

In states where there is need for such provision, the practical desirability of the proposal is obvious. In many administrative proceedings copies of a wide variety of documents—*e.g.*, personnel records, financial statements, medical records—are frequently offered in evidence. In something over ninety-nine per cent of the cases, it is fair to estimate, no question is raised as to the authenticity of the copy. It would therefore involve an unnecessary and unwarranted expense of time and money to require all such records to be proved by bringing in the various books of original entry from which they were derived, and having witnesses testify to each step from, say, the original invoice to the journal entry to the ledger to a trial balance sheet to a final financial statement.

The Revised Model Act therefore provides in Section 10(2) that copies may be used, whenever the original document is not readily available. It further provides (in order to facilitate re-

---

[192] Section 10(2).

ducing the bulk of the record) that if the document or copy thereof is lengthy, the parties may introduce only the relevant excerpts. At the same time, to avoid possible mistake or misfeasance, the right to examine the original, upon request, is guaranteed.

The provisions of the Revised Model State Act have already been adopted in some states.[193] A substantial number of states have adopted in substance the provisions of the original Model State Act, which provided, in Section 9 (2):

> All evidence, including records and documents in the possession of the agency of which it desires to avail itself, shall be offered and made a part of the record in the case, and no other factual information or evidence shall be considered in the determination of the case. Documentary evidence may be received in the form of copies or excerpts, or by incorporation by reference.

The draftsmen of the Revised Act believed that the requirement as to incorporating in the record all documents relied on could more appropriately be covered in the sections prescribing the necessary form and content of the hearing record; and these requirements are set forth and made more specific in Sections 9(e) and 9(g) of the Revised Act. The provision for incorporation by reference was dropped. In many cases, such incorporation is accomplished by agreement of the parties.[194] In cases where the parties cannot so agree, there is danger that a statutory right to incorporate documents into the record by mere reference might interfere with the rights of cross-examination guaranteed elsewhere by the Revised Model Act.[195] Accordingly, there were deleted the provisions of the original act which might be interpreted as granting a right to introduce, by the device of "incorporating by reference," documents which perhaps might not be in the hearing room for the examination of the parties. States having enacted the substance of the above-quoted provision of

---

193 Georgia (CODE ANN. § 3A-101); Hawaii (SESS. LAWS 1961, Act 103, § 10(a)); Oklahoma (STAT. tit. 75, § 310); Rhode Island (GEN. LAWS ANN. § 42-35-10).

194 *E.g.,* State *ex rel.* Utilities Comm'n v. Southern Ry., 256 N.C. 359, 124 S.E.2d 510 (1962), where a record of proceedings before the Interstate Commerce Commission was introduced by stipulation in proceedings before a state public utility commission.

195 Section 10(3).

the first Model State Act respecting documentary evidence are noted below.[196]

Other enactments of particular interest are found in the states of Maine, Missouri, and Virginia. The Maine statute[197] provides that whenever a party proposes to introduce documentary evidence (other than official records as recognized by statute) he shall give advance notice of his intention to all other parties, who may then demand the right to cross-examine the author of the document; and the statute further provides that if the author is not produced for cross-examination following such demand, the document shall be excluded as hearsay.

The Missouri statute[198] is somewhat more guarded than is the Revised Model Act in its provisions for introduction of copies of documentary evidence. It provides that copies may be introduced without proof of the unavailability of the originals only if it shall be shown—by testimony or otherwise—that the copy is a true copy. The statute also contains provisions affording a party whose documentary evidence is excluded because of his failure to make such proof, an opportunity at a later date to establish by other evidence the facts sought to be proved by the excluded document.

The Virginia statute[199] provides that secondary evidence of the contents of a document may be received only if the original is not readily available; requires the agency to balance the importance of the evidence against the difficulty of obtaining it; and declares that the more important the evidence is, the greater effort should be made to produce the original document.

(J) Effect of Exclusion of Proper Evidence

The exclusion of proper evidence may vitiate the agency's decision, if it appears that its exclusion may have affected the result. State courts agree with decisions in the federal courts that refusal to receive competent and material evidence may be a

---

196 Maine (Rev. Stat. Ann. ch. 20-A, § 10—which also has other noteworthy provisions explained below); Maryland (Ann. Code art. 41, § 252); Massachusetts (Gen. Laws Ann. ch. 30A, § 11); Michigan (Stat. Ann. § 3.560-(21.5)); Minnesota (Stat. § 15.0419(2)); Nebraska (Rev. Stat. § 84-914); Oregon (Rev. Stat. § 183.450); Washington (Rev. Code § 34.04.100).

197 Me. Rev. Stat. Ann. ch. 20-A, § 10.

198 Mo. Rev. Stat. § 536.070.

199 Va. Code Ann. § 9-6.11.

denial of due process.[200] The requirement that proper evidence be received is a necessary counterpart of the rule that the agency must give due weight to all the evidence before it; refusal to consider proper evidence which has been duly proffered falls within the condemnation that voids arbitrary administrative action.[201]

If it appears that the excluded evidence could not materially have affected the outcome of the case—if a remand to receive and consider the evidence improperly excluded would amount to nothing more than "a postponement of the inevitable," the error committed is not prejudicial.[202] But normally it is impossible for a reviewing court to be assured that the outcome could not have been affected by the consideration of the excluded testimony, and in the usual case the necessary result of the exclusion of proper testimony is to void the administrative order.[203]

Section 4

What Evidence Is Required to Support a Finding

(A) TESTS OF "SUBSTANTIALITY" OF EVIDENCE AFFECT PROOF-TAKING PROCEDURES

Underlying the entire proof-taking processes of administrative agencies are the requirements and implications of the substantial evidence rule. For this reason, some reference to the substantial evidence rule is appropriate in this chapter, despite the fact that its consideration and application ordinarily arises only in connection with judicial review of agency decisions. The substantial evidence rule is important in two ways: (a) it constitutes the criterion to test the validity of agency findings of fact; (b) it accounts in large measure for the practices adopted by the agencies in receiving evidence. The first aspect of the rule—its appli-

---

200 NLRB v. Burns, 207 F.2d 434 (8th Cir. 1953); Donnelly Garment Co. v. NLRB, 123 F.2d 215 (8th Cir. 1941)—reviewing many authorities; People *ex rel.* Hirschberg v. Board of Supervisors, 251 N.Y. 156, 167 N.E. 204 (1929); People *ex rel.* Packwood v. Riley, 232 N.Y. 283, 133 N.E. 891 (1922).

201 Gallant's Case, 326 Mass. 507, 95 N.E.2d 536 (1950); Prince v. Industrial Comm'n, 89 Ariz. 314, 361 P.2d 929 (1961).

202 Pittsburgh Plate Glass Co. v. NLRB, 313 U.S. 146, 85 L. Ed. 1251, 61 Sup. Ct. 908 (1941); 113 F.2d 698, 702 (8th Cir. 1940).

203 See, in addition to the cases cited in notes 199, 200 and 201 *supra,* Hunt's Adm'rx v. Fuqua, 311 Ky. 497, 224 S.W.2d 917 (1949).

cation in judicial review proceedings to test the validity of agency findings of fact—will be discussed in Chapter XIX. The second aspect—its bearing upon the practices adopted by the agencies in receiving evidence—will be considered here.

Ever conscious that their findings may be challenged in the courts on the ground that they are not supported by substantial evidence, the agencies attempt to make sure that the evidence on which they base their findings will meet the requirement of "substantiality" imposed by the courts. This, likely, is one of the reasons for the general tendency of many agencies to follow in the main the rules of evidence as they are applied in civil non-jury cases in the courts.

Fundamentally, the substantial evidence rule has two aspects. The first denies the quality of substantiality to evidence that fails to meet certain fundamental prerequisites. If they are not met, the court need go no further; the evidence is not substantial. If, however, these basic requirements are satisfied, the second phase of the "substantiality" test comes into play; and the court proceeds to determine whether the whole record clearly precludes the agency's findings "from being justified by a fair estimate of the worth of the testimony."[204]

The first aspect is ordinarily described as the "legal residuum" rule. Under this rule, it is said that a finding cannot be deemed to be supported by substantial evidence unless at least a residuum of the supporting evidence would be competent under the exclusionary rules. For example, if the supporting evidence were all hearsay, it could not be deemed substantial.

It is this rule which directly affects the proof-taking practices of the agencies; and it will therefore be considered in this chapter, in connection with the preceding discussion concerning the question as to what evidence may be admitted.

The second aspect of the "substantial evidence" rule—involving the appraisal of the "substantiality" of the evidence on the record considered as a whole—will be discussed in connection with the examination to be made in Chapter XIX of the grounds on which administrative findings and orders in a contested case may be reversed by the courts on appeal.

---

204 Universal Camera Corp. v. NLRB, 340 U. S. 474, 490, 95 L. Ed. 456, 71 Sup. Ct. 456 (1951).

(B) The Legal Residuum Rule in the State Courts

Most of the state courts that have spoken on the question since the promulgation of the first Model State Administrative Procedure Act in 1946[205] have continued to support the legal residuum rule, which first gained currency long before administrative law was thought of as a separate aspect of the corpus juris.[206] Decisions from twenty-one states demonstrate the continued vitality of the rule (although it may be noted that in some of the cases cited, the same result could have been reached on the basis that the evidence relied on was not substantial, in the second sense described above):

1. *California.* In California, the question is in large part ruled by statute. The Government Code,[207] applicable to some half hundred agencies, specifies that hearsay evidence shall not be sufficient in itself to support a finding unless it would be admissible over objection in a civil action. However, with respect to workmen's compensation proceedings, another statute[208] provides that no order shall be invalidated because of the use, as proof of any fact in dispute, of any evidence not admissible in court proceedings. Before the above-mentioned provision in the Government Code was adopted, the California court declared that unless specially permitted by statute, hearsay evidence is not competent and does not constitute substantial evidence.[209]

205 Neither the original nor the Revised Model State Administrative Procedure Acts makes specific provision concerning the legal residuum rule. The original version provided in Section 12(7)(e) that the reviewing court could reverse administrative findings not supported by competent, material, and substantial evidence. The inclusion of "competent" supported a suggestion that the residuum rule was by indirection imported into the original Model Act. The revised version provides, in Section 15(g)(5), that the court may reverse agency findings that are clearly erroneous in view of the reliable, probative, and substantial evidence. The omission of the adjective "competent" makes it clear that the statute does not of itself require the adoption of the residuum rule.

206 While it is often said that the rule was "born" in the decision of the New York court in *Carroll v. Knickerbocker Ice Co.,* 218 N.Y. 435, 113 N.E. 507 (1916), it had in fact been applied in earlier cases, *e.g.,* Reck v. Whittlesberger, 181 Mich. 463, 148 N.W. 247, 52 L.R.A. (n.s.) 930 (1914).

207 Cal. Gov't Code § 11513.

208 Cal. Labor Code § 5708.

209 Walker v. City of San Gabriel, 20 Cal. 2d 879, 129 P.2d 349 (1942). In *Johnstone v. Daly City,* 156 Cal. App. 2d 506, 319 P.2d 756 (1958), it was held that a discharge from civil service position cannot be based wholly on hearsay; and in *Stout v. Department of Employment,* 172 Cal. App. 2d 666, 342 P.2d 918 (1959), it was said that to base an administrative order solely on incompetent hearsay is an abuse of discretion. Again, in *Dyer v. Watson,* 121 Cal. App. 2d 84, 262 P.2d 873 (1953), the court said that hearsay evidence alone does not constitute substantial evidence.

2. *Colorado.* In a workmen's compensation case, the Colorado court said that the award may not stand if based wholly on hearsay.[210]

3. *Delaware.* The Superior Court reversed an order of the unemployment compensation commission, because its findings were based solely on hearsay evidence.[211]

4. *Idaho.* The Idaho court set aside a finding of the public utilities commission which was based solely on correspondence. The decision appears to accept the residuum rule.[212]

5. *Illinois.* In 1958,[213] the Illinois court continued its long-standing support of the residuum rule.[214]

6. *Maine.* In a workmen's compensation case, the court held that although hearsay admitted by consent may properly be considered as corroborative of competent evidence, hearsay will not alone support a finding.[215]

7. *Massachusetts.* Construing a provision of an unemployment compensation act that "the findings of the board of review as to the facts, if supported by any evidence, shall be conclusive," the Massachusetts court held that this meant "supported by substantial evidence such 'as a reasonable mind might accept as adequate to support a conclusion'" and ruled that exclusively hearsay evidence is not substantial evidence "even before an administrative tribunal."[216]

8. *Missouri.* The court set aside a revocation of a license where the finding was supported only by hearsay evidence, remarking that "hearsay testimony is not 'competent and substan-

---

210 Johnson v. Industrial Comm'n of Colorado, 137 Colo. 591, 328 P.2d 384 (1958). *Accord:* Williams v. New Amsterdam Cas. Co., 136 Colo. 458, 319 P.2d 1078 (1957); *cf.*, Banking Bd. v. Holyoke Industrial Bank, 383 P.2d 318 (Colo. 1963).

211 Geegan v. Unemployment Compensation Comm'n, 45 Del. 513, 76 A.2d 116 (1950).

212 Application of Citizens Utils. Co., 82 Idaho 208, 351 P.2d 487 (1960).

213 Menning v. Department of Registration & Educ., 14 Ill. 2d 553, 153 N.E.2d 52 (1958).

214 *E.g.*, Sidney Wanzer & Sons, Inc. v. Industrial Comm'n, 380 Ill. 409, 44 N.E.2d 40 (1942).

215 Goldthwaite v. Sheraton Restaurant, 154 Me. 214, 145 A.2d 362 (1958).

216 Sinclair v. Director of Div. of Employment Security, 331 Mass. 101, 102, 117 N.E.2d 164 (1954). In another case, the court held that an award in a workmen's compensation case may not be based solely on hearsay. Buck's Dependents' Case, 342 Mass. 766, 175 N.E.2d 369 (1961).

tial evidence' and could not provide the legal basis for a finding."[217]

9. *Michigan.* The Michigan court adopted the legal residuum rule in 1914[218] and appears to continue to insist that an administrative finding cannot stand if there is "no competent evidence" to support it.[219]

10. *New Jersey.* Under the leadership of Judge Vanderbilt, the New Jersey court repeatedly insisted that administrative findings, to be sustained on appeal, must be supported by a residuum of legally competent evidence. In a 1950 decision,[220] that court said that while the workmen's compensation board, not being bound by the rules of evidence, may receive hearsay, nevertheless hearsay cannot form the basis of an award of compensation. Similar rulings were made in 1957,[221] and 1961.[222]

11. *New York.* In New York, the legal residuum rule was first enunciated in a workmen's compensation case,[223] holding that an award could not be based on hearsay statements attributed to a deceased workman as to an alleged accidental injury. Subsequently, the statute was amended to provide "declarations of a deceased employee concerning the accident shall be received in evidence and shall, if corroborated by circumstances or other evidence, be sufficient to establish the accident and the injury."[224] While the court has held that the statute may be applied to statements by claimants who, as a result of injury, have lost understanding and the power of speech; it has not repudiated the legal residuum rule entirely, even in workmen's compensation cases.[225] In 1954, the court declared: "It is the decisional

217 Dittmeier v. Missouri Real Estate Comm'n, 237 S.W.2d 201, 206 (Mo. App. 1951). In *Ellis v. State Dep't of Pub. Health & Welfare,* 365 Mo. 614, 285 S.W.2d 634 (1956), the court set aside an agency decision because it appeared to have been based upon a piece of evidence (a physician's certificate) which was not legally competent.

218 Reck v. Whittlesberger, 181 Mich. 463, 148 N.W. 247, 52 L.R.A. (n.s.) 930 (1914).

219 Simpson v. Matthes, 343 Mich. 125, 72 N.W.2d 64 (1955).

220 Andricsak v. National Fireproofing Corp., 3 N.J. 466, 70 A.2d 750 (1950).

221 Gilligan v. International Paper Co., 24 N.J. 230, 131 A.2d 503 (1957).

222 Black v. Mahoney Troast Constr. Co., 65 N.J. Super. 397, 168 A.2d 62 (1961).

223 Carroll v. Knickerbocker Ice Co., 218 N.Y. 435, 113 N.E. 507 (1916).

224 N.Y. Laws of 1922, ch. 615.

225 Altschuller v. Bressler, 289 N.Y. 463, 46 N.E.2d 886 (1943); Ptaszynski v. American Sugar Ref. Co., 280 App. Div. 905, 115 N.Y.S.2d 543, *aff'd,* 305 N.Y. 833, 114 N.E.2d 38 (1953).

law, of course, that while hearsay evidence is admissible in compensation proceedings, there must be a residuum of common-law evidence."[226] The appellate division has also ruled that an order suspending a liquor license may not be based exclusively on hearsay.[227]

12. *North Carolina.* An oft-cited 1938 ruling[228] enunciating the residuum rule has been followed consistently.[229]

13. *Ohio.* The Ohio court continues to apply the legal residuum rule.[230]

14. *Oklahoma.* The Oklahoma court has followed the residuum rule in a number of cases,[231] and in some cases has apparently held it to be error even to admit evidence incompetent by common-law tests;[232] but in other cases has apparently ignored the rule.[233]

15. *Pennsylvania.* In Pennsylvania, too, the legal residuum rule continues to be supported.[234]

16. *Rhode Island.* Admission of incompetent evidence in a workmen's compensation case, over proper objection, was held to be prejudicial error, the commission being bound by the rules of evidence.[235]

17. *South Carolina.* The rule is that while an administrative agency is not governed by the legal rules of evidence, still an

---

226 Doca v. Federal Stevedoring Co., 308 N.Y. 44, 52, 123 N.E.2d 632 (1954); *cf.* Graham v. Nassau & Suffolk Lighting Co., 308 N.Y. 140, 123 N.E.2d 813 (1954).

227 Magee v. New York State Liquor Authority, 13 App. Div. 2d 649, 214 N.Y.S.2d 1 (1961).

228 Plyler v. Charlotte Country Club, 214 N.C. 453, 199 S.E. 622 (1938).

229 Little v. Power Brake Co., 255 N.C. 451, 121 S.E.2d 889 (1961); Pearson v. Peerless Flooring Co., 247 N.C. 434, 101 S.E.2d 301 (1958); Penland v. Bird Coal Co., 246 N.C. 26, 97 S.E.2d 432 (1957); Johnson v. Erwin Cotton Mills Co., 232 N.C. 321, 59 S.E.2d 828 (1950).

230 Chesapeake & Ohio Ry. v. Public Utils. Comm'n, 163 Ohio St. 252, 126 N.E.2d 314 (1955).

231 G. T. Harvey Co. v. Steele, 347 P.2d 802 (Okla. 1959); *cf.* Mid-Union Drilling Co. v. Graham, 184 Okla. 514, 88 P.2d 619 (1939).

232 Patrick & Tilman v. Matkin, 154 Okla. 232, 7 P.2d 414 (1932); F. W. Merrick, Inc. v. Cross, 144 Okla. 40, 289 Pac. 267 (1930).

233 Grison Oil Corp. v. Corporation Comm'n, 186 Okla. 548, 99 P.2d 134 (1940); Croxton v. State, 186 Okla. 249, 97 P.2d 11 (1939). Many cases are collected in MERRILL, ADMINISTRATIVE LAW 331 (1954).

234 Glen Alden Coal Co. v. Unemployment Compensation Bd. of Review, 168 Pa. Super. 534, 79 A.2d 796 (1951); Phillips v. Unemployment Compensation Bd. of Review, 152 Pa. 2d 75, 30 A.2d 718 (1943).

235 Cole v. New England Transp. Co., 88 R.I. 408, 149 A.2d 352 (1959).

order founded only on hearsay or other improper evidence will not be sustained.[236]

18. *Texas.* In a decision typical of the area in which the question seems most often to arise, it was held in Texas that testimony as to statements of a deceased employee will not support an award of workmen's compensation.[237]

19. *Utah.* The workmen's compensation commission may receive and consider any kind of evidence, but there must be a residuum of evidence of a type that would be legal and competent in a court of law to support an award; a finding cannot be based wholly on hearsay.[238]

20. *Wisconsin.* In a number of decisions, the Wisconsin court has adhered without deviation to the residuum rule.[239]

21. *Wyoming.* The Wyoming court has held that hearsay alone will not support a finding.[240]

(C) Will the Legal Residuum Rule Survive?

Despite the seeming vigor with which many courts continue to insist that there must be a residuum of legally competent evidence to support an administrative finding (and it is perhaps significant that many of these decisions involve claims for workmen's compensation, where the dangers of basing awards on self-serving claims of interested witnesses are obvious), there is some doubt whether the rule will survive as a general requirement.

The long-standing disagreement among the federal courts of appeal[241] may come to be reflected, to a greater extent than has yet appeared, in the decisions of the state courts.

Already, many state court decisions can be cited in support of the proposition that the courts tend to ease the rigor of the rule,

---

236 Richards v. City of Columbia, 227 S.C. 538, 88 S.E.2d 683 (1955).

237 Bean v. Hardware Mut. Cas. Co., 349 S.W.2d 284 (Tex. Civ. App. 1961).

238 Hackford v. Industrial Comm'n, 11 Utah 2d 312, 358 P.2d 899 (1961).

239 State *ex rel.* Ball v. McPhee, 6 Wis. 2d 190, 94 N.W.2d 711 (1959); California Packing Co. v. Industrial Comm'n, 270 Wis. 72, 70 N.W.2d 200 (1955); Wisconsin Tel. Co. v. Industrial Comm'n, 263 Wis. 380, 57 N.W.2d 334 (1953).

240 Jennings v. C. M. & W. Drilling Co., 307 P.2d 122 (Wyo. 1957).

241 The split of authority noted in Cooper, Administrative Agencies and the Courts 193 (1951), continues. *E.g.,* John W. McGrath Corp. v. Hughes, 264 F.2d 314 (2d Cir. 1959); NLRB v. Englander Co., 260 F.2d 67 (9th Cir. 1958).

in cases where the evidence appears convincing, by holding competent as part of the *res gestae* hearsay statements made considerably after the event;[242] or by upholding as a valid inference from circumstantial evidence findings which are in large part based on hearsay.[243]

Legal scholars have long criticized the residuum rule. It is charged, for example, that the mere circumstance that there is some residuum of proof pointing in one direction or another has nothing to do with the making of the administrative finding, because the agency is influenced by the preponderance of the testimony, not by the residuum thereof. As observed by Wigmore:[244] "It is obviously fallacious to assume that one or more pieces of 'legal' evidence are 'per se' a sufficient guarantee of truth." The rule, in short, is branded as artificial.[245]

On the other hand, it is urged that the existence of the rule has accomplished considerable good, because the fear that it may be invoked has led agencies to insist on careful presentation and detailed examination of the evidence offered in contested cases; and because it has had the effect of inducing agencies to apply the rules of evidence in much the same fashion as they are applied by judges sitting in non-jury civil cases.

In most cases, to be sure, it makes no difference whether the court accepts or rejects the legal residuum rule, because there is usually more than a residuum of legally competent evidence pointing both ways; the agency decision would be supported by at least a residuum of legally competent evidence, whichever way the case was decided.

---

242 *E.g.,* Commissioners of Roads & Revenues of Fulton County v. Dowis, 107 Ga. App. 647, 131 S.E.2d 144 (1963); American Security Co. v. Minard, 118 Ind. App. 310, 77 N.E.2d 762 (1948); Gifford v. Iowa Mfg. Co., 243 Iowa 145, 51 N.W.2d 119 (952); Sligh v. Newberry Elec. Coop., Inc., 216 S.C. 401, 58 S.E.2d 675 (1950); Truck Ins. Exch. v. Michling, 358 S.W.2d 697 (Tex. Civ. App. 1962).

243 *E.g.,* Carney v. General Cable Corp., 303 N.Y. 885, 105 N.E.2d 108 (1952). Remarks in the following cases indicate, in some degree, a repudiation of the legal residuum rule: Hudgens v. Industrial Comm'n, 83 Ariz. 383, 321 P.2d 1039 (1958); Shindhelm v. Razook, 190 Kan. 80, 372 P.2d 278 (1962); Standard Oil Co. of New Jersey v. Mealey, 147 Md. 249, 127 Atl. 850 (1925); Collins-Dietz-Morris Co. v. Richardson, 307 P.2d 159 (Okla. 1957). Many cases indicating a relaxation of the legal residuum rule are cited in 2 DAVIS, ADMINISTRATIVE LAW TREATISE § 14.12 (1958).

244 1 WIGMORE, EVIDENCE § 4 (3d ed. 1940).

245 It is criticized also by BENJAMIN, ADMINISTRATIVE ADJUDICATION IN THE STATE OF NEW YORK 189 et seq. (1942).

(D) Other Requirements

It is required, of course, that there must be *evidence* to support the finding. The state courts agree with the statement of Justice Brandeis in *United States v. Abilene & S. Ry.*,[246] that: "A finding without evidence is beyond the power of the Commission. Papers in the Commission's files are not always evidence in a case. . . . Nothing can be treated as evidence which is not introduced as such." As the requirement was phrased by the California court: "Administrative tribunals exercising quasi-judicial powers which are required to make a determination after a hearing cannot act on their own information. Nothing may be treated as evidence which has not been introduced as such."[247]

Section 5

Official Notice

(A) The Problem

Administrative agencies, in the decision of contested cases, may take official notice of matters which the courts would notice judicially. Within these limits, no difficulties are encountered. The problem arises only in connection with the question how much beyond these limits the agencies may go in relying on conclusions developed as a result of their intensive experience in their specialized fields of activity, as a basis for making factual findings as to matters of a general nature which their experience has taught them to be true.

The rule is now clearly emerging that an administrative agency may take official notice of any generally recognized technical or scientific facts within the agency's specialized knowledge, subject always to the proviso that the parties must be given adequate advance notice of the facts which the agency proposes to note, and given adequate opportunity to show the inaccuracy of the facts or the fallacy of the conclusions which the agency

---

[246] 265 U.S. 274, 288, 68 L. Ed. 1016, 44 Sup. Ct. 565 (1924).

[247] La Prade v. Department of Water & Power, 27 Cal. 2d 47, 51, 162 P.2d 13 (1945); *cf.* Sultan Turkish Bath, Inc. v. Board of Police Comm'rs, 169 Cal. App. 2d 188, 337 P.2d 203 (1959), holding that a hearing examiner's view of a turkish bath establishment, in connection with license revocation proceedings, when such inspection was made with the consent of counsel, could be treated as evidence in the case.

proposes tentatively to accept without proof. To satisfy this requirement, it is necessary that a statement of the facts noticed must be incorporated into the record. The source material on which the agency relies should, on request, be made available to the parties for their examination.

(B) Statutory Provisions

The principles above described are embodied in the Revised Model Act, which provides:[248]

> Notice may be taken of judicially cognizable facts. In addition, notice may be taken of generally recognized technical or scientific facts within the agency's specialized knowledge. Parties shall be notified either before or during the hearing, or by reference in preliminary reports or otherwise, of the material noticed, including any staff memoranda or data, and they shall be afforded an opportunity to contest the material so noticed. The agency's experience, technical competence, and specialized knowledge may be utilized in the evaluation of the evidence.

States which have adopted legislation concerning official notice have followed, in general, the same pattern as that found in the Revised Model Act, which involves three basic requirements: (1) limitation as to what types of facts may be noticed; (2) provisions for giving the other parties to the case ample notice of what asserted facts the agency proposes to notice; (3) guarantees of adequate opportunity to explain or refute the asserted facts.

The provisions limiting the types of fact of which notice may be taken are of particular significance. It needs no argument to demonstrate that agencies may not take notice of the "litigation facts" involved in a particular case; to do so would be to shift the burden of proof and make a mockery of the hearing procedure. The doctrine of notice should be limited to facts of a general nature, representing generalizations distilled from repeated demonstrations.

But just what are facts of a "general nature"? Some agencies, operating under the phrase found in the original Model State Act—"general, technical, or scientific facts" (a phrase found in the statutes of several states)[249]—construed the term "general"

---

[248] Section 10(4).

[249] Colorado (Rev. Stat. Ann. § 3-16-4); Maine (Rev. Stat. Ann. ch.

as embracing congeries of asserted facts of rather narrowly circumscribed applicability. It was to correct this tendency that the draftsmen of the Revised Model Act adopted as the key phrase "generally recognized technical or scientific facts." This phrase is beginning to appear in the state statutes.[250] A very similar phrase—"generally accepted technical or scientific matter"—appears in the statutes of Alaska and California.[251] Other variants of phraseology occur, such as "technical or scientific facts,"[252] or "any generally recognized fact or any established technical or scientific fact."[253]

The statutes in all of the above-mentioned states[254] provide, in one form of language or another, that the other parties to the case must be given notice, before a final order is entered, of the asserted facts which the agency proposes to notice, and must be afforded opportunity to explain or refute them.

Even in the absence of statute, of course, an agency may take notice of facts which a court would judicially notice; and at least one state[255] provides that the scope of facts officially noticed must be limited to those of which a court of record could take judicial notice.

The Florida statute[256] does not limit the facts which an agency may officially notice, but does provide that when an agency order rests on official notice of a material fact not appearing in the evidence of record, any party shall on timely request be afforded an opportunity to show the contrary.

The California and North Dakota statutes are of particular interest. The California statute[257] provides in careful and meticu-

---

20-A, § 10); Maryland (ANN. CODE art. 41, § 252); Massachusetts (GEN. LAWS ANN. ch. 30A, § 11); Michigan (STAT. ANN. § 3.560(21.5)); Minnesota (STAT. § 15.0419); Nebraska (REV. STAT. § 84-914); New Mexico (STAT. ANN. § 67-26-11—licensing act); Oregon (REV. STAT. § 183.450); Washington (REV. CODE § 34.04.100).

250 *E.g.*, Georgia (CODE ANN. § 3A-101); Hawaii (SESS. LAWS 1961, Act 103, § 10); Oklahoma (STAT. tit. 75, § 310); Rhode Island (GEN. LAWS ANN. § 42-35-10).

251 ALASKA STAT. § 44.62.480; CAL. GOV'T CODE § 11515.

252 MO. REV. STAT. § 536.070.

253 WIS. STAT. § 227.10.

254 Alaska, California, Colorado, Georgia, Hawaii, Maine, Maryland, Massachusetts, Michigan, Minnesota, Missouri, Nebraska, New Mexico, Oklahoma, Oregon, Rhode Island, Washington, Wisconsin. See the statutory citations set forth in notes 249-53 *supra*.

255 VA. CODE ANN. § 9-6.11.

256 FLA. STAT. § 120.24(2).

257 CAL. GOV'T CODE § 11515. The same provisions appear in ALASKA STAT. § 44.62.480.

lous detail that the parties present at the hearing shall be informed of the matters to be noticed; and requires that those matters be noted in the record, referred to therein, or appended thereto. It further provides that any such party shall be given a reasonable opportunity on request to refute the officially noticed matters by evidence or by written or oral presentation of authority, the manner of such refutation to be determined by the agency. The North Dakota statute[258] in some respects goes further than do those of other states in describing the scope of matters that may be established without formal proof. Going somewhat beyond traditional concepts of official notice, the North Dakota statute provides that when an agency desires to avail itself of any relevant information in its possession or furnished by members of its staff, or secured from any person in the course of an agency investigation, it may do so after first transmitting a copy of such information (or an abstract thereof) to each party of record, and affording each party on request an opportunity to examine such information and cross-examine the person furnishing the information and presenting evidence in connection therewith.

(C) Court Decisions

Generally, the court decisions reach approximately the same results as those required by the Revised Model Act.

(1) Matters Judicially Noticed

Agencies may take official notice of matters that a court would notice judicially. It may, for example, notice its own prior orders.[259]

(2) Broad Notice Permitted, if Parties Given Notice and Opportunity to Refute

The New Jersey court, speaking through Chief Justice Vanderbilt, adopted (without benefit of statute) substantially the same rule as that set forth in the Revised Model Act. The court declared:

---

258 N.D. Cent. Code § 28-32-07.

259 Harding Glass Co. v. Arkansas Pub. Serv. Comm'n, 229 Ark. 153, 313 S.W.2d 812 (1958).

> Beyond question the use of expert knowledge gained by the Department is a desirable attribute of the administrative process, but it need not be applied in a manner which is unfair. By taking appropriate official notice of such material and making such facts part of the record and giving the parties fair oportunity to meet, explain, or refute it, the Commissioner can satisfy the requirements of fairness and adequately protect the interests of all concerned.[260]

(3) Substituting Notice for Proof Disapproved, Where No Warning Given

In cases where an agency assumes to take official notice of an asserted fact within its specialized knowledge, but one which would not be judicially noticed, the courts insist that the agency must give notice to the other parties, and afford them an opportunity for refutation. Thus, it was error for a workmen's compensation commission, without affording such opportunity, to take official notice as to the harmfulness of silicon dioxide dust.[261] The Florida court held that the state real estate commission could not take notice whether a certain individual was a registered salesman.[262] In Massachusetts, it was held to be error for the department of public utilities to rely on its own information in determining the cost of a utility's capital.[263] The New Jersey court has set aside tax equalization orders, because the taxing officials relied on their own data to determine average assessment ratios, and failed to afford the local taxing districts an opportunity to examine such data and undertake to refute them;[264] and has reversed the state board of optometrists for undertaking to determine, without the benefit of evidence, that a slight variance was not within allowable standards of tolerance, remarking, "a board of experts, sitting in a quasi-judicial capacity, cannot be silent witnesses as well as judges."[265] In Vermont, a rate order was set aside because it was based on official notice

---

[260] Elizabeth Fed. Sav. & Loan Ass'n v. Howell, 24 N.J. 488, 507, 132 A.2d 779 (1957).

[261] Orosco v. Poarch, 70 Ariz. 432, 222 P.2d 805 (1950).

[262] Thorn v. Florida Real Estate Comm'n, 146 So. 2d 907 (Fla. App. 1962).

[263] Salisbury Water Supply Co. v. Department of Pub. Utils., 344 Mass. 716, 184 N.E.2d 44 (1962).

[264] Borough of Little Ferry v. Bergen County Bd. of Taxation, 18 N.J. 400, 113 A.2d 768 (1955); City of Passaic v. Passaic County Bd. of Taxation, 18 N.J. 371, 113 A.2d 753 (1955).

[265] New Jersey State Bd. of Optometrists v. Nemitz, 21 N.J. 18, 28, 90 A.2d 740 (1952).

that a six per cent rate of return was just.[266] The Wisconsin court held that in workmen's compensation proceedings, the agency could not determine by official notice the going rate of pay for a particular occupation in a given community;[267] and the Indiana court disapproved of the action of a public utility commission in taking official notice of the ownership of a utility's stock for a period of time subsequent to the hearing.[268]

(4) Relaxation of Rule, if Parties Not Prejudiced

Sometimes, if the court is convinced that the other parties to the case were not prejudiced, an agency may be permitted to take notice of unproved facts even though it has not complied with the customary formalities as to notice. Typical is a Michigan case, where on an appeal from an order fixing electrical rates, a municipality objected that the public service commission was not authorized to take official notice of information contained in its files but not formally offered in evidence. Finding that the municipality knew that the reports of the electric company were relied on by the commission, that it had had adequate opportunity to study such reports, and that it had not objected at the hearing to the failure to introduce them in evidence, and that it made no claim the information had been misinterpreted, the court found no prejudicial error had been committed.[269] The Missouri court, though criticizing the public service commission for giving consideration to data furnished by its own engineers, found that the other parties had not been prejudiced thereby.[270]

(5) Parties May Disprove Facts Noticed

While text writers and, seemingly, the courts are in disagreement whether the parties in court proceedings may disprove

---

[266] City of Newport v. Newport Elec. Div., 116 Vt. 103, 70 A.2d 590 (1950).

[267] Springfield Lumber, Feed & Fuel Co. v. Industrial Comm'n, 10 Wis. 2d 405, 102 N.W.2d 754 (1960).

[268] Public Serv. Comm'n v. Indiana Bell Tel. Co., 235 Ind. 1, 130 N.E.2d 467 (1955).

[269] City of Ishpeming v. Michigan Pub. Serv. Comm'n, 370 Mich. 293, 121 N.W.2d 462 (1963). See also, permitting an agency to notice facts set forth by the party in a report it had filed with the agency, Application of Montana-Dakota Utils. Co., 111 N.W.2d 705 (N.D. 1961).

[270] State *ex rel.* Hotel Continental v. Burton, 334 S.W.2d 75 (Mo. 1960).

facts which a court judicially notices[271] it seems clear that in administrative proceedings the parties have, independent of statute, the right guaranteed by the Revised Model Act to refute facts outside the scope of judicial notice which an agency proposes to notice officially. This, of course, is the very purpose of requiring agencies to give the other parties to a proceeding notification as to the facts which the agency proposes to notice. Indeed, the statute apparently accords the parties the right to refute any asserted facts which the agency proposes to notice, whether they be "judicially cognizable facts" or "generally recognized technical or scientific facts."

(6) Agencies May Not Notice Litigation Facts

The principle of official notice is based on the premise that administrative tribunals should be permitted to utilize their special information and knowledge built up over many years of intensive study of a specialized field, and should not be required to treat each case as an isolated phenomenon in the consideration of which their accumulated knowledge must be excluded. This premise does not apply to a case where an agency may be inclined to rely on ex parte reports of investigators as to the particular factual details peculiar to a given case. Information gathered privately by an agency with reference solely to a particular case at hand does not bear the hallmark of expert knowledge. It is rather to be compared, from the standpoint of reliability, with the report of a private detective agency. There is no reason to permit an agency to rely on such information as a basis for decision, and the state courts consistently refuse to do so. As the Kentucky court said: "While an administrative body may take notice of matters of common knowledge and may even act upon its own expert knowledge or information, it cannot by personal investigation develop its own evidence to support its finding."[272] This principle has been applied in a number of cases.[273]

---

[271] The authorities are collected in 2 DAVIS, ADMINISTRATIVE LAW TREATISE § 15.09 (1958).

[272] Bauer v. Alcoholic Beverage Control Bd., 320 S.W.2d 126 (Ky. 1959).

[273] *E.g.*, English v. City of Long Beach, 35 Cal. 2d 155, 217 P.2d 22 (1950); Smith v. Department of Registration & Educ., 412 Ill. 332, 106 N.E.2d 722 (1952); Petition of New York Water Serv. Corp., 283 N.Y. 23, 27 N.E.2d 221 (1940); Civil Serv. Comm'n v. Polito, 397 Pa. 538, 156 A.2d 99 (1959).

(7) Agencies May Utilize Experience in Appraising Evidence

In the process of decision, as distinguished from the process of proof, agency officials are at liberty to give the fullest play to their expert knowledge and experience in evaluating the evidence that is in the record and drawing conclusions therefrom. Such utilization is not only permissible, but desirable.[274] This, of course, is quite a different thing than the utilization of special experience and asserted knowledge as a substitute for evidence and as a basis for making factual findings as to matters not proved by evidence in the record. As the Iowa court said, in connection with the issuance of a certificate of convenience to a common carrier, the commission "can and should consider the general transportation problem that affects this state as well as the nation as a whole. It is not alone restricted to the evidence that is presented at the hearing but may take into consideration other factors and information of which it has knowledge."[275]

(8) Use of Record in Another Proceeding

Not infrequently, agencies incorporate into the record of a particular proceeding, either by introduction of bulky exhibits or by reference to the agency's files and records, a transcript of proceedings in another case. This really involves a problem as to the right of cross-examination, rather than a problem of official notice; and the primary issue is the right of the other parties to insist upon examining the files of the cases referred to, and meeting by their own proofs whatever adverse factual data such files may contain. However, one Pennsylvania case questions the right of an agency to take notice of its records in a prior case involving the same party.[276]

---

[274] Ebersole v. Beck Mining Div., Inc., 276 P.2d 201 (Okla. 1954); Kaiser Aluminum & Chem. Corp. v. Department of Labor & Industries, 45 Wash. 2d 745, 277 P.2d 742 (1954). See BENJAMIN, ADMINISTRATIVE ADJUDICATION IN THE STATE OF NEW YORK 209-10 (1942); Report of Attorney General's Committee on Administrative Procedure, S. DOC. No. 8, 77th Cong., 1st Sess. 71 (1941).

[275] Haas v. Iowa State Commerce Comm'n, 241 Iowa 333, 338, 41 N.W.2d 98 (1950).

[276] *In re* Shenandoah Suburban Bus Lines, Inc., 355 Pa. 521, 50 A.2d 301 (1947).

(9) Notice More Freely Permitted, Where Agency Is Acting in Non-Judicial Capacity

Where an agency exercises legislative or executive functions, it is not ordinarily required to show any basis of substantial evidence to support its ruling (except where a statute imposes such a requirement) and therefore in reaching its conclusions it would seem that it may rely as fully on its own experience as on any other factor—that the usual doctrines of official notice do not apply. Thus, in zoning cases, where the agency's function is not ordinarily strictly judicial, a broad measure of reliance on the agency's own knowledge of the district involved is often allowed.[277] However, the New Jersey court has indicated that it may insist on the agency's giving advance notification, and an opportunity to refute, even where the agency is exercising rule-making powers. In a case where a public utilities commission was engaged in the formulation of rules governing safety practices on railroads, following a disastrous train wreck, the agency had taken notice of an attorney general's report, and of its own findings in a connected proceeding, in formulating its order. While the court regarded the proceedings as primarily legislative, it said that ". . . in due time during the course of the hearing the Board should have formally advised the Pennsylvania [Railroad] that these matters were being officially noticed and made part of the hearing record. However, we fail to see how the Pennsylvania was in anywise prejudiced by the omission."[278] The inference would seem to be that had prejudice been shown, the same requirements as to official notice would have been applied in a rule-making proceeding as are ordinarily applied in contested cases.

---

[277] *E.g.,* Burke v. Board of Representatives, 148 Conn. 33, 166 A.2d 849 (1961); Parsons v. Board of Zoning Appeals, 140 Conn. 290, 99 A.2d 149 (1953); Woodbury v. Zoning Bd. of Review, 78 R.I. 319, 82 A.2d (1951).

[278] Lehigh & H.R. Ry. v. Department of Pub. Utils., 14 N.J. 440, 102 A.2d 633 (1954); Pennsylvania R.R. v. Department of Pub. Utils., 14 N.J. 411, 429, 102 A.2d 618 (1954).

Section 6

The Record for Decision

(A) What Should Be Included in Record

In cases where evidence is taken, the administrative decision should be based exclusively on the record made at the hearing. That record should comprise the seven elements discussed below. The inclusion of all of them is important in the attainment of two objectives: First, that the administrative decision be a fully informed decision; second, that the administrative record afford a proper foundation for judicial review.

(1) Pleadings, Motions, Intermediate Rulings

The requirement of the Revised Model State Act[279] that the record in a contested case shall include the pleadings, motions, and intermediate rulings, is designed to bring into sharp focus, and compel a decision on, each point relied on by respondent. It is designed to proscribe the practice of conveniently ignoring objections which it is difficult to answer on logical and persuasive grounds. A number of the more recently enacted state administrative procedure acts include such a provision.[280]

(2) Evidence Received or Considered

The Revised Model State Act[281] requires the inclusion in the record of all evidence which is received and of all evidence which is considered. This provision is important in two respects: First, it means that all evidence which is received at the hearing must be included in the record, even though the agency decided the evidence was irrelevant or without probative value, and accordingly refused to consider it. In view of the circumstance that (sometimes by statute and sometimes by practice) parties to contested cases are frequently permitted to introduce whatever evidence they desire, even though the hearing officer believes it

---

279 Section 9(e)(1).

280 California (GOV'T CODE § 11523); Georgia (CODE ANN. § 3A-101); Hawaii (SESS. LAWS 1961, Act 103, § 9(e)); Indiana (ANN. STAT. § 63-3009); North Carolina (GEN. STAT. § 150-25—licensing act); North Dakota (CENT. CODE § 28-32-06); Oklahoma (STAT. tit. 75, § 309(e)); Rhode Island (GEN. LAWS ANN. § 42-35-9).

281 Section 9(e)(2): "The record in a contested case shall include: . . . evidence received or considered."

to be without significance, this provision serves an important purpose—that of assuring that such evidence will be preserved for subsequent judicial review. Secondly, the provision of the Revised Model Act guarantees that any evidentiary material which the agency considers in its decision must be incorporated into the record.

Thus, the provision is a more precise statement of the objectives of the cognate section of the original Model State Act, which provided in Section 9 (2) that "all evidence, including records and documents in the possession of the agency of which it desires to avail itself, shall be offered and made a part of the record in the case, and no other factual information or evidence shall be considered in the determination of the case." A number of state statutes incorporate the substance of this provision of the original Model State Act.[282]

A number of court decisions illustrate the utility of such statutory provisions. Thus, in one Michigan case, the court set aside an order of a water resources commission requiring a company to install a waste treatment system after a "hearing" which was really nothing more than a conference, and which had the following incurable defects: the witnesses were not sworn; no exhibits were identified; materials and data relied upon by the commission were not introduced into evidence; and the record of the so-called hearing did not purport to be full and complete.[283] Again, the Arizona court held void an order of the state corporation commission revoking respondent's motor carrier certificate, on the ground that he was not "a fit and proper" person. Pointing out that no proper record had been made or preserved for judicial review, the court said:

> The Commission has not certified to this Court any record of a hearing held on that date. Indeed, the evidence indicated that if what purported to be a hearing was held, it was attended by no more than one Commissioner and such record does not indicate a majority of the Commission gave its approval to any finding; that a court reporter was not present; that no transcript of evidence or

---

[282] Maine (REV. STAT. ANN. ch. 20-A, § 8); Maryland (ANN. CODE art. 41, § 251); Massachusetts (GEN. LAWS ANN. ch. 30A, § 11); Michigan (STAT. ANN. § 3.560(21.4)); Minnesota (STAT. § 15.0418); Missouri (REV. STAT. § 536.-070); Nebraska (REV. STAT. § 84-913); Washington (REV. CODE § 34.04.090 (1)); Wisconsin (STAT. § 227.11).

[283] L. A. Darling Co. v. Water Resources Comm'n, 341 Mich. 654, 67 N.W. 2d 890 (1955).

testimony was taken; and that there was no entry in the Commission docket of what action, if any, was taken with regard to petitioner's certificate.[284]

The Wisconsin court has had occasion to point out that reports in the commission's file, but not put in evidence, do not constitute competent evidence;[285] and Indiana has held that evidence outside the administrative record may not be relied on to support the order.[286]

Other states, in various forms, provide for the inclusion in the record of a complete transcript of all the proceedings before the agency.[287]

(3) Statement of Matters Officially Noticed

There should be included in the record, of course, a statement of all matters officially noticed. Only in this way can it be made sure that the other parties to a contested case have had an opportunity to exercise their right to undertake to refute the correctness of the agency's assumptions as to what the facts are.[288] The provision of the Revised Model State Act,[289] that the record in a contested case shall include "a statement of the matters officially noticed," is reflected in several of the more recently adopted state acts.[290]

The requirement that the record include a statement of matters officially noticed implies that where the agency's decision is predicated in part on its view of the premises, it must include in the record a statement of the conclusions it reached on the

284 Dallas v. Arizona Corp. Comm'n, 86 Ariz. 345, 348, 346 P.2d 152 (1959).

285 Unruh v. Industrial Comm'n, 8 Wis. 2d 394, 99 N.W.2d 182 (1959); *accord,* Public Utils. Comm'n v. Cole's Express, 153 Me. 487, 138 A.2d 466 (1958).

286 Jones v. State *ex rel.* Indiana Livestock Sanitary Bd., 240 Ind. 230, 163 N.E.2d 605 (1960).

287 California (GOV'T CODE § 11523); Florida (STAT. § 120.24); Hawaii (SESS. LAWS 1961, Act 103, § 9(e)); Indiana (ANN. STAT. § 63-3009); North Carolina (GEN. STAT. § 150-25—licensing act); North Dakota (CENT. CODE § 28-32-06); Ohio (REV. CODE ANN. § 119.09); Oklahoma (STAT. tit. 75, § 309(e)); Oregon (REV. STAT. § 183.420); Pennsylvania (STAT. ANN. tit. 71, § 1710.31); Rhode Island (GEN. LAWS ANN. § 42-35-9).

288 See § 5 (c)(5) of this chapter.

289 Section 9(e) (3).

290 Alaska (STAT. § 44.62.480); California (GOV'T CODE § 11515); Colorado (REV. STAT. ANN. § 3-16-4(8)); Georgia (CODE ANN. § 3A-101); Hawaii (SESS. LAWS 1961, Act 103, § 9(e)); Oklahoma (STAT. tit. 75, § 309(e)); Rhode Island (GEN. LAWS ANN. § 42-35-9).

basis of such inspection. Thus, the New York court set aside an order of a zoning board of appeals which granted a variance on the basis of a report submitted by a committee of three board members who had inspected the site and on the basis of their visit had recommended that permission be granted to erect a medical building in a residential neighborhood, since "although this is a very nice neighborhood," it "would be difficult to use" the lots in question "for the purposes for which they are presently zoned." The court pointed out that this report was insufficient to create a proper record, since it consisted merely of conclusions and not facts, and provided no proper basis to permit the court to review the committee's conclusions. The court said: "The Board may act upon its own knowledge of conditions, but in the return it must disclose those facts upon which a reviewing court can determine that, under the statute, the Board had power to grant a variance."[291] In another zoning case, the New York court reiterated that while a zoning board is entitled to act on its personal knowledge and inspection, it must set forth in the record the facts so ascertained; mere conclusionary statements are insufficient.[292]

There is some tendency to relax the rule, where an agency notices only its own prior proceedings involving the same parties.[293]

(4) Offers of Proof and Objections

Section 9 (e) (4) of the Revised Model State Act provides that the record in a contested case must include "questions and offers of proof, objections, and rulings thereon." These related requirements are all designed to assure the completeness of the record. It means that, at the very minimum, if the hearing officer sustains an objection and refuses to permit the witness to answer a question, the record must at least show the question, thus giving an indication of the line of inquiry which the party proposed to pursue—so that if the agency or a reviewing court finds that such inquiry was relevant, the case may be remanded

---

291 Forrest v. Evershed, 7 N.Y.2d 256, 263, 196 N.Y.S.2d 958, 164 N.E.2d 841 (1959).

292 Community Synagogue v. Bates, 1 N.Y.2d 445, 136 N.E.2d 488 (1956).

293 Fink v. Cole, 1 N.Y.2d 48, 150 N.Y.S.2d 175, 133 N.E.2d 691 (1956); Application of Montana-Dakota Utils. Co., 111 N.W.2d 705 (N.D. 1961); Allstate Ins. Co. v. Commonwealth, 199 Va. 434, 100 S.E.2d 31 (1957).

for the taking of further evidence. Further, the section inferentially provides that, in the event an objection is sustained, the party proffering the evidence may make a statement on the record as to what the excluded evidence would have shown. In practice, this is often accomplished by making a separate record of the excluded testimony—a practice which has as much to commend it in administrative proceedings as in non-jury cases in the courts. Finally, by requiring the record to incorporate the statement of the objection and the ruling thereon, the act provides a means for bringing into sharp focus the precise point on which the question of relevancy or materiality arises.

Similar provisions are beginning to appear in the administrative procedure acts of the states. Some of them, such as California[294] specifically provide that exhibits which are rejected by the hearing officer shall nevertheless be included as a part of the record, thus assuring the availability on appeal of all the evidentiary materials which any party considers significant. The Missouri statute[295] provides that evidence to which an objection is sustained shall, at the request of the party seeking to introduce the same, or at the instance of the agency, nevertheless be heard and preserved in the record (together with any cross-examination with respect thereto, and any rebuttal thereof) unless it is wholly irrelevant, repetitious, privileged, or unduly long. Predictably, provisions such as those found in the Revised Model Act and in the statutes of California and Missouri will find general acceptance as more states adopt administrative procedure acts.[296]

(5) Proposed Findings and Exceptions

One of the most effective devices that can be utilized, either in judicial or administrative proceedings, to reveal clearly and specifically the precise issues that are critical to the case (and to require hard, clear thinking thereon and a specific resolution thereof) is that of filing proposed findings of fact and conclusions of law, requiring the decision-making authority to rule

---

294 CAL. GOV'T CODE § 11523.

295 MO. REV. STAT. § 536.070.

296 *Cf.* California (GOV'T CODE § 11523); Georgia (CODE ANN. § 3A-101); Hawaii (SESS. LAWS 1961, Act 103, § 9(e)); Indiana (ANN. STAT. § 63-3009); Missouri (REV. STAT. § 536.070); North Dakota (CENT. CODE § 28-12-06); Ohio (REV. CODE ANN. § 119.09); Oklahoma (STAT. tit. 75, § 309(e)); Rhode Island (GEN. LAWS ANN. § 42-35-9).

thereon, and affording the parties an opportunity to argue their exceptions to such rulings. It was to serve these purposes that provision is made in Section 9 (e) (5) of the Revised Model State Act that the record on appeal must contain the proposed findings and exceptions. This provision, too, is finding general acceptance with the state legislatures, and is often being included in the newer statutes.[297]

(6) Report of Hearing Officer

The report of the hearing officer may tend to confirm, or to cast doubts upon, the correctness of the findings and decision of the agency (in cases where, as is often true, the report of the hearing officer is only the first step in the decisional process). Therefore, its inclusion in the record is helpful. Concurrence between the hearing officer and the institutional staff in their findings and conclusions may afford an indication that the case is purely run-of-the-mine, raising no new questions of statutory interpretation but merely applying well-settled principles to facts clearly established by the evidence. On the other hand, comparison of the report of the hearing officer with that later prepared by the agency staff may disclose discrepancies so remarkable as almost to suggest that they involve different cases. In such event, reference to the report of the hearing officer may disclose important issues that were ignored in the staff report. Further, as the United States Supreme Court had occasion to observe: "The evidence supporting a conclusion may be less substantial when an impartial, experienced trial examiner who has observed the witnesses and lived with the case has drawn conclusions different from the Board's."[298]

The New Jersey court, in a trenchant opinion by Chief Justice Vanderbilt, found that there was a deprival of due process where an agency in determining a case considered a report by a hearing officer which had not been made available to respondent. The court declared that such a report may not lawfully be used as an aid in the administrative decision process unless a copy of

---

[297] Florida (STAT. § 120.26); Georgia (CODE ANN. § 3A-101); Hawaii (SESS. LAWS 1961, Act 103, § 9(e)); Indiana (ANN. STAT. § 63-3009); North Dakota (CENT. CODE § 28-32-06); Oklahoma (STAT. tit. 75, § 309(e)); Rhode Island (GEN. LAWS ANN. § 42-35-9).

[298] Universal Camera Corp. v. NLRB, 340 U.S. 474, 496, 95 L. Ed. 456, 71 Sup. Ct. 456 (1951).

it has been made available to respondent, who "has a right not only to refute it but, what in a case like this is usually more important, to supplement, explain, and give different perspective to the hearer's view of the case."[299]

The Massachusetts court held, under statutes requiring, respectively, the inclusion in the record for review of "a transcript of the entire record in the proceedings" (Milk Control Act) and "the official report of the proceedings" (Public Utilities Law) that it was proper to include the report of the hearing officer as a part of the record.[300]

The newer state statutes quite uniformly require the inclusion in the record of any decision, opinion, or report by the officer presiding at the hearing.[301] This is the provision of Section 9 (e) (6) of the Revised Model State Act.

(7) Staff Memoranda

One of the most significant (and controversial) provisions in the Revised Model State Act is the requirement found in Section 9 (e) (7) that the record in a contested case shall include "all staff memoranda or data submitted to the hearing officer or members of the agency in connection with their consideration of the case."

This provision is addressed to a situation which exists in many state agencies, as well as in most federal agencies—the existence of a case load which renders it impossible for agency members to achieve the type of personal mastery of the record contemplated by the United States Supreme Court, which in deciding the *Morgan* case[302] declared that "the officer who makes the determinations must consider and appraise the evidence which justifies them," because "the weight ascribed by the law to the findings . . . rests upon the assumption that the officer who makes the findings has addressed himself to the evidence and upon that evidence has conscientiously reached the conclusions which he

---

299 Mazza v. Cavicchia, 15 N.J. 498, 515, 105 A.2d 545 (1954).

300 Norwood Ice Co. v. Milk Control Comm'n, 338 Mass. 435, 155 N.E.2d 758 (1959); Fortier v. Department of Pub. Utils., 342 Mass. 728, 175 N.E.2d 495 (1961).

301 California (GOV'T CODE § 11523); Florida (STAT. § 120.24); Georgia (CODE ANN. § 3A-101); Hawaii (SESS. LAWS 1961, Act 103, § 9(e)); Oklahoma (STAT. tit. 75, § 309(e)); Rhode Island (GEN. LAWS ANN. § 42-35-9).

302 Morgan v. United States, 298 U.S. 468, 482, 80 L. Ed. 1288, 56 Sup. Ct. 906 (1936).

deems it to justify. . . . The one who decides must hear." In many agencies, the agency members do not comply with this requirement. They are compelled to place principal reliance on memoranda, reports, and recommendations for decision prepared by their assistants, whose suggested decisions are made without the benefit of having heard either the testimony or the arguments of counsel—with the result that the agency order represents decision second-hand, twice removed.

As a result, counsel representing respondents too often experience the frustration that is said to accompany the activity of punching a pillow. They present their evidence and their arguments to a hearing officer whose report may for most practical purposes be disregarded, or at least accorded second-rate importance, in the subsequent process of agency decision. They mail briefs to the agency; but have no certain conviction whether their briefs will be read—or, if so, by whom.

If they are accorded the privilege of oral argument before the agency members, they are not able to argue with greatest possible effectiveness if (as in many agencies) they are not permitted to see the staff memoranda which furnish the actual basis of agency decision. Deprived of access to such memoranda, they have no opportunity to point out to the agency members that the case would take on a different complexion if consideration were given to matters not mentioned, or inadequately treated, in the staff memoranda.

The result is that when the case is argued before the members of the agency, counsel are in the anomalous position of being required to address their arguments to the published report of the hearing officer, while the members of the agency are addressing their attention to the secret report of the staff—which may present quite a different picture of the case. The agency members, not having read the transcript of testimony nor the report of the hearing examiner, are not able to follow the argument of counsel. On the other hand, counsel—not knowing the contents of the staff report from which the agency members derive their sole knowledge of the case—are unable to address themselves to the points with which the agency members are concerned.

Under such circumstances, the effectiveness of participation of counsel representing respondents in the process of agency decision is unfortunately diminished. As every trial lawyer knows, the opportunity to cross verbal swords with the person who will ultimately make the decision—to learn by oral argument what issues principally concern him, to direct his attention to counsel's arguments respecting those issues, and to correct any misapprehensions which he may have formed—are all of crucial importance to effective advocacy. But when the staff memoranda on which decision is to be predicated are withheld from counsel, this opportunity for effective argument is denied.

If all staff memoranda prepared for the assistance of the agency members (and purporting to enable them to obtain a "mastery of the record" by reading a brief synopsis thereof—often only three or four pages in length) were made a part of the record, it would enable counsel to participate more effectively in the process of decision; and it would, moreover, serve as an effective check against the possibility that decision might be predicated on synopses that were inadequate or inaccurate. It was for these reasons that the draftsmen of the Revised Model State Act required the inclusion of such memoranda in the record.

There are those who object to such proposals. Many agencies object; their objections in the main reflect their position as parties to the case—they complain that to reveal their staff memoranda is comparable to requiring one party litigant to reveal to his opponent the contents of his confidential notes. Others object that if the staff memoranda were subjected to scrutiny and criticism by the other parties, it would be necessary to spend more time and care on their preparation. More plausibly, it is also urged that if the staff memoranda were included in the record, so many objections and exceptions would be urged as to the correctness of the staff memoranda that the agency members would become lost in the welter of exceptions and disagreements, and the result would be a compounding of confusion, which could be cleared up only by going to the transcript of testimony itself—something the agency members do not have time to do.

Weighing the conflicting arguments, the draftsmen of the Revised Model Act decided it would be best, on balance, to require the staff memoranda to be included in the record. Legislatures in a number of states that have adopted administrative procedure acts since the promulgation of the Revised Model Act have concurred in this judgment.[303] An earlier North Dakota statute[304] requires the inclusion in the record of all "reports or memoranda."

(B) Requirement That Decision Be Based Solely on Record

It is important that the record of a contested case be complete; and it is equally imperative that the decision be based exclusively on matters that appear in the record. Otherwise, the hearing could be reduced to a mere talisman; and judicial review would become meaningless.

Independent of statutory requirements, indeed, the courts have often held that the administrative decision must be based exclusively on the record made at the hearing.

In holding that an agency cannot base a decision on information received by it otherwise than at the hearing, the California court declared: "The action of such an administrative board exercising adjudicatory functions when based upon information of which the parties were not apprised and which they had no opportunity to controvert amounts to a denial of a hearing."[305]

In a leading case, Chief Justice Vanderbilt declared for the New Jersey court:

> In any proceeding that is judicial in nature, whether in a court or in an administrative agency, the process of decision must be governed by the basic principle of the exclusiveness of the record . . . . Unless this principle is observed, the right to a hearing itself becomes meaningless. Of what real worth is the right to present evidence and to argue its significance at a formal hearing, if the one who decides the case may stray at will from the record in reaching his decision?[306]

The Florida court, holding that the industrial commission was not justified in considering or relying on extraneous evidence, obtained either within or outside its official files, in passing on a motion to dismiss a claim for compensation, observed: "It is

303 Georgia (CODE ANN. § 3A-101); Hawaii (SESS. LAWS 1961, Act 103, § 9(e)); Oklahoma (STAT. tit. 75, § 309(e)); Rhode Island (GEN. LAWS ANN. § 42-35-9).

304 N.D. CENT. CODE § 28-32-17.

305 English v. City of Long Beach, 35 Cal. 2d 155, 158, 217 P.2d 22 (1950).

306 Mazza v. Cavicchia, 15 N.J. 498, 514, 105 A.2d 545 (1954).

established law . . . that findings based upon matters *dehors* the record or not supported by evidence in the record submitted to us for examination will not be permitted to stand."[307]

On similar grounds, the Indiana court set aside an order of the state public service commission based upon the commission's own investigation, made after the hearing and without notice to the parties.[308] The principle has been recognized and applied by the courts of other states.[309]

Supplementing the basic proposition that the decision must be based exclusively on the record is the corollary that the record must contain evidence justifying the agency's order.[310]

These court-imposed requirements are fortified by the provision found in Section 9 (g) of the Revised Model State Act, which requires that "findings of fact shall be based exclusively on the evidence and on matters officially noticed."

A substantial body of statutory enactment imposes similar requirements.[311]

Section 7

Written Transcripts

In cases where a right to judicial review exists, it would seem that parties to a contested case are entitled to insist that the proceedings be recorded stenographically, so as to make it possible to prepare a transcript of the record for purposes of judicial

---

307 Hodges v. State Road Dep't of Florida, 112 So. 2d 593, 596 (Fla. 1959).

308 Monon R.R. v. Public Serv. Comm'n, 241 Ind. 142, 170 N.E.2d 441 (1960).

309 Lewis v. Board of Educ., 348 S.W.2d 921 (Ky. 1961); Moore v. Macduff, 309 N.Y. 35, 127 N.E.2d 741 (1955); *cf.* Town of Smithtown v. Moore, 11 N.Y.2d 238, 228 N.Y.S.2d 657, 183 N.E.2d 66 (1962).

310 Coleman v. Watts, 81 So. 2d 650 (Fla. 1955); Thorn v. Florida Real Estate Comm'n, 146 So. 2d 907 (Fla. 1962); Town of West New York v. Bock, 38 N.J. 500, 186 A.2d 97 (1962); *cf.* Von Kohorn v. Morrell, 9 N.Y.2d 27, 210 N.Y.S.2d 525, 172 N.E.2d 287 (1961).

311 Georgia (CODE ANN. § 3A-101); Hawaii (SESS. LAWS 1961, Act 103, § 9(g)); Indiana (ANN. STAT. § 63-3010); Maine (REV. STAT. ANN. ch. 20-A, § 10-II); Maryland (ANN. CODE art. 41, § 252); Massachusetts (GEN. LAWS ANN. ch. 30A, § 11(4)); Michigan (STAT. ANN. § 3.560(21.5)); Minnesota (STAT. § 15.0419); Nebraska (REV. STAT. § 84-914(3)); North Dakota (CENT. CODE § 28-32-06); Oklahoma (STAT. tit. 75, § 309(g)); Oregon (REV. STAT. § 183.450(2)); Rhode Island (GEN. LAWS ANN. § 42-35-9); Virginia (CODE ANN. § 9-6.11(d)); Washington (REV. CODE § 34.04.100(2)).

review,[312] although occasionally review is based on a de novo hearing in court.

The Revised Model State Act provides[313] that "oral proceedings or any part thereof shall be transcribed on request of any party." Similar provisions are found in many states. Frequently, it is specified that the party requesting a transcript must pay the cost thereof.[314] In other states, the statutes make general provision for the furnishing of a transcript on request.[315]

---

312 Johnson v. Village of Cohasset, 263 Minn. 425, 116 N.W.2d 692 (1962). *Cf.*, State *ex rel.* Baumann v. Quinn, 337 S.W.2d 84 (Mo. 1960), holding it competent for the legislature to provide that the private party must make his own arrangements for having the hearing reported.

313 Section 9(f).

314 Alaska (STAT. § 44.62.560); California (GOV'T CODE § 11523); Colorado (REV. STAT. ANN. § 3-16-4); Indiana (ANN. STAT. § 63-3009); Massachusetts (GEN. LAWS ANN. ch. 30A, § 11); Minnesota (STAT. § 15.0418); Missouri (REV. STAT. § 536.070(4)); North Dakota (CENT. CODE § 28-32-12).

315 Hawaii (SESS. LAWS 1961, Act 103, § 9(f)); Maine (REV. STAT. ANN. ch. 20-A, § 8); Maryland (ANN. CODE art. 41, § 251); Michigan (STAT. ANN. § 3.560(21.4)); Nebraska (REV. STAT. § 84-913); Ohio (REV. CODE ANN. § 119.09); Oklahoma (STAT. tit. 75, § 309(f)); Oregon (REV. STAT. § 183.-420); Rhode Island (GEN. LAWS ANN. § 42-35-9); Washington (REV. CODE § 34.04.090(1)).